Swedish Handcraft

SWEDISH HANDCRAFT

by Anna-Maja Nylén

translated by Anne-Charlotte Hanes Harvey

VAN NOSTRAND REINHOLD COMPANY
NEW YORK CINCINNATI TORONTO LONDON MELBOURNE

Acknowledgments

Swedish Handcraft is largely based on materials in Nordiska Museet, Stockholm. For the access to its collections, photographic material, and data, I am deeply grateful. Except where otherwise noted, all illustrations are courtesy of Nordiska Museet. All who work at Nordiska Museet, each in his or her way, have contributed to the end result of *Swedish Handcraft*, and I thank them all.

I also wish to thank the Berlingska Boktryckeri, Lund, for its interested and exacting preparation and presentation of my manuscript.

My warm thanks go to my translator, Anne-Charlotte Hanes Harvey, for her diligent work to find English equivalents for regional or dialectal terms. By her keen interest and knowledgeable scrutiny of the text, she has prompted me to clarify and amend the presentation.

I also wish to thank my colleague, Dr. Marta Hoffmann of Oslo, Norway, for her gracious and valued assistance in checking specific terms of textile technology.

The Author

Library of Congress Catalog Card Number
75-28331

ISBN 0-442-26090-3

Printed in Sweden. Berlingska Boktryckeriet, Lund 1977

This book was originally published in Sweden under the title *Hemslöjd* by Håkan Ohlssons Förlag, Lund.

Copyright for *Hemslöjd* by Anna-Maja Nylén 1968

Published in the U.S.A. in 1977 by Van Nostrand Reinhold Company
A Division of Litton Educational Publishing, Inc.
450 West 33rd Street
New York, New York 10001

Van Nostrand Reinhold Limited
1410 Birchmount Road
Scarborough, Ontario M1P 2E7, Canada

Van Nostrand Reinhold Australia Pty. Ltd.
17 Queen Street
Mitcham, Victoria 3132, Australia

Van Nostrand Reinhold Company Ltd.
Molly Millars Lane
Wokingham, Berkshire, England

16 15 14 13 12 11 10 9 8 7 6 5 4 3 2 1

Library of Congress Cataloging in Publication Data
Nylén, Anna-Maja, 1912–1976
Swedish handcraft
Translation of Hemslöjd
Bibliography: p.
Includes index
1. Handicraft—Sweden—History. I. Title
TT89.N9513   746'.09485   75-28331
ISBN 0-442-26090-3

Translator's note

A map has been added for the convenience of readers not familiar with the geography of Sweden. As far as possible, this map includes all place names mentioned in the text. All geographical names in the text retain their Swedish spelling, except those of places outside Sweden and those of international features (e.g., the Baltic Sea), which are given in English. Names of museums, associations, etc., have generally been left in the original language, although, where pertinent, a translation is given in parentheses immediately following the name. Similarly, titles of books mentioned in the text which have not appeared in English translation are followed by a translation in parentheses, thus: Ingers, *Flamskvävnad* ("Flemish weaving").

Quotes and references for which no other source is given are based on Nordiska Museet's collection of oral reports, resulting from questionnaires administered in the various craft regions in the 1930s.

Unless otherwise noted, quotes in the text are my own translations of the original.

Many terms in the original text have regional or dialectal overtones which cannot be rendered exactly in translation. Other terms lack English equivalents entirely. I have then preferred to retain the original term (in italics), often directly followed by a literal translation in parentheses.

Terms denoting geographical or administrative divisions are translated as follows: *landskap* (province), *län* (county), *härad* (hundred, district), and *socken* (parish). *Tingslag* and *lappmark* are explained, though not translated, in the text.

The term "peasant" has been chosen as the closest equivalent of the Swedish *bonde* (noun) and *allmoge* (adjective). It should be noted that the Swedish *bonde* was always a free man who owned his own land. "Peasant" is here used entirely without derogatory connotations.

The Swedish *borgare* has been alternately translated "burgher" and "bourgeois." When the emphasis of the text is on a recognized class of society, e.g., the Estate represented in the Swedish parliament, I have used "burgher." When the emphasis is on a milieu, an outlook, or a value system, I have preferred "bourgeois." Generally, this has resulted in the use of "burgher" when speaking of the time up through the eighteenth century, and "bourgeois" when speaking of the eighteenth and nineteenth centuries.

For certain historical terms, I am indebted to E. Heckscher, *An Economic History of Sweden,* and I. Andersson, *A History of Sweden.* In matters of ethnological terminology, I have consulted Åke Hultcrantz, *General Ethnological Concepts: International Dictionary of Regional European Ethnology and Folklore.* My authority on textile terminology has been E. Strömberg et al., *Nordisk textilteknisk terminologi,* the official dictionary of CIETA (Centre International d'Etudes des Textiles Anciens).

For the convenience of English-speaking readers, the number of illustration references in the text has been increased by the author, and explanatory footnotes have been added.

I wish to thank the author for her untiring cooperation and personal interest, without which this translation could not have been completed. My thanks go also to Dr. Michael Harvey for valuable suggestions and criticisms.

Anna-Maja Nylén passed away on February 27, 1976, and never had the opportunity to read the galley proofs of the translated edition. Inga Wintzell of Nordiska Museet, Stockholm, and Dr. Marta Hoffmann of Norsk Folkemuseum, Oslo, assumed some of Dr. Nylén's responsibilities in the final stages of preparation of this edition. For their generous and invaluable assistance I am deeply grateful.

We all hope that the finished product will be a fitting reflection of and tribute to Anna-Maja Nylén's many and lasting contributions to her field.

Contents

1 Lake Siljan
2 Lake Mälaren
3 Lake Vänern
4 Lake Vättern
5 Lake Storsjön
6 Torne River
7 Dalälven (river)
8 Göta River
9 Fårö
10 Sollerö
11 Visingsö
12 Frösön
13 Västra Vingåker
14 Bollnäs
15 Rengsjö
16 Vemmenhög
17 Garsås village
18 Ovansjö
19 Asarum
20 Hällaryd
21 Österåker
22 Sorunda
23 Ramsele
24 Ovanåker
25 Alfta
26 Östervåla
27 Lindome
28 Urshult
29 Bergkarlås
30 Risa
31 Vattnäs
32 Nusnäs
33 Bonäs
34 Våmhus
35 Flymen
36 Väne
37 Kulling
38 Visseltofta
39 Västerfärnebo
40 Revsund
41 Rätan

42 Sveg
43 Hede
44 Gnosjö
45 Kimsta
46 Ekshärad
47 Mo
48 Gårdsby
49 Ödenäs
50 Sandhult
51 Virsemark
52 Lerbäck
53 Boxholm ironworks
54 Stora Kopparberg
   mine
55 Gripsholm Castle
56 Tosterup Castle
57 Kägleholm Castle
58 Torpa Castle
59 Karlberg
60 Hook Manor
61 Kjörtingsberg Manor
   cottage industry
62 Marieby Church
63 Dal Church
64 Södra Råda Church
65 Fogdö Church
66 Grödinge Church
67 Överenhörna Church
68 Skog Church
69 Överhogdal Church
70 Marby Church
71 Kyrkås Church
72 Tännäs Church
73 Oseberg
74 Gokstad
75 Birka
76 Arnö
77 Vendel
78 Valsgärde
79 Gerum
80 Åsle bog

Scandinavia
---- Country boundary
••••• Province boundary

Introduction

The history and development of Swedish handcraft corresponds to the development of handcraft in several western European countries. Swedish handcraft may be particularly representative and rewarding to study, however, in that it offers a wealth of clear and accessible historical examples of that development. In some areas of Sweden, existing craft traditions have never been broken, spanning the years of transition from an agrarian society to today's industrialized state. Furthermore, Sweden has a well-established tradition of research, study, and publication in the general areas of cultural anthropology and folklore.

Swedish Handcraft was written primarily as a comprehensive resource for prospective workers in the Swedish handcraft organizations and for use by teachers of design in industrial and vocational schools. But it is also a historical presentation aimed at a wider, general reading audience. I have strived to avoid too technical an approach, and the work is generously illustrated.

In some respects, the intended use of *Swedish Handcraft* as a text for contemporary handcraft societies has affected its emphasis and scope. Textile crafts have been given more space in this treatment than have, for example, woodcraft or metalwork. Textile crafts, women's crafts, were generally the ones to survive in unbroken tradition when, in the late 1800s, industrialization absorbed much manpower from the traditional households. At the birth of the Handcraft Movement textile crafts therefore played a significant role, and have since come to dominate contemporary handcraft manufacture. Further, some handcrafted products, such as heavy tools and boats, have even been omitted, as I felt a discussion of their construction to have limited appeal.

Swedish Handcraft is largely based on artifacts and material dating from the Renaissance through the second half of the nineteenth century. In the late 1800s, industrial production became so extensive that home craft production progressively lost its dominant position. With this development appeared the Handcraft Movement, which to some extent has been organizing and directing home craft production ever since. The activities of the Handcraft Movement and the concurrent formal organization of craft production introduced a new element in the historical picture, further justifying, I feel, a cut-off point for this study at the end of the nineteenth century.

I believe that anybody concerned with environmental questions will be better able to understand today's complex problems by seeing them from a wider historical perspective. I have therefore tried to give an overall view of the evolution of crafts and craft products, and their close interdependence on cultural milieu, physical environment, and function. Accordingly, I have organized the material under three headings: "Handcraft as a Form of Production," "Milieau and Function" (with the summarizing chapter "Handcraft and Cultural Milieu"), and "The Products of Handcraft."

I hope that this approach will also introduce the reader to some of the great gains made in the general field of cultural anthropology during the last twenty-five years in the areas of Nordic ethnology, cultural geography, and economic history. A number of scholars have made pioneering contributions fundamental to the present work. There is a wealth of published material in the field, mostly in the form of articles in a great number of publications and periodicals.

A comprehensive study like *Swedish Handcraft* naturally draws on such already published material: special studies, abstracts, and interpretations of the existing primary source material. Above all, this presentation is based on the findings of Gösta Berg, Åke Campbell, Albert Eskeröd, Sigurd Erixon, John Granlund, Eli Heckscher, Per Nyström, Sigfrid Svensson, and Gustaf Utterström. My treatment is also based on a number of special studies of textile history by, among others, Ernst Fischer, Agnes Geijer, Margrethe Hald, Gunnel Hazelius-Berg, Ingegerd Henschen-Ingvar, Marta Hoffmann, Sven T. Kjellberg, Elisabeth Strömberg, Vivi Sylwan, and Emilie von Walterstorff.

My task has been mostly to extract from the varied sources what I, on the basis of my own experience, deemed essential to this work. In some instances, my experience has also enabled me to present some conclusions and findings of my own.

As the presentation makes no claim to be an original scientific study, I have not wished to encumber the text with bibliographic footnotes. For each area of interest, however, a selected bibliography is appended. These bibliographies are merely intended to direct the reader's attention to the published sources so that he may, should he so desire, investigate any area in greater depth than is feasible in this treatment.

Handcraft as a form of production

What is handcraft?

In modern Sweden, the concept *hemslöjd* (literally, "home craft"; handcraft) is primarily linked with the production of craft items under the auspices of the various handcraft societies. Actually, the term *hemslöjd* refers originally to all production taking place in the home. Clearly, most consumer goods are today produced industrially, mechanically, and on special premises, in workshops and factories. The home remains, however, even today, a very important producer of goods for home consumption: food products, textiles for clothing and interior decoration, and articles of other materials, such as wood and metal, for furnishings and other purposes. Up to about 1850, the home and the household were the country's largest producers of all articles required for clothing, food, house and home, tools, and means of transportation. *Hemslöjd,* domestic manufacture for private consumption or for sale, can be defined as manufacture in the home by the members of the household to supplement their main livelihood, generally farming. Like all definitions, this one does not always apply, especially not to historical reality.

Besides the handcraft carried on in the home, we must also consider the professional crafts and industry. The purpose of this work is to study the products of various home crafts, their milieus and functions. But, as we shall find, this cannot be accomplished without taking into account the two other forms of production, professional craft manufacture and industry.

Home crafts, professional crafts, and industry

Characteristic of home craft production is that a particular product is made in the home, as a sideline, uncommissioned, and is sold by the producer directly to the consumer. The professional craftsman, however, has special training for a certain type of manufacture, which is carried out in a workshop. His products are made to order and sold directly to the customer. Industrial production has a more complicated organization with an employer who possesses the necessary capital for the acquisi-

1. Woman on her way to sell homemade textiles. Öxabäck, Västergötland, beginning of the twentieth century.

tion of raw materials and tools or machinery, but who need not himself know the manufacturing process for which he employs and compensates workers. The finished products are sold through entrepreneurs, either by himself or by salesmen employed by him.

In other words, there are distinct differences between these three forms of production in theory. However, in reality, they blend imperceptibly into each other and develop through mutual interaction.

We know that handcraft for household use and for sale is extremely old. It is also clear that specialized professional artisans existed as early as the Stone and Bronze Ages. At what point industrial production emerged is more difficult to establish, since the decisive criterion is not the nature of the final product but economic and organizational factors. However, it is known that cloth manufacture was industrially organized in Europe as early as the Middle Ages; moreover, this industry was the first to be operated on a large scale.

In the 1630s, the Swedish state began taking an interest in and encouraging the founding of various industries, especially the textile industry. In its efforts to create industrial production, the state came into conflict with the home manufacture of craft products for sale. This conflict was very sharp, especially at times during the eighteenth century. The restrictive measures of the state came to oppose the handcraft production, because the latter was the major competitor for the consumer. To a great extent, this opposition had to do with the complex condition of the national industries in seventeenth- and eighteenth-century Sweden.

Professional crafts and home crafts

Since agriculture and animal husbandry completely dominated the national industries as late as the twentieth century, the agrarian population, through the ages, has constituted, without any comparison, the majority of the population. In 1850 it was 75 percent of the total population, in 1870 around 70 percent, and in 1900, 55 percent. Household industry for home consumption was, on the whole, an unavoidable supplement to the livelihood of the agrarian population. The production in burgher homes, rural and urban, was also considerable. In the year 1870, the urban population constituted only 13 percent of the country's total population; at the turn of the century this figure had increased to 22 percent. It was not until the latter part of the nine-

2. Sale of woven goods at the large annual Larsmässo Fair in Göteborg, 1907.

3. Some of the linens and domestic textiles which were in the possession of the Ekström family, Yxnaholma, Höör (Skåne), in 1965. These represent part of the accumulated efforts of four generations since the end of the eighteenth century.

4. Itinerant peddler from Västergötland, or *knalle*, hawking a skein of yarn. Over his shoulder are slung his *knalle* sack and a length of woven material; from his wrist hangs an ell rule. Painting by Pehr Hilleström, second half of the eighteenth century.

5. Wall hanging painted on linen weave, attributed to Johannes Nilsson (1757–1827), Laholm, Halland. Various craftsmen are represented: glazier, mason, carpenter, tailor, cooper, shoemaker, painter, cabinetmaker, hatter, coppersmith, woodturner, and blacksmith. Dated 1804.

teenth century that the towns ceased contributing agricultural products. As late as the nineteenth century, the burghers in the cities kept cows, pigs, and other stock. Also, outside the town proper, they would have outlying pasture land, tilled plots, and vegetable gardens, from which they obtained necessities for household consumption. Textile materials were also processed.

It has always been—and still remains—extraordinarily difficult to determine the total output of handcraft production in the area of production for household use. When it comes to handcraft products made for sale, there is a certain accounting in statistical reports.[1] As far as professional crafts go, the possibility of estimating their significance, based on actual figures, is far better. At the middle of the eighteenth century, which marks the beginning of Sweden's population statistics, specialized craftsmen constituted only 4–5 percent of the total population. On the other hand, these professional craftsmen were occupied full time. Their output must, nevertheless, have been relatively small compared with that of the spare-time craftsmen.

Since the twelfth century, free craftsmen or artisans have joined together in so-called guilds, i.e., professional leagues with certain standards of training and skill for those who wished to join and to be licensed to ply their trade. A proficiency test was required for advancement from apprentice to journeyman. The journeyman then had to improve his skills by working for several masters. To that end, and to gain experience generally, he undertook long travels, often abroad, during his journeyman years. This type of training, in which the journeyman amassed a store of technical knowledge, patterns, and models, was a most important factor in the dissemination of new styles. The condition for the foundation of a guild was the existence of at least four professional craftsmen of the same or similar crafts within one town. Medieval Sweden had only a few towns of the requisite size. Stockholm, Visby, Kalmar, Norrköping, Malmö (in Skåne, at that time a Danish province),[2] and a few more towns harbored practically all guild-regulated crafts in Sweden.

In the Middle Ages there were also specialized professionals attached to monasteries and large noble estates. After the dissolution of the monasteries in Sweden in the sixteenth century, the nobles continued to keep craftsmen and artisans on their estates. They were granted the privilege of keeping these manorial craftsmen outside of the guilds. These craftsmen have also been of great importance in the dissemination of new styles from the landed gentry to the peasantry and the latter's craft milieu.

In Stockholm, where the majority of Swedish craftsmen was to be found, the number of craftsmen increased somewhat during the eighteenth century. Not until this time did the guild system reach the smaller rural towns. And only in exceptional cases did this expansion affect the countryside itself. Most country parishes had only one or two craftsmen in the same trade, most often operating outside of the guild system. They were called *gärningsmän* (journeymen)[3] and were employed by the county governor on the recommendation of the parish council. Most prominent among the rural craftsmen were the tailor and the shoemaker. But for luxury items, such as jewelry, hats, fine leathergoods, printed textiles, and decorative hardware, and for certain pieces of furniture and wood articles, one would turn to specialized craftsmen (fig. 5). Even by the time the guild system was abolished by statutes in the 1840s and 1860s, it had not spread to the countryside to any noticeable extent. This differentiation between urban industries and rural industries had been part of Swedish economic policy in the Middle Ages, as well as in the Age of Empire and the Age of Freedom.[4]

Since the late Middle Ages, the creation of towns had been encouraged by the Crown. The burghers, artisans, and merchants of the cities were granted the privilege of selling and buying up goods in the countryside at specific fairs, whereas the farmers were generally prohibited

6. A Västergötland peddler, *knalle,* buying up lengths of woven material in a farmhouse. Painting by J. W. Wallander, 1850s.

7. Selling baskets outside a churchyard wall. Ekshärad, Värmland, beginning of the twentieth century.

What is handcraft?

8. Especially in the "Seven Hundreds" in Västergötland, handcraft production for sale was organized by merchants with capital, so-called *förlagsmän* or merchant-employers.—*Förlagsmän* Johan Lundberg and his wife. Toarp, Västergötland.

9. Craftsmen would usually sell their own products. Sale of textiles, baskets, toy horses, etc. Kyrkhult, Blekinge.

from trading. This prohibition of rural trade was stiffened during the Vasa era.[5] Craft production by peasants was also prohibited. The whole country was divided into precisely drawn-up trade districts (*uppland*) surrounding those market towns to which farmers were obliged to bring their goods for sale. The cities, in turn, were designated as inland cities for domestic trade only (*uppstäder*), or staple cities, with exclusive rights to overseas trade.

Handcraft products intended for sale

Trade has been regulated from the beginning of recorded time by the coming together of buyers and sellers from separate locations. Traditionally, they would meet at certain agreed on places at certain times, e.g., to celebrate religious holidays, to attend church, or to attend the *ting* (originally, an assembly of freemen with legislative and judiciary powers; here, "district courts"). A relic of the custom to buy and sell whenever a sizable crowd assembled was the Sunday commerce on the church green. In spite of resistance from the clergy and the authorities, this practice continued to flourish as late as the nineteenth century, and, in exceptional cases, even later (fig. 7).

Some of these rural markets and fairs have been of great importance since at least the Middle Ages, attracting buyers and sellers from afar. Some such annual fairs still exist in various parts of the country and attract a large attendance (fig. 2).[6]

To these large annual fairs, as well as to the weekly markets in town, peasants would come with their products. But apart from this government-regulated trade, the peasants traditionally sold handcraft products in town and country by traveling around and selling directly to consumers (figs. 4, 6, 9, 10). It was this unchecked trade which the authorities wished to prevent. However, for the rural population this manufacture and retailing was a necessary complement to its livelihood.

In certain areas the craft production for sale has been more important than agriculture to the economy of the household. Farming, cattle raising, hunting, and fishing gave an immediate return in the form of foodstuffs. The making of craft products for sale, on the other hand, aimed at creating trade objects with which to acquire the barest necessities for those either completely lacking foodstuffs or producing them in insufficient amounts.

Craft provinces and provincial crafts

As far back as conditions in Sweden are known, there have been regions which have had to compensate for their lack of food products by providing services or by specialized manufacture of certain craft products. These were areas where the soil did not yield sufficiently, and where the labor market reached a high degree of specialization in the production of trade objects and services. Such was the case in Bergslagen, Sweden's first industrial area, where mining and forest industries swallowed up the work force and created a shortage of consumer goods. A similar situation existed in the urban centers of the Lake Mälaren district where merchants, officials, and craftsmen made up a significant stratum of consumers for handcraft products and foodstuffs. Stockholm and other larger cities in the

Mälaren valley and Bergslagen have, magnet-like, attracted handcraft products from the immediately surrounding countryside as well as from Dalarna, Hälsingland and other Norrland provinces, southeastern Sweden, Gotland, and Finland.

The handcraft production for sale was, however, not directed merely from the provinces to the urban centers, but also from province to province. There existed an exchange of goods over great distances without the cooperation of middlemen.

The supply of raw materials of certain kinds, e.g., flax, wool, iron, and wood, and the supply of labor have created distinct craft districts, specializing in certain kinds of products. Agriculture has been developed and able to fully support the people in a few regions only: the wide farmlands in Skåne, Småland's coastal

10. The districts of Östra Göinge and Västra Göinge in northern Skåne are traditional woodcraft regions. Even today, "Göinge wagon loads" arrive in cities and towns on market days. Kristianstad, Skåne, 1951.

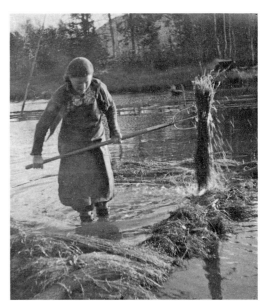

11. In the provinces of southern Norrland, flax products have been an important economic factor since the Middle Ages.—The flax is pulled. Ljusdal, Hälsingland.

12. Flax retting. Hanebo, Hälsingland.

15

13. Breaking and clubbing the flax. Umeå, Västerbotten.

14. Hackling the flax. Ljusdal, Hälsingland.

15. A skein of handspun linen yarn. Sollerö, Dalarna.

areas, the plains in Östergötland and Västergötland, the Mälaren valley, and the land around Lake Storsjön in Jämtland. But in the forest areas, handcraft for sale as a sideline to farming has consistently been of major importance. In these areas, the supply of wood has created favorable conditions for woodcrafts of various kinds. Consequently, a production of coopered vessels, splint boxes, baskets, and other wood objects has developed in Sweden's forest regions. Since woodcraft products are bulky and cumbersome to transport, they have generally been offered for sale in nearby towns and on adjacent nonwooded farmlands (figs. 18, 20, 23). Thus, Swedish woodcraft has generally been sold in proximity to the place of manufacture, with the exception of the woodcraft of Västergötland, which will be further discussed below.

On the whole, woodcraft was man's work. In forest areas, the contribution of women to craft production for sale consisted of textile materials (figs. 13, 17). Access to forest pasture land increased the feasibility of keeping a large stock of cattle. On the Baltic islands of Gotland (fig. 156) and Öland, sheep raising has always been favored by climatic and soil conditions; in Småland and Halland there have been favorable pasture lands for sheep and dairy cattle. Hälsingland, Ångermanland, and Västerbotten—three provinces in northern Sweden—have offered favorable conditions for flax growing and flax processing. The same is true, to a certain extent, of the *härad* (district or hundred)[7] of Mark in Västergötland and some parts of Småland. Through their textile production, these areas, especially rich in raw materials, have developed into highly productive and competitive manufacturing districts of great importance.

Textiles have been more suitable than other products for interregional trade as they are easy to transport. Since prehistoric times, cloth has been an object for commercial speculation, creating commercial and industrial centers earlier than any other branch of industry. Also in the Swedish home craft production for sale, textiles were objects of long-range trade. The major production areas—in Norrland for flax products, and in southern Sweden for both wool and flax products—emerged early as the major suppliers of textiles and retained this position as late as the mid-nineteenth century (see map, fig. 26).

To a certain extent, similar conditions prevailed also for iron forging. The main area with iron-ore deposits was Bergslagen (southern Dalarna and Västmanland), where Stora Kopparberg ("The Great Copper Mountain") had been mined since the thirteenth century. On a smaller scale, there was also mining in northern Östergötland (fig. 19), Södermanland, Uppland, Gästrikland, and—from the end of the seventeenth century—in Härjedalen and Norrbotten. Since prehistoric times, lake and bog ore supplies have been extracted, particularly in Dalarna and Småland. Smelting and further processing of the ore was carried out in small furnaces as a peasant industry. From

16. In the western Swedish craft region, textile production for sale was so extensive that it occupied men, women, and children alike. Mark district, Västergötland, about 1900.

17. As a rule, every country household raised sheep and processed wool.—Carding the wool. Mangskog, Värmland.

17

18. The supply of labor or of a certain raw material, e.g., wool or wood, has helped create distinct craft regions.—The spinning-wheel maker E. O. Berglund with his children and grandchildren. Malå, Västerbotten.

19. Nail smith. Häradshammar, Östergötland, 1921.

20. Coopering. Planing the interior of an iron-banded tub. Örkelljunga, Skåne.

the end of the seventeenth century, processing of the ore mined in Bergslagen took place at the ironworks (*bruk*) in Värmland, Närke, Västmanland, Uppland, and Gästrikland. Some of the ore was, however, still processed by the peasants in Västergötland, Småland, and northern Skåne. In connection with the large-scale production at the ironworks there also grew up a certain production on a smaller scale for household consumption and for the market.

Handcraft production for sale has long taken place in two major areas. These areas, the western Swedish craft region and the northern Swedish, or Norrland, craft region, are in several respects quite unlike each other.

The western Swedish craft region

It is known that, shortly before the middle of the sixteenth century, wadmal (coarse fulled and napped woolen cloth) and linen tabby were spoken of as products of Västergötland. The linen from the district of Mark was especially noted as a quality product. Not until the middle of that century did textile manufacture reach such an extent that there was any surplus to trade. In 1604, when Karl IX proposed a curtailing of rural crafts, the clergy objected on the grounds that the soil in Norrland and Västergötland could not fully support the peasants.

When the city of Borås was founded in the 1620s, the Västergötland production of craft

21. Basket weaving. Töllsjö, Västergötland.

22. Plaiting of straw for straw hats. Ärtemark, Dalsland.

23. Planing splints for basket weaving. Örkened, Skåne.

24. "Västergötland coverlet" from Bjuråker, Hälsingland. Weft-patterned tabby, type *upphämta*, linen ground with pattern weft of colored woolen yarn.

to this manufacture (figs. 140, 141). They offered these vessels for sale all over the country. They would also take the opportunity to replenish their stores by settling temporarily wherever raw materials were to be had for little or nothing.

During the latter part of the seventeenth century and all of the eighteenth, textile crafts received a tremendous boost and became the most important crafts of the western Swedish region.

When Borås was granted town privileges in the 1620s, its trade was limited to textiles and iron and wood products. It was intended that the Borås merchants would, from then on, limit their trading to Västergötland, and that the lively peasant trade would be channeled through Borås. Such, however, was not the outcome. The peasants of Västergötland continued their trading throughout the country, and the Borås merchants continued to buy and sell, as before, in the towns of Bergslagen. The towns of Bergslagen complained, and even succeeded in having Borås's town privileges

items for sale was already well under way, apparently along well-established lines.

As elsewhere in the country, the route of the regular ox drives from the south to Bergslagen constituted the main channel of the country's various trade and exchange of goods. As a border province—adjoining the then Danish provinces of Skåne and Halland on one side and the then Danish Norway on the other—Västergötland maintained a lively commerce with parts of the Danish kingdom. Simultaneously, Västergötland traded with central Sweden. People from Västergötland, Småland, and Östergötland sold oxen in Bergslagen, even outside of the fixed fairs. They also sold wrought-iron products, wood products, fine woolen cloth, wadmal, and fish.

In the sixteenth century, it was reported that

there were particularly great numbers of blacksmiths in the districts of Mark, Gäsene, and Kind; later also in the districts of Ås and Veden. Among their products were nails, horseshoe nails, locks, scythes, saw blades, trivets, braziers, grills, pots, bits, sleigh bells, and Jew's harps. This production probably reflected a regional specialization, tied in with the prehistoric extraction of lake and bog ore in Småland. During the Middle Ages and later, farmers would buy their iron from Bergslagen instead. Woodcraft was then less important than blacksmithing.

During the seventeenth and part of the eighteenth centuries, woodcraft products in the form of turned vessels were more prevalent. The farmers, especially those of the districts of Mark, Kind, and Redväg, devoted themselves

25. Coverlet seal with the legend "Ulricehamns rev. hallstempel," indicating that this coverlet was made in the western Swedish craft region.

temporarily suspended. In the eighteenth century, however, the Borås merchants were given the right to bring their wares to all cities in the realm and to man booths and stands during fairs. These rights were unique, confirming the extent and importance of the Västergötland trade. Peasants, too, from Västergötland would traverse the country, crisscrossing their own province as well as the rest of the country. Far north into Norway and across the Baltic into Finland they wandered with their sacks or loaded packhorses, side by side with the Västergötland merchants—the peasants hiding furtively behind the merchants' well-earned privileges. However, in the eighteenth century, the peasants succeeded in pushing through their demands to trade legally all over the country.

Thus, both the Västergötland peasants themselves and the merchants of Borås—through traveling salesmen—sold their wares; the peasants sold the products of their own crafts, the merchants what they had bought up at markets in the province. But it did not stop at that. The Borås merchants were said to "buy the quill while still on the goose, the wool before the sheep is shorn, the ox in the stall, and the grain in the granary." Their efficiency was founded on a wide network of connections, which had been established and was maintained through repeated personal efforts. It is known that the Borås merchants found their way across the Baltic to Gotland as early as the seventeenth century. There they bought up wool and wadmal. Furthermore, they had the right to buy up textiles in the west coast town of Varberg and its surroundings. In reality, then, their activity encompassed all of Halland. Their method of operation consisted of buying up raw materials, wool on Gotland, cow hair in Småland, or iron in Bergslagen, then placing these materials for processing or finishing in the provinces of Småland, northern Skåne, Halland, and Västergötland, where there was a surplus of available labor. The Västergötland *knalle* (figs. 4, 6), or itinerant peddler, could then sell the manufactured products in Bergslagen, the cities of the Lake Mälaren valley, in Värmland, Norrland, Norway, and Finland. The manufacturers (figs. 1, 16) were paid for their work and were provided with materials

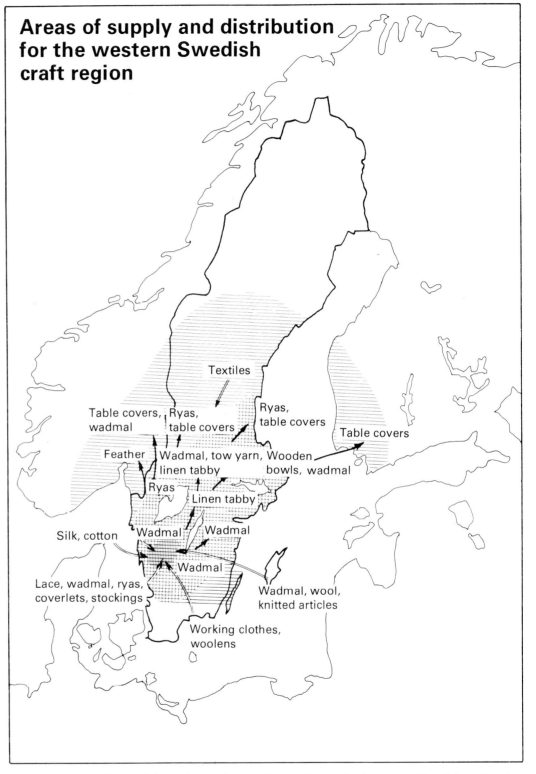

26. In the seventeenth and eighteenth centuries, textile manufacture in the western Swedish craft region developed into the region's most important industry. Its products were distributed by itinerant salesmen throughout large parts of Sweden, Denmark, Norway, and Finland.

by a merchant of substantial means, a so-called *förlagsman* (fig. 8). This organization was known as the *förlag* system, i.e., the merchant-employer or putting-out system. It was a form of industrial organization, but an industry in the home, decentralized, as opposed to factory-located industry. In addition to this manufacture, various domestic crafts were also practiced in the home. To distinguish between the products of these two systems is hardly possible, and no attempt has been made here to do so.

The business connections made by the traveling salesmen in the provinces were far-reaching and complex. The salesmen probably operated on a kind of installment plan; in several places they found business partners among peasants, burghers, and ironworkers. The merchants would finance the sales trips which required post horses, feed, expense accounts, and merchandise. Moreover, the merchants had permanent headquarters where the salesmen could lodge, organize their trade, and replenish their stores. Thus, a network of business connections, suppliers of raw materials, and manufacturers organized the entire country into specified buying and selling areas (fig. 26).

The Norrland craft region

The Norrland craft region differs from the western Swedish region in products as well as organization. Here the manufacture was based on locally produced raw materials; the finished product was, by and large, sold by the producer directly to the consumer. In other words, there existed no putting-out system, and the manufacturer himself received the profit.

The most important craft locality within the region was the linen-producing parishes in the provinces along the Baltic. As early as the Middle Ages, coarse linen goods and processed flax were extensively produced here and sold widely to the coastal towns of Norrland and to central Sweden (figs. 13, 14). The Norrland flax production was further developed during the eighteenth century, but, unlike the western Swedish textile production, it lost its market with the introduction of cotton at the beginning of the nineteenth century.

Dalarna

The province of Dalarna offers the most conspicuous and best-known provincial craft production in Sweden. Its poorly developed agriculture and its archaic inheritance customs[8] have made a developed craft production imperative. A remarkable specialization has given rise to a specific manufacture in each parish, e.g., the casting of small bells and buttons—so-called Gustafs buttons—in Gustafs parish; the making of coopered vessels (fig. 519) and splint baskets in Mora (fig. 553) and Venjan; the painting of cabinetry and purely decorative painting in Leksand and Rättvik (fig. 27); boat building in Sollerö; iron extraction, smithery, and the making of chimney bricks in Älvdalen; the making of grindstones in Orsa; and the tanning of hides and the making of leather garments in Malung.

Here, too, the distribution took place without middlemen by retailing directly to the consumers during trips, especially to Bergslagen, the Lake Mälaren area, and Stockholm (fig. 135).

Handcraft production and industry

From the middle of the seventeenth century, the state carried on an intensive activity supporting industrial enterprise by direct subsidies, by protective tariffs, and by legislation directed against home craft production for sale.

In his book *An Economic History of Sweden* (see Bibliography), Eli F. Heckscher has thrown light on the position of the handcrafts in this situation, which came to a head during the eighteenth century. The economic literature of the day exhibits a united front against handcraft, which is condemned in no uncertain terms. It is referred to as "kladdandet och klåpandet" (the dabbling and bungling) in the countryside. This displeasure was directed especially against those who carried on a domestic craft production for sale, "these dabbling and bungling craftsmen, who peddle their makeshift wares illegally to divers buyers and the common populace, servants and the like." The bitterness towards the peasants' domestic production and trade was based on contemporary views of the national economy. To make

commerce and industry flourish, it was considered advisable to locate what was regarded as urban industries in the towns and prohibit their practice by the peasants. In spite of the strong state support lavished on the manufacturing industries during the eighteenth century—direct cash subsidies, alms, privileges, and protection against competing foreign goods—these industries rarely turned out to be the basis for the later rapidly expanding industrial development of the nineteenth century. The nineteenth-century textile industry especially was, ironically, a direct heir of the maligned domestic industry so persistent in certain areas.

Heckscher writes, "Contemporaneous reports [also] agree that the domestic industry increased considerably during the eighteenth century. Especially weaving and spinning were taken up in province after province where there had been no textile crafts in the preceding century. For this result the industrial policy of the time must be assumed to be largely responsible, although its aim was an entirely different one and, in fact, directly opposed to such a development. When protectionist policies raised the prices of foreign goods, the products of household industry rather than those of domestic manufacturers filled the void. Their qualities as well as the way in which they were distributed fitted the needs of the population far better."[9]

During the eighteenth century, especially, handcraft production, particularly textile manufacture in *Sjuhäradsbygden* (the "Seven Hundreds"),[10] changed over from a domestic industry to modern industrial factory production. The first mechanized cotton mill in Sweden, Rydboholm, outside Borås, developed from the extensive putting-out system that had been organized by a peasant woman named Mother Kerstin of Stämmemad. In 1834, her son, Sven Erikson, reorganized her establishment into a factory. The "Seven Hundreds" are today the center of Sweden's textile industry, directly developed out of domestic industry. This region also boasts an unusual number of mail-order firms. There probably exists a direct connection between these firms and the distribution organization built up by the itinerant peddlers. They brough their wares to their customers and took their orders, much as mail-order firms now offer service directly to the home. However, as late as the 1920s and '30s, the peddlers continued their trade, their sacks now filled, not with handcraft, but with factory products.

Within other craft regions, domestic production for sale has been converted in a similar fashion to factory production and/or household production for domestic consumption. Such is the case with the textile production in Västra Vingåker, Södermanland, and in certain Dalarna parishes; with the forest industries in the forest areas of Dalarna, Småland, northern Skåne, Västergötland, Östergötland, and Uppland; and with the metalcraft in Dalarna, Småland, and northern Skåne.

During the latter part of the nineteenth century, the interplay between various branches of industrial production and domestic industry became increasingly more complicated. Handcraft societies, the educational system, as well as the general dissemination of culture, came to play increasingly prominent roles. Material touching this interplay from the last one hundred years—an epoch of vital importance which cannot yet be surveyed—exists in vast, though unprocessed, amounts. The present work deals with this epoch only in those cases in which a craft product's design has grown out of a strongly traditional milieu. From around the mid-nineteenth century, one must take into account a great increase in the number of new industrial products for all classes of society. In all areas, industrial mass production created a number of special forms: on one hand, by reaching out directly to all strata of society; on the other, by stimulating the crafts still practiced in the households. Thus, to begin with, industrial production had a stimulating effect on home production.

Handcraft and decorative art work

Some handcraft products emphasize a more conscious aesthetic intention. Their function is nonutilitarian, purely ornamental, as in certain textile products, wood carvings, and decorative painting on built-in furnishings, pieces of carpentry, and wall hangings. These must be

27. Within the production milieu of domestic crafts, there also existed provincial artists with a conscious aesthetic intent. Many of them signed their works; others are known to us through other sources.— Painting on paper, *The Horse Trading,* signed EAS i Ullvi. Leksand, Dalarna.

judged artistic creations, evidently executed by individuals with a distinct aesthetic gift. They are not infrequently signed, which points to a highly developed sense of identity (figs. 27, 28). These artists were well-known and acknowledged specialists in their respective spheres. They were the ones to be commissioned for projects of a more official or public nature, e.g., the erection and embellishment of churches and "bridal chambers," rooms for receiving wedding guests. Their names have lived on for generations in the provinces in oral tradition and, in some felicitous cases, in official documents. However, for the most part,

this type of provincial professional, working outside the urban craft guilds, has been extremely difficult or impossible to trace in contemporary official records. Occasionally, research efforts have unearthed artists whose talent and interest for their work brought them into contact with workshop production and other, more professionally oriented, manufacture. At times they attracted assistants and founded workshops with a wide variety of activities and a large market. Some of these workshops continued for several generations. Certain of these provincial artists also handcrafted everyday wares. Thus, it is obviously

What is handcraft?

28. Wall hanging painted on textile, "Ahasverus gästabud som stod i 180 dagar" (The banquet of Ahasuerus, which lasted for 180 days). Breared, Halland.

often difficult to distinguish between handcraft and decorative art work; although there are pure strains of decorative art work or artistic production which decidedly fall outside of the scope of this work. Among the latter I count the painting of wall hangings, wood carving, and finer carpentry for interior decoration of churches. All three emerge as, or constitute, well-defined groups, classifiable as workshop production. Decorative art work exists within practically every type of handcraft. Hence, although the more aesthetically conscious craft production will not be treated here, certain perspectives on this related area will be included. The emphasis of this work, however, is on the contribution of the anonymous craftsman.

Handcraft and the Handcraft Movement
The Handcraft Movement, that is, the activity carried on by societies and private individuals

in order to further the production and distribution of handcrafted items, developed rapidly towards the end of the nineteenth century. *Föreningen för Svensk Hemslöjd* (The Society for Swedish Handcraft) was founded in 1899, soon followed by the majority of the fifty-six now active societies. The background to this lively organizational activity was primarily the difficulties of handcraft in holding its own against the greater volume and more efficient distribution of industrial production. Even earlier, the agricultural societies had worked for the improvement and encouragement of handcraft—especially the cultivation and spinning of flax. In the 1840s, several agricultural societies employed instructors in weaving as well as straw plaiting and basket weaving. In the 1870s, straw-plaiting instruction was offered in seventeen counties, basket weaving in twelve, weaving in eight, lace making in two, and carpentry in two. Sporadically, courses were also offered in clog

making, wood carving, wrought-iron forging, etc. The agricultural societies also strived to acquire patterns and models. In several counties there were such collections; pamphlets were printed up, and copies of J. E. Ekenmark's weaving manual[11] were purchased for distribution. Handcraft exhibitions were arranged at which rewards were given (fig. 29); retail centers were also set up to facilitate distribution. In 1863, permanent exhibitions of handcraft were created in Kalmar and Karlstad. During the 1860s and '70s, the agricultural societies exhibited a lively and active interest in supporting handcraft production. The state also gave some subsidies. The immediate reason was the need for state support in such regions where handcraft, previously important, had been driven out of business by industrial production at the same time as agriculture was hit by crop failure. Later, however, the agricultural societies' interest in handcraft was somewhat dampened, and the state grants were diverted to the pedagogical aspect of craft production. It was in this situation that the organization of handcraft societies began. One of the driving forces was Lilli Zickerman around the turn of the twentieth century (fig. 32). Her energetic propaganda activity created a favorable start for the Handcraft Movement. This movement at once engendered a strong response, permeated as the time was by ideas of national romanticism.

Even earlier, two associations had already awakened an interest in Swedish peasant craft by praising its high technical and aesthetic quality. These two groups were the *Svenska Slöjdföreningen* (The Swedish Society for Industrial Design), founded in 1845, and *Föreningen Handarbetets Vänner* (The Friends of Textile Art Association), founded in 1874. The further acceptance of the Handcraft Movement and its products was significantly boosted by the great successes at the international exhibitions in Vienna (1873 and 1909), Berlin (1907), and Budapest (1910), as well as the Stockholm Exhibition of 1897 and the Baltic Exhibition in Malmö, in 1914.

Organizationally, a consolidation began in 1912 with the formation of *Svenska Hemslöjds-föreningarnas Riksförbund* (The National As-

30. Mrs. Degerlund, weaver from Karlshamn, worked for the Handcraft Society in Karlskrona.

31. Johanna Brunsson (1846–1920), art weaver and weaving teacher, came from the western Swedish craft milieu. In 1889 she started Brunsson's Weaving School, which until its closing in 1958 was one of Sweden's foremost training centers for weaving instructors.

29. Handcraft production for sale lost its position as the country's greatest producer of goods in the mid-nineteenth century. Through the efforts of the Handcraft Movement it has lived on in the form of quality production.—The Agricultural Society's craft hall in Karlskrona.

What is handcraft?

sociation of Swedish Handcraft Societies). In 1928, a common sales organization with wholesale and retail outlets in Stockholm was created, *Hemslöjdsförbundet för Sverige* (The Swedish Handcraft Industries Association). Further-

32. Lilli Zickerman (1858–1949), textile artist who organized and carried out a countrywide inventory of handcraft. In 1899, she founded *Föreningen för Svensk Hemslöjd* (The Society for Swedish Handcraft).

33. Handcraft retail outlet. The Handcraft Society of Mora, Dalarna.

more, a joint jury-screening procedure was instituted to maintain the quality of handcraft products on a consistently high level.

Most of the agricultural societies have continued their teaching activity through trained handcraft consultants. Carried out in cooperation with the handcraft societies, their work with courses and guidance of craftsmen is today's guarantee for a continuation of the manual tradition and for the perpetuation of Swedish handcraft production. Through their retail shops the handcraft societies have created a chain of sales outlets for handcraft products (fig. 33) and, at the same time, have emerged as centers for Swedish design in the various provinces by virtue of their exacting standards for products and milieus alike.

Handcraft: Milieu and function

Settlement and dwelling

The center of the household is the fireplace (fig. 34). It gives warmth and contains the fire over which food is prepared. All other activities in the home, however elaborate they may have become with time, revolve around these two basic functions. Many other functions of the dwelling have been added: to safeguard property, and to provide areas for sleep, work, and fellowship with one's family, relatives, and friends. The latter social function has, perhaps more than any other, contributed to the development of the dwelling and its furnishings. It has created new, more differentiated needs and has stimulated new forms of architectural and interior design.

Rural tradition

Home furnishings—household utensils, furniture, textiles, and built-in furnishings—have always adapted to the form of the dwelling. Thus, the strong influence from Sweden's rural heritage—in the form of living and eating habits, holiday customs, and social-value systems—can still be felt, even in the modern homes of today's industrialized society.

The overall milieu, i.e., the adjustment of the dwelling to adjacent buildings and their relationship to local environment and industry, is also important. Different types of industry have given rise to characteristic types of settlements. The fishing villages of Bohuslän are adapted to the fishing industry and the needs of a fishing population. The large villages in Dalarna are an expression of that province's social structure and economic conditions (fig. 37). The patriarchally organized ironworks created the typical ironworks community with its ironmaster's residence, workers' lodgings, and workshops. The town reflects the requirements of trade, workshop manufacture, and industry. The sawmill community, the railroad junction, etc. are fairly recent types, successively created by new industries, new routes of communication, and new power supplies. Thus, a wide range of settlements exists in today's Sweden, from socialized communities for

34. Interior of fire-house. Rockvallarna *fäbod*—outlying summer dairy farm—Funäsdalen, Härjedalen, 1957.

35. Lapp hut, *kåta,* of permanent wood construction, used by permanently settled Lapps. Jokkmokk, Lappland, 1938.

36. Cityscape. Högdalen, outside Stockholm, 1962.

37. Village clustered around a crossroads. Sollerö, Dalarna, 1920s.

the production of nuclear energy to temporary villages of nomadic herders (figs. 35, 36). These settlements constitute part of the cultural milieu in which we live and to which our furnishings must be suited. It is obvious that rural traditions still play an important part in the city as well as the countryside. They have also, to a great extent, been a decisive factor in the shaping of Swedish housing in all social strata, up to the time of, and far beyond the breakthrough of, industrialism.

Centuries of traditions shape our present dwelling milieu

Because of their permanence in time and space, settlements, house types, and dwellings join to create a milieu reaching back a couple of hundred years in time, in some cases several centuries. This milieu encompasses the life of past generations, their habits, social customs, household goods, and aesthetic consciousness. Thus, we live not only in the present but also in the past. In our present environment we can trace and illustrate the development of housing and household goods in time and space, and their manifestations in different social groups. Among the Lapps, e.g., we can study the layout of a nomadic cattle raiser's *kåta*—a conical tent or hut of turf and wood—and what func-

tions the *kåta* fulfills (figs. 35, 101). We may compare the *kåta* to today's colossal buildings with hundreds of apartments, each comprising several rooms, all under a single roof (fig. 36). We may also compare the furnishings of the *kåta* with our own highly specialized furnishings, reflecting our widely diversified society and life-styles.

Today, we have access to graphic examples of differentiation in dwellings and furnishings, without having to resort to museums. The following is a selection of the most important milestones in the development of housing and furnishings, with an emphasis on their functional differentiation. The purpose is to demonstrate the dependence of the form of the furnishings on that of the dwelling.

29

Settlement and dwelling

Town and country

Building customs in the countryside naturally vary widely according to prevailing economic conditions. They reflect the social stratification, from the unpropertied poor to crofters and yeomen, to ironmasters, to landed gentry. The houses of well-to-do burghers and the rural upper class have naturally been of great importance in adopting and transmitting new ideas to the surrounding countryside. However, towns and country manors are far from exhibiting a homogeneous style. Generally, only buildings of an official or public nature are stylistically consistent. The dwellings of simple people, e.g., the cottage of the soldier, the fisherman, and the boatswain, and the lodgings of the workshop and factory worker, have all retained the character of rural settlements (see

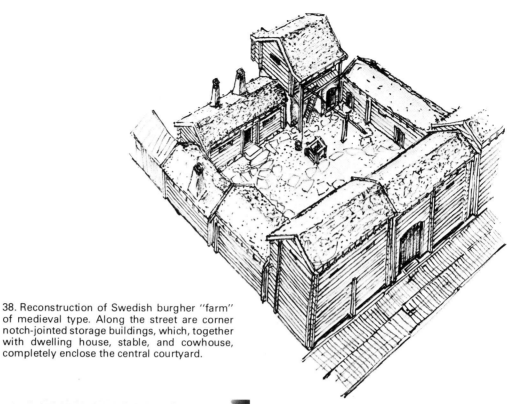

38. Reconstruction of Swedish burgher "farm" of medieval type. Along the street are corner notch-jointed storage buildings, which, together with dwelling house, stable, and cowhouse, completely enclose the central courtyard.

fig. 49 and further text on page 37). Add to this the fact that, as late as the nineteenth century, townspeople kept farm land, or at least pasture land, cabbage patches, small garden plots, cows, chickens, and pigs, which helped supply the household's required foodstuffs. It is easy to understand that the life of townspeople in many respects did not differ too much from that of farmers or landed gentry. Up to the mid-eighteenth century, many towns were little more than peasant villages elevated to townships, or more or less permanent settlements grown up around marketplaces and churches (figs. 38, 39).

Wood dominates Swedish building tradition

Houses of wood still give the Swedish countryside its distinct character. In northern and central Sweden, wooden buildings are, in spite of changes in the exterior, still traditionally

39. "Farm" in town of medieval type. Ystad, Skåne.

40. The "farms" of Kila village are laid out with their barns flanking the main street. Hycklinge, Östergötland, 1912.

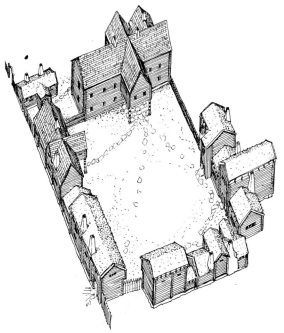

41. View of Stockholm around the middle of the seventeenth century, showing the House of Nobles (second from the left), private palaces, and the Grayfriars' Church (Riddarholmskyrkan). From Erik Dahlberg's seventeenth-century pictorial atlas of Sweden, *Suecia Antiqua et Hodierna* (1661–1716).

42. Reconstruction of a manor (Sörbo, Västergötland) from the mid-seventeenth century. All buildings are of log construction.

grouped, and built with traditional methods on traditional plans (fig. 37). The cities—small, medium-sized, and large ones, even Stockholm —were also predominantly rural milieus fifty to one hundred years ago (fig. 41). Town lots included stables, cow sheds, barns, and storage sheds, built around a courtyard and connected to the dwelling house. Far into the nineteenth century, these town blocks were built of wood. Stone and brick architecture was of some importance in Stockholm and Visby (on Gotland). In Skåne, towns were built in half-timber construction (fig. 39).

Manors, official residences, and parsonages were also built of wood (figs. 42, 45). On the whole, they had the appearance of largish farms as late as the eighteenth century.

Village and city planning

Through certain efforts by the authorities, village lots were regulated as early as the Middle Ages. Two types of villages are characterized by long narrow lots, forcing the house clusters close together. These types are especially common in central eastern Sweden, the provinces around Lake Mälaren, in Östergötland, and along the coast of Småland down to the Blckinge border. They are called *radbyar*, line-type settlements: single *radby*, with houses lined up along one side of the main village street, and double *radby*, with houses on both sides (fig. 40). Most villages had a more irregular layout, *klungbyar*, or cluster villages (fig. 37). Because of its regular, centralized arrangement, a *radby* often gave the impression of being a town, especially as many towns barely could be distinguished from villages, anyway, because of the farming activities and cattle raising of the burghers. As in the country, the farms in the towns were laid out on a square, enclosing a central courtyard with loft houses and gateways (fig. 38).

The two-story loft house, with or without outside gallery, was initially a foreign phenomenon, imported into Sweden during the Middle Ages. It spread from the towns to the countryside during the seventeenth and eighteenth centuries and became most popular in central Sweden, especially in Bergslagen, Da-

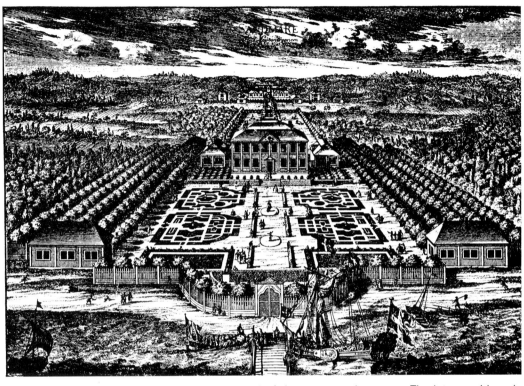

43. View of the Noor estate in Uppland at the end of the seventeenth century. The layout, with main building, wings, and formal garden, is patterned on contemporary French models. From Erik Dahlberg, *Suecia Antiqua et Hodlerna* (1661–1716).

larna, and Härjedalen. The loft house was used for storage, the upper story also, often, for sleeping quarters. The Age of Empire (1600–1720) brought Sweden into closer contact with the Continent in all respects. Architecture and building activity, particularly, were greatly stimulated by the nobility's self-esteem and economic resources, newly boosted by participation in the Thirty Years' War (1618–48). The palatial establishments designed by contemporary French architects were the model for the Swedish nobles (fig. 43). During the latter part of the seventeenth century and throughout the eighteenth century, symmetrically laid-out complexes, consisting of a main building with one or two pairs of flanking wings, replaced the older, traditional manor type (figs. 44, 45).

The dwelling house

In its simplest form, the dwelling house is a single room with a hearth. Such a simple type of dwelling can still be seen in the *eldhus* (firehouse)[1] of the *fäbod*, the outlying dairy farm. The fire-house is a one-room structure, with entrance in one of the gable walls, protected by a kind of porch or overhang created by the projecting roof. Some few *fäbodar* still have a raised hearth for an open fire in the middle of the packed dirt floor (fig. 37). The smoke, it is hoped, escapes through an opening in the ceiling—there are no windows. The smoke may, however, swirl around the room, be sucked out the doorway, or fill the upper part of the room, so that one must crouch to avoid getting it into lungs and eyes. It is advisable to sit on the small, low stools, about eight to

44. Painting showing the main building of the ironmaker residence Sveden. Stora Kopparberg, Dalarna, 1819.

45. Drawing of Skogaholm, a manor from the province of Närke, now at Skansen, the open-air museum in Stockholm. Built at the end of the seventeenth century of red-painted logs, it was plastered in the eighteenth century and painted yellow. Like grander models, it has a main building (1) with a pair of wings (2, 3), pavilions (4, 5), a folly or gazebo (6), and a parterre, a formal garden of French type (7).

46. Skabersjö Castle, Skåne, with courtyard to the left and cowhouse to the right. Drawing by G. Behrman, 1680.

twelve inches high, made of tree stumps. There is no other freestanding furniture. Along the walls run built-in benches to sit on while working or eating. The bedding consists of a skin underneath, and, on top, another skin, or a coverlet or wool or woven rags. It is placed in a corner or wherever desired on the wall benches. A round-bottomed cauldron hangs in a movable trammel over the fire. The cauldron has no legs but a handle by which it is suspended over the fire. Chopped pine or tender willow leaves are strewn on the dirt floor. On the walls hang shelves for assorted vessels. As a rule, there are, nowadays, modern housewares at hand: coffee cups and plates of china, stainless-steel buckets and vats for milk and cream. Before World War I, however, the original wooden forms had an especially natural place in the *fäbod* fire-house: old furnishings were sent to the *fäbod* from the main farm, whenever the latter was being modernized.

In a large number of today's *fäbod* fire-houses, however, the fireplace is located in one of the corners. Generally, it is a bricked, open fireplace with chimney, adjacent to which is placed an iron range. As a rule, there are also windows and a wooden floor. At the *fäbod*, there is often a separate storage shed for the *fäbod*'s dairy products, various food supplies, and tools. This shed is placed directly across from the fire-house, with gables and entrances facing. The projecting roof of this shed meets the roof of the fire-house, so that a "room" is created in the middle. It is a characteristic, traditional building custom in Sweden—as well as in the rest of Europe—to thus combine one or several independent units rather than, as is the modern custom, erecting larger buildings with several rooms (fig. 47).

This combination of fire-house with storage shed recurs so frequently that it may be called typical. By providing the two houses with a joint roof, a house type is created which has two rooms, one on either side of a common entry.

The parstuga—the Swedish two-room house

A house with two rooms on either side of an entry is called a *parstuga* (literally, "two-house

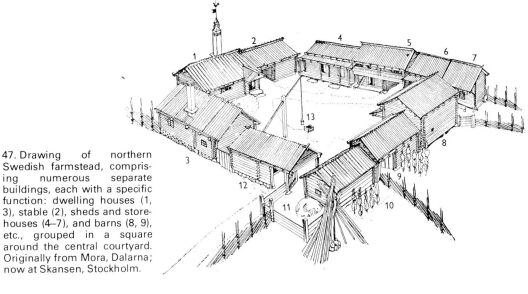

47. Drawing of northern Swedish farmstead, comprising numerous separate buildings, each with a specific function: dwelling houses (1, 3), stable (2), sheds and storehouses (4–7), and barns (8, 9), etc., grouped in a square around the central courtyard. Originally from Mora, Dalarna; now at Skansen, Stockholm.

house").[2] This type with its several variants is without question the most common house plan in Sweden. In central and northern Sweden the *parstuga* was the standard house plan, flourishing especially in the seventeenth and eighteenth centuries. In its older form, the *parstuga* maintains the original functions of the two rooms, the one room being living quarters with hearth and the other, storage space. The *parstuga* has,

48. *Parstuga,* exterior and plan. Salem, Södermanland, 1930.

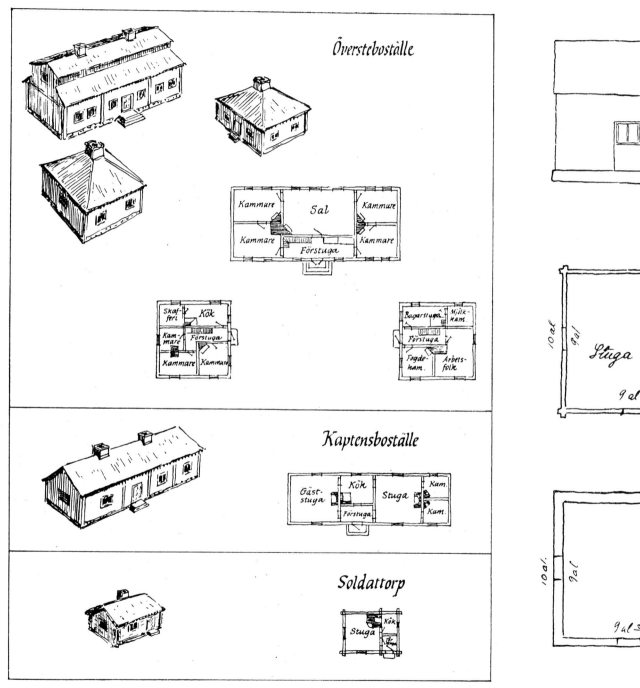

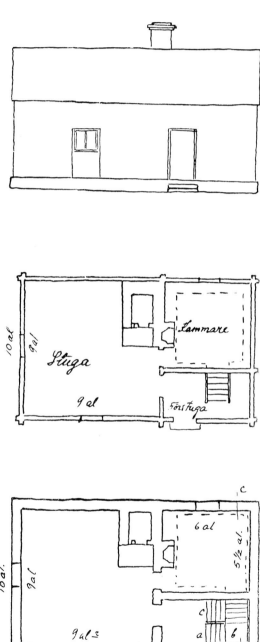

49. Military residences, top to bottom: colonel's residence, captain's residence, and soldier's cottage. According to approved plans by Erik Dahlberg and models in Armémuseum, Stockholm.

50. Plan and elevation of *enkelstuga*, or one-room house, drawn by Carl Wijnblad, 1766. Suggested dwelling house for one-fourth of a homestead.

however, turned out to be an extremely tenacious form, adaptable to the most varying milieus and requirements, and has therefore evolved through several stages (fig. 48).

The reorganization of the armed forces in the 1680s led to the building of state-owned residences for officers (fig. 49, 50). To that end, the famous field marshal Erik Dahlberg was commissioned to work up suitable architectural plans. For cavalry and infantry captains, the house plan consisted of a *parstuga*, a two-room house, with a pair of chambers at one gable end and a separate kitchen. For lieutenants and ensigns, Dahlberg suggested an *enkelstuga*, a one-room house, expanded by additional chambers. Even the parsonages were built on the basic plan of the *parstuga*, enlarged as needed. During the eighteenth century, the plans for military residences as well as parsonages evolved further with the addition of double side chambers, and often a second story.

The enkelstuga—the Swedish one-room house
As a result of a reduction in the minimum taxable homestead in the latter half of the eighteenth century, one-room houses were quite frequently erected, at least in central Sweden. During the nineteenth century, this house plan became the one most frequently used by common people. The *enkelstuga* has one room with a hearth, an entry, and a small chamber sectioned off from the entry (fig. 50). It became widespread as a result of the lowered living standard on the smaller, divided homesteads.

The Southern Götaland house type
In southwestern Sweden, branching out into Västergötland, Bohuslän, and Öland, a somewhat different house plan was used. It consisted of a one-story *stuga* with a hearth, flanked on one or two sides by a two-story storage house, annexed to the *stuga* with passageways in-between (figs. 53, 55, 56). The type is called the Southern Götaland house type, or *högloftstugan*, the "bower *stuga*."

The residential wing of the Skåne farm does

51. Interior of *stuga*, kitchen-living quarters combination, showing the entrance wall with corner cupboard and plate rack. Lima, Dalarna.

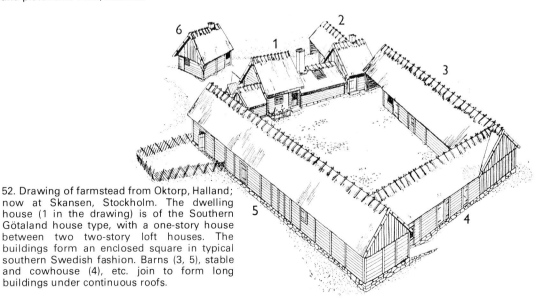

52. Drawing of farmstead from Oktorp, Halland; now at Skansen, Stockholm. The dwelling house (1 in the drawing) is of the Southern Götaland house type, with a one-story house between two two-story loft houses. The buildings form an enclosed square in typical southern Swedish fashion. Barns (3, 5), stable and cowhouse (4), etc. join to form long buildings under continuous roofs.

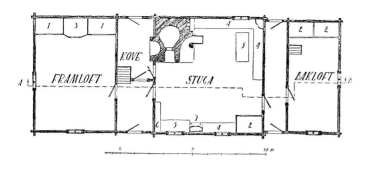

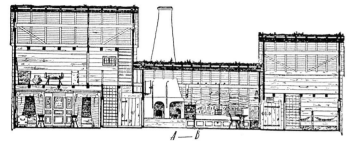

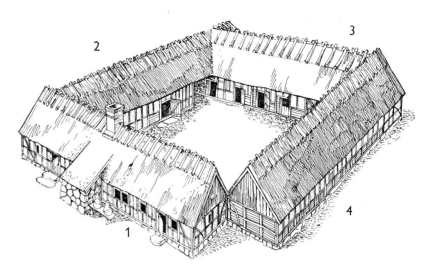

53. Drawing of dwelling house from Kyrkhult, Blekinge; now at Skansen, Stockholm. Example of the Southern Götaland house type, plan and section.

54. The Skåne variant of the Southern Götaland house type, though built on the same general plan, lacks the characteristic flanking loft houses. Dwelling house (1), barn (2), woodshed and stable (3), and cowhouse and barn (4) enclose the central courtyard.—Farmstead from Ravlunda, Skåne; now at Skansen, Stockholm.

55. The *stuga* in a house of Southern Götaland type, decorated for the holidays with hangings and fringed borders on the walls and the sloping ceiling. Drawing inscribed July 2, 1884, Vippentorp, Ysby, Laholm (Halland).

not exhibit the typical two-story storage parts: every unit is single-storied and joined under one roof (figs. 54, 57). In spite of this difference in the exterior, the ground plan is principally the same, with a hearth in the central part and storage areas flanking it.

Both the *parstuga* and the Southern Götaland house type were extended by the addition of chambers on the gable ends. These variants were largely a result of the influence of upper-class housing, especially of official residences and parsonages.

The stuga—the kitchen-living quarters combination

The *stuga* with its hearth was originally used as kitchen, workshop, and bedroom. In the wintertime, the whole household would sleep there, in all perhaps a dozen people. For this reason, the arrangement of furniture was dictated by the need for sleeping space, to be found in built-in two-story bunk beds, on benches, and on the floor (fig. 70). The other part of the *parstuga,* called *nystugan* (the new *stuga*) or *anderstugan* (the other *stuga*), or whatever other local name it might have had, originally served as storage space. To begin with, this space lacked a hearth, but later it generally had a fireplace in the inner corner. At weddings, funerals, and other celebrations, it was cleared out to provide room for the guests. In central and northern Sweden, great care was lavished on the decorative articulation of this part of the dwelling house, corresponding to its social and ceremonial function. The die-hard parlor tradition may be traced to this functional separation of the *parstuga* and the ornamentation of its "guest" part.

The separate kitchen

Throughout the seventeenth and eighteenth centuries, strong Continental influences brought about a change of far-reaching consequences in the plan of the dwelling house. The fireplace and associated household chores were moved to a separate room, often the chamber that was partitioned off from the entry. In Swedish building tradition the combination

56. Southern Götaland house in Jämshög, Blekinge. Drawing by R. Mejborg, dated June 29, 1883.

57. Central part of Skåne dwelling house, cross section.

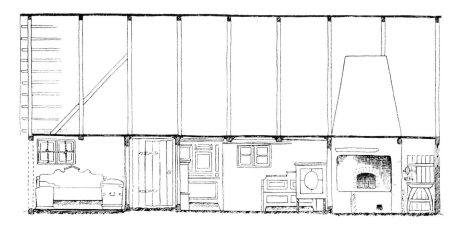

58. The *stuga* was used as kitchen, workshop, bedroom, and living room. *Stuga* in Storsjö, Härjedalen, 1927.

kitchen-living quarters is still used extensively, especially in Norrland. To use the *stuga* as living room, bedroom, and kitchen is a deeply engrained Swedish custom. Thus, the separate kitchen is not yet completely accepted in central and northern Sweden. As early as the Middle Ages, kitchens on large estates and castles were placed in a separate house. From the seventeenth century, manors often had the kitchen in a separate wing (fig. 45). In Skåne, a separate kitchen developed also in peasant homes during the seventeenth and eighteenth centuries (fig. 57).

The flue—an important step in the development of the dwelling house

Castles and manors have continually been influenced by western European architectural styles. Important innovations which changed the shape of the dwelling house gained acceptance during the sixteenth and seventeenth cen-

59. Interior of *stuga.* The girl is strewing the floor with fresh leaves, a common practice at holidays. Bruksvallarna, Härjedalen, 1909.

61. *Stuga* with open fireplace and trammel. Ore, Dalarna, 1924.

60. *Stuga* interior, Halland. The woman is churning butter, the man carving a wooden ladle. Woodcut by Severin Nilsson, end of the nineteenth century.

62. *Stuga* interior, showing fireplace with built-in iron range. Trosa, Södermanland, 1938.

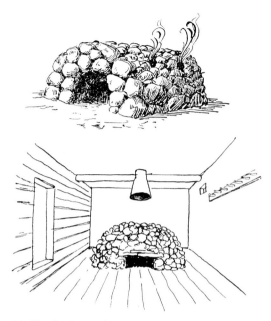

63. The flueless *rökugn* or smoke oven is a pile of rocks heaped over a vaulted chamber holding the fire. In southern Sweden, the type survived in the dwelling house up to the mid-1700s; in Finnish settlements, sauna-dwelling combinations could be found as late as the nineteenth century. In the rest of Sweden, the *rökugn* was used only in kilns designed to dry grain and flax or smoke meats. The same word (*bastu*) was used for these kilns as for saunas. Today, the same heating principle is found in the sauna.—Top, sauna oven, Bredestad, Småland; bottom, sauna interior, Överkalix, Norrbotten, 1933.

turies. In town architecture, the flue was introduced as early as the Middle Ages, probably first appearing on the island of Gotland. As a consequence, the hearth moved from the middle of the room to one of its corners. From the sixteenth century on, this type of fireplace can be assumed to have spread also to larger farms in central and northern Sweden. However, the transition from ceiling apertures to windows in the walls came generally first during the seventeenth and eighteenth centuries. In some parts of southwestern Sweden, people retained the fireplace without flue, the so-called *rökugn* (smoke oven), as late as the mid-eighteenth century. The *rökugn* consisted of a pile of rocks, heaped over a vault or chamber,

where the fire was kept (fig. 63, top). This oven was an improvement over the open hearth, insofar as the rock pile, once warmed up, would retain the heat longer. In that way, fuel would be conserved. Also, there would be no smoke during the periods when the fire was not going. However, whenever there was a fire,

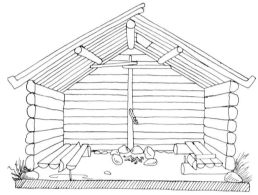

64. Model of fire-house. Central fire without flue for heating, cooking, and illumination. Trammel of wood. Mörsil, Jämtland.

65. Model of fireplace with flue, baking oven, and light niche for illumination. Kedum, Västergötland.

the smoke would escape into the room, as there was no chimney or flue. The *rökugn* was especially widespread in eastern Europe, and came to Skåne from the south, probably in the early Middle Ages. Through Finnish settlers it was introduced to the area known as the "Finnish woods" in Värmland.[3]

In northern and central Sweden, the open hearth of the fire-house was retained (fig. 64). During the Middle Ages it was combined with the baking oven and, in the sixteenth century, also with the chimney. The fireplace was then generally moved from its old place in the middle of the room to one of the corners. The three functions of the hearth—to give warmth, light, and heat for food preparation—were gradually taken over by separate arrangements and devices (fig. 65).

Hearth, baking oven, and stove

On the typical Skåne farm, there exists a fireplace complex totally different from those used in the rest of Sweden. In this complex, which was developed and widely adopted during the eighteenth century, the fireplace proper is partitioned off from the *stuga* by walls. Standing in this "stove room," one is directly underneath the chimney and surrounded on three sides by the cooking area. The baking oven is bricked into the wall straight ahead, from which it protrudes like a half-cupola on the outside of the house. From this stove room are fired an oven extending into the *stuga*, a brewing cauldron, and a kiln for drying malt. In other words, this room functions as a kind of central heating plant. Once the *stuga* was rid of kitchen chores, its interior decoration took on a somewhat different aspect, compared with that of farm kitchens in other provinces.

Already existing in towns, the iron stove for heating appeared in the countryside around the middle of the seventeenth century, especially in the former Norwegian and Danish provinces.

Hearth, dwelling house, and furnishings

The development from a hearth with an open fire in the middle of the room and without chimney to a hearth with chimney and oven

66. In the twentieth century, the separate kitchen became the rule in most of Sweden. The iron range was used for cooking, while illumination was provided by kerosene or electric lamps. Drawing with color wash by Carl Larsson, 1900.

meant a great deal for the design and plan of the dwelling house and its furnishings. The fireplace itself has also helped shape cooking pots and other cooking utensils and has, of course, also influenced our eating habits. Round-bottomed cooking pots belonged to the open fire (fig. 60), over which they were suspended from a movable trammel. The tripod

was an indispensable accessory to the round-bottomed cauldron, which only gradually acquired legs (figs. 34, 61). To the open hearth also belonged the waffle-iron, the grill (fig. 574), the roasting spit, and the hearthstone on which bread was baked. When special heating arrangements were introduced in the dwelling house, the stove became more specialized.

67. With the spread of the faïence stove from manorial milieu to other social strata in the nineteenth century, new rooms, such as this chamber, were added to the traditional building plans. Ekstad, Gotland, 1937.

68. In court milieu, the bedroom figured prominently in ceremonial functions. Here, at the levee, the Monarch would grant audiences.—The bed alcove in Queen Hedvig Eleonora's bedroom, Drottningholm Palace.

69. *Stuga* with two built-in bunk beds, in the daytime hidden from view by bed curtains, *förlåtar*. Sollerö parish, Dalarna.

70. In the wintertime, the whole household would sleep in the *stuga*. Orsa, Dalarna. Ink drawing, entitled *Reveille in Orsa*, by Fritz von Dardel, 1893.

From open hearth to electric light

The iron range came into general use in the nineteenth century and brought with it a completely different set of pots and pans with flat bottoms and flanges (fig. 66). The heating function of the fireplace was retained, but nothing of its illuminating function. For a long time the hearth had been the most important light source in the house. In the *stuga* and elsewhere resinous pine sticks also were used to light one's way. In some types of fireplace there was a separate niche fired only for illumination (fig. 65). In certain parts of the country, oil lamps of iron or clay were of some importance, e.g., in southwestern Sweden and Bohuslän and on Gotland. Tallow candles were

45

71. In the summertime, sleeping quarters were found in a variety of places: storehouses, lofts, and barns.—Twin bunks in storehouse, Malung, Dalarna.

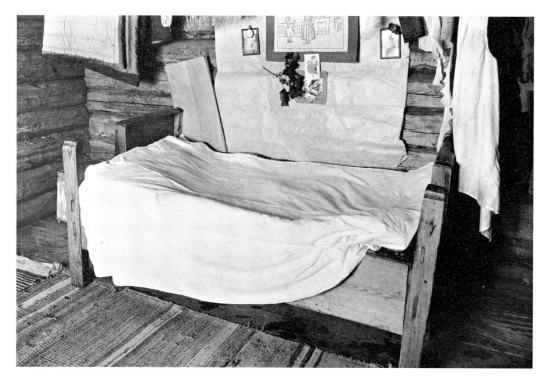

72. Bed in storage loft, so-called *pigbo* (servant-girl's nest). Norrbärke, Dalarna, 1926.

used only at Christmastime and other holidays.

Among the upper classes, tallow candles and wax candles were used. Lamps using colza oil and kerosene appeared first in the 1870s. Electricity as a source of energy for the home was introduced somewhat later—an electric company was founded in Stockholm in 1892.

From open hearth to central heating

The separation of the hearth with its activities from the living room-bedroom combination is a milestone in the articulation of the dwelling space. This separation occurred, as noted above, through influence from Continental models. The heating function of the hearth was taken over by more efficient sources of heat. The faïence stove is an offshoot of the heating and baking oven (fig. 67). In the Middle Ages, conical clay cups were first cemented into the outer surface of the oven to increase its effective radiation surface. Gradually, these cups developed into square tiles, which were used as an integral building material for the stove.

In the eighteenth century, the Swedish faïence stove was improved by the invention of a smoke duct making several loops, which gave the stove greater capacity for heat retention. As late as thirty-five to forty years ago, the faïence stove was still the major heating apparatus in Sweden.

The separate bedroom

The access to a separate source of heat, such as the faïence stove, contributed considerably to the continued specializiation of the rooms in the dwelling house. As most families, in the country and in the towns, usually had one single room aside from the *stuga,* the former became both bedroom and parlor. In upperclass houses, as well, the bedroom was used not only for sleeping, but also as a salon as late as the end of the seventeenth century. In the royal circle, the levee and dressing in the morning and the undressing and going to bed at night were all solemn events of an official nature, blending private and public functions. The model was, of course, French (fig. 68).

73. As a rule, the chamber was used as the first separate bedroom, while also acquiring the function of parlor.—Chamber with extension sofa, pushed in and piled high with bedding. Gryt, Östergötland.

Settlement and dwelling

The toilette of the ladies, likewise, assumed the character of a social gathering, at which one would receive friends and acquaintances.

Not until the eighteenth century did the bedroom start to become a room for the sole purpose of sleeping. During the nineteenth century, this specialization became increasingly common in upper-class or urban milieu, though for a long time the bedroom was in a suite of rooms with social function. As late as the 1870s and '80s, families in Stockholm assembled in the mistress's bedroom until the footman announced that dinner was served. After dinner, the party retired to the same bedroom to take their coffee. Not until the end

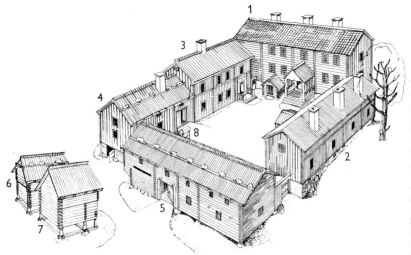

74. In the mid-1900s, the expanding lumber industry brought prosperity and a higher living standard. In Norrland, the larger farms were built out to a point where they could be most aptly described as "wooden castles."—Perspective drawing of a farmstead from Delsbo, Hälsingland, now at Skansen, Stockholm. The farm buildings include main building (1), guest wing (3), wing for the farmer's old parents (2), cowhouse (4), stable and barn (5), and storehouses (6, 7).

75. Well-to-do farm. Right, the dwelling houses; left, the cowhouse. Bollnäs, Hälsingland, 1929.

of the nineteenth century did the custom of using the bedroom for social functions start to disappear. Then the bedroom became a place for sleeping only—with greater privacy, access to fresh air and light, and equipped with more and more furnishings for personal hygiene.

In rural mileu, this differentiation was found only after the two World Wars. There was no question of separate bedrooms, especially as a bed of one's own was not seen as necessary or even especially desirable. In the wintertime, all the people on the farm would find a place to sleep in the *stuga* (fig. 70), where it was warm. During the warm season, one would find sleeping quarters in a variety of places: storage houses, lofts, and barns (fig. 72). In northern Sweden, one might also sleep in the scrubbed cow shed, vacated by the cows when they left for the *fäbod*. Sleeping quarters and bedstead would vary and mattered little. On the other hand, the bedding was of primary importance and could be laid out almost anywhere, depending on the circumstances.

The chamber

The chamber, the small room added to the *parstuga*, took on the dual function of parlor and master bedroom. If the bed was an extension sofa, it would be pushed in and made up with a coverlet or bedspread thrown over it in the daytime (fig. 73). Servant girls and hired men would, however, continue to sleep in the kitchen, in tables with built-in drawer beds, on extension sofas, or whatever else was available.

The two-story house

As early as the last part of the eighteenth century, two-story dwelling houses began to appear, in southern Sweden even in peasant milieu. By the 1820s, the two-story plan had become widespread in Blekinge, Småland, Västergötland, and central Sweden.

In Värmland, Dalarna, and Norrland, the increased economic role of the forest and the expansion of the lumber industry around the middle of the nineteenth century brought considerable prosperity, resulting in increased building activity. The new houses were erected

76. The *sal*—the reception hall on the first or second floor—became the center for entertainment and formal functions. Here rugs were first introduced, as were curtains, faïence stoves, and other newfangled furnishings. Stora Tuna, Dalarna, 1926.

in two stories with a profusion of windows (fig. 75). These windows were, as a rule, not meant to be opened. Apparently, the family only needed fresh air in the communal sleeping quarters, the *stuga,* on the ground floor. Governors' Reports from the counties in Norrland criticize the farmers' inclination to build too many and too large houses. Doubtless the near-palatial farmhouses in Norrland express self-assertion and a hunger for prestige. The added living areas, especially those on the second floor, were not intended for everyday use (fig. 78). They served mainly as formal apartments, but could also be left unfinished and used to store clothes, textiles, and tools and equipment for the making of textiles.

The sal—the reception hall or drawing room

On large farms, as previously on manorial estates, entertaining and other social functions helped to further differentiate the living quarters. From the mid-1800s, modeled on the pattern of contemporary manors, a large hall was added directly inside the entry. Sometimes one or two such halls were placed together with guest rooms on the upper floor.

In Hälsingland and other parts of Norrland, there were even special guest houses built, with painted, splattered, or stenciled walls and sumptuously outfitted beds (figs. 74, 75). The furnishings of these houses, demonstrating the farm's prosperity and the skill of its womenfolk, were a strong incentive for textile crafts.

77. The *sal* developed into a dining room or a room for social gatherings and entertainment, i.e., a "best" room or drawing room. This *sal* is on the first floor.

78. *Sal* or reception hall on the second floor. An opened-up gateleg table dominates the center of the room. Ekshärad, Värmland, 1957.

Furniture and household articles

The dwelling house and its floor plan have played a major part in determining the design of furniture, which, in turn, has influenced the function and design of other household articles. Earlier, the living room-kitchen combination, the *stuga*, served all functions. Not until the late eighteenth century and throughout the nineteenth century were these various functions delegated to separate rooms.

The traditional furnishing system
Traditionally, the furniture in the *stuga* was placed along the walls. In the fire-house with its central hearth, built-in benches along the walls were the only furnishings. They were used for sleeping, eating, sitting, and working. The *stuga* with a corner hearth was furnished according to the same principle (fig. 81). Separate movable pieces of furniture included a table and a few stools or seats. The benches, the bedstead, the shelves for the cooking vessels, and the corner cupboards belonged to the room's permanent furnishings. The fireplace in the inner corner of the room was the focal point for the table, which often was placed diagonally opposite the fireplace. The bed was built into one of the long walls across from the table. The shelves for cooking pots were opposite the hearth. In the *anderstuga* there were usually benches attached to the wall, a trestle table, and a built-in cupboard. This strongly wall-oriented furnishing system survived even in upper-class residences as late as the beginning of the nineteenth century (fig. 80). Older room types have, however, retained the traditional types of furniture and their placement far longer. New types of furniture were naturally associated with new room types. Hence, it was the chamber, the reception hall, the parlor, and the salon that gradually introduced other and new ideas about furniture and its placement. The magnet which was to draw the furniture away from its fixed position along the walls was the circular table (fig. 82).

79. The old furnishing system was characterized by built-in benches and beds. The few movables were also placed along the walls.—*Stuga* from Slöinge, Halland. Oil painting from about 1850.

The table
In its oldest and simplest form, the table consisted of loose boards, either individual wooden boards or trenchers resting on each person's knees, or large communal table boards laid on trestles. In his book *Folklig möbelkultur* ("Folk furnishings"), Sigurd Erixon characterizes the custom of sitting at table: "To sit at table together is a social function, a form of communion, which does not belong to primitive life. It is actually a ceremonial custom created

by and for the feasting males." (Fig. 83.) Before the advent of the table, the hearth was, with all certainty, the focal point at mealtimes and drinking bouts, as it still is among the Lapps today. In everyday peasant milieu one would eat at the hearth (fig. 85). The pot was placed near the hearth on a seat, on a board with mortised legs, or on a folding table-chair —a combination which served as a table when the top was lowered, as a chair when it was raised. The long table, consisting of loose

80. The wall-oriented furnishing system was the rule also in bourgeois milieu up to the mid-1800s, as seen in this interior from a well-to-do home in Stockholm. Drawing with color wash, 1798.

81. The original part of the dwelling house, the *stuga,* retained its built-in benches, crockery shelves, and simple seats. New furnishings were introduced with the new room types: the chamber, the *sal* or drawing room, and the parlor.—A typical *stuga.* Sollerö, Dalarna, 1937.

82. The round table shattered the old placement system and "pulled" the furniture away from the walls.—*Stuga* with a central circular table, surrounded by chairs. Sandhult, Västergötland.

boards resting on more or less temporary supports, is known from prehistoric times. The table with a skirt came to Sweden in the seventeenth century and was, to begin with, not common among the lower and middle classes. Not until the nineteenth century did it become generally accepted, in a changed and simplified form. The gateleg table appeared towards the end of the seventeenth century, becoming quite widespread during the eighteenth century (fig. 78). It can also be found with semicircular drop leaves, resembling the matching semicircular end tables introduced in the eighteenth century (fig. 90).

It is characteristic of all these types of table that they were designed to be placed next to the wall when not in use. The trestle table had the advantage that it could be completely disassembled. The drop-leaf table could be folded to occupy minimal space along the wall; the semicircular tables, when not in use, were likewise placed against the wall. This arrangement was in accordance with the older furnishing system. When the circular table permanently took its place in the middle of the floor, it effectively shattered the old placement system. This change happened in bourgeois milieu in the first half of the nineteenth century, in provin-

Häradsrättens afslutande i Tingshuset, wid Leksands Kyrka, att dricka Skålar med Spel och fjolmusik, för alla Stånd, från det högsta till fjerdingsmännernas Skål. Samt derefter Bön och Sång. ~ R. af Petrus petrifilius. ~ år 1863 ~

83. The closing festivities of the district court in Leksand, Dalarna, marked by solemn toasting. The jury members drink from four-tipped bowls, the judge's assistants from goblets. Painting by Petrus Petrifilius, 1863.

84. Everyday meals were taken informally around the hearth.—Lapps take a meal break at the campfire. Akkajaure, Lappland, 1937.

85. A meal is served next to the hearth on a long seat. Potatoes from the trough are dipped in the pan drippings. Mangskog, Värmland, 1910s.

cial milieu between 1870 and 1930. The change took place above all in the new room types: the chamber, the reception hall directly adjoining the entry, or the reception hall on the second floor. The circular table and the parlor group began turning up in the homes of farmers and laborers at the turn of the century, dining-room furniture already in the 1870s (fig. 77).At the same time more differentiated table forms were introduced, such as circular-top window tables with pillar or baluster pedestal on a tripod or tetrapod, round or oval sofa tables, square tables with two flat end supports ending in two splayed legs.

So long as the dwelling house retained its old components—the living room-kitchen combination, the *stuga,* and the storage or guest part—the old wall furniture remained. So long as the *stuga* itself with the hearth stayed undifferentiated, for so long did its furniture also remain unchanged.

Serving utensils

Whereas everyday meals, by virtue of their simple form, long retained their primitive character, feasts and formal occasions came to require richly developed utensils and customs associated with food and drink (figs. 87, 88). In sixteenth-century court milieu, even at large banquets, one made do with the fingers as eating utensils. This custom survived in backward areas until modern times (fig. 85). Neither did the diner use a plate or bowl. Meat, fish, etc. were rolled up in a thin bread-cake or eaten on a piece of bread. In the Middle Ages the fork was a rarity, in the sixteenth century still a luxury item. From the seventeenth century on, the fork was somewhat more widely used among the upper classes, and was brought as a personal utensil to banquets. In the eighteenth century, it became a more common table accessory; in farm homes, however, it was not in general use until the nineteenth century. The spoon, on the other hand, already existed in the Stone Age and played a major role, not only in the eating of liquid and half-solid foods such as soup, porridge, and gruel, but also in drinking customs. Milk, mead, ale or beer, and aquavit were "supped" with or without spoon

from a bowl or drunk by means of a dipper from a large communal vessel (fig. 83).

Serving dishes for solid foods

From the customs surrounding the serving of food and drink evolved in all social strata a wide range of table utensils mainly made of wood, or treen. Bread and coldcuts were placed on wooden disks or platters. In Skåne these have survived in the form of *sillabräden* (herring boards). They could be long enough to lie across the knees of the diner. Wooden platters have been reintroduced into modern Sweden from Denmark, where they survived in the form of small individual wooden boards for bread and butter. As a rule, the early wooden plates were round boards without raised rim or bowl (fig. 87). Little by little, these elements were incorporated, probably as a result of influence from pewter, silver, and china plates. The early plates are found all over the country. They are usually unpainted and of turned hardwood, indicating an origin in Sweden's oak and beech regions (fig. 485). Their distribution can probably be attributed to the itinerant peddlers from Västergötland. Especially in southern Sweden, the plates were at times decoratively painted.

In Jämtland and Härjedalen there are still round and artfully turned disks without rim or bowl for serving cheese and butter.

The original place setting was complete if it included a wooden disk, a spoon, and one's personal knife. Additional equipment—salvers, bowls, piggins, chalices, or buttersticks—was all more or less designed to display the food. Butter, cheese, porridge, and, especially, bread were served in impressively decorated serving dishes and the courses themselves were molded and garnished (figs. 485, 486).

Carved and turned wooden bowls and dishes with or without pedestal base or legs came in graduated sizes, from that of a small saucer to about three feet in diameter. They exhibited little differentiation in basic design—just as the diet offered little variation—and were used interchangeably for fish, meat, and butter. Generally, a certain differentiation will result from the introduction of new and different

86. The Duke of Berry at table. The table is covered with a cloth in twill variation. The food, which is carved at the table, is served on wooden disks. There are no forks or knives in the place settings. Drinks are served from a separate table by the wine steward. After P. Durrieu, *Les Très Riches Heures de Jean de France, duc de Berry.* Early fifteenth century.

materials. This phenomenon was naturally seen more often among the wealthy, where pewter, silver, and stoneware had been in use for household utensils since the Middle Ages. The shapes and forms of wooden vessels were therefore at an early stage influenced by the corresponding metal prototypes, an influence particularly seen in drinking vessels.

Serving vessels for drink

Turned goblets, deep, round, hemispherical bowls with a pronounced inverted lip, four-tipped bowls, tumblers or noggins,[4] *kåsor*—double-handled bowls, often staved and willow-bound—and beakers have more or less assimilated form or decoration from their metallic counterparts (fig. 92). The particular manner of drinking has greatly influenced the shape and form of drinking vessels. In general, the development has been from communal forms to forms for individual use. Beer or ale[5] is an ancient beverage, associated with celebrations, so much so that these festivities were traditionally called *öl* (ale, beer), as in the compound words *gravöl* (funeral *öl*, "wake"), *barnsöl* (child *öl*, "christening party"), *taklagsöl* (roofing *öl*, "barn raising"), etc. Water was seldom drunk by itself, but rather mixed with sour milk or beer. There is preserved a splendid variety of serving vessels for ale and beer, from the legendary horn (fig. 564) and the magnificent *kåsa* (fig. 498)—described and depicted by Sweden's great sixteenth-century historiographer Olaus Magnus—to the beer bottle and glass so prevalent in the nineteenth century. The storage of beer or ale required coopered barrels or kegs which

87. Wedding banquet, *Brölopet i Kanan* [sic] (The Marriage in Cana), wall hanging attributed to Per Svensson of Schönhult, Knäred, Halland. The table is set with tablecloth, knives and forks but no plates, serving platters with roast suckling pig, cheese-cakes, pretzels, and other breads; also beakers, carafes, tankards, and bowls.

88. Detail of painting showing a banquet where the prodigal son is "wasting his substance with riotous living." Painting attributed to Anders Svensson, Ön, Halland. Early nineteenth century.

were kept in cool storage in the cellar. To serve the beer, it was poured into turned *tappskålar* (tap bowls), large bowls with a short spout or pouring lip, especially common in Bohuslän and Västergötland (fig. 487). These bowls were emptied into tankards, which in turn conveyed the beer to beakers or stoups. A more ancient mode of serving was to offer the beer in a large bowl, often a brass cauldron in which the beer had been heated, from which everyone helped himself by means of small bird-shaped dippers,

ölgäss (literally, "ale geese") (fig. 496). These bird-shaped vessels were widespread, especially in northern Sweden. A particular type with a narrower mouth and a handle occurred in Västergötland, Småland, and Halland. Drinking customs, inspiring a rich variety of artistic forms, have created individualized works of art especially in the carving and painting of dippers and floating vessels.

One particular type of drinking vessel is the so-called *snibbskål*, the four-tipped bowl. It is

89. Wedding banquet in aristocratic milieu in the 1670s. The dishes are carried in to musical accompaniment (*Tafelmusik*) and drinks are served from an elegantly appointed "bar" on the side. Ink drawing from L. Magalotti, *Resa i Sverige år 1674* ("Travel in Sweden in 1674").

a low, round, turned wooden bowl with a square rim, or four projecting "tips," remaining after the turning process. They are, as a rule, colored red, with painted decoration and humorous or moralizing inscriptions (fig. 485, center). Sigurd Erixon is of the opinion that these four-tipped bowls belonged to guilds or brotherhoods and that they served an almost ritualistic function. Several eighteenth-century sets of four-tipped bowls have been preserved; these sets were used at village festivities or village council meetings. The most remarkable is probably the matched set which was once used by the jury members at the closing festivities of the district court in Leksand, Dalarna (fig. 83). Most of the four-tipped bowls, however, come from Västergötland, Östergötland, Småland, and parts of the adjoining provinces. They were reportedly at one time sold by traveling Västergötland peddlers.

Other types of turned vessels associated with beer drinking have included tankards, covered flagons, stoups, beakers, and goblets. One group, especially widely used in southern Sweden with some distribution as far north as southern Dalarna, was painted or decorated with turned moldings and bone knops. These vessels belonged primarily in well-to-do homes in town and country, but there are some examples preserved from peasant milieu. Similar vessel forms were also made with bound staves. Larger vessels for transporting beer indoors or out were preferably coopered. A special variant is the *tvebottnakanna* (literally, "two-bottomed tankard"), a staved wooden jug, named for its two "bottoms" or "heads," one on the bottom and the other one on top. This type is found particularly in northern and central Sweden, most commonly in Dalarna, Värmland, and Västmanland, but also in Småland, Västergötland, and Dalsland. The *tvebottnakanna* has an extended stave serving as handle, a lid cut in the top "bottom," and a spout (fig. 92, second from right on top shelf).

During the eighteenth century, aquavit became a popular drink. It was taken throughout the day, starting with the morning meal, and was a standard item in packed meals and travel provisions. As such, it was transported in and drunk from small coopered kegs or canteens

90. As late as the eighteenth century, table utensils in all social strata were generally made of wood. To some extent, pottery, pewter, copper, and brass were also used. When china dishes were introduced in the eighteenth century, they became the status goods *par preference.*—The China Pantry, Tureholm Castle, Södermanland.

91. Individual plates and flatware were not standard equipment in the majority of Swedish homes until the nineteenth century.—Mealtime in a peasant household, Västra Klagstorp, Skåne, 1902.

92. Drinking customs and ceremonial toasts have inspired a wealth of decorative vessel forms.— A selection of drinking vessels in various materials and forms: bowls, horns, *kåsor*—two-handled cups—and tankards, goblets, chalices, stoups, jugs, and beakers.

of the same kind used for gruel and sour milk. The aquavit kegs were, however, often decoratively painted and equipped with a metal mouthpiece. At festive occasions aquavit was "supped" with a spoon or a small dipper from a larger vessel, a brass cauldron, a wassail bowl, or a four-tipped bowl. In more affluent urban and rural homes, aquavit was also taken in small hemispherical tumblers or noggins and in *kåsor* of silver.

Kåsa (plural, *kåsor*) is a term which has been applied to vessels of quite varying sizes. In its most magnificent form, the *kåsa* is equipped with a pair of handles, elaborately carved and up to two feet high, which branch out and join overhead like an arbor. This type of *kåsa* developed among the nobility. Most preserved examples date from the sixteenth and seventeenth centuries, though a few were used in farmers' homes in isolated areas as late as the nineteenth century. The *kåsa*'s strongly ritualistic function has been established. Smaller vessels in wood, turned or staved, and quite small vessels of silver, resembling dram cups, have also been called *kåsor*. Their common denominator is that the bowl itself is round, widening upwards, and provided with two handles ending in animal heads, stylized animal forms, or birds' heads and tails. The latter's asymmetrical form points to a connection with the bird-shaped drinking vessels, a generally accepted interpretation of the origin of the *kåsa*.

Certain uniquely individualized bowls for food or drink or both are made from hollowed-out burls, especially birch burls. The woodcarver has "read" animal forms into the irregular patterns of the wood, which he has then extended into fantastic animal shapes (fig. 497 and color fig. 54).

Table textiles

Formal occasions, not everyday living, have stimulated the development of new forms and functions. This phenomenon has been noted above in connection with table utensils. The same is true of table linen.

The custom of covering the dining table with a cloth is known at least from the Middle Ages (fig. 86). Available data from the period

93. In the seventeenth century, linen damask tablecloths became an indispensable accessory to the festive table. Dutch damask, especially, was imported to Sweden. It was clearly intended for the Court and the highest social strata.—Damask tablecloth with motifs from the life of Samson, monogrammed ORS/LGS and dated 1615.

before 1500 in Sweden is scanty. But the more extensive information about Continental practices offers certain points of departure for an evaluation of the contemporary conditions in Sweden. During the Middle Ages, painted tabletops were common in western European upper- and upper-middle-class milieus. The custom of painting the tabletop was still in fashion in Sweden in the sixteenth century, apparently having filtered down into peasant milieu. There are two trestle tables from Delsbo, Hälsingland, with painted tops, dated respectively 1545 and 1595, and one from Jämtland, dated 1653.

Tablecloths

Whether the table was covered with a cloth during meals is not known, but somehow the painting on the table top must have been displayed. A number of Continental banqueting scenes from the Middle Ages show the guests sitting at long tables covered with white cloths. In Holland and Flanders—centers for flax cultivation and linen weaving—there was a lively manufacture of linen weaves in twill variations and block-patterned damask. Swedish import records from the sixteenth century indicate that the importation of these weaves was con-

siderable (fig. 199). There is therefore good reason to believe that white tablecloths have been in use in Sweden's wealthier homes since the late Middle Ages. From the sixteenth and seventeenth centuries, historical sources overflow with descriptions of banquets in words and pictures, conveying a strong impression that the activities of the age centered on the pleasures of the table (figs. 89, 93, 94).

It was required of the banquet that it should not only offer culinary sensations, but also be a dramatic spectacle, an entertainment with con-

stantly changing scenes. The various courses—their combinations, the sequence in which they were served, their decorative form—the lavish table decorations, and the resetting of the table with new courses, new tablecloths, and new table decorations gave a strong stimulus to the development of the entire range of dining accessories, not the least of which was the tablecloth. The lack of plates and the necessity of using one's fingers to eat with made it quite natural to wipe one's fingers on the tablecloth. In the Middle Ages, a special length of ma-

94. The banquet offered not only culinary sensations with food sculptures and other lavish dishes, but also a varied visual spectacle. The table was reset several times with new dishes, new centerpieces, and new tablecloths.—In this engraving, showing the Swedish banquet celebrating the Peace of Nuremberg in 1649, a number of platters with birds in full plumage are carried in under the supervision of the steward. Musicians in the four corners of the hall provide musical accompaniment.

terial was introduced for this purpose—a long napkin, which was spread over the knees of the guests the entire length of the table. Such long napkins were used as late as the eighteenth century, and have survived in a few samples. However, the napkin in the modern sense of the word, i.e., the personal napkin, had been introduced as early as the sixteenth century. Ever since the Renaissance it ranked with the foremost ornaments of the festive table, folded in an endless variety of decorative shapes (fig. 95). During this era, there was a tremendous development in Holland of rich pattern weaving of table linen and linen damask. From there, fine linen for the table spread also to Sweden. At first fine linen tablecloths were imported, but from the end of the seventeenth century, they were also manufactured domestically.

During the seventeenth century, the place settings of the nobility included a separate napkin or mat under the plate on the tablecloth. The custom of using this mat survived in Sweden only at the royal table. In other countries, it is more common. Recently, the mat has returned from English and American table customs in the form of the place mat, an inexpensive replacement for the full tablecloth.

The white table covers from the eighteenth century, once in everyday use, have today been reserved for the festive table, because of the expense and time involved in their upkeep.

To what extent did tablecloths actually reach the lower strata of society? It appears as if the white tablecloth was not in common use until cotton became inexpensive at the beginning of the nineteenth century. Cotton also considerably increased the supply of available textile raw material and freed labor so that even smaller households in areas with small or insignificant linen production could obtain or weave tablecloths. It is, however, quite clear that the flax regions in Norrland as well as Skåne, and parts of Småland (figs. 87, 88) and Östergötland, were well provided with table linen, as evidenced in a still-existing very rich inventory of linen and half-linen diaper weaves. The napkin also appeared in peasant milieu, at least in name. In the eighteenth century, napkins frequently appeared in inventories. In

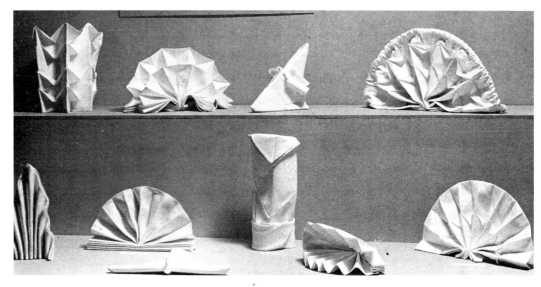

95. As the custom of eating with one's fingers was the rule in the sixteenth and seventeenth centuries, napkins were definitely called for. Decorative ways of folding linen napkins were developed especially at this time.—Artfully folded napkins from the exhibit "Lin och linne" (Flax and linen), Nordiska Museet, 1944.

most cases, however, the napkin belonged to the costume, either as headcloth or handkerchief. In the nineteenth century, it was common in peasant homes, used, as a rule, not as a table accessory, but as a decorative covering for a small table (fig. 76).

Table covers

Already in the Middle Ages magnificent coverlets were laid on tables for decoration. The first oriental rugs brought to Europe were used this way, a tradition still surviving in Holland. Richly patterned weaves have also been used this way. From the sixteenth and seventeenth centuries, there are some superb richly embroidered coverlets from noble households. The use of these coverlets was probably quite undifferentiated, as was the case also with coverlets in peasant homes. They could serve as table covers, bedspreads, or wall hangings. However, there are a few long embroidered seventeenth-century table covers of wool ex-

tant, whose form and decor indicate that they were intended for the new type of long, impressive skirted table on turned legs introduced in the Renaissance. In peasant milieu there was nothing corresponding to these showpieces until the nineteenth century. There are, however, woven coverlets in pick-up double cloth, *upphämta* technique (figs. 112, 131), *krabbasnär, rölakan,* etc., which were used in decorative furnishing and festival customs. The occurrence of coverlets in upper-class milieu correlates directly to the development of cabinetry. When veneered furniture acquired polished surfaces, and table tops were inlaid with different woods, ivory, tortoise shell, metal, and polished gemstones, these tops became the aesthetic focal point instead of the table coverings. In peasant homes, generally, veneered furniture did not appear until the mid-nineteenth century. Previously, the painted table top played an important role in the furnishing of the home. There, it was an imitation of the rich veneer and marquetry work of period furniture.

Decorative tablecloths

As the highly decorated tops on tables, chests of drawers, and fall-front bureau-desks disappeared at the beginning of the nineteenth century, an extraordinary variety of decorative cloths rapidly developed. The appearance of the circular table, placed in the middle of the floor, contributed greatly to this development. There were cloths especially made for bureau tops, for small window tables, for tall fall-front bureau-desks, for square dining tables, for nightstands, salon tables, and sofa tables. This variety of tablecloths encouraged the development of textile decorative patterns (figs. 76–78, 82, 96, 99, 100, 106, 118).

Sitting furniture

Sitting on the ground and crouching in the fetal position are primitive resting positions still used by, e.g., the Lapps (fig. 84). These positions naturally spring from their life in the wilderness and around the open fire in the center of the *kåta*. The stool also belongs in this milieu, whereas the above-mentioned built-in benches or seats were developed in conjunction with the fire-house and the *stuga* with a corner hearth. These benches and seats were intended for several persons. The chair, the individual seat, originally existed only in isolated instances as a seat of honor for the master of the house, a judge, a bride, and, in its most elevated state, as a throne for a king. The log chair, a hollowed-out tree trunk with backrest and removable seat lid, is a prehistoric form once common to all of Europe. Though it was earlier in use throughout the country, it now exists only as a relic in the northern parts of Sweden. The turned chair, somewhat like the New England Brewster chair, was brought

97. Built-in benches were decorated, at least on special occasions, with cushions or pads. Some single chair, a seat of honor, might also have a seat pad. As late as the seventeenth century, loose seat pads were the rule also among the affluent. In peasant milieu, especially in southern Sweden, they could be found well into the nineteenth century.—*Stuga* on large farm, Veberöd, Skåne.

96. The appearance of the centrally placed table—in the middle of the *sal,* the drawing room, or as the focus for a group of furniture in parlor or salon—contributed greatly to the development of decorative textile furnishings.—Stockholm interior, table with boldly patterned tablecloth. End of nineteenth century.

to Sweden in the early Middle Ages, and was also used as a seat of honor. It survived in peasant milieu well into the nineteenth century as, among other things, bridal seats in churches and judge's seats in courthouses. Also chairs of Renaissance or baroque types, when appearing in peasant milieu, functioned as seats of honor and were trimmed accordingly (fig. 97). The Gustavian[6] chair with square-sectioned, vertical slats in the backrest was the first truly common type of individual seat in Sweden. With its introduction, built-in benches and seats were gradually ousted from the guest part of the house. The placement of the chairs, however, continued to be wall-oriented (figs. 98, 99). Manorial reception halls served as models for the furnishing of corresponding rooms on larger farms: the guest *stuga*, the

anderstuga, the *nystuga,* or whatever the local equivalent term might have been.

The spindle-back chair was Sweden's first factory-made production-line chair. In this form, the individual seat, i.e., the chair, was introduced into chamber and kitchen areas. The predecessor of the Swedish turned chair is the English Windsor chair. The nineteenth-century Windsor type, however, came to Sweden not from England but from the United States, probably through channels opened by the late nineteenth-century mass emigration to America. It is reported that in Sweden American Windsor chairs were first factory-made in northern Småland around 1850 under the guidance of Mrs. Henriette Killander of Hook Manor, Småland. Industrial manufacture started in several places in the late 1870s (fig. 481).

98. Not until the first half of the nineteenth century did the chair become common in peasant milieu. On the model of manorial reception halls, peasant drawing rooms acquired rows of chairs along the walls. Stora Kopparberg, Dalarna, 1926.

99. Chairs with padded seats were first introduced in seventeenth-century upper-class homes, and began to reach peasant homes in the mid-1800s. Sundborn, Dalarna, 1926.

Cushions and seat covers

Cushions especially fashioned for sitting furniture have existed since the Middle Ages. Built-in benches were provided with weavings running along the walls as protection against cold and damp. They were called *rygglakan* (literally, "back covers") and were of various kinds, from simple wadmal to sumptuous weaves of a kind which came to be especially associated with these backwarmers, hence called *rölakan* or *röllakan*, a derivation of *rygglakan*. Bench coverings may have been a plain length of material, but in the Middle Ages padded cushions were already used (fig. 119), their front or topside made of some patterned weave, and the back or underside of some simpler material or hide. Seat cushions on benches and chairs were, as a rule, loose until the mid-seventeenth century in bourgeois milieu. In peasant milieu, the custom remained until the mid-nineteenth century—in other words, as long as sitting furniture consisted largely of settles and benches. Benches, as well as the few existing chairs, were constructed with a depression in the seat for the cushion. Around the middle of the seventeenth century, another chair construction was introduced in upper-class milieu, namely, the chair with skirt. In this form, the chair also acquired an upholstered seat. Loose chair cushions, upholstery on chairs, benches, and sofas (figs. 229, 230, 243, 345, 346), as well as carriage cushions (figs. 263, 344), were some of the textile elements of interior decoration and home furnishing which became special focal ponts for aesthetic ambitions (figs. 217–230, color figs. 19–24). Most chairs from the seventeenth century preserved in their original state are leather covered. A few have survived with textile covering of velvet or shag, silk damask, cross-stitch embroidery, or so-called Flemish tapestry.

During the first half of the eighteenth century, cross-stitch embroidery · was especially fashionable, but leather, silk, and velvet continued to be used. Flemish weaving, however, went out of fashion. Nevertheless, there is reason to pay particular attention to this textile technique, as it was transmitted from bourgeois milieu to peasant milieu, especially in Småland and Skåne, and gave rise to a rich, locally distinctive production. Aside from Flemish weaving, *rölakan* and *krabbasnår* weaves were also used for cushions in southwestern Sweden, i.e., Blekinge, Skåne, parts of Småland (figs. 144, 217, 227, 352–54, 356–60; color figs. 36–40), Halland, and southwestern Västergötland.

In central and northern Sweden, bench pads are missing in peasant milieu, but isolated examples of Flemish weaving exist. They probably originally came from bourgeois or parsonage milieu. Embroidered cushions have existed throughout the country, with distinct local variations.

Pillows

During the latter part of the nineteenth century, completely cloth-covered and upholstered sitting furniture appeared in connection with the use of springs to make sofas and armchairs as comfortable as possible. This new type of sitting furniture entered the parlors of peasant homes towards the end of the century directly from the factory. As a rule, it had no influence on the household's own manufacture of craft items, either for consumption or for sale. The loose cushions and pads survived in the form of purely decorative throw pillows, which were lavishly and zealously decorated (figs. 99, 100).

Storage

Furniture and household articles for storage purposes belong among the most primitive equipment in the dwelling house. The need to keep left-over foodstuffs and to safeguard valuables is a basic ingredient of primitive life. The Lapps, for example, have a type of small storehouse, the *njalla,* for food storage, and carry their valuables with them in a type of coffer, the *kisa* (fig. 107).

Food storage

The earliest materials for storing food and other household necessities were animal skins, hides, intestines, bladders, etc. (fig. 101). A sausage was originally a container to store left-over food. Salt and spices, expensive and

100. Bourgeois Stockholm home, around 1880, with a superabundance of textile furnishings: wall-to-wall carpeting, curtains, drapes, completely upholstered sitting furniture, tablecloths, pillows, and antimacassars.

highly prized means of flavoring and preserving foodstuffs, were also kept in animal skins. Whole flayed cat skins were used for holding spices and also for keeping money—so-called money cats. Flour was stored either in similarly treated calfskins with the hair side out, or in cloth bags.

Overall, until today, wood has been the most important material for storage vessels and containers. It has been worked in a number of techniques: it has been hollowed out and turned, in stands and boxes; coopered in barrels, kegs, piggins, and tubs; molded in thin sheets into boxes of every conceivable size; and braided and woven in strips into baskets

for various purposes and commodities (figs. 102, 519–29). For each new stage in the development of food storage, new materials and new forms of containers have been added. The processes of drying and smoking are conditioned by storage in animal skins; pickling, fermentation, and brining by storage in coopered or hollowed-out wooden vessels. Ceramic goods —e.g., the characteristic and still popular crocks from Höganäs—have been used for such purposes in southern Sweden and in bourgeois milieu. Elsewhere in peasant milieu, stoneware was generally reserved for more formal occasions. Tin canisters and molds appeared during the nineteenth century and had, like glass and

101. Interior of a *kåta* or Lapp hut. Animal bladders filled with blood and a reindeer stomach filled with dry milk are suspended from the *kåta* poles. Vittangi, Lappland, 1932.

102. With the introduction of glass and tin came canning as a method of food preservation, and the use of wooden vessels for storage or preservation declined.—Larder, Lidingö, 1968.

103. Food storage with flour bin of boards and nails and coopered vessels for salt-brined meat, fish, and other foods. Dried meats and sausages hang from the ceiling. Mangskog, Värmland, 1919.

china goods, their heyday when canning was introduced as the newest and most sensible preserving technique of the nineteenth century. In our time, the technique of freezing has created its own forms of storage containers: plastic bags and refrigerator equipment of different synthetic materials, as well as ready-made disposable packaging of cardboard and foil which continually diminish the need for permanent storage containers.

Storage of textiles and clothing
Coopered tubs, pails, troughs, and vats have played a central part in the household, not only

in food storage but also in washing and cleaning. Woodcraft production has, therefore, to a high degree, focused on the manufacture of coopered vessels for sale. However, coopered containers were not used for storage of foodstuffs and for washing only, but also in earlier times for clothes storage. During the early Middle Ages, the chest appeared. It retained its prominent place as late as the nineteenth century, in spite of the competition offered by the cupboard—a significant status piece from the seventeenth century—the introduction of

104. The chest has long remained popular for storage of clothes and textiles, especially in Skåne. —Chest chamber built as late as the 1920s, with six old chests and two linen cupboards. Espö, Skåne, 1966.

105. A well-filled linen closet. Höör, Skåne, 1965.

106. In northern Sweden clothes and textiles were kept in separate rooms or loft houses, often highly decorated.—Clothes storage, "guest *stuga*," from Boda, Dalarna.

the chest of drawers, and the fall-front bureau-desk in the nineteenth century. These types have all been used for storage of clothing and textiles (figs. 104–8). In Swedish peasant milieu, it has also been customary to store clothes and bedding in separate rooms, clothes closets or wardrobes, and often in the guest *stuga* and in loft houses, where guests were customarily lodged (fig. 72). Such was the situation especially in Dalarna and Hälsingland, where the clothes in these closets often were decoratively arranged on rails suspended from the ceiling or hung on special wicker hangers on the walls, in such a fashion that each garment was not only stored with proper care, but also decoratively displayed (fig. 106). In a way, these rooms served as a sort of exhibition hall, showing off the material assets of the house. Another place for storing the textile wealth of

the house was the reception hall on the second floor, where beds with bolsters, quilts, and pillows demonstrated the economic status of the household and the weaving skill of its womenfolk. In southern Sweden, particularly Skåne, the *kistekammare* (chest chamber)—corresponding to central and northern Sweden's storage room, the *anderstuga,* the guest *stuga,* or the loft house—had lining the walls rows of chests in which clothes and home decorating textiles were stored (fig. 104). Here were also beds for guests, and hangings adorned the walls. Storage-display was important in the social life of the household: the joy of ownership was given superb aesthetic expression in household fixtures and movables.

The closet and the wardrobe existed in upper-class homes from the eighteenth century on as storage areas and servant quarters. In the

beginning of the nineteenth century, the so-called *klädkontor* (clothes office) appeared in connection with the bedroom, and from the end of that century, the closet became common in Stockholm apartment buildings. The wardrobe has reappeared in today's urban homes and city apartments in the form of the larger walk-in closet.

Storage of decorative items

The cupboard was the most ostentatious piece of furniture in the home. The best housewares and the home's decorative items were also kept here: pewter, silver, brass, pottery, and whatever china the household might possess (figs. 76, 78, 96).

Imitations of the silverware, crystal, and china of the well-to-do in cheaper materials,

107. Lapps traditionally kept their valuables in a *kisa* or box of molded wood splint.—From the permanent exhibit "Samisk kultur" (Lapp culture), Nordiska Museet.

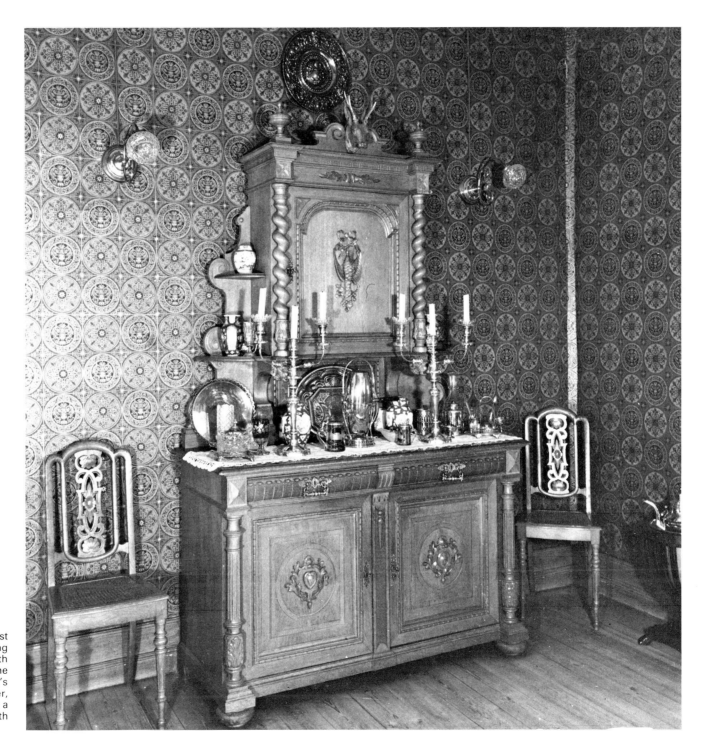

108. The cupboard was the most ostentatious piece of furniture during the eighteenth and nineteenth centuries in all social strata. It became a display case for the household's status symbols, especially silver, glassware, and china.—Buffet from a Stockholm home, late nineteenth century.

Furniture and household articles

109. The bedding existed before the bedstead and was not tied to any particular piece of furniture. It could be laid out directly on the floor, on a berth, a bunk, a bench, or in some other place.—This bottom sheet of rag weave was functional and easy to care for on a bed of twigs, hay, or straw. Venjan, Dalarna.

such as nickel, silverplate, and pressed glass, began to appear during the second half of the nineteenth century. Everyday articles of this cheaper kind were affordable by the common man. Finer glass and china services were placed in the dining-room buffet or sideboard. The profusion of bric-à-brac was kept in cupboards with glassed doors or displayed in special shelves, whatnots, or étagères. The buffet became the showpiece of the home, decorated with crystal bowls, spice-, fruit-, and knife-racks, silver and china bibelots—a grandiose display case designed to demonstrate the economic and social standard of the household (fig. 108).

Bedstead and bedding

Bed and bedstead

The bed and bedding existed before the bedstead, and were made up of simple components. The bed could be laid out directly on the floor, on a berth, a bunk, a bench, or some other place (fig. 34). The bed was not associated with any particular piece of furniture, being placed now here, now there, on temporary foundations. Nor was the shakedown bed tied to any particular room. In some parts of Sweden this custom has survived into the twentieth century, thus providing an opportunity to study a type of sleeping arrangement with prehistoric roots. When the bedstead appeared, bed conditions changed and new forms, materials, and decoration emerged. The components of the bedding changed with the changing role of the bedstead in interior decoration, depending on whether it was built-in or freestanding, merely a support for the bedding, or a status-conferring piece. The equipment of the bedstead is an interesting chapter, inextricably bound up with Swedish dwelling tradition. The fell or fur rug (figs. 58, 71), the rya[7]—the knotted pile rug—(figs. 250, 251), and the padded or quilted coverlet (fig. 117) represent three different stages of chronological development; yet, all three can still be found, side by side, in different social milieus and in different parts of the country.

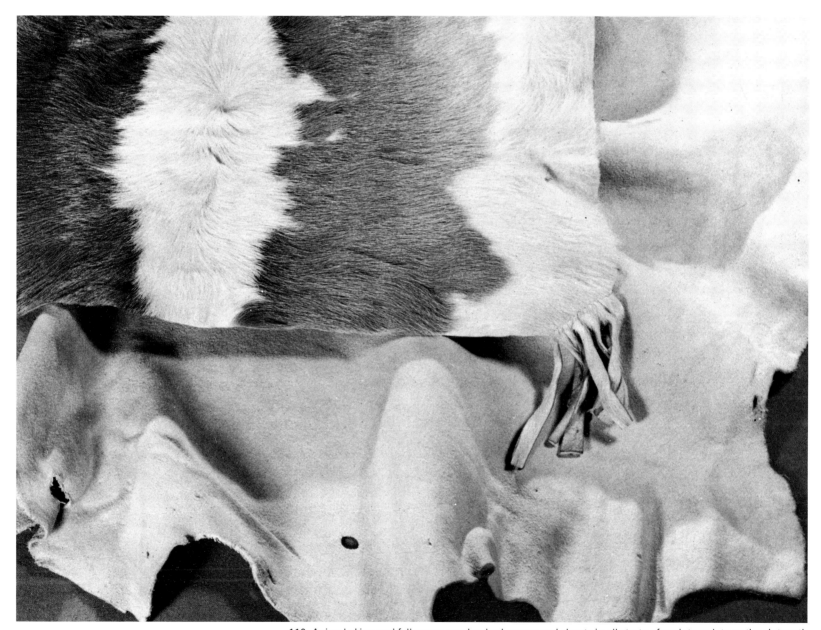

110. Animal skins and fells were used as bed covers and sheets in all strata of society as late as the sixteenth century. For climatic reasons, they are still in use in Norrland.—Sheets of untanned calfskin and chamois. Hälsingland and Dalarna.

Hay, straw, and animal skin

In the *fäbodar* in Norrland, one may still encounter a built-in berth or bunk with a bed of hay covered by a rag spread—the *umbrea* or *unnerbrea* (bottom "sheet") or a reindeer skin (figs. 109, 110), topped by a sheepskin rug sewn to a coverlet, the *åkläde* (fig. 216). The *åkläde* could also be ripped from the sheepskin rug and used separately during the hottest summer months. It is understandable that this ancient type of bedding has survived in northern Sweden, as nothing retains the heat so well as fur rugs and reindeer skins in poorly insulated *fäbod* buildings when it is really cold outside (fig. 34). Furthermore, padded and quilted coverlets and mattresses are not suited to dwellings from which cold and damp can never be completely expelled. Hay, on the other hand, is an excellent bedding material, as it can be changed when it is matted or damp. A fabric with rag weft makes suitable bottom sheets on hay because it will not slip, and hay or straw cannot penetrate the rags. A bottom sheet woven with rags is therefore preferable wherever hay or straw is used in the bed. Thus, sheets with rag weft are still found all over northern Sweden and in Värmland. Isolated examples in Småland and Östergötland seem to indicate that rag sheets were once common also in the southern parts of Sweden. A fell and straw or hay have also been used in combination with bottom sheets and pillowcases of calfskin, tanned or untanned, or of chamois (fig. 110). There is reason to believe that the use of skin sheets was a widely accepted custom in all classes of society. Castle inventories from the sixteenth century list skin sheets trimmed with red skin, obviously lavish ensembles for the highest social stratum. From peasant milieu in more recent times, there are whole mattress covers of brown tanned hides as well as pillowcases of the same material.

The sheepskin rug with sewn-on coverlet exists all over the country from Blekinge north, as do coverlets without fur rug. In Norrland, fells have occasionally been made with rabbit fur, no doubt considered luxury items (fig. 112). These fells are not made of whole pelts but of woven fur strips. One castle inventory in central Sweden lists fells of squirrel skin.

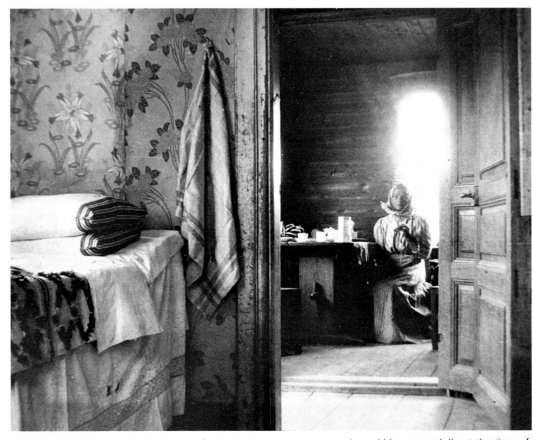

111. To possess fine textile furnishings for the bed was every woman's ambition, especially at the time of marriage. The dowry consisted largely of textiles, primarily bedding. In Hälsingland, with its highly developed flax cultivation, the bed received richer trappings than anywhere else.—Bed with hanging sheet, top sheet, bottom sheet, pillowcases with decorative "caps," and rag coverlet with inserted cloth strips. Järvsö, Hälsingland.

Whether they were made with woven strips or whole pelts is not known.

Hair, feathers, and cloth

The foundation of the bed has generally consisted of straw in those parts of the country where the grain crops provided an adequate supply, and of hay in other parts. Also, elk hair, reindeer hair, and cut-up rags have frequently made up the bottom layer, not only in rural milieu but also in poor urban milieu. Whereas hay or straw can be used loose, the latter materials require a closed covering, as do feathers and down. The supply of these filling materials for bolsters and mattresses is dependent on the availability of sources. Elk and reindeer hair are abundant in northern Sweden, from where they have also been exported south. Chicken and geese have long been kept in the southernmost provinces. They were not introduced farther north until quite late, and then only into the wealthier strata of society. Bolsters filled with feather or down therefore have existed in southern Swedish peasant milieu from the seventeenth century,

112. Fell-backed coverlet. Fell, with weft of jackrabbit-fur strips and linen warp; coverlet in *upphämta* on ground of linen warp and cotton weft with pattern weft of wool. Ljungdalen, Storsjö, Härjedalen.

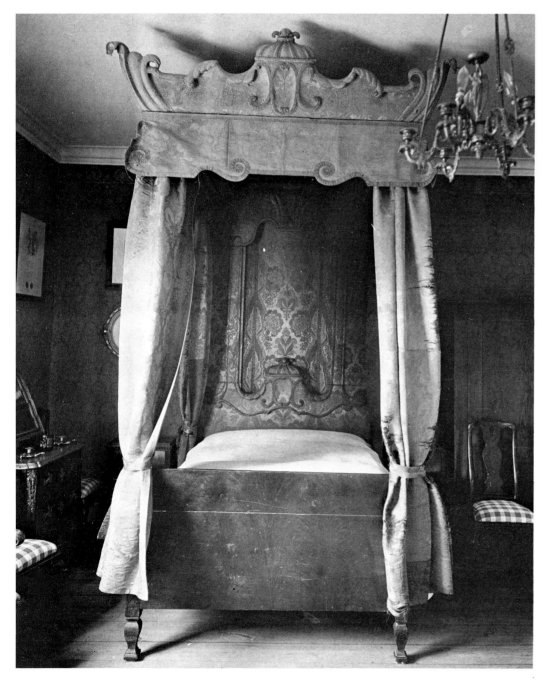

113. In seventeenth- and eighteenth-century upper-class milieu, the bed was a showpiece and the bedroom a room for social gatherings. The textile accouterments added significantly to the bed's decorative and status value.—Bedstead from the beginning of the eighteenth century, Sturefors Castle, Östergötland.

whereas in the rest of the country they have been found exclusively in castle, manor house, or well-to-do urban homes. Down can also be obtained from wild birds, primarily the eider. Access to such feather or down supply has, in other words, also given rise to local production of feather or down bolsters. In Småland, mattresses and bolsters were sometimes filled with pig's hair. Another stuffing material was the pods from cotton grass and cattail.

With the use of this kind of stuffing a tick is necessary. It should also be taken into account that the appearance of freestanding bedsteads increased the need for a closed casing for the bottom filling material. The above-mentioned bolster tick of skin, however, seems to have been relatively rare, at least judging from surviving examples. Instead, woven bolster ticks were more common and are preserved in far greater numbers. Bolster ticks show a distinct local differentiation, as does the complete bedding. In peasant milieu, the use of hay and straw survives into modern times in the *fäbod* region, the bed retaining also the rag-weft bottom sheet and the fell. In other parts of the country, the mattress or bolster (figs. 114, 117) came into use in combination with rya and coverlet, with feather or down comforter, or with quilted coverlet.

The social function of the bed
The rya is nowadays used as floor covering or wall decoration. Originally it served as a bed cover. As late as the sixteenth century it was in common use on all social levels. Castles belonging to the Crown sorted their pile covers according to quality—the best for gentry, the poorer for servants. In the course of the sixteenth century, the quilted coverlet started to spread from the Continent to Sweden. In the seventeenth century, it had become common among the upper classes; in the eighteenth century it was taken up, to a limited extent, by the rural population. Skåne, like Denmark, had already accepted the down-filled bolster or comforter in the seventeenth century. The rya did survive in bourgeois milieu, however, as a decorative cover or bedspread. In peasant homes, the pile rug continued to serve in its

original function until the end of the nineteenth century, especially in western Sweden and in eastern Sweden from Blekinge in the south to Uppland in the north. The use and design of the rya is related to the development of the bedstead and living habits. The formal display nature of the bed in seventeenth-century upper-class homes has already been pointed out: there, the bedroom functioned also as a room in which to receive guests (fig. 68). From the mid-seventeenth century, when Sweden's contact with Continental culture increased, the combination bedroom-sitting room took on a formal, ceremonial nature. The bedstead became a status item with increasingly more lavish accouterments (fig. 113). Another circumstance influenced this change, namely the increased importance of the bedding as the woman's contribution to the house. Hence, it became a social ambition for every family— and, of course, especially, for any bride-to-be— to demonstrate social and economic standards by rich bedding and textiles in general. These conditions acted as significant incentives on all social levels. An enormous effort was put forth on textile furnishings far in advance of the wedding. Not only were sheets and pillowcases monogrammed—as is still customary—but also coverlets, bolsters, pillows and cushions, pile covers, bed curtains, and decorative bedspreads (figs. 116, 195, 207, 210, 211, 218, 250, 381, 382). The emphasis on bedding gives a clear indication of the bed's status. Obviously, all these items were intended to be seen. Just as the buffet became the display case for housewares, often received as *lysning* gifts,[6] so did the bed exhibit the bride's textile assets. One may well imagine that this bedding by no means was intended for everyday use—a supposition borne out by available evidence.

Linen and silk

From the sixteenth and seventeenth centuries, sheets and pillowcases have been preserved which were made with extraordinary care. They are of linen tabby with wide borders of embroidery. Dates and initials show that they were made for the weddings of socially prominent people. Splendid examples of extravagant

114. Down-filled bolsters, comforters, and cushions of striped woolen ticking are found in peasant milieu in southwestern Sweden and Blekinge as well as on Öland and Gotland.—Bedding from Asarum parish, Blekinge, shown at an exhibition in Karlshamn in the 1910s.

115. Canopied bed at a *fäbod.* Modeled on eighteenth-century upper-class bedsteads, this bed sports curtains of white cotton tabby embroidered in red with hanging sheet and pillowcases to match. Bjuråker, Hälsingland.

display in connection with weddings are found in coverlets, canopies, bed curtains, embroidery, weaves, laces, knittings, fringes, and borders (figs. 113, 115, 364, 372, 403, 404). All types of decorative techniques were called upon to create rich and varied accessories for the bed. In the seventeenth century, the most prestigious era of the bed, a certain type of pillowcase developed. This type featured an embroidered "cap" on one of the pillow's short ends, designed to give one "show" side to the pillow, as the bed was placed with one side along the wall (figs. 111, 335). The bottom

sheet was bordered all around and hung down, visible below the coverlet spread over the bed. The top sheet had a wide border to turn down over the edge of the coverlet (fig. 115). There is reason to suppose that linen sheets initially were not intended for everyday use, even in the homes of the gentry. Among peasants this was the case, to a certain extent, as late as the end of the nineteenth century; although the standard was usually high in Hälsingland and the coastal provinces in southern Norrland with their highly developed flax cultivation. In these areas, finer bedding was therefore al-

116. The prodigal son reclining on a bed piled high with bolsters and covered with a striped coverlet.— Wall hanging of painted linen tabby by Johannes Nilsson of Gyltige, end of the eighteenth century. Kvibille, Halland.

117. Bed from the middle of the nineteenth century, made up with wedding sheets and pillowcases with embroidered top. From the exhibit "Lin och linne" (Flax and linen), Nordiska Museet, 1944.

ready well developed in the eighteenth century. Embroidered hanging sheets with solely decorative function also appeared here. These, however, have existed elsewhere, though at times in the form of a mere embroidered strip or half a sheet folded over the edge of the coverlet. In Hälsingland, the guest beds were impressive sights, exhibiting the fine linen of the province and its resultant wealth. The pillows were piled two or three high, and there were hanging sheets, top sheets, bed curtains, and decorative rag pile coverlets of linen with inserted pattern strips (fig. 111, 115). For everyday use, however, the bedding did not include sheets here either. The bottom sheet of rag weave sufficed. In Jämtland, Härjedalen, and on Öland and Gotland, bottom sheets of wool have been used—in the former provinces to keep out the cold, in the two latter ones to ward off the damp, raw weather. In both cases a plentiful supply of wool has probably also contributed to the development of woolen sheets, whereas flax in these provinces had to be bought from the outside.

It is worth noting that sheets were not used for hygienic reasons until quite late. Their predominant function was to display wealth. Linen long remained a status symbol both in furnishings and in dress. The bedding's heat-conserving properties were of prime importance in northern Sweden, which contributed significantly to the region's conservatism in bedding. Only with the coming of a higher living standard and more efficient heating of the dwelling house did this situation change. Nevertheless, the upper-class bedding for display was responsible for a curious local development not limited to linen articles.

Coverlet and rya
The quilted coverlet was probably, originally, only a decorative bed cover. In the seventeenth century, it had a thin layer of padding between a top layer of silk and a lining of linen tabby. It must have had an exclusively decorative function, whereas heat retention was provided by something else, perhaps a rya. The Västergötland peddlers' sales of ryas were by no means limited to peasant milieu. Certain descriptions of pile covers from Västergötland in inventories from eighteenth-century upper-class homes agree quite well with the few preserved examples, indicating the transition from the practical rya to the decorative rya. In Uppland, Gästrikland, Hälsingland, and other Norrland provinces, the decorative rya appears in peasant milieu (color fig. 28), but not the practical rya. Apparently the fell was here never replaced by the rya, until the latter was introduced as decorative coverlet or bedspread.

The rya, then, survives as a warming bed cover in Uppland, parts of Östergötland and Närke, the coastal areas of Småland, and Blekinge (figs. 255, 261). The fact that the rya replaced the fell in coastal areas generally, and that the quilted coverlet did not gain acceptance here, is probably connected with the pile cover's usefulness in damp climates. The rya pile resists humidity, something the fell and the quilted coverlet are unable to do. The rya's survival in Bohuslän is partly due to this property, partly to other factors which are discussed below.

Bed curtains and bedspreads
In Skåne the rya did not survive the seventeenth century, when the down-filled bolster came into use. In southwestern Sweden, in the region of the Southern Götaland house type with its characteristic plan, an antiquated textile furnishing concept lived on. Simultaneously, yet another type of bedstead and bed placement developed in central and eastern Sweden, in the region of the *parstuga* house type. Under influence from Gustavian and Empire-style furniture, the freestanding bedstead, still placed in a corner, was equipped with a cornice, attached to the ceiling, or a tester or canopy frame, supported by corner posts (figs. 113, 115, 321). From this cornice, bed hangings of linen were suspended; in the nineteenth century, hangings of cotton as well. The second innovation was the Gustavian extension bed, a combination of the old chest-settle or extension bed with a sofa, resulting in a new, characteristically Swedish, type. The Gustavian extension bed has a telescoping frame which extends the bed's long side out into the room. It was usually placed in a corner, the traditional place for the bed. Especially during the nineteenth century, it became the piece of furniture typical of the bedroom-parlor chamber, where it stood in state during the day, telescoped, piled high with bedding, and adorned with a bedspread, generally white (fig. 73). Among people of the higher classes, the white coverlet of linen or, in exceptional cases, of thinly quilted and stitched cotton, was already in use at the end of the seventeenth century. It retained its popularity in spite of competition from more colorful silk coverlets, and dominated completely from the end of the eighteenth century throughout the nineteenth century. The definitive breakthrough of the white crocheted, knitted, or woven coverlet or bedspread was in part attributable to the increased use of cotton and to the introduction of the so-called Imperial bed, a bed with a high headboard and a lower foot board (fig. 117). It was intended to stand with the headboard against the wall, but in peasant homes it was placed in the traditional corner. Not until separate bedrooms became common did the beds extend, often in pairs, out from the middle of the wall.

In grander circumstances, the canopied bed had, of course, been extending from the wall, visible from all sides, since the sixteenth century. At that point, the textile furnishing for the bed was complemented by bedspread and decorative throw-pillows. The Imperial bed with its dominant position in the room exposed new areas of the bed to view, thus further stimulating the embellishment of the bedding. The pillow ornamentation, initially decorating one end of the pillowcase, now filled its entire top (fig. 117). Indeed, the bed and its accessories have been one of the great sources of inspiration for textile production in Sweden.

Textiles for walls and ceiling
Show towel and hanging cloth
As late as the sixteenth century, it was customary, on all social levels, to eat with one's fingers. Hence, it was necessary to offer washbasins and towels in connection with the meal. In modern times this custom lives on in the use of finger bowls, e.g., after eating shellfish. The decorative towel therefore developed out of banqueting customs, not—as long as hygienic arrangements were more or less cursory—out of any need for textiles for personal hygiene. When personal cleanliness eventually was encouraged by the introduction of specialized furniture, such as the commode and the washstand, the towel also developed accordingly (fig. 118).

From the eighteenth century on, the commode is commonly found in well-to-do homes. In peasant homes, the water trough or pail was used, later the sink or a washbasin, which was placed on a chair and, after use, hung on the wall. The upper strata of the peasant population did not furnish the guest room with a commode until the latter part of the nineteenth century. Above the commode was hung a shelf on consoles for the show towel. The showpiece nature of the towel was emphasized by its rich ornamentation. Compared to the show towel, the hand towel was of minor importance. The hand towel was also a relatively late cultural acquisition. Fabrics made expressly for toweling probably did not exist in peasant milieu until the mid-nineteenth century. The

118. The hand towel is a later cultural acquisition than the show towel, the latter being related to hanging cloths decorating walls and ceiling. When special furniture for personal hygiene was introduced, the show towel was given a specific function and lavish ornamentation.—Chamber with show towel hanging over commode. Västrum, Småland, 1946.

show towel is undeniably related to the hanging cloths—fringed and sometimes patterned cloths, which were hung up for festive occasions between the door to the chamber and the door to the entry, or as decorations hung on various furniture, grandfather clocks, cupboards, crown rails,[9] etc. (figs. 51, 71). With the introduction of the commode, the decorative cloth or hanging acquired a new raison-d'être, a more specialized function, and an appropriately adjusted form.

The towel, then, has a dual origin; it derives, on one hand, from table customs; on the other, from the more general use of decorative textiles in older house types. As long as the hearth lacked a flue, any permanent covering or decoration of the walls was futile. Its design

would soon have been obliterated by soot. Thus, there was a strong desire at festive occasions to create a sharp contrast to the sooty everyday room. In Icelandic literature there are descriptions of the amazing interior transformation of a chieftain's dwelling house that took place in preparation for a banquet: walls, ceiling, and benches were all covered or hung with textiles. The verb for this type of decoration was [to] tjälda (Old Norse, tjaldr), now surviving in the name for a lace weave, myggtjäll (literally, "mosquito netting"; mock leno weave). According to linguistic authorities tjälda (verb) and tjäll (noun) are probably related to tält (tent), and it is very conceivable that the thus trimmed interior did indeed present a tentlike appearance. A similar scheme

of textile decoration is found in the houses of southern Halland and southern Småland. At holidays, these houses were completely lined with hangings of various sizes and shapes, carefully fitted to the sloping ceiling, the low walls above the permanent benches, the purlins, and the rafters themselves (figs. 119, 133, 401). Some drawings from the 1880s show interiors which are definitely tentlike (fig. 55).

Although the fireplace in affluent homes was already equipped with a flue in the Middle Ages, the custom of dressing the walls with textiles persisted. Some seventeenth-century walls were painted to resemble walls hung with draped textiles (fig. 120). From parsonage and castle inventories, from other archival records, and from literary sources, it is known that the walls of a room could be draped with lengths of woven material in two or more colors, the ceiling hung with fabrics and darned net strips, and that entire rooms could be lined with wadmal or fine woolen cloth. When King Gustaf II Adolf died (1632), the Queen had her own and other rooms in the royal palace completely hung with black woolen cloth. This was by no means an unusual expression for intense personal grief, but rather an accepted custom for those who had the means to observe it. The Danish cultural historian, Fredrik Troels Lund, gives numerous examples of this tradition in his comprehensive work, Dagligt liv i Norden ("Daily life in the Nordic countries"). At weddings as well as at funerals, hangings were borrowed from relatives and neighbors. In upper-class milieu, textile wall dressings for special occasions were retained into the seventeenth century. However, lengths of wadmal and linen tabby (preferably patterned), linen, wool, or silk were later permanently attached to the walls in the form of tapestry or wall "paper." In peasant milieu this custom survived in many areas beyond the mid-nineteenth century.

Painted and woven hangings for walls and ceiling

Alongside the removable textile furnishings on the walls and the ceiling, decorations were painted directly on the whitewashed plaster or

80

wood walls as early as the Middle Ages. Decorative painting directly on the wall, or on lengths of linen tabby, *bonader,* flourished in upper-class milieu and inspired similar decorations in peasant milieu.[10] The painting of wall hangings appeared first in Bergslagen, Hälsingland, and adjoining Norrland provinces at the end of the seventeenth century, and developed during the latter half of the eighteenth century and the beginning of the nineteenth century in Halland and in southwestern Småland (figs. 5, 28, 87, 88). Thus the stages in the development of the dwelling house are reflected in its furnishings: first, the detachable textiles associated with the older house type without flue; second, permanent wall decorations, painted either directly on the wall or on canvas fitted to the wall or into wall panels, a practice connected with stoves with flue.

Northern and central Sweden

In northern and central Sweden even peasant houses had a fireplace with flue by the sixteenth century. Where this arrangement occurred and a generally high living standard existed, there were separate guest houses with wall paintings (figs. 106, 120). Here, the room's textile furnishing in the form of wall hangings or ceiling cloths had been replaced by painting, either directly on the wooden walls or on canvas, permanently affixed to the walls of the room.

Southern Sweden

In southern Sweden, however, the prevalent Southern Götaland house type and the dwelling customs associated with it have perpetuated the old tradition of detachable wall decorations, thus keeping alive textile traditions of

119. Interior of Skåne *stuga,* decorated with wall runners between the ceiling and the benches. Painting by unknown artist, mid-nineteenth century.

120. Interior of "guest *stuga,*" "wedding *stuga.*" Rättvik, Dalarna.

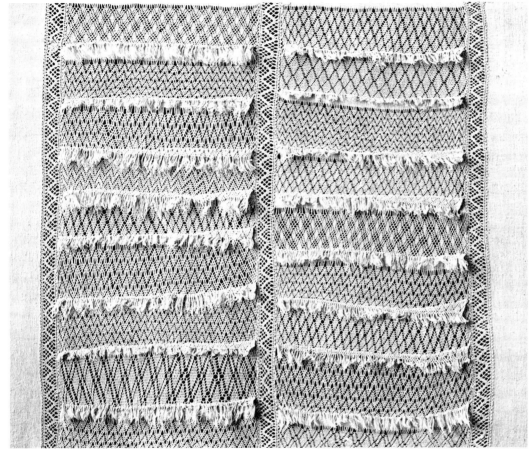

121. Wall hanging of white linen tabby with insertions of bobbin lace (the vertical strips) and braiding. Ore, Dalarna. (For detail, see fig. 412.)

medieval and prehistoric origin. As late as the mid-eighteenth century, the farmhouse did not, as noted above, possess a chimney. The smoke escaped through the ceiling window, encrusting the ceiling and walls with soot. Only when the authorities intervened, decreeing the building of chimneys, were the farmers forced to remodel their fireplaces. However, by force of habit painted and woven wall hangings and hanging cloths continued to be put up only at holidays. This custom prevailed in the region dominated by the Southern Götaland house type, i.e., Halland, Blekinge, southwest-ern Småland, southwestern Västergötland, and Skåne. The decorative hanging tradition has caused the creation of Sweden's perhaps most magnificent works of textile folk art: the *duka-gång*[11] hangings from Skåne (figs. 119, 241, 242), the hanging cloths and woven wall hangings from Blekinge and Halland, and the ceiling cloths from Västergötland (figs. 133, color fig. 17). This textile tradition has an offshoot of rare beauty and variety in the painted wall hangings from Småland and Halland. A latter-day representative of the wall-hanging tradition was the rectangular hanging embroidered with mottoes, devices, or quotations. This type of hanging was rarely missing in any late-nineteenth-century or early-twentieth-century Swedish home.

In southern Sweden, local variations have developed. In Blekinge, there were so-called *dragdukar* (hangings) on the walls and across the rafters. They were rectangular, measuring about two by five feet, and embellished with patterns in transverse borders, in *dukagång, upphämta,*[12] laid-in, or—as was common in the Bräkne district in the late eighteenth century—embroidered with rococo and Gustavian-inspired flowers (figs. 320, 362, 363).

In Halland, the hanging cloths were very narrow, about ten inches wide, and between seventeen and thirty-five feet long. They had transverse borders, embroidered or woven in *upphämta* with laid-in patterns (figs. 267, 268). There were also wider so-called *sparradukar* (rafter cloths), which were decorated with embroidered or woven patterns. In addition to these woven wall hangings, painted hangings were also used (fig. 133). Ceiling cloths, or rafter cloths, were used especially in Väster-götland (fig. 400).

In Småland, long hangings were used, a good three feet wide and approximately twenty-seven feet long, with transverse borders in *upphämta*. They were often finished along the bottom edge with a braiding or a checkered border with fringe. Painted hangings were not infrequently executed on worn-out wall hangings of this type or on other old woven wall hangings.

In southeastern Skåne there were the impressive woven wall hangings in *dukagång,* two widths wide and up to eighty feet long, with rhythmically repeated, boldly stylized borders in dark blue. Narrower cloths were also hung on the walls or in the ceiling across the room. In northern Skåne these cloths resemble those of Småland; in eastern Skåne, those of Blekinge. Within the entire southern region these cloths and woven wall hangings have been trimmed with plaited fringe. In Västergötland the large ceiling cloths, intended for the incline of the ceiling, were executed in knotted net with a pattern in darning or embroidery (figs. 400–402).

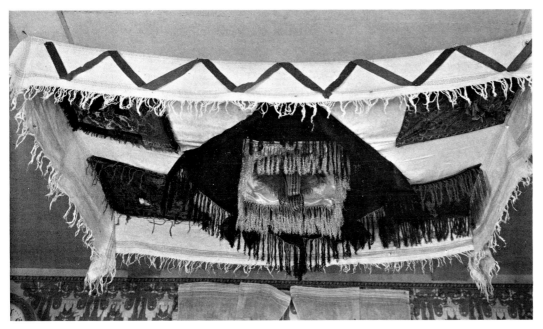

122. Canopy made up of a white patterned cotton coverlet with fringe, decorated with pinned-on red ribbons along the edges and with silk kerchiefs in the four corners and—in several thicknesses—in the center. This canopy was hung up at weddings and on other festive occasions. Mora, Dalarna.

during the marriage vows (fig. 89). A number of magnificent textile objects have been created around this ceremonial function in different parts of the country. Aside from these specially made canopies, some areas, especially in northern Sweden, have used other richly patterned textiles as canopies. In Floda, Dalarna, coverlets from Västergötland were thus used, in Skåne coverlets in *rölakan* technique,[13] and in Leksand, Dalarna, coverlets in rosepath. In Bohuslän, coverlets in double weaves or *upphämta* were hung on the walls with a row of handkerchiefs above them and silk kerchiefs in the corners of the room. This practice clearly demonstrates a lack of functional differentiation in textile furnishings, further underlined by the fact that decorative weavings were indiscriminately used to spread on the bed, to hang on the wall, or to lay out on benches and seats.

Textiles on the floor

Decorating the floor for special occasions was done in peasant milieu by spreading more or less infrequently used coverlets on the floor. In upper-class milieu the rug came into use in the sixteenth and seventeenth centuries, although to a very limited extent. As late as the end of the eighteenth century, pictures of bourgeois homes show bare wooden floors, strewn with chopped juniper or spruce (fig. 80). Rugs must also have been used, however, as memoirs from the beginning of the nineteenth century note that cloth patches and rags were saved for use as filling in rug weaving. Runners in diaper patterns (figs. 124, 127) existed no later than around the mid-nineteenth century, coarse linen tabby rugs with printed or stenciled pattern even earlier (fig. 126). The use of rugs in manor houses seems to have acted as a strong incentive for farm homes, where rugs were regarded as a sign of social distinction.

The general acceptance of floor coverings from the middle of the nineteenth century by all social classes must of course be viewed against the background of an overall improvement in living conditions, including improved housing conditions, especially as seen in the addition of rooms with differentiated functions.

Remnants of a more extensive textile furnishing have, however, survived also in central and northern Sweden. Here can be found hanging cloths, of moderate size, in linen tabby and trimmed with braidings, which were hung on festive occasions over various pieces of furniture. They were also used at funerals to sling under and carry the coffin. In Ore parish, Dalarna, larger hanging cloths have also appeared, nearly the size of wall hangings and consisting of linen tabby lengths interspersed with braiding and laces (figs. 121, 412). The whole *stuga* would be hung with these cloths. In addition, it was customary at funerals throughout central and northern Sweden to hang the whole house, or at least the room of the wake, with white sheets, covering the walls and the windows. At weddings and sometimes also at christenings, the walls of the *stuga* were hung with sheets, decorated with cutouts of colored paper. Sometimes a family would pool all its silk cloths and kerchiefs with those of

relatives and neighbors and use them as wall and ceiling hangings (fig. 122).

Ceiling cloth and canopy

The table canopy was an important element in the ceremonial furnishing of the house. It was used in the manor house, where it figured prominently on formal occasions or at holidays. In the Middle Ages and in the sixteenth century, a woven cloth was suspended from the ceiling to catch falling or flaking soot particles. This was especially desirable above the dining table. The canopy therefore came to be traditionally associated with the table—an association continued even later, when there was no risk of any soot falling in the food (fig. 94). Also in other situations, the utilitarian ceiling cloth gradually acquired a symbolic function. The cloth became a ceremonial symbol and attribute, e.g., at coronations, processions, or weddings, when it was held over the couple

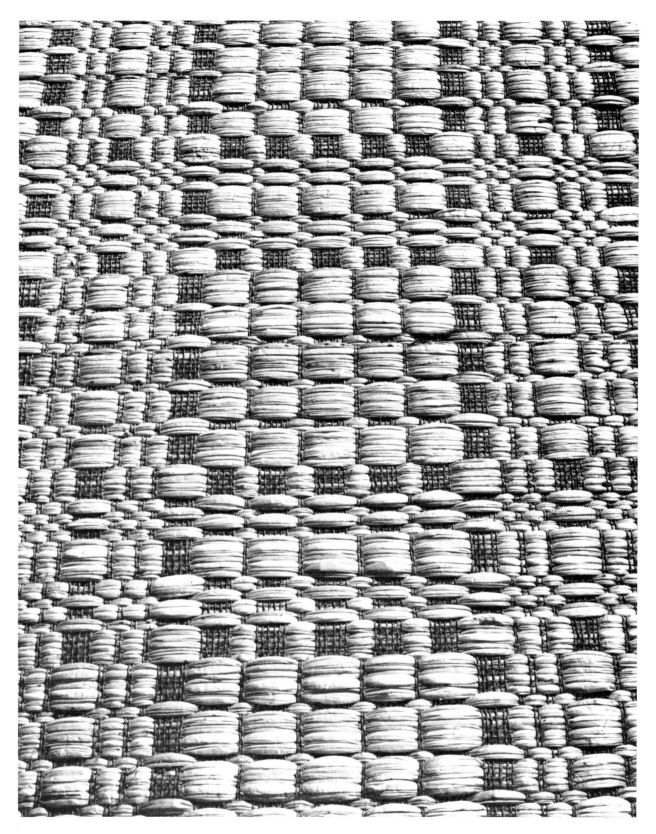

123. Runner, pattern weft of rushes on blue cotton ground. Riala, Uppland.

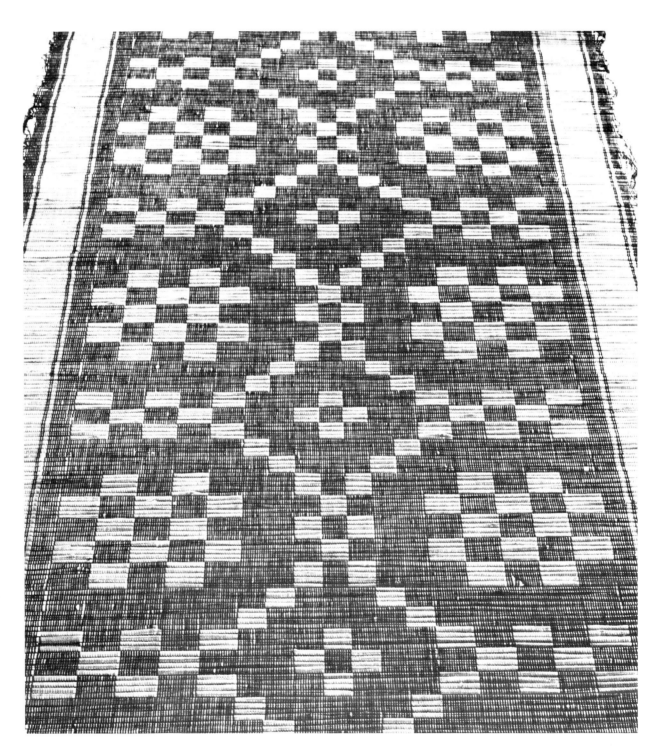

124. Runner, black cotton ground with weft of blue cotton yarn and straw. Öde-borg, Dalsland.

125. Runner of rag weave. Linen warp with weft of white and brown rags of linen and cotton plus some wool yarn in natural color and white. Bjuråker, Hälsingland.

Not until houses were built with several rooms was it feasible to think of a permanent decorative covering for the floors. Thus, if a house had a chamber, the rugs would be spread in there, since there was too much traffic in the *stuga*.

Decorating the floor

Decorating the floors for the holiday is an old Swedish custom, well documented throughout the country. A small sampling gives an idea of the different ways of dressing floors. From Dalarna come the following reminiscences (from the Nordiska Museet's collection of interviews and questionnaires): "Floor coverings began to be used in the 1880s, when rag rugs were first used. Before the advent of rugs, straw was spread on the floor at Christmastime. Some people might have had straw on the floor also at New Year's, and a few allowed it to stay on until past New Year's. Furthermore, finely chopped spruce was strewn on the floor on Sundays in the wintertime (fig. 79). During Lent, many people had clean, fine sand on their floors, and the sand was swept into wavy patterns and swirls with a broom. In the summer we would pick new shoots of spruce and spread them on the floor Saturday evenings. At Midsummer, aspen leaves were raked together and spread on the floor." (Fig. 59.)

On Öland in the 1860s there were no rugs; the floors were bare and scrubbed clean. In the winter and in damp weather, a thin layer of dry white sand was sprinkled on them. This sand was kept in readiness in piles on kitchen and living-room floors. On Sundays and holidays chopped spruce was strewn over the sand. At the end of the 1860s, rag rugs were first woven for the entry, the living room, and the kitchen. At the same time, runners of wool appeared in the parlors. The runners were bought in town. In Småland and other prov-

126. Runner, coarse linen tabby with printed black pattern. The ground shows traces of yellow color. Beginning of the nineteenth century.

127. Parlor with ribbed rugs in diaper patterns. Sundborn, Dalarna.

inces in central Sweden, affluent farm homes used straw mats around the mid-nineteenth century (figs. 123, 124). Sometimes rags would be inserted in these mats—rags were readily available in the home as they were usually saved to be sold to be reprocessed as paper. There was also a kind of straw mat, made of four-end braids sewn together, used under the bedding. Rag rugs appeared in more modern farm homes around 1860 (fig. 77). To start with, these rugs were used only on formal occasions or at holidays, never for parties or purely social gatherings. The reason was that "we cannot afford to have people traipsing around on our new rugs."

In Bohuslän, mats of straw and rushes seem to have been common. The warp was natural-colored plied yarn and the weft was straw. If an especially decorative effect was desired, cloth strips could be cut out and inserted into the weave so as to create the effect of cloth "patches" of different colors forming a zigzag pattern. The mats were placed on the floor, either completely covering it or leaving a few inches of flooring showing between them. After straw mats, rag rugs became the vogue. They were laid, like the mats, closely together, covering the entire floor. When ribbed-weave rugs appeared, these were also laid out closely together, in a similar fashion (fig. 127).

In Värmland and Västergötland, straw and rags have been alternately used as weft. In Skåne and Blekinge, floors were not covered with rugs or mats until the 1880s. Until that time, the floors were strewn with sand and chopped juniper on Sundays and holidays. From Uppland it is reported that wide runners were woven with yellow linen warp and weft of gray bast fiber, obtained from the mats in which rye from Russia was imported. A similar report from Ångermanland indicates that Russian flour sacks of bast fiber were torn up for use as weft in rugs.

It seems to have been quite common, to begin with, to restrict the use of rugs or mats to holidays, funerals, and weddings. In Hälsingland, it is reported that rugs were used on holidays in the 1850s–'60s. In Kimstad, Östergötland, new rag rugs were spread from the carriages to the church stairs for wedding guests and the bridal couple to walk on. There was also a custom of laying down fine coverlets and shawls as a bridal mat before the bridal kneeler during the ceremony and at the bridal bed.

Rugs
The custom of using rags as weft began as an expression of frugality, out of sheer necessity. Today's seemingly limitless material resources make it difficult for us to understand how strong the need to save and reprocess once was. In Hälsingland, in the 1850s–'60s—when rugs were first introduced at holidays—there was a religious sect named the Hedbergians after its leader, a Pastor Hedberg. He preached, among other things, that it was wasteful, hence sinful, to use rugs on the floors. Woolen materials in clothing were also reused, over and over again. They were unraveled and rewoven. The need for such intensive utilization of the material logically suggests the use of rags or strips of material as filling or weft in the weave. As mentioned earlier, rags were used widely in bottom sheets to spread over the bed straw, especially in Norrland up to our time. In Gästrikland and Hälsingland decorative coverlets with patterns of inserted short cloth strips in different colors were common. The earliest such coverlet known to the Nordiska Museet dates from 1834.

Wood pulp and rag rugs
The use of rag rugs started to spread around the middle of the nineteenth century and achieved acceptance during the 1860s–'90s. The origin of rag weaving in Sweden is unknown. Was the idea indigenous or was it imported? This question cannot be answered without a knowledge of the history of rag weaving in other countries. The wider use of rugs in general was attributable to the improved living standard, as mentioned above. But why rugs with rag weft? Threshed straw, previously the predominant material in floor coverings, was not as usable for mats after the introduction of mechanized threshers, leaving rags the cheapest material available. Furthermore, changes in the raw material

128. Paper blind, painted to look like partially raised curtains of striped cloth behind two flower urns on the window sill. Farm from Delsbo, Hälsingland, now at Skansen, Stockholm.

supply to the paper industry were probably also of great importance. Earlier, linen rags had been used for paper manufacture. With increased use of wood pulp, the demand for rags, and their prices, slumped. Old rags could no longer be sold as profitably as before, so many preferred to use them for rugs. In addition, manufacture and consumption in general increased with the breakthrough of industrialism, which resulted in a greater supply of rags.

Curtains
Curtains became a necessity only when windows increased in size. In the Middle Ages, windows were still, as a rule, only small apertures, which could be closed by shutters. Gradually these openings were made in the

form of frames, covered with transparent skin, horn, or paper. During the course of the sixteenth century, window glass was widely introduced, at first as small greenish pieces joined by lead cames. In the seventeenth century clear glass appeared on the market, and it was possible to create larger panes with less leading. In the eighteenth century, curtains became more common, as a result of the increasingly more intensive exposure to contemporary Continental practices (fig. 129). In peasant milieu, they appeared first at the end of the eighteenth century, and became the rule in the nineteenth century. They were first used in the chamber and on the second floor—in northern Sweden in the guest house—i.e., in the newer parts of the dwelling house. The window shade arrived before the long or swag curtain. It was made of linen tabby, plain, checked, or striped. Paper blinds, painted to look like woven curtains behind flower pots, were used especially in the large two-story houses in Hälsingland to give the houses a solid and respectable appearance (fig. 128).

The first curtains to appear in the *stuga*—the oldest part of the house—were white tier curtains, hung from a wire half-way up the window. Later a valance was added at the top. Before the 1850s, long curtains were found especially in areas with well-developed textile culture and close contacts with manor and urban milieus, such as Skåne, Östergötland, the provinces around Lake Mälaren, and Bergslagen. In the southern Norrland flax region, especially in Hälsingland, long curtains were first put up in pairs in the 1850s–'60s. The curtains preserved from this time are woven in *myggtjäll* or with strips in open weave. They are always white and apparently reflect the influence of the Gustavian and Empire styles. The arrangements of the curtains, with their straight or slightly curved cornices, are influenced by these styles as well (figs. 76–78, 98, 99, 106).

129. Curtain arrangement from the beginning of the nineteenth century. Long swag curtains of weave-patterned white cotton, under valances of silk with ball fringe, festooned over a gilt curtain rod. Rosersberg Castle, Stockholm.

Handcraft and cultural milieu

We have now made a brief overview of the functional differentiation of the dwelling house and its furnishings. This overview indicates that changes in the floor plan of the house, in the number of room units, and in their respective uses, are reflected in the types of furniture and their form, the latter in turn influencing also housewares and textiles.

The dwelling house constitutes a milieu around a particular life-style, with its everyday and holiday activities. In this milieu can be seen a complex network of related phenomena, conditioned by the area's geography, history, and social structure. Furnishings which are strongly tied to a particular milieu are usually products of that milieu—handcraft products for home consumption—and therefore exceedingly difficult to treat in a continuous chronological fashion. Much remains to be researched and explored before such a treatment can be made. Technically, peasant crafts deal in forms and shapes harking back to prehistoric time and of such basic kinds that they are found all over the world. Design and pattern can, to a limited extent, give a few stylistic pointers for the purpose of dating, if not the object, at least the type. On the whole, the inventory of peasant ornament is characterized by retention of styles long after they have gone out of fashion elsewhere. This phenomenon, cultural lag, makes it difficult to date an object with certainty. Though made in the nineteenth century, it may have a medieval pattern, as is often the case with *dukagång* and *rölakan* weaves (figs. 136, 219, 241). On the other hand, this circumstance provides the information that a medieval ornament at one time was taken up in one particular social milieu, in one region, and for use on a particular type of object, and has continued to be used until today. Style retardation has also affected elements from other distinctive epochs: the Renaissance, the baroque and rococo periods, etc. Thus, there has been a strong influence from the prevailing styles of various epochs. Continental styles were transmitted in various ways with the assistance of the most mobile strata of society: clergy, merchants and urban crafts-

men, officials, and the nobility with its participation in the country's domestic and foreign affairs—all groups who, for one reason or another, maintained connections with the Continent. By his ties to the soil the peasant has always constituted a static factor in Swedish culture. This means that traditions, arising out of local conditions and maintained in a particular area, province, or country, with regard to house construction, furnishings, dress, etc., have had a better chance to survive in the peasant class. However, peasant culture has demonstrated a highly variable degree of receptivity to influences from other milieus, depending on the particular region and epoch in question.

Home craft manufacture for sale, a standardized production

As already emphasized, until around the middle of the nineteenth century handcraft was the major form of production in Sweden. Handcraft products for sale were retailed by their makers or by special salesmen in various parts of the country and in various social milieus. The demands filled by craft products for sale were very similar throughout the country, in spite of wide variations in living conditions. In general demand were linen tabby, diaper weaves, wadmal (color figs. 3–5, 8–10), fine woolen cloth, striped fabrics, and such articles of clothing as stockings, ribbons, mittens, gloves, neckerchiefs or scarves, simple knitted jackets, skirts, and pants. Of textile furnishings there was a general demand for cushion covers, bolster ticks, wall hangings, table covers (figs. 130, 131), coverlets, and horse blankets. Rough coopered vessels for storage and laundry (figs. 103, 520, 522, 533), turned wooden plates and bowls, simple baskets and splint boxes, nails, tacks, hardware, and similar items also belong in this list, among what we today would call standard housewares. The composition of the itinerant peddler's pack of goods for sale was no doubt based on generations' accumulated experience of the supply and demand situation in various parts of the country. Inventories from different social groups almost constantly list some kind of

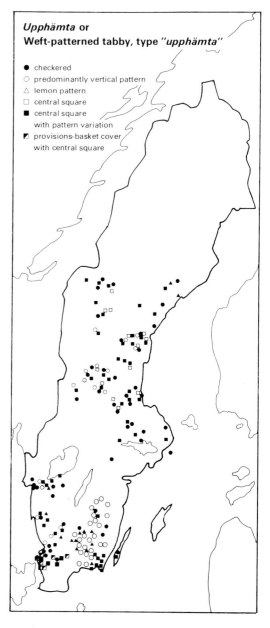

Upphämta or
Weft-patterned tabby, type *"upphämta"*

● checkered
○ predominantly vertical pattern
△ lemon pattern
□ central square
■ central square with pattern variation
◪ provisions-basket cover with central square

130. Map showing the distribution of Västergötland coverlets in *upphämta* (see fig. 131).

Borås or Västergötland product, such as aprons, bed cushions with so-called Borås ticking, tea tablecloths, curtains, pillowcase "caps," skirts, and bodices. In theory, it should be possible to distinguish handcraft items made for sale and retailed generally by a careful study of existing materials and archival sources. However, a study of existing objects only would probably not be sufficient. In spite of the sizable collections in museums and elsewhere, the majority of these handcraft products have, because of their nature, worn out and disappeared long ago.

However, on the basis of sparse descriptions in customs records and other sources, it has been possible to identify some of the products sold by the Västergötland peddlers. Indeed, a certain type of coverlet in *upphämta* was such a typical item that it was called "Västergötland coverlet," and was found in southern as well as northern Sweden (figs. 130, 131). Such is the case also with coverlets and ryas, which, according to a description from 1822, were bought in Halland by Borås salesmen and sold in Norway or Norrland for twice the price. They were made of cow hair, usually with a pile of dyed cow hair. Turned wooden bowls and plates of hardwood are found far up in Norrland, where such material is not indigenous. A certain type of *krabbasnår* coverlet,[14] typical of the Västmanland part of Bergslagen, was originally brought there from Småland and northern Skåne by the Västergötland peddlers and inspired a locally distinctive production. This was true also for the technique of knitting, which was disseminated by the Västergötland trade and in certain places resulted in local manufacture. In the same manner, a group of simple decorative ryas, prevalent especially in Gästrikland and Dalarna, was apparently brought there by the Västergötland trade, and with time inspired the local women to start making knotted pile covers (fig. 258). The pile spreads were also brought to Värmland by itinerant salesmen, but disappeared when the Västergötland salesmen ceased to carry them.

The Västergötland handcraft production for sale is especially noteworthy. It concentrated on standard goods for differing social and

131. Table cover in *upphämta,* so-called Västergötland coverlet, with trace of hallmark seal in one corner. Delsbo, Hälsingland.

local milieus. It was thus forced to adjust to rural demands as well as the demands of bourgeois customers for rough, practical everyday wares. Handcraft products from Västergötland and other provinces have appeared in the upper-class inventories. To mention a few examples, peasants from Hälsingland sold linen products; women from Vingåker (in Södermanland) sold wadmal and linen tabby (fig. 135); and people from Dalarna sold both wood and textile products in homes and market places in Stockholm and other cities.

The wide variety of customers and their respective needs have certainly also influenced the production. Particularly the well-organized western Swedish craft production, with its putting-out system, led the way in shaping the

craft production for sale according to customer demand. The contact between different social and local milieus was established and maintained by the Västergötland peddlers, and, as will be seen, also exerted a decisive influence on the local craft production for home consumption.

The textile industrial enterprises which were started from the middle of the seventeenth century on taught, wittingly or unwittingly, technical know-how and transmitted patterns and models by drawing on labor from the surrounding areas. This dissemination contributed to the great expansion of commercial craft production during the eighteenth century and it naturally also stimulated handcraft production for home consumption.

Legend

Southern Götaland house type

Extended Southern Götaland house type with chambers

Skåne house type

Hanging cloths, wall hangings, purlin borders

132. Map showing the distribution of the Southern Götaland house type with related house types and textile furnishings. Shown are the respective areas of the extended Southern Götaland house with chambers, the Skåne house type (figs. 53, 54), and rich textile furnishings in the form of hanging cloths, wall hangings, shelf edgings, etc. (fig. 133).

Craft production for home consumption shows local adjustment

A closer look at the range of craft products, known to have originated in the areas supplying Västergötland salesmen and merchant-employers, makes it quite clear that craft products for home consumption have differed to a certain extent from items made for sale. Of exported wares, more examples have been preserved in the sales area than in the production area (see figs. 131 and 452; also pages 189 ff.). This circumstance may lead to erroneous conclusions regarding local characteristics of handcraft items.

As previously noted, many craft products are strongly shaped by the form of the dwelling, the hearth, and the furniture. Such is the case especially with the distinctive wall runners, ceiling cloths, and wall hangings used in Skåne, Blekinge, Halland, and parts of Västergötland. In spite of the fact that these areas—with the exception of the Skåne plains—are known for their craft export, these textiles are not found in these provinces' respective sales areas. Obviously, for some reason, they have not been marketable outside of their production areas. The explanation can hardly be determined merely by studying the particular textile material, its technique, or pattern. If, on the other hand, these factors are seen in the context of the dwelling house, its construction, and people's living habits, the most compelling reason becomes evident. The distribution of ceiling cloths, hanging cloths, and wall runners is tied in with the occurrence of the Southern Götaland house type and its variants, e.g., the Skåne farmstead (fig. 132).

The occurrence and the form of other craft products—whether belonging to furnishings, dress, bedding, or the table—have of course primarily been influenced by customs of living, dressing, sleeping, and eating.

Distinctive local traits and provincial division

Variations in folk culture are in general thought to correlate with the division of the country into provinces. Since the days of Arthur Hazelius (1833–1901), founder of the Nordiska Museet and Skansen, the collections

133. Interior of *stuga* in house of Southern Götaland type. Walls and ceiling are decorated with painted and woven hangings and purlin borders with braiding. Josnahult, Knäred, Halland.

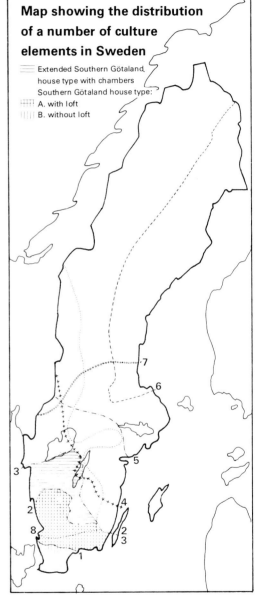

Map showing the distribution of a number of culture elements in Sweden

≡ Extended Southern Götaland, house type with chambers

Southern Götaland house type:
▦ A. with loft
▥ B. without loft

of the Nordiska Museet of peasant craft products, furniture, and furnishings have been organized by province, even to a certain extent as late as 1954. No doubt this exhibition plan has actively contributed to propagating and confirming the impression that provincial boundaries have been and continue to be cultural boundaries as well.

Since the second decade of the twentieth century, the identification of local cultural variations and their causes has had top priority among Swedish ethnologists. Cartographic representations of the diffusion of various cultural elements have been carried out, and do provide some basis for a better understanding of cultural differentiation.

Cartography

One of the Swedish pioneers in cartography was Gerda Cederblom, who made an investigation of spinning implements, "Våra äldsta spånadsredskap och deras ättlingar" ("Our oldest spinning implements and their descendants"), published in *Fataburen* in 1909. This investigation was the preliminary study for her cultural historical atlas, planned to encompass all the Nordic countries. A major atlas of Swedish folk culture appeared in 1957 with Sigurd Erixon as editor and main contributor. This work is the first to throw light on the problems of local cultural variations.

Emilie von Walterstorff's examination of the Swedish textile tradition, *Svenska vävnads-*

134. Map showing the distribution of a number of culture elements: (1) Southern boundary for Southern Götaland house type with loft houses. (2) Northern boundary for Southern Götaland house type without loft houses (Skåne house type). (3) Northern boundary for extended Southern Götaland house type (with chambers). (4) Eastern boundary for the cleft-stail hayrake. (5) Northern boundary for the separate kitchen. (6) Southern and western boundaries for the hay barn with outward leaning walls. (7) Southern boundary for the transverse hole-swippled flail. (8) Northern, eastern, and southern boundary for the arched smoke hood.

135. Peasants at Skeppsbron in Stockholm. The woman in the foreground is from Västra Vingåker, Södermanland, and carries bolts of woven materials under her arm and a sieve in her hand. Detail of aquarelle from the 1830s by G. W. Palm.

the cultural behavior patterns are so similar that they can be classified as distinct ethnological units, has of course always been influenced by geographical factors. Climate and vegetation form the economic basis for human industry. The access to raw materials directly influences the form of the culture produced. Rugged terrain, unpopulated areas, or areas with poorly developed communications all contribute to the creation of cultural barriers. The true driving force is, however, man himself. His will and ability to exploit certain given resources and, individually or as a group, to create new forms to take advantage of these resources, have overcome all natural barriers. Other factors influencing local differentiation in craft production are the economic condition, the social stratification, and the course of political events.

Handcraft and the national industries

In studying, for example, von Walterstorff's investigations of weaving techniques and pattern types to obtain some idea of the frequency and diffusion of culture elements, one is continually struck by the dominant position occupied by Skåne—even allowing for the province's relatively dense population. To ascribe Skåne's position merely to its inhabitants' predilection for and knowledge of textile crafts would be to confuse cause and effect.

First of all, one must, of course, always consider the supply of raw materials and labor. Living conditions are extremely varied in a country like Sweden. This was especially true of Swedish rural life before the coming of modern industry, when self-sufficency was the dominant feature of the economic system. The Lapps with their nomadic life practiced crafts, used tools, procured and used raw materials, and needed objects entirely unlike those of the permanent agricultural population. Between those two extremes of environment and cultural milieu there were—and still are—a number of intermediary forms. In these forms, cattle raising, fishing, industry and mining, trade, etc., singly or in combinations of two or more, have constituted the population's economic foundation.

tekniker och mönstertyper ("Swedish weaving techniques and pattern types"), was published in 1940 as part of this atlas. Her work is mainly based on the Nordiska Museet's collections of artifacts and data. Another invaluable source for this research has been the archive of The Society for Swedish Handcraft, assembled by Lilli Zickerman. Emilie von Walterstorff's distribution maps of techniques and patterns constitute a firm foundation of extraordinary value for continued research in Swedish peasant textiles, while also helping to clarify the overall picture of Swedish culture geography, with its variations and interrelationships (fig. 137). However, on the basis of this cartography alone it is hardly possible to arrive at

an understanding of the actual causes of these variations and interrelationships. This is the case with all culture elements when viewed out of context, whether they have to do with dress, housewares, furniture, house types, vehicles, customs, or beliefs. Each culture element is an integral part of a functional whole, in which all elements are interdependent. Any speculation regarding reasons and causes for regional differentiation must thus take a number of other factors into consideration.

The basic conditions for regional culture

The diffusion of culture elements and the demarcation and creation of areas, within which

136. Detail of coverlet in *rölakan* tapestry weave, showing an animal figure within a squat octagonal frame. Southwestern Skåne, 1801.

Textile home crafts, in Sweden generally practiced by women, exemplify a division of labor between the sexes, which is significantly and intimately associated with a region's particular type of industry.

Favorable conditions for textile production have existed in those areas where agriculture provided such a solid foundation for the economy that the women did not have to earn supplementary income. The needs of the household in those areas were more than satisfied.

Such a situation existed on the Skåne plain, where the rich soil has been able to give its tillers a good livelihood. But such soil also demanded intensive cultivation, absorbing virtually the entire male labor force in agriculture. As a result, and because of lack of raw materials, woodcrafts were poorly represented in these areas.

The *fäbod* region offers a completely different set of conditions. It is a region where the agriculture has had less opportunity to

Handcraft and cultural milieu

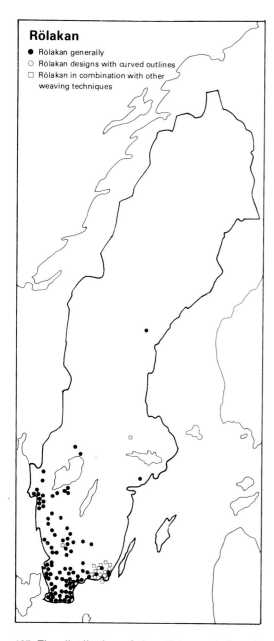

Rölakan

- ● Rölakan generally
- ○ Rölakan designs with curved outlines
- □ Rölakan in combination with other weaving techniques

137. The distribution of the *rölakan* technique in Sweden.

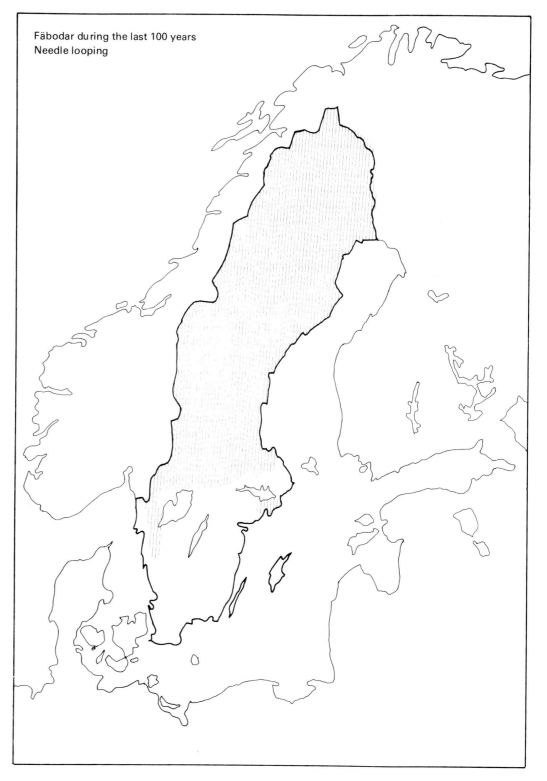

Fäbodar during the last 100 years
Needle looping

138. Map showing the occurrence of *fäbodar*—outlying summer dairy farms—and needle looping.

139. Samples of techniques: top, needle looping; bottom, knitting with two ends, showing the characteristic structure of the reverse side.

develop and cattle raising has been predominant and, as a rule, carried on within the *fäbod* system.

In order to feed its cattle, the population had to utilize the grass supply over such large areas that, in the summer, people and cattle periodically had to be stationed in outlying places quite distant from the farm in the village. They might have to move between two, even three or four, such *fäbod* settlements, in other words, lead a half-nomadic life. The women's function under these conditions was to follow the cattle, manage the cow house, and collect and process the animal products, mainly milk. All this was carried on outside of the regular household work. In some places

the women have also taken care of part of the farming. In upper Norrland, for example, the housewife alone took care of the sowing. With such a large portion of the livelihood depending on female labor, it is obvious that there was little time left for the making of textiles. Neither was the half-nomadic life during part of the year conducive to weaving. On the other hand, textile techniques demanding fewer and easier-to-handle tools were favored in these parts of the country. Such techniques include knitting (figs. 138, 139), band weaving (figs. 281, 282, 290), embroidery, lace making, and sprang (knotless netting on a frame).

On one hand, a surplus of labor or materials has created producing areas all over the country; on the other hand, a lack of either labor or materials or of both has created consuming areas. These conditions existed even before the advent of industrial production. An exchange of products or services, without middlemen, in the form of commodities, as well as by the use of money, has always existed. It has created continuity and exchange of spiritual as well as material goods. It has disseminated a knowledge of patterns, techniques, working methods, and raw materials, as well as of customs and associated beliefs.

Although the Skåne plain emerges as one of the foremost textile producing areas in Sweden, it does not belong among those exporting textiles. Supplementary income from handcraft production for sale has not been necessary. Whereas the Skåne textiles have remained in the milieu for which they were created, a different situation exists in, e.g., the above-mentioned western Swedish craft region—including Västergötland's forest areas, the inland parts of Halland, and large parts of the Småland plateau. In spite of the fact that the region's textile production has been at least as intensive as that of Skåne, it does not emerge as distinctly in preserved artifacts and, consequently, not as distinctly in cartographic representation. Along with other crafts—wood crafts, blacksmithing, iron forging, and furniture making—this region's textile production was of vital importance for the very existence of the population.

Bergslagen and the Mälaren valley emerged

as lively market areas because of their early developed, industrially organized production and because of their greater social differentiation and urban development.

Connections with the Continent
The Scandinavian peninsula is on the outer periphery of the European culture area. Those cultural currents that have emanated from the civilizations around the Mediterranean since prehistoric times and from western Europe since the Middle Ages have followed sea trading routes and traveled like waves towards the Scandinavian coast. They have washed in over Skåne, Blekinge, Gotland, over Halland, Bohuslän, and—via these provinces—seeped into southwestern Småland, Västergötland, and Norway to Jämtland and Härjedalen. Waterways were previously the best traffic routes. Rivers, lakes, and inland seas, such as the Baltic Sea, Skagerrak, and the North Sea, have united more than they have divided. For that reason, the Danish realm included the southern Swedish coastal provinces until 1658.

Intensive trade within these coastal areas was carried on, possibly as early as the Age of Migrations. In the Middle Ages, it was monopolized by the powerful trade organization, the Hanseatic League, which bought up herring, dried fish, furs, oxen, and horses, and sold primarily salt and fine wooden cloth as well as great amounts of other consumer goods. Through its two northern outposts, Visby in the Baltic and Bergen on the Norwegian coast, the Hanseatic League encompassed the whole Scandinavian peninsula in its sphere of influence until 1530, when Gustav Vasa began the liberation of Sweden from the Hanseatic monopoly (figs. 149, 150). Swedish trade with northern Germany, Holland, and Flanders did not suffer as a result. An intensive influx of goods continued and—perhaps more significant—there took place an immigration of craftsmen and merchants, who brought with them tools, methods, and workshop traditions.

Gustav Vasa's sons consciously strove to bridge the gap between Sweden and the Continent. As a result of the Thirty Years' War (1618–48) and Sweden's ensuing position as a

140. Top, turned bowl with two "ears" or handles, so-called Västergötland bowl, manufactured primarily in the red beech region in Västergötland and northern Småland. Villstad, Småland. Bottom, turned wooden bowl, *bolle*, with inverted lip. Ljusdal, Hälsingland.

world power, the contact with the Continent increased very rapidly during the latter part of the seventeenth century. Sweden's administrative center, Stockholm, and the Mälaren valley attracted nobles who established their estates in the area. Merchants, artisans, and industrial entrepreneurs followed.

The cultural currents from the Continent via Denmark over Skåne and Halland to Bohuslän and Norway were, thus, curtailed. Instead, direct connections between the Continent and eastern central Sweden were strengthened, at the same time as a reorientation took place toward English and French markets (fig. 151). The wars of Karl XII (1699–1718) were followed by a long period of peace, which gave commerce and industry a great upswing.

Turned vessels

141. Map showing the distribution of turned bowls of the types in fig. 140.

142. Detail of knitted jacket or sweater in red and green wool. Halland.

Prosperity and social changes in the eighteenth century

An important change in the social structure occurred during the eighteenth century with the emergence of a class of entrepreneurs, merchants, and industrial managers, who by force of their economic clout achieved great influence alongside that of the landed gentry and nobility. The population increased greatly in the eighteenth century, resulting in, among other things, a division of the homesteads. Thus, the rural population was forced to experience a lowered living standard. In addition, the number of unpropertied poor in the rural areas increased, people without any land of their own who served on others' farms and manors. From this class, the *statare*—a nine-

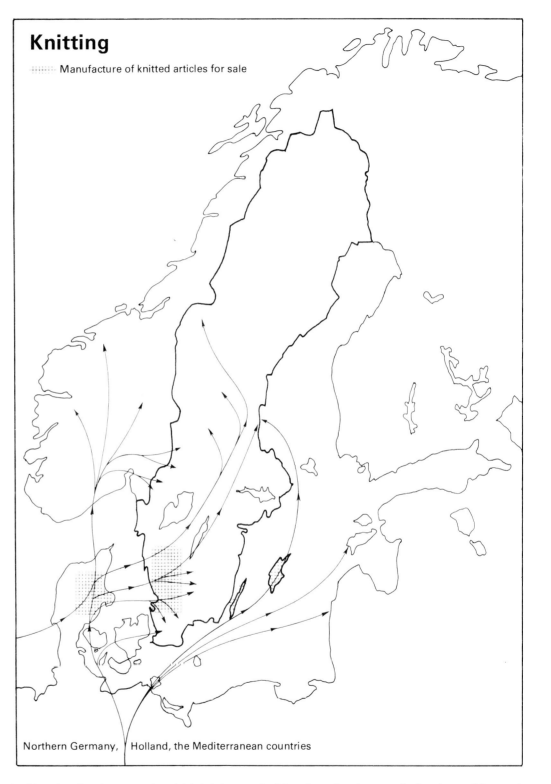

Knitting

:::::: Manufacture of knitted articles for sale

Northern Germany, Holland, the Mediterranean countries

143. Map showing the routes by which knitting reached Sweden; also the areas in Sweden and Denmark with important manufacture of knit articles for sale, and the probable distribution of the latter within Scandinavia.

144. Carriage cushion in Flemish weave, detail showing a lion. Torna, Skåne.

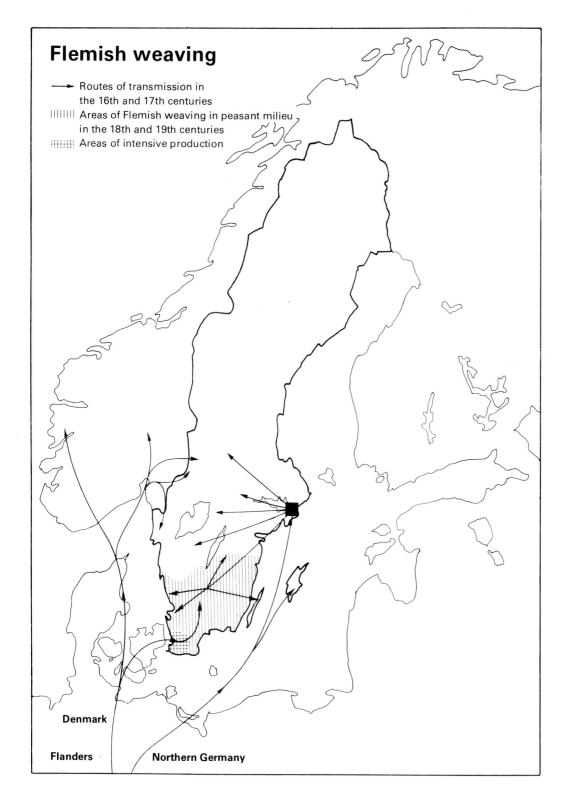

Flemish weaving

→ Routes of transmission in the 16th and 17th centuries

||||||| Areas of Flemish weaving in peasant milieu in the 18th and 19th centuries

▦ Areas of intensive production

Denmark

Flanders   **Northern Germany**

145. Map showing the distribution of Flemish weaving in Sweden.

teenth-century type of landless laborer on large estates—were later recruited, and somewhat later, the factory workers. The development roughly sketched here formed the basis for the social and economic tendencies of various areas to accept or reject cultural impulses from the Continent.

Stylistic development reflects the cultural situation

The styles imported via tradesmen and craftsmen have had a varying impact on the indigenous craft production. In the southern parts of Sweden, situated close to the Continent, the Renaissance and the baroque styles permeated thoroughly, as these parts were under Danish rule up to the mid-1600s. Farther north, the Renaissance style made itself felt to a very limited extent. Instead, medieval traditions survived in many places as late as the end of the seventeenth century. The economic and political trends of the seventeenth and eighteenth centuries put the peasantry in central Sweden into contact with the baroque, the rococo, and the Gustavian styles. This overview is obviously a simplified picture of the immensely complicated course of events which constitute a local culture's acceptance or rejection of period styles. Thus, elements of various styles survived in different parts of the country long after they had gone out of fashion elsewhere.

Style retardation and local distinctive characteristics

The phenomenon called cultural lag or style retardation gives, to a great extent, peasant crafts their varying local character. Very primitive traits have in this manner been preserved in handcrafts. In a study of Skåne *rölakan* and *dukagång* weaves (figs. 136, 148, 219, 241), Professor Andreas Lindblom maintains that their patterns, in spite of comprehensive transformation, have retained distinguishable connections—via many intermediaries—with ornamental Byzantine motifs. This supposition opens staggering stylistic and historical perspectives: but connections of this nature do exist and demand an explanation. The Middle Ages,

146. Pillow for making bobbin lace with *réseau,* showing the revolving roller, the pricked parchment with pins, and the bobbins.

the Renaissance, the baroque, and the succeeding eras have, to a varying degree, put their stamp on Swedish crafts. Thus, stylistic elements from the most diverse epochs can be isolated in these crafts.

This occurrence was by no means a question of mere indiscriminate copying. By being translated into another technique or material, the original motifs received from the major Continental styles were disarranged, dissolved, and jumbled in an often incomprehensible new "order." From this chaos something new and original gradually emerged. Various stylistic elements were interwoven, often resulting in new styles with new decorative values. A spectacular example of this phenomenon is the Flemish weaving of Skåne and Småland (figs. 222–230).

Culture areas and cultural boundaries

Questions regarding culture areas and cultural boundaries are so complicated that no clear and unequivocal picture has yet been drawn by ethnological research. Ethnologists are currently mapping the cultural lines of force in Sweden's magnetic field, to discover what were the poles and their respective charges. This much can, however, be stated with certainty: there have been no fences around parishes, districts, or provinces, preventing the free exchange of spiritual and material goods. On the contrary, such goods have freely flowed back and forth according to a certain system. To return to the magnetic image for a moment, trade has followed certain lines of force, at least some of which have been mapped or sketched in already.

The notion that cultural boundaries coincide with parish, district, or provincial boundaries —a common misunderstanding of the nature of handcraft—does not stand up to scientific scrutiny. Thus, although there have existed many distinct variations in Swedish folk culture, certainly also from one province to another, we are today beginning to distinguish boundaries and areas cutting across provincial boundary lines as well (fig. 152).

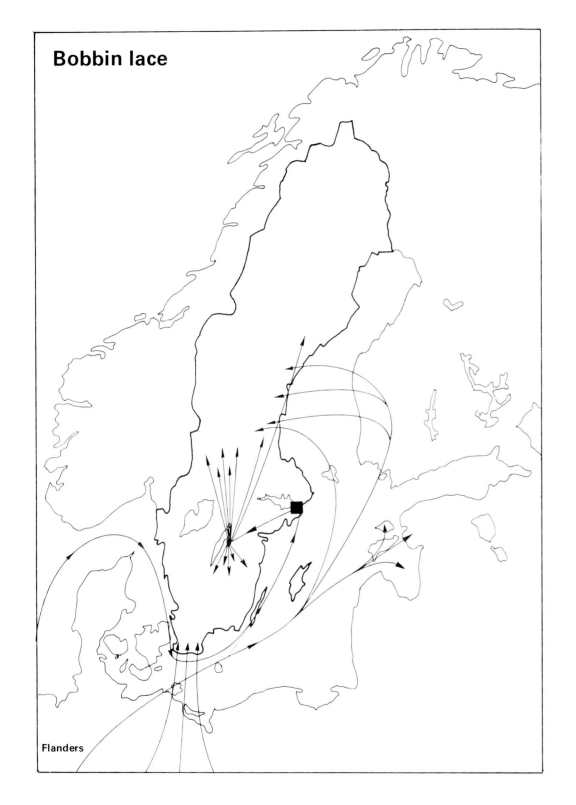

Bobbin lace

Flanders

147. Map showing probable routes of transmission for bobbin-lace making in the eighteenth and nineteenth centuries.

148. Silk with double-headed eagle in roundel, surrounded by animal figure motifs. Spanish-Moorish origin, eleventh century. After Heinrich J. Schmidt, *Alte Seidenstoffe*.

Southwestern Sweden and northwestern Sweden
The cartographic representations published by Sigurd Erixon in *Svenska kulturgränser och kulturprovinser* ("Swedish cultural boundaries and culture provinces") and *Atlas över svensk folkkultur* ("Atlas of Swedish folk culture"), in 1945 and 1951, respectively, indicate that a number of phenomena seem to be identified with a geographical area incorporating Blekinge, Skåne, southwestern Småland, and Hal-

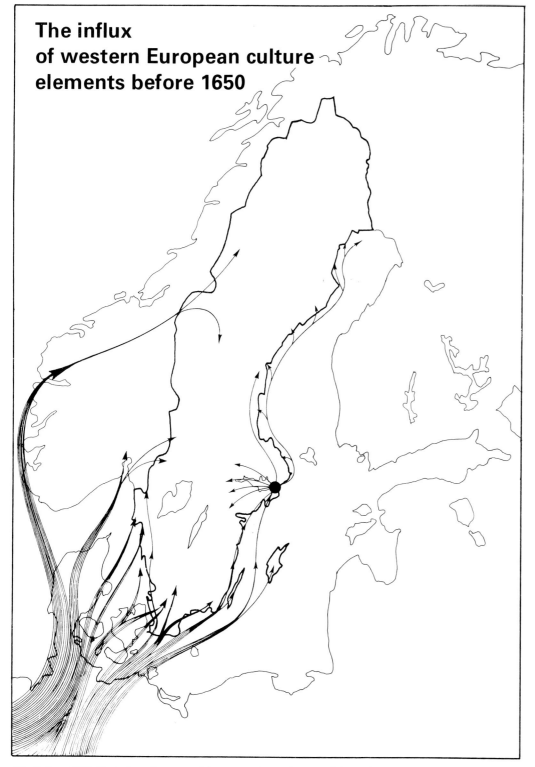

The influx
of western European culture
elements before 1650

149. Before 1650, the influx of western European culture elements followed the trade routes of the Hanseatic League. Skåne and southwestern Sweden belonged to Denmark and were not far removed from its capital, Copenhagen.

land (figs. 132–34, 149). Sometimes a feeler from this area reaches into southwestern Västergötland, along the coast of Bohuslän, and into Värmland, disappears from there into Norway only to reappear again in western Härjedalen and Jämtland. In many instances, the same types are thus found in the southwestern and western Swedish provinces as well as in Norway. The connection between the northwestern and the southwestern Swedish regions was, in fact, maintained via Norway. Such was the case with the techniques of *rölakan,* double weaving, and Flemish weaving (figs. 137, 145). Sigurd Erixon has in many ways substantiated western Sweden's cultural contact with Norway and western Europe. He has emphasized that the two large land masses flanking Skagerrak and Kattegat have, at different times and in different ways, undergone a similar development. Repeated interaction has further helped form a cohesive cultural unit.

The fäbod region
Parts of upper Dalarna have been especially conservative, particularly the parishes around and above Lake Siljan. The peasant culture of Hälsingland, Jämtland, and Härjedalen has many traits in common with that of Dalarna, although the former has also been influenced in a curious way by rococo and Gustavian forms. On the whole, the peasant culture of all of northern Sweden bears the stamp of the *fäbod* system and the attendant life-style. As pointed out above, this common life-style has resulted in certain similarities also in the craft products of the various parts of this region (fig. 138).

Eastern Sweden
In Bergslagen, central eastern Sweden including Östergötland, and the east coast with Gotland, the peasant culture has been molded by a more continuous influx of new goods and ideas. There are several reasons for this molding. The country's political, economic, and cultural center was, and still is, located here, in the midst of eastern Sweden's agricultural

. Portrait of the German merchant Jergen Gisze, painted in
2 by Hans Holbein the Younger. Gisze lived in London and
s probably a member of the powerful Hanseatic League.

areas with Baltic ports (figs. 145, 147, 151).
Shipping along the Baltic coast has been very
lively, and a large number of larger or smaller
ports have transmitted a constant stream of
impulses in the form of merchandise to all
strata of society, including the farmers. Local
traditions in eastern Sweden are therefore less
distinctive. Eastern Sweden, inland Svealand,
and Bergslagen have long been the main industrial region of the country, open to cosmo-
politan influences which have diminished the
local characteristics of the region's crafts.
Much handcrafted merchandise was brought
here from southern Sweden by Västergötland
peddlers (figs. 130, 131, 141–43). The island

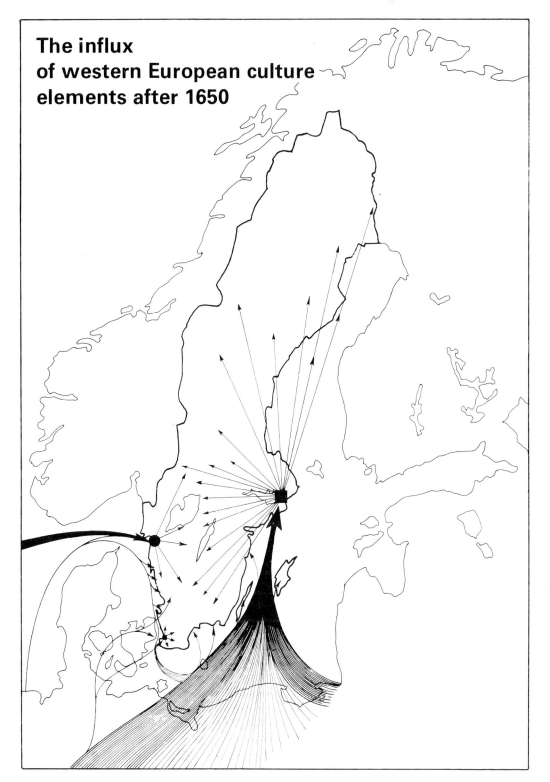

The influx
of western European culture
elements after 1650

151. The influx of western European culture elements followed other routes after the end of the Thirty
Years' War (1648). Stockholm, the administrative center of the Swedish Empire, attracted most of the
country's trade and commerce. From there, impulses were transmitted to the rest of the country.

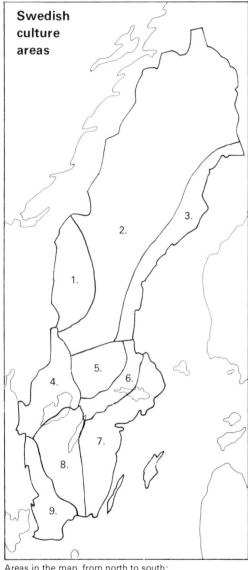

Swedish culture areas

Areas in the map, from north to south:
1 Northwestern Sweden
2 The fäbod region
3 Norrland coastal region
4 Upper western Sweden
5 Bergslagen
6 Central Svealand
7 Eastern Sweden
8 Central southwestern Sweden
9 [Coastal] Southwestern Sweden

152. Swedish cultural boundaries and culture areas.

province of Gotland has been a recipient of impulses thanks to its location favorable to trade and shipping. Perhaps more than any other part of the country, Gotland has had a peasant population with an almost urban culture.

Norrland's coastal region
Norrland's coastal areas also exhibit a number of phenomena of relatively recent origin, pointing to a cultural renaissance of sorts around the end of the eighteenth century and the beginning of the nineteenth century. However, it was not until later—after the mid-1800s—that Norrland's forest industry became especially important for its peasant culture, although the peasants in many places had earned a significant supplementary livelihood from the forest since the seventeenth century.

Local characteristics and industrialism
During the last century, the switch to industrial production actively contributed to the transformation of locally conditioned cultural milieus. Much has been written and said about the urbanization of the countryside. But a significant factor is also the reverse process, the ruralization of cities and towns. In certain respects, rural cultural traditions have thus been given wider scope. They are by no means obliterated, surviving in modern Sweden's cultural life, imparting a distinctive character to it. Modern Swedish handcraft is one of several examples of the vitality of the cultural heritage.

Some tendencies of local differentiation of Swedish handcraft have been pointed out. The three most important ones may be summarized as follows:

First of all, commercial craft production manufactured standard goods, suitable for varying local and social milieus and, as a rule, lacking any local characteristics. This craft production was distributed throughout the country or channeled to specific market areas. It is therefore to be expected that many handcraft items, preserved today in homes or museum collections, were found in a place altogether different from that of their origin.

A dominant commercial craft production within a certain area does not, however, preclude the existence in that area of a craft production for household consumption, catering to local tastes and demands.

Secondly, commercial craft regions are far less distinguishable in terms of the quantity of existing preserved artifacts than those areas dominated by craft production for household consumption. Commercial craft products were exported, whereas craft products for home consumption remained in the area. The textile crafts of the Skåne plain are a case in point.

Thirdly, craft production for household consumption is the locally distinctive production, made according to local traditions and needs.

153. Vegetable fibers and yarns. Left side of picture, left to right, top row: scutching tow yarn, tow yarn line linen; center row: scutched and hackled flax; bottom: skein of dyed linen yarn above a skein of ikat-dyed linen yarn for chiné patterns. Right side of picture, top to bottom: braid of machine-spun hemp yarn, ball of linden bast, balls of cut rag strips, prespun cotton, and spun cotton yarn.

The products of handcraft

The supply of textile raw materials

The use of skins for clothing and of fells for covers is common all over the world, from the polar regions to the equator. The step from pelts to fabrics of spun animal hair would seem a natural one. But there is no way of knowing for a certainty whether the technique of spinning animal hairs to thread and yarn was first used in spinning animal or plant fibers. Clearly, fibers of one kind or another, used to bind or tie things together, were used by primitive man. The use of fibers is far older than any weaving technique, and all conceivable types of fiber have been employed, from bast to sinews and leather thongs. A large number of fibers can be used in their natural state without first being twisted or spun together, e.g., the fibers of certain palms and banana trees and the bast fibers from elm and linden trees. Of the some four hundred plants which yield spinnable fi-

bers, around fifty have proven suitable and are to a certain extent still used in this capacity. Hemp, flax, cotton, jute, coconut, and sisal are encountered every day. Less well known are hops, nettles, certain grasses, such as banana grass and ramie (China grass), and a number of palms and cacti. The most important textile fibers are linen and hemp, known to man for at least 7,000 years, and cotton, used for about as long in India, but probably not introduced into Europe until the first millennium B.C.

Among spinnable animal fibers, sheep's wool is the most important, having been used for textiles since the Stone Age. Other animal fibers have also been spun into yarn, e.g., cow hair, goat hair, horse hair, boar bristles, hare and rabbit fur, dog hair, human hair, and llama wool. Silk is also an animal fiber, obtained from the cocoon of the silk worm. Silk can be used without being spun; moreover, a single cocoon may yield up to 3,000 feet of continuous silk filament. Silk manufacture in Europe began in the eighth century A.D., but

154. Animal fibers and yarns. Left, spun and unspun silk, skeins of embroidery silk; center, a lock of wool, carded wool, spun and dyed yarn in skeins and balls; right, horsehair, balls of cow-hair yarn, goat-hair yarn, churned shoddy, spun shoddy in balls, and tufts of human hair.

had probably been known in the Far East by around 1500 B.C.

The spinning of the thread marks the first step towards the making of a woven fabric. However, clothing has also been made from fabrics other than woven materials.

Bark and straw, grass, root fiber, and bast have been used—and played a far from insignificant role—in the manufacture of clothing. In the South Sea Islands, bark has been used to make bark cloth, so-called *tapa. Tapa* cloth is made from the inner soft fibers of the bark from certain trees. By soaking and pounding the fibers are made into a light and soft, though somewhat brittle, cloth. Lengths of *tapa* up to 170 feet are made by "gluing" the edges of the pieces together. In Sweden a similar material has been utilized: birch polypores have been beaten soft and used for headwear.

The thread, i.e., the spun fiber, has, however, turned out to be the starting point for most useful fabrics. Some of these fabrics are made with one continuous filament, such as those produced by the techniques of needle looping, sewing, knitting, crocheting, and knotting. Other techniques are based on a system of a varying number of threads, which may be felted, twisted, arranged, braided, or tied together, as in the techniques of braiding, sprang (knotless netting on a frame), lace making, macramé, or felting. The system most capable of technical development, however, is weaving, which is based on two sets of threads crossing each other at right angles. There are a great number of simple looms consisting only of a frame for the stretching of the lengthwise threads—the warp—in which the crosswise threads—the weft or filling—can be introduced. The simpler the weaving tool, the greater the possibilities it offers for freestyle patterns. The more complicated and technically perfected the loom as a time- and labor-saving device, the more the weaver is restricted to certain combinations in the interlacing of the threads.

Wool and woolens

The oldest find of textile material in the Nordic countries consists of some coarse nets of bast from the Stone Age. The oldest find of a woven material consists of articles of clothing made of woolen fabric, found in tombs in Denmark from the early Bronze Age (ca. [1800] 1500–1100 B.C.). Judging from these finds, wool was the earliest weaving material in prehistoric Scandinavia. The earliest Swedish find also dates from the Bronze Age. It is the famous Gerum cloak, found in a peat bog on the Gerum Mountain in Västergötland and dated to the end of the early Bronze Age or the beginning of the late Bronze Age (around 1200–1000 B.C.). Danish Bronze Age tombs have yielded a number of amazingly well-preserved articles of clothing. They were found in coffins of split and hollowed-out oak logs, which had hermetically sealed in the corpses (fig. 155). All animal components within had been preserved by the tannic acid in the wood and by certain favorable conditions, whereas any vegetable fibers that may have been present had been destroyed by the chemical environment. Linen, for example, would have been unable to resist the effects of the humic acids, a chemical component of most of the soil in Scandinavia and the rest of Europe. One European site in which the chemical factors contributed favorably to the preservation of plant fibers is the prehistoric so-called Swiss Lake Dwellings, dated to circa 2500–2000 B.C. Tabby weaves of linen or bast fiber, some of them with brocaded patterns, bear witness to an advanced plant-fiber processing and a developed weaving technique. In the same find were also some extraordinary complicated braidings of bast fiber, partly with knotted-in pile.

In the Nordic Bronze Age finds, wool is the only material—with the exception of one sprang cap of horse hair. The wool is of natural color, brown or brownish black. Certain claims about mixed-in deer hair have been disproven by analysis. It must therefore be accepted as fact that sheep were already kept at that time for their fleece. The earliest documented wool shears date from the time of the Gothic migrations. However, even more primitive methods for harvesting wool have remained in use until quite recently; in the nineteenth century in the Faeroe Islands, wool was pulled or combed out of the pelt, a practice heretofore prevalent

155. Early Bronze Age oak coffin grave from Egtved, Denmark, dated to about 1400–1200 B.C. The body, that of a woman sixteen to eighteen years old, is lying on a cowhide. She is dressed in a short jacket with elbow-length sleeves and a short corded skirt.

all over northern Europe. Textile fragments preserved in the Nordic countries from the Roman Iron Age and the first part of the Age of Migrations (A.D. 200–500) were all made of wool. There is evidence that blue dye from woad and also red and yellow dyes were used. Impressions of flax seeds have been found on some artifacts. From around A.D. 500–700, there are a number of important finds in

156. Sheepshearing. Eksta, Gotland, 1937.

158. Wool sample. From the Berch Collection, 1760s, now in Nordiska Museet.

159. Wool sample. The Berch Collection, Nordiska Museet.

157. Wool shears of iron. Småland.

Denmark, Norway, and Sweden. From the latter part of the Age of Migrations (A.D. 600–800), the finds are richer and the presence of flax can be established in Sweden, in the form of all-linen fabrics, or linen warp in woolen fabrics. From the Viking Age there is a wealth of archaeological data. Several very rich sites confirm the existence of an indigenous manufacture of linen and wool materials, as well as import of articles of linen, wool, cotton, and silk. By the increasingly closer ties with the Continent, merchandise of all kinds was introduced, not the least of which was textiles. It must be remembered that there did exist a considerable social stratification. Thus, an economically privileged upper class maintained connections abroad and strived to acquire foreign goods.

Also in the Middle Ages, the indigenous supply of raw materials was based on domestic sheep breeds. In the sixteenth century, so-called *schäferier* (from German, *Schäferei,* "sheep ranch") were founded, i.e., stations for more efficient sheep breeding using imported German, Spanish, and English breeds. The object was to produce a breed which by cross-breeding with native stock would give fleece suitable for clothing materials. These stations were especially intended to produce sufficient wool for the cloth manufactories, founded with state support in the sixteenth and seventeenth centuries in Stockholm, Kalmar, Norrköping, Göteborg, and other towns. The energetic efforts to stimulate Swedish wool production resulted in a large sheep stock. However, the attempts of the authorities to improve the stock resulted in sheep with widely divergent characteristics in different parts of the country. One could therefore hardly speak of any uniform Swedish sheep breed. And the finest wool still had to be imported. At the end of the seventeenth century, the state's interest in improving the domestic wool production cooled, as first-grade wool could be obtained from the Swedish province of Pomerania. In the eighteenth century, the high protective tariffs on fine woolen cloth in support of the fledgling Swedish textile industry resulted in a strong stimulus for the home crafts and their products (figs. 158–60). The Swedish wool production and sheep stock increased again. Minor fluctuations have subsequently occurred as the result of war or blockades.

Spinning implements

The invention of the spinning wheel was of major importance for textile crafts by increas-

ing the production of raw material. Spinning with a hand spindle (fig. 162), and, simpler yet, spinning with a *farsadh* or spinning hook, or rolling the fibers together against the cheek or thigh (fig. 161), have been preserved in localities where the spinning wheel was an encumbrance to the mobile life. Thus, these older spinning methods were retained in the *fäbod* region of Dalarna and among the Lapps in northern Sweden until the end of the nineteenth century and the beginning of the twentieth century. On the Continent, the spinning wheel already existed in a primitive form with a hand-turned wheel in the thirteenth century, with a flyer in the 1480s, and with a treadle in the 1530s. Before the founding of the first cloth factories in Stockholm—before 1550—there were no spinning wheels listed in contemporary Swedish records and inventories. In the beginning of the sixteenth century, it is

162. Spinning with spindle and distaff. Orsa, Dalarna. Drawing by J. F. Höckert, mid-nineteenth century.

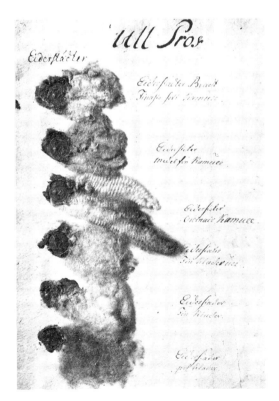

160. Samples of wool attached to a stiff board with sealing wax. "Finest, medium fine, ordinary wool, fine and coarse wool for woolen cloth." The Berch Collection, Nordiska Museet.

161. Lapp woman twisting sinews by rolling them against her cheek.

163. Women carding wool and spinning with the aid of a spinning wheel. Gesäter, Dalsland, early twentieth century.

164. Spinning machine. Tidafors wool factory, Nyed, Värmland.

reported that seventy-seven wives spun four *skeppund* and thirteen *lispund* (about 1,800 pounds) of wool. The large number of spinners for the amount of wool produced indicates that only spindles were used. When a cloth manufactory was founded in Kalmar in the 1560s, a list of required equipment included four spinning wheels. The first recorded importation of spinning wheels took place in 1552, when three treadle wheels were imported to Stockholm from Lübeck.

The pedagogic activity of the cloth manufactories

Since the cloth manufactories to a large extent put out wool to be spun in homes, there is reason to suppose that the spinning wheel (fig. 163) was spread via these manufactories into the countryside. The standards and output of handcraft production were no doubt improved by the superior technical equipment and the professional personnel at these factories. These professionals were supposed not only to produce woolen cloth, but also to instruct. The markedly increased productivity of handcrafts during the eighteenth century must be viewed against the background of the distribution, to all strata of the population, of technically more advanced tools and methods during the seventeenth and eighteenth centuries. Thus, writes one author in 1781: "As rare as it was seventy years ago to see a spinning wheel in the homes of the *bergsmän* (literally, "mountain men"; ironmakers), so rare is it now to find any household without spinning wheels and looms."

The sheep-raising stations and cloth manufactories founded with Crown support were, as a rule, associated with pedagogic activity, which benefited the immediate neighborhood. The neighborhood, in return, was expected to supply a certain amount of wool, as well as carry out carding, combing, and spinning of their own as well as imported wool. Instruction was found to be especially needed for the processing of the imported wool fibers, which were longer and finer than the domestic varieties. As it was, the peasants mishandled the finer wool. Instead of shearing their imported sheep once a year, as instructed, to obtain longer

165. Medal struck to commemorate the coronation of Adolf Fredrik and Lovisa Ulrika in 1751. The inscription reads: "Til heder för den qvinna som fint och snält kan spinna" (Honoring the woman who is a fine and nimble spinner).

wool, they insisted on shearing them twice a year and got short wool. In addition, this short wool, intended for the manufactories, instead often found its way to hatters in the towns. Moreover, the Swedish Board of Commerce soon expressed fear that instruction of the peasantry would increase the home manufacture of woolens to the detriment of projected sales by the cities' factories.

Nevertheless, spinning schools were started in 1741: three in Stockholm, three in Västergötland, four in Västmanland, and one in Norrköping, Östergötland. Later, one was added on Gotland. In these schools primarily worsted spinning was taught. Spinning instruction was further organized during the eighteenth century so that every parish regularly would send womenfolk to cities with cloth manufactories, where they would become proficient in the art of spinning, so that they might instruct others upon their return home. This was part of the attempt by the weaving industry to organize and regularize its raw material supply. A com-

mittee of experts recommended that spinning done in the homes should be expanded. A division of the country was made thus: flax would be put out for spinning in all of Finland, except Österbotten; in southern Norrland; parts of Västmanland, Halland, Västergötland, and Småland; and around Vadstena, Östergötland. Other parts of the country would be entrusted with the spinning of combed wool, and Dalarna was especially singled out for cotton spinning. Spinning for the cloth manufactories was carried out also by permanent employees, and by orphans and inmates in "spinneries" and other correctional facilities. Because of the abhorrent conditions under which this spinning was carried out, people became prejudiced against the activity. But since spinning was necessary to keep the factories running, a campaign was launched to counteract this prejudice by the award of distinctions and medals for superior spinning. In this context, a medal was struck at the coronation in 1751 of Adolf Fredrik and Lovisa Ulrika. The inscription read:

"Til heder för den qvinna som fint och snält kan spinna" (Honoring the woman who is a fine and nimble spinner) (fig. 165).

The strict division of the country into wool-, flax-, and cotton-spinning areas met with many obstacles in the implementation. The peasantry did not heed the rulings by the Board of Commerce. In addition, the factories competed with each other for the labor force. The commissioners tried to lure workers from other districts into their own. A so-called spinnery in the eighteenth century was often actually composed of several parishes or districts, within which the merchant-employer had exclusive rights to enlist spinners. For example, in Närke, Kjörtingsberg manor had a cottage industry with a spinning district of eighteen parishes. In Kristianstad county, Skåne, there were 150 spinners of combed wool in the district of Albo, Jerrestad, and Ingelstad in 1785–86. However, several hundred more could have been given work had there been sufficient wool and spinning wheels to go around. In Småland, as well, there was a lack of wool, and the number of spinners was so large that there was not enough work for all of them. On Gotland, there were 331 spinners in Visby alone and 400 in the countryside. In the neighborhood of Alingsås, Västergötland, spinning almost entirely ceased with the decline of the manufacturing plant in Alingsås. In the provinces of southern Norrland, wool spinning declined for another reason: the peasants did not consider it desirable to allow wool spinning to infringe on the highly developed and lucrative flax processing.

During the latter part of the eighteenth century, carding and spinning machines were invented (fig. 164). They greatly increased the yarn production for the cloth manufactories. The import of wool also increased, a result of removed tariffs and of active state support for the wool trade.

Sheep raising and wool supply
During the beginning of the nineteenth century, there was great interest in sheep breeding and the production of coarse wool. In the

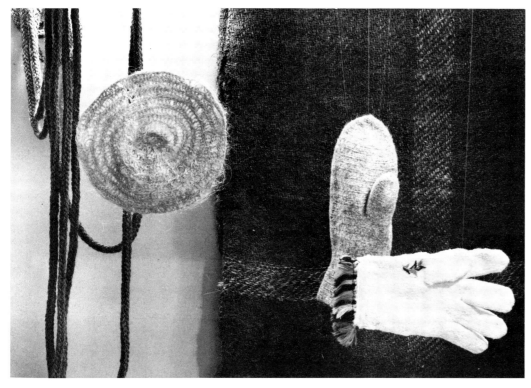

166. Reins of woman's hair and needle-looped strainer of cow's-tail bristles, Ore, Dalarna; horse blanket, woven of cow hair, Frösö, Jämtland; needle-looped mitten of goat hair, Dalby, Värmland; bride's mitten knit of sheep's wool mixed with jackrabbit fur, Äppelbo, Dalarna.

Gotland wool would be traded from parish to parish.

Fleece for wool production was thus supplied largely by domestic sources. Imported fleece went to the factories in Stockholm, Norrköping, and Göteborg. A fair amount of hair from hides was also imported. From Jutland in Denmark it came via Göteborg and Halmstad in western Sweden's craft region.

Other animal fibers

To a large extent, various kinds of fibers have been added to sheep's wool for the spinning of yarn (fig. 154). For coarser fabrics cow hair, boar bristles, and goat hair have been blended in with the sheep's wool. Dog hair, jack-rabbit fur, and woman's hair have substituted in periods of short supply. This practice has ancient roots and is a remnant of a primitive gathering culture. The use of different animal fibers does have some advantages, however. Each fiber has certain properties, which have been utilized for specific purposes (figs. 166, 167). Textiles made of cow hair, goat hair, and boar bristles are quite resistant to cold and dampness. The same is true for articles of woman's hair, which was considered especially suitable for outer mittens for fishing and work in the forest. Dog hair and jack-rabbit fur gave softness and warmth. Rabbit fur was also whiter than sheep's wool and therefore used in children's mittens and elegant holiday mittens (fig. 166). Goat hair, preferably mixed with wool, was used for insoles with a toe cap. Cow hair was obtained from the tanner, who sold it by the sack. As it was heavily coated with lime, it first had to be beaten to remove the lime dust. After scrubbing and carding, it was spun unmixed into hair yarn, which was woven into horse blankets (color fig. 5), "tarps" for wagonloads in transport, blankets for carriages, and bedcovers. It was also used in a wool mixture as weft in coarse clothing materials and as the main weft in knotted pile covers.

Hair yarn was also mixed in to extend the wool. Horse hair, cow's tail bristles, and goat hair were used for needle-looped articles, such as milk strainers and clothing accessories. The yarn's water-repellent properties made it espe-

middle of the nineteenth century, sheep were commonly raised by peasants, especially by the poor and unlanded. Pasture land and feed for a few sheep could always be scrounged. Townspeople also kept sheep, which were "boarded" in the country. The payment for this service might be part of the wool yield. Dealers in wool yarn and woolen fabrics could have flocks of several thousand sheep boarded with peasants in exchange for the mutton and some wool. This was especially the case in Västergötland. The sheep-flock size varied widely: twenty-five to a hundred head were common in Västra Göinge in Skåne, in Halland, in Jösse district in Värmland, and on Gotland. Elsewhere, ten to twenty sheep were usually kept in the summer, two to six in the winter. Thus, peasants generally had access to wool.

Servants were paid their wages in wool. Those who for some reason lacked wool went around begging for some. In many localities the supply of animals was so great that some of them would be sold off, as in Halland, from where large herds were driven into Småland to be sold. As a rule, surplus wool was sold in its unprocessed state.

Traveling buyers from the spinneries took their share; and the peasants brought the rest in wool sacks to the town markets. Large wool fairs were held, for example, in Sala and Norrköping. Wool was used as a trade item by the merchants in town and general-store owners in the country. Localities lacking in wool would get wool by barter with other localities. Women in Älvdalen in northern Dalarna walked to Härjedalen for wool, and on

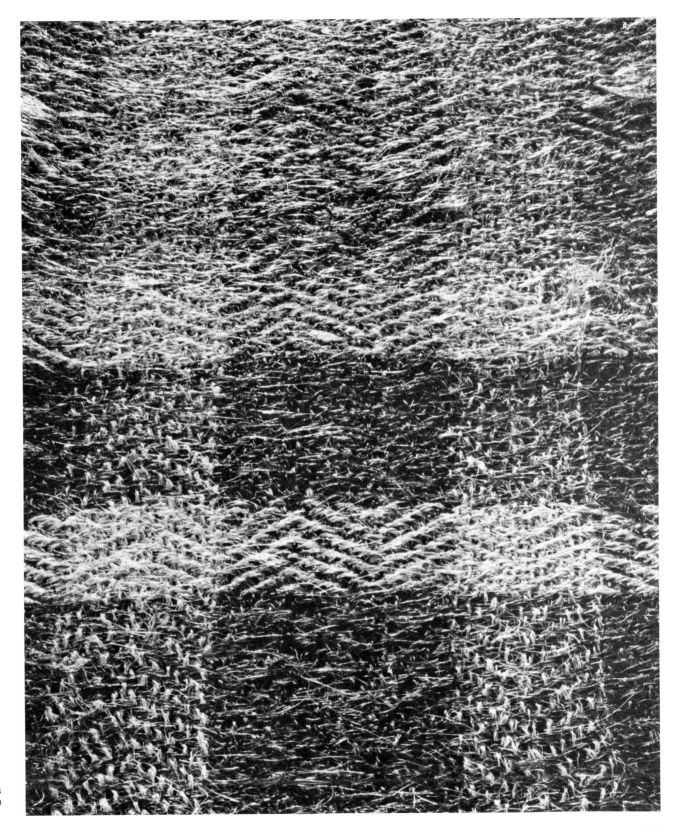

167. Blanket of cow hair in various natural colors, check pattern in chevron twill. Borgsjö, Medelpad.

The supply of textile raw materials

cially suitable for mittens, stocking feet, and insoles (figs. 166, 437).

Shoddy

Worn-out woolen articles were cut up or garnetted into shreds, which were soaked and pounded in a churn with hot water, until the threads returned to a fibrous state. This was called shoddy. After drying and beating, it was scrubbed and carded together with new wool and spun to be woven again. The resulting fabric was used in everyday work clothes.

Flax and linen

It is quite difficult to ascertain the extent of the domestic supply of raw material for flax processing. Import lists show that fine linen goods were imported in the sixteenth century and later, only in limited quantities, for an exclusive market. The importance of linen as tax payment—taxes could be paid in kind—in certain parts of the country shows that a surplus production already existed in the Middle Ages. In the twelfth century, the Archbishop of Uppsala collected a tax in linen tabby from Hälsingland. Apparently flax cultivation in this province is of ancient origin. Later, Hälsingland continued to stand out as a major producer of flax and linen. Västergötland was first noted for its textile products, linens and woolens, at the time of Gustav Vasa.

A look at the importation of flax seed can give some idea of the extent of the flax cultivation. In the latter part of the eighteenth century, this import increased considerably. For the most part, the imported seed went to the southern Norrland provinces. The flax seed was brought in from Russia, as were considerable amounts of flax and tow, which were shipped to Stockholm or Göteborg. The Stockholm import decreased as the import of flax seed increased. However, the Göteborg import increased because the linen production in western Sweden, which was dependent on imported raw materials, was stepped up. In Västergötland, flax was cultivated only in one district, the district of Mark. Much flax was sown there, but the domestic harvest was not sufficient for even the local linen production. The

remainder was obtained from the counties of Jönköping, Halland, and Skaraborg, and also from Hälsingland and abroad. Those of the population who did not themselves cultivate flax would nevertheless spin flax which they had bought, or flax put out by merchant-employers. In other parts of the country, domestic flax cultivation gradually increased, providing the basis for a well-documented upswing in linen production. From 1815 to 1819 there was even a limited export of Swedish linen. Up to 1820, flax growing expanded throughout the country, creating conditions for an improved supply of linen to the domestic market. The total linen production consisted of—in equal parts—domestic processing of flax for home consumption and domestic processing of flax for sale.

The improved flax supply in northern Sweden, in contrast to that of western Sweden, was the result of an increase in planted acreage. It was centered in the southern parts of Norr-

168. Water-powered flax brake. Hanebo, Hälsingland, 1946.

169. Seals of quality. Top, wax seal made with stamp from Flor workshop, Mo, Hälsingland. Bottom, lead seal with inscriptions, on one side, "Flors linne hall stemp" (Flor linen hallmark); on the other, the date, 1760. Property of Per Flordal, Hälsingmo.

land: Hälsingland and southern Västerbotten. Some flax was also grown in Medelpad and Gästrikland, most of it, however, for home consumption.

Most of the work in making linen is related to the processing of the raw material. The increased linen production in Norrland was decisively influenced by a number of inventions made in the eighteenth century by local clergy to facilitate and lighten the work involved in these time-consuming procedures. Water-powered flax brakes and scutchers appeared in Hälsingland's waterways in the early 1700s, though they were rare in other parts of the country (fig. 168).

The significance of the spinning wheel for spinning and spinning schools has already been touched on. The Flor damask workshop in Mo, Hälsingland, and its pedagogic activity in the field of spinning were crucial factors in the development of the southern Norrland linen production.

116

Cotton

Cotton is mentioned in the Viking Age in Icelandic literature as a rare and precious material. Although it later became less of a rarity, it remained an expensive import item, almost, but not quite, on a par with silk. As late as the eighteenth century, cotton as raw material was of negligible significance in Sweden. But the import of cotton and cotton yarn increased relatively sharply until the end of the century. To start with, most of the trade was channeled through Stockholm, but later Göteborg became the greatest importer of cotton. This was transmitted to the western Swedish textile factories and the domestic handcraft market. Apparently, the major production of Swedish cotton materials in the eighteenth century was located in eastern Sweden (fig. 170). It is known that Dalarna, by statute from the Board of Commerce, was specifically singled out for cotton spinning. By the 1770s, however, cotton spinning was also recorded in Mark district, Västergötland. In the 1820s, Göteborg and the western Swedish textile region absorbed half of the cotton import, and subsequently an increasingly greater portion of it. As previously noted, the western Swedish textile producers were highly dependent on imported raw materials, even before the introduction of cotton. The supply of raw materials was based on the putting-out system and the economic cooperation of merchants with capital in Göteborg with the manufacturers in the "Seven Hundreds." It was therefore not difficult to change from one imported raw material to another within the region.

For southern Norrland, where the linen production was founded on domestic raw materials and on capital invested in flax growing acreage, the adjustment to the new development of the raw-material market was far more difficult. Norrland was also poorly situated, geographically, to import cotton, which was shipped to Sweden from the United States and England.

Before the major inventions which facilitated the processing of the raw materials and the spinning, far more time was taken up by spinning than by weaving. It was estimated that three or four spinners were required to keep

170. Woman spinning cotton on a great wheel. Painting by Pehr Hilleström, 1760s.

one weaver busy. When machine-spun yars replaced homespun yarn, the number of work hours freed for weaving consequently increased. For this reason, improvements in spinning technique were of greater significance than inventions facilitating weaving.

At first, cotton was only used for scarves, as weft in apron materials, and as warp. Cotton was considered finer than linen and was therefore used in weaves that allowed the cotton to show on the right side of the fabric. All-linen fabrics were considered coarse and old-fashioned. Cotton was used in various cloths, sheets, and white coverlets, instead of tow yarn and linen tabby (fig. 190).

Hemp

As the hemp fiber can be distinguished from flax fiber only by microscopic analysis, it is possible that many preserved coarser linen articles are actually made of hemp. It is difficult to obtain exact data about the extent of Swedish hemp cultivation in the past. Around 1870 hemp occupied 1,000–1,200 acres, compared to 40,000 acres for flax. During the nineteenth century, the cultivation of both plants declined. Earlier, the state had taken a great interest in hemp growing, as hemp was the most important raw material for cordage for the Navy. The wet strength of hemp made it as important for the fleet as oak and tar. Towards the end of the eighteenth century, Halland, Västergötland, Västerbotten, the Torneå valley in northernmost Sweden, Jämtland, and Gotland were the major hemp-growing regions. Hemp was also grown generally for household consumption: it was used in coarser clothing materials (fig. 171), as warp in tow yarn fabrics, bottom sheets, knotted pile covers, coverlets, and harnesses, and also as raw material for rope. Hemp is a plant related to hops and nettles, originally growing wild in Central Asia. It was cultivated already about 3000 B.C., but came to Europe much later. It was reported in Greece around 500 B.C. as a novelty. It was introduced into the rest of Europe by two routes: from the east via Russia and the Baltic States, and from the south via the Mediter-

ranean countries. Russian and Italian hemp exhibit quite different properties. The latter is far finer and can be spun in yarns corresponding to linen number 80. The Russian hemp yarn is no finer than number 25. Swedish hemp belongs to the latter variety, and it is therefore safe to assume that it came to Sweden from the east. It is generally believed that this occurred in the Viking Age and that domestic hemp growing was quite common in the Middle Ages. According to traditional accounts of conditions in the latter part of the nineteenth century, hemp seems to have been commonly used as raw material for coarser fabrics.

The relationship between flax, hemp, nettle, hop, and other plant fibers, especially in prehistoric times and the Middle Ages, is an interesting field of study, offering certain problems. In her work *Det textila arbetet i Norden under forntid och medeltid* ("Textile work in the Nordic countries from prehistoric times through the Middle Ages"), Agnes Geijer has presented some thought-provoking opinions in this matter. Her views will be briefly summarized here.

Medieval French sources indicate that linen fabric was a luxury item even in the thirteenth century. The occupation of linen weaver is not mentioned in these sources as existing even in Paris, western Europe's largest city at the time. Instead, professional French weavers were called *cannevassiers,* from the French word *cannevas,* or hemp cloth, which apparently was a common and major commodity.

Woven textiles of plant fibers, presumed to be flax, have been found in the prehistoric Swiss Lake Dwellings from the Stone and Bronze Ages. It has been assumed also in other prehistoric finds of vegetable fibers that these were flax fibers. However, flax and hemp fibers both have a natural twist, that of flax corresponding to the S-twist in spinning, that of hemp, to the Z-twist. A microscopic analysis of plant-fiber fragments from prehistoric times and the Middle Ages surely could help establish the true identity of these fragments, giving a better basis for estimating the then existing supply of raw materials and for evaluating the often contradictory evidence given by preserved artifacts and documentary sources.

Other plant fibers

There are extensive descriptions of the use of various wild plants as textile raw material. In the Nordic countries, Germany, and eastern Europe, nettles have been mentioned as being used for thread and cloth, especially in times of deprivation, when regular materials, such as linen and hemp, were scarce (fig. 153). In Norway, it was even cultivated at one time. There is reason to suspect, as in the case of other culture elements with a wide distribution, that the spinning of nettles is very old. Cloth of nettle fiber dating from the early Iron Age, has been found in Denmark and Norway. The continued usage of nettles is documented in Sweden, and is also mentioned in 1761 in an essay in the records of the Royal Academy of Sciences. A frequent term in inventories from the eighteenth century and the beginning of the nineteenth century is *nettelduk* (nettle cloth). In these cases, however, the term usually had nothing to do with a cloth of nettle fiber, but with a grade designation for very fine linen or cotton fabrics. Similarly, the term "batiste" is nowadays used to indicate a thin cotton or linen fabric.

Hops have reportedly been spun and woven in Sweden. Nordiska Museet owns an actual specimen of such a fabric in the bottom half of a shift (fig. 171).

Bast

Bast of linden, pine, or spruce was a material of great economic importance as late as the eighteenth century. Bast was used to make ropes, fishing implements, cordage for logging, charcoal-kiln baskets, net bags, *höbågar* or folding frames for carrying hay, harnesses, and mats. Two textile techniques predominated, namely looping with slip knots and weaving. The latter technique, weaving bast strips, was used only for mats and rugs. Mats from the ninth-century Oseberg ship burial find in Norway have bast in both warp and weft. The use of bast has been especially widespread in eastern Europe. The bast from the linden tree comes from the inner part of the bark, preferably taken when the tree is in sap.

At that time, the bast layer can be laid bare and separated from the bark. At other times, the bark must be retted, i.e., gathered in bundles and placed in water. Depending on the thickness of the bast layer, it takes between two weeks and several months to ret bast. The art of preparing linden bast has been widely known in the linden-growing region. Bast bundles and finished products of bast were sold to the larger farms in the area.

Wood bast is made from pine and spruce. After cutting and lengthwise splitting, the wood is heated in a fireplace or baking oven or boiled in a cauldron to facilitate the removal of the bast. Linden bast as well as other wood bast give a partially processed raw material for ropes and other products. This material is twined without tools and extended by the continuous feeding of bast into the twining. A spinning wheel or swift has also been used to twine linden bast.

Preparation of linden bast is of prehistoric origin. In Denmark, bast nets of slip knots have been found in some Stone Age sites. The technique is identical with that still used in twentieth-century Swedish bast fyke nets. In the sixteenth century, fyke nets and other nets of knotted bast were mentioned. Today, carrying bags and mats are still made with slip knots of wood bast. Semicircular and square mats and runners, sometimes dyed red or green, are made in Ödenäs and Sandhult in Västergötland. They have been and still are distributed primarily via Göteborg. Since the 1850s they have also been exported to Denmark.

In Virsemark in Dalsland, fyke nets of wood bast were made which were exported by the wagonload to Norway. The weaving of bast mats occurred sporadically in Sweden. In eastern Europe, it was very widespread. There, bast mats were used as sacking for, among other things, export goods. These so-called *ryssmattor*, "Russian mats," came to Sweden especially as sacking for the grain imported from Russian in the 1860s. These bast mats were saved and unraveled and used, e.g., in rag rugs.

With regard to material and technique, bast articles are throwbacks to the time before the introduction of cultivated plant fibers.

171. Sark or shift, bottom part of mixed hemp and hop fiber, top of hemp. Bogvattnet, Jämtland.

Weaving implements

As mentioned above, woolen textiles dating from the Bronze Age ([1800] 1500–500 B.C.) have been found in the Nordic countries. A number of significant observations have been made about these finds, especially about the rich contents of the Danish oak coffin graves. These observations should be applicable to Swedish conditions as well. Extremely careful analyses by the Danish textile researcher Margrethe Hald constitute the basis for our knowledge of early weaving techniques in the Nordic countries. A dissertation by the Norwegian researcher Marta Hoffmann, *The Warpweighted Loom*, has further widened our knowledge about the oldest weaving tools and techniques in Scandinavia. The conclusions summarized below have appeared in several major publications (figs. 172–75).

The garments preserved from the Danish Bronze Age—four women's and three men's garments—are all made from a coarse tabby. Some garments consist of very large pieces, the

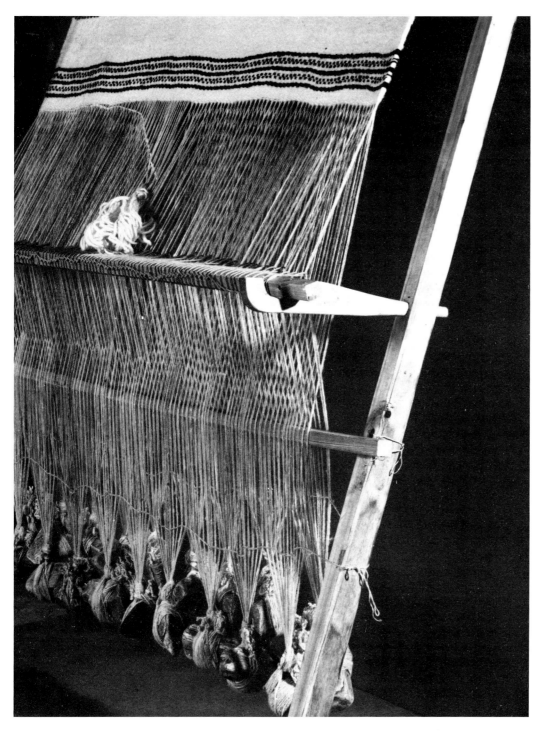

largest 211 centimeters wide and 390 centimeters long (approximately seven by thirteen feet). The warp yarn is in most cases of a different twist from the weft yarn. The remarkable width and the existence of selvage on three sides of the weave pose the question of what kind of loom would have produced these weaves. It has long been theorized that the warp-weighted vertical loom was used in Bronze Age Denmark. This loom was used, until quite recently, in Norway and is still in use among Norwegian Lapps. Support for this theory is provided by the particular warping apparatus used in conjunction with the latter-day warp-weighted loom. The warping frame is combined with a band loom thus: Every pick of the band weft is pulled out into a long loop of the same length as the warp in the intended weave, and laid around the pegs of the warping frame. To dress the loom, the band is attached at the top, on the beam, with its long weft threads hanging down to form the warp, the threads of which are connected in pairs. In these threads are hung stones, which must be as equal in weight as possible. In this fashion, the fabric acquires its three selvages, i.e., actually two selvages and one starting border at the upper end of the warp. The loom consists of uprights with a transverse warp beam at the top, resting in crotches. The frame is leaned against a wall, whereby a natural shed is formed by the vertically suspended and weighted warp threads, of which every other one is bound up on a heddle-rod (fig. 174). To form a shed, the heddle-rod is lifted and placed on the heddle-rod supports inserted in pegholes in the uprights. It has been surmised that two people simultaneously worked at the loom, because in fabrics from these looms there are often double weft picks crossed over each other, and then brought back to their respective selvages. Greek vase paintings from about 600 B.C. (e.g., fig. 175) show precisely this type of loom with two women weaving. The con-

172. Vertical warp-weighted loom, made in 1957 by Nils Oppervoll. Troms, Norway.

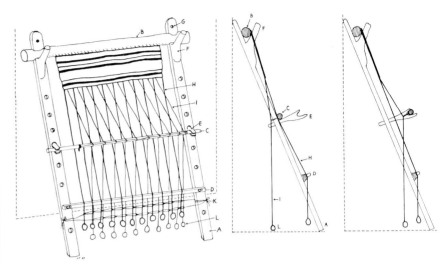

174. Front view and section of the warp-weighted loom: (a) uprights, (b) beam, (c) heddle rod, (d) shed rod, (e) supports for the heddle rod, (f) crotches for the beam, (g) hole for nailing the upright to the wall or to a beam, (h) front threads, (i) back threads, (k) chained spacing cord, (l) loom weights, rocks. After Marta Hoffmann, *The Warp-weighted Loom.*

175. Weaving on a loom with weighted warp. Scene from Grecian vase, ca. 600 B.C. After Marta Hoffmann, *The Warp-weighted Loom.*

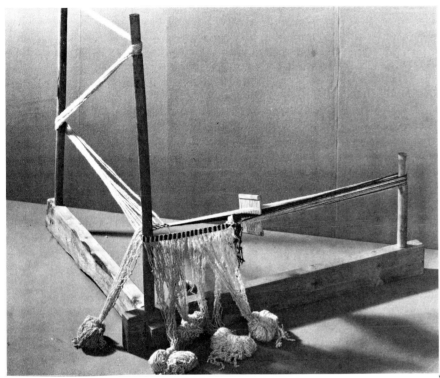

173. Warping frame to be used in conjunction with the loom in fig. 172.

siderable width of the aforementioned woven piece also argues for this practice, as does the fact that no shuttle was used and the filling had to be introduced into the shed with the fingers. The weft was battened upward with a so-called sword beater which did not extend the full width of the warp. The Grecian loom in fig. 175 agrees on all important points with that in fig. 172.

No loom from the Bronze Age has been preserved. It may seem odd that not even warp weights from the Bronze Age have been found, whereas fired-clay weights from the Iron Age have been preserved. One explanation might be that the Bronze Age loom made use of rocks in their natural state—as is the case with the latter-day warp-weighted looms in Norway—which are not identifiable by the archaeologists as warp weights. Weights from the

tenth century, found in Iceland, confirm that the loom was brought to that country from the mother country, Norway. An Icelandic illustration from 1788 of a loom with weighted warp confirms that looms of this type were still in use in Iceland at the time.

The cloth of the Swedish Gerum cloak is superior in quality to the Danish Bronze Age

fabrics. It has a greater warp thread count (sixty-five to seventy-four threads per ten centimeters) compared to the Danish fabrics (fifty-six to sixty-five threads). It is a four-shaft (2/2) twill of wool in two colors, creating a checkered pattern.

Margrethe Hald is of the opinion that simultaneously with the warp-weighted loom there may also have existed a loom with two warp beams, an opinion supported by the occurrence of tubular weaves in the Danish Bronze Age finds. Marta Hoffmann shares Margrethe Hald's opinion that a two-beam vertical loom was being used, and considers it possible that the cloth for the Gerum cloak was woven on such a loom.

The earliest examples known so far of fabrics woven in three-shaft twill were found in Vendel and Valsgärde, and in Birka, dating from the seventh century, and the ninth to tenth centuries respectively. These fabrics were probably imported. From the late Middle Ages on, weaves in three-shaft twill were well known in Denmark, Norway, and Sweden. They are totally missing in Iceland and Greenland finds, whereas one single example has been found on the Faeroe Islands. It is natural to associate the appearance of the three-shaft twill and a partially new terminology in medieval Nordic sources with the introduction of the loom with horizontal warp. The date for this significant milestone in Swedish textile history cannot be fixed by any preserved artifacts or written documents. A patient collecting of pertinent data has been carried out by several textile researchers, in the hopes that they might be able to establish the general period in which this important innovation was introduced. Certain findings of these researchers are summarized below.

In the city of Sigtuna, founded around the year A.D. 1000, a loom pulley has been unearthed, dating from no later than the thirteenth century. Pulleys are part of the horizontal loom. In the fourteenth century, the term *solv* (heddle) first appears in both Danish and Swedish. The heddle also belongs to the new loom type. In the fourteenth century, the term *fyrskaft* (four-shaft) is first used. The warp-weighted loom has a natural shed. On the Faeroe Islands and Iceland, where this type survived until the end of the eighteenth century, and where consequently an older terminology appears in written sources, the term *enskaft* (literally, "one-shaft") denotes what today is known as *tuskaft* (two-shaft tabby weave). Four-shaft weaves were, correspondingly, called "three-shaft," a logical ter-

176. Professional weavers working at loom with horizontal warp. Manuscript illumination from Ypres, 1363. Reproduced in *Folkliv,* 1939.

minological distinction. There is also negative proof of the introduction of the horizontal loom in the Middle Ages. Finds of warp weights are numerous in Sweden from the Viking Age and, to a certain extent, from the Middle Ages. In Denmark, they do not date beyond the Viking Age. In Norway, however, considerable numbers of warp weights have been found, from the Middle Ages and later. In Germany, the warp-weighted loom seems to have been in use throughout the Middle Ages, judging from archaeological data, while it disappeared from western Europe and England after the ninth century. On Europe's periphery it has lived on: in Norway until today; in Iceland and the Faeroe Islands until the nineteenth century.

On the Continent the change in technical equipment naturally took place earlier than in Sweden. A number of circumstances indicate that this change happened some time around the year A.D. 1000. Data about and pictures of the horizontal warp loom with treadles exist from the twelfth century. Thus, for some time the two loom types apparently existed simultaneously and in the same localities, though in different production milieus.

Weaving as professional craft and industry
It is evident that, concurrent with the introduction of the horizontal warp loom in western Europe, a technical and administrative reorganization of weaving was begun. Handling the new loom with horizontal warp became man's work and developed quickly into a professional male craft (fig. 176). In some areas, the warp-weighted loom survived for weaving

done by women in the home. Already in the Middle Ages, textile manufacture became the first and most important industrially organized production in Europe, preceding and overshadowing even iron and copper production. Textile production laid the foundation for the first European industrial centers. In Flanders and Artois, textile centers grew up which sold their products all over Europe and also to the Near East. Ypres, Ghent, Arras, Douai, and other cities supported themselves by their textile industry. Around the middle of the fourteenth century, there were 4,500 weavers in Ghent—not counting professionals in related and supportive occupations: wool washers, carders, fullers, spinners, dyers, sizers, etc. In the thirteenth century, textile manufacture was already organized in certain areas, above all

177. Woman weaving on a horizontal loom. Engraving by J. F. Martin, second half of the eighteenth century.

Flanders and Florence, as a putting-out industry, where the merchant-employer put out materials to independent craftsmen, who carried out, in their own workshops, any one of the around twenty-five different steps required in the preparation of the finished cloth. The craftsmen were highly economically dependent on the merchant-employer. Aside from these putting-out enterprises, there were also local craftsmen working for the domestic market, though this production was relatively insignificant.

Looms with horizontal warp thus laid the foundation for manufacture with extensive specialization and division of labor. Its products were far superior to those of home craft production in appearance and, especially, finish. The horizontal loom had warp ends of considerable length, wound on a movable beam. The loom was equipped with treadles, beater, shuttles, and automatic shedding device.

The preparation of the raw material was still handled largely by women. In towns, as well as in the surrounding countryside, male and female spinners worked for the town-based weavers. The loom with horizontal warp was developed in a production milieu where the object was to weave a high-quality product in as large amounts as possible for the largest market possible—in other words, a standardized mass production. The horizontal loom was constructed to meet these demands. The weaver can sit at his work. The dressing of the loom takes more work, but once dressed, the loom is easy to operate. The harnesses allow a quick change of sheds by means of the treadles, an equally rapid introduction of the weft by means of the shuttle, and a less strenous beating of the filling with the beater. The basic shafts could, furthermore, be supplemented with a draw system or the mechanical execution of complicated patterns more quickly than on the warp-weighted loom. To start with, however, the decisive appeal of the new loom was its greater productivity. All weaves previously woven on the warp-weighted loom could be executed also on the horizontal loom, with the exception of weaves in various tapestry techniques, which, even today, are worked on a vertical warp (fig. 178).

Summary

Finds of loom weights indicate that the older loom type continued to exist for a long time side by side with the new loom type. In Scandinavia, it was retained longest in Norway. In certain Norwegian localities all textiles, except for everyday fabrics like wadmal and linen tabby, were long woven on vertical looms. In Sweden, there are, as far as can be ascertained, no traces of the warp-weighted loom after the thirteenth century.

In short, there is evidence that textile production in Sweden began as early as the Bronze Age. The loom used was a vertical warp-weighted loom, on which were woven a number of weaves: tabby, four-shaft twill, weaves with brocaded discontinuous pattern (corresponding to what is now known as *krabbasnår* and *dukagång*), weaves with continuous brocaded patterns (corresponding to *upphämta*), soumak, weaves in various tapestry techniques, double weave, and knotted pile weaves. Very little is known about the possible role of the vertical loom with two beams. The type of tapestry technique used at the time need not have been executed on such a loom. The simple shedding mechanism was conducive to pattern weaving by the introduction of a separate pattern weft.

However, the vertical warp-weighted loom was heavy to operate and poorly suited to mass production of clothing materials. It is generally agreed that the use of the horizontal loom began in Sweden in the thirteenth century. The older loom type with weighted hanging warp was probably used for some time concurrently with the new type, although we do not have any evidence, archaeological or documentary, of its continued existence in Sweden after the thirteenth century.

The vertical loom with two warp beams used for Flemish weaving (fig. 178) cannot be traced back farther than the sixteenth century, when it was brought into Sweden from the tapestry-weaving centers in western Europe through the channels of professionally organized crafts.

178. Upright tapestry loom for Flemish weaving. Torna, Skåne.

Fabrics

Broadcloth and wadmal[1]

In the Middle Ages, fine woolen cloth or broadcloth dominated professionally organized textile production. Cloth differed from earlier woven fabrics in the careful finishing procedures which the fabric had to undergo before being marketed: napping, fulling, gigging or teaseling, shearing, and pressing. The fabric undergoing this treatment had to be made from especially soft wool. The resulting fabric was distinguished by its softness and its shiny, smooth surface; qualities which only the finishing processes could impart. It is understandable that the majority of professional workers in cloth manufacture were finishers. In 1270, for example, one French source indicates a proportion of 300 finishers to sixty weavers to twenty dyers.

In the Middle Ages, broadcloth had a market encompassing the whole contemporary known world. Great consumers were the Baltic provinces, to which Flemish and English cloth was brought by the Hanseatic League. Broadcloth dominated Swedish import, around 1550 accounting for 25 percent of the total import. The cloth trade followed certain already well-established trade routes. These routes formed a rich and complex network in which Sweden was naturally included by virtue of earlier Viking Age trade connections eastward. On the Continent, the textile production was standardized for retailing in an area extending from the Mediterranean in the south to the Baltic in the north. The major production centers gradually developed certain types of cloth of a standardized thickness and quality and fixed dimensions. These were introduced on the international market, i.e., at the large international textile fairs, in, for example, Constantinople, Alexandria, Bruges, and Paris. These textile products were all woolen cloth of the type we would call broadcloth and were named after their place of origin. Worsted woolen cloth was introduced first in the sixteenth century (fig. 179). Also in Sweden, woolen cloth was the dominating clothing material in the Middle Ages. A lively import of broadcloth was carried on, whereas no import of the fine fleece

179. Cloth packers. Woodcut by Jost Amman, first half of the sixteenth century.

from which it was made is documented. The biggest importer of broadcloth was the state, which used it to clothe the army. Nobility and burghers confirmed their social standing by using broadcloth. As late as the eighteenth century, cloth was a mark of social distinction. For the Swedish peasantry, homespuns were the standard clothing material. This was the case into the twentieth century (fig. 180). Early sources mention home-manufactured fabrics such as wadmal. The Swedish word for wadmal, *vadmal,* is derived from *vådmått,* i.e., the measure of one length of fabric. The term figures in the earliest written sources—the National Codes for the countryside, the town codes, and other documents—as a most important trade object and an accepted medium of exchange. The domestic wadmal manufacture must therefore have been quite extensive. In a royal ordinance of 1380, the peasants were granted the right to use wadmal as a trade object and to sell it to each other; broadcloth trade, however, remained the exclusive province of the city merchants. Today, wadmal is used to designate a two-shaft or four-shaft woolen material, fulled but not shorn. It is not clear when this definition of wadmal became commonly accepted. It is, however, considered probable that wadmal earlier denoted certain woolen fabrics woven on a warp-weighted loom. They were woven in pieces of standard measurements, hence the name and its derivation. In Iceland, where this loom type was in use up to the end of the eighteenth century, written records indicate that the term wadmal had earlier been associated also with unfulled cloth but always a four-shaft twill. As mentioned above, fulling and shearing became important procedures in conjunction with the rise of the professionally organized manufacture based on the horizontal loom.

Fulling

Fulling, a long-known process, occurs naturally when wool is washed. The introduction of the water-powered fulling mill was undoubtedly a result of the greater emphasis on finishing processes in the Middle Ages. It is not known when and where the fulling mill was introduced, but the earliest mention is from Normandy in the eleventh century.

Until today, wadmal has been the most significant clothing material for the common man. It was used especially in male dress. In female dress, it was most commonly used for bodices, jackets, and skirts into the eighteenth century—in some old-fashioned parts, e.g., Dalarna, as late as the nineteenth century. In inventories, white, gray, black, or blue woolen jackets or woolen coats were mentioned as often as the qualifying phrase, "of wadmal" (color fig. 3). Whether this distinction reflects an inconsistent vocabulary or an actual difference is difficult to determine. Judging from preserved material, it does, however, seem likely that simple patterned unfulled tabby was particularly common in female dress. Skirts, especially, were made of fabrics with woolen weft and linen warp—from the eighteenth century, with cotton warp (color figs. 1, 6, 7). In

180. Two bolts of woolen fabric, one fulled and napped, the other unprocessed. Woven at the beginning of the twentieth century. Odensala, Uppland.

Västra Vingåker, Södermanland, a thin, soft woolen twill was used in the old-fashioned long jackets worn by men and women alike. Wadmal was used in the man's long frock coat and the woman's *livkjol* (literally, "body skirt"), a high-waisted skirt with attached bodice. Broadcloth was used, to a limited extent, in holiday costumes.

According to existing sources, a soft woolen twill in white or gray was used also for sheets and pillowcases in Jämtland and Härjedalen,

and on Öland and Gotland. The same kind of material was also used for shifts and skirts in Jämtland and other parts of Norrland, and for a type of shirt called *bussarong* (color fig. 4),[2] designed to be worn outside the pants, and especially common in the coastal provinces of Norrland. It would be gray for everyday wear and red or blue for holidays. Previously quite common, these simple coarse woolen weaves were used primarily for clothing and, incidentally, for interior furnishings.

125

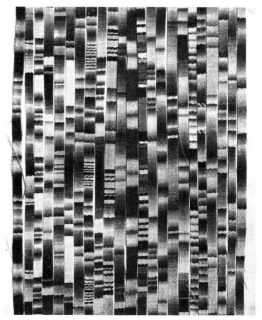

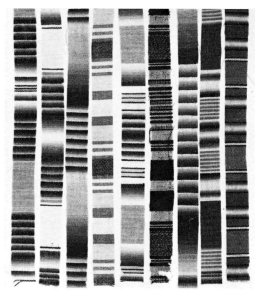

182. Page from sample book with twenty-three different calamanco patterns. "Striped calamancos made in Norwich." The Berch Collection, Nordiska Museet.

183. Samples of striped camlets from the 1750s. The Berch Collection, Nordiska Museet.

181. Samples of stuffs—any materials other than woolen cloth—including, among others, various shags, calamanco, flowered calamanco, wool damask, and printed fabrics. Manufacturing samples submitted to the Board of Commerce. Riksarkivet.

184. Russian merchants in long coats and high caps offering their wares in the courtyard of the Town Hall (now Stockholms Stadsmuseum), the main floor of which housed their stocks. Engraving dated 1691, from Erik Dahlberg, *Suecia Antiqua et Hodierna* (1661–1716).

Patterned woolen materials

Aside from the cloth factories there were also factories for so-called stuff (German, *Stoff*; Fr. *étoffe*), denoting all materials other than fine woolen cloth. The first stuff factory was founded in 1662 in Stockholm by a Scot, David Young, later elevated to noble rank by the name Leijonancker. Several types of materials were manufactured there, such as *trip*, a shag-like material, shalloon, serge, camlet, and tabinet. Most of these types of stuff were, however, imported. During the eighteenth century, several stuff factories were founded in Stockholm, Norrköping, Malmö, Alingsås, Marie-

stad, Västervik, and Sundsvall (figs. 181–83). Patterns were woven or printed on fabrics. From the end of the seventeenth century, several printing factories were active. The manufacture of richly patterned materials, whether woven or printed, reflected very closely the prevailing taste in the first half and the middle of the eighteenth century; dress as well as interior decoration were at that time characterized by lively and colorful patterns. After 1780, during the Gustavian era and the Empire, patterns became considerably more restrained.

Domestic manufacture was encouraged in

all conceivable ways to counteract textile import. The consumption of foreign luxury items was strictly—though not always efficiently—prohibited. In the sixteenth and seventeenth centuries, the state had already acted to restrict imports. But during the eighteenth century, the state went so far as to issue new sets of decrees against "superfluities" practically every decade. In 1727, for example, a decree was issued for the wives of cavalry men, dragoons, soldiers, and boatswains and for servant girls, prohibiting the wearing of any other jackets than Swedish-made jackets of wool. When women—and men—did not heed these regulations, it was suggested that violators be jailed for eight days on water and bread. At the same time, the state wished to encourage domestic production, so people were allowed to wear jackets made of any material that they themselves or others had woven—so long as it was made within the country. The state's measures to encourage domestic factory production included high tariffs on foreign materials, awards and prizes to domestic manufacturers, dress regulations requiring the wearing of domestic products, and extensive pedagogical activity by cloth and stuff factories among the urban and rural population. Thus, the factories' production increased. So did—and, incidentally, to an even greater extent—home craft production. With improved techniques of spinning and processing of wool and linen and with better implements, the home crafts could actually compete with the textile industry, which labored under great initial difficulties. The weaving of materials for household consumption was carried on not only in farm homes, but also in the towns, and on larger manors and estates. The provincial Governors' Five-Year Reports reflect a generally increased interest in and knowledge of all kinds of weaving. It was no longer a question of weaving only the old fabrics, wadmal and linen tabby, in the home, but also of weaving patterned materials. In Stockholm County, according to the Governor's Report of 1751, peasants and people of quality wove their own supply of everyday textiles. The same report indicates that, after the prohibition of imported fabrics in 1739, all finer spinning and

weaving improved and developed. Only the finishing procedures, shearing and calendering, were handled by professional craftsmen. Some people did not weave only for their own consumption, but were able to weave enough to sell the surplus. This was, reportedly, the case in the 1750s in the Södermanland cities of Eskilstuna, Torshälla, Trosa, and Strängnäs; also in Blekinge, on Gotland, and in western Norrland. The towns in Västerbotten were originally able to supply more than 50,000 ells (approximately 62,500 yards) of surplus wadmal annually for selling to the Lapps alone. However, when the peasants stopped buying broadcloth for their coats and started to use wadmal instead, the production of wadmal could not keep up with the demand. Large amounts had to be bought from the Russians, who would cross the border each winter to trade (fig. 184). Actually, the Lapps preferred the Russian wadmal, as it had cow hair mixed in and therefore was better able to withstand cold and damp.

In the western Swedish textile region, the putting-out system started to flourish in the eighteenth century. In 1742, a cloth manufactory was founded in Halland for the purpose of allowing the peasants to weave a medium-fine woolen cloth, just as was done in certain localities in England. At an inspection in 1746, it was found that the peasants in the parishes around Halmstad, Halland, were weaving coarse as well as finer half-width woolen cloth. This weaving activity was soon discontinued, but was taken up by the weavers in Borås.

In 1760, in Dalsland, the peasantry were reportedly unable to spin and weave enough for their own consumption. Instead, they would buy what they needed from Västergötland peddlers. However, after acquiring better sheep stock and after the women had started to compete with each other in spinning and weaving, the peasants of Dalsland were even able to sell textiles to Borås.

Stripes and checks
In the 1760s, the Board of Commerce complained that the width of wadmal did not adhere to regulation standards. In the opinion

of the Board, the reason for this was that the peasants of Kind (Västergötland), Halland, and Skåne refused to change their traditional weaving techniques, which, in turn, were conditioned by the type of loom used. This complaint is a starting point for estimating which textiles were made in the homes. Apparently the fabrics were limited to those which could be woven on the common handloom with its simple shedding mechanism, at times supplemented with extra shafts. Easiest to weave on this loom were, aside from wadmal, various striped and checked fabrics in simple bindings. The striped calamanco especially became a favorite model, spawning an impressive number of striped patterns in most Swedish provinces. As a rule, these patterns were used for clothing material and bolster ticking (figs. 114, 185, 186). Bodices and vests in Swedish folk costumes, for example, are predominantly striped. Articles of purchased calamanco have been found throughout the country, indicating that models and inspiration for the weaver of striped patterns were never far away. In some regions the use of striped material was limited to bodices or vests, while skirts and jackets were made of wadmal or half-wool tabby. This was the case, above all, in the most old-fashioned parts of Södermanland, Värmland, Dalarna, and Norrland. But for the rest of the country, striped skirts and jackets were common in female dress. In Skåne, striped materials were used extensively for aprons (color fig. 7), sparingly in other articles of clothing, and most of all for wide-striped bolster and cushion ticks of half-wool. Around the middle of the eighteenth century, striped materials exhibited broad, richly shaded stripes, which were especially characteristic of factory-made calamanco and striped camlets (figs. 182, 183). The homemade counterparts were not as colorful, and they naturally did not have the same fine finish.

During the last third of the eighteenth century and in the beginning of the nineteenth century, a lighter color scheme with narrower stripes on white ground came into fashionable dress (fig. 191). The new color scheme was the result of the introduction and general acceptance of cotton as a clothing material; from the

1820s on, it became increasingly important in popular costume (fig. 192). The intricately patterned materials of wool or silk from the mid eighteenth century could not, as a rule, be woven on the common handloom. Such novelty materials as flowered calamanco and woolen damask, silk damask, *ras de Sicile*, cut or uncut velvets, brocades, and printed cottons were no doubt very attractive to the home weavers, but impossible to duplicate and difficult to approximate. Only weavers in a few regions, e.g., Västergötland, Bohuslän, and Halland, attempted to imitate these fabrics in wool with laid-in patterns. As might be expected, these

were regions with a long-developed textile industry and a rural population knowledgeable and experienced in factory weaving techniques.

The linen production in Norrland

Already in the twelfth century, Hälsingland emerged as a province with a surplus of flax and linen. The Harmånger, Jättendal, and Gnarp parishes were known for their linen products, which under the collective name of *nordanstigsväv* (literally, "northern road weaves"; so-called after the central road leading north through the province of Hälsingland)

185. Striped fabrics in satin weave of cotton, linen, or half-wool, intended for cushions and pillows. Woven around 1900 by the members of one family. Höör, Skåne.

186. Pillow tick. Brown and white wool twill. Jämtland.

were in wide demand. On the whole, linen production was widespread. In the eighteenth and nineteenth centuries, northern and southern Hälsingland had their distinct specialties. The southern part sold scutched flax (line linen), with the exception of Järvsö, which also sold linen. The northern part manufactured coarse fabrics: coarse hemp or linen plain weaves and bolster tickings. The weaving centers were Järvsö, Färila, Ljusdal, Bjuråker, and Delsbo. The Hälsingland parishes were also somewhat differentiated. From the northeastern parishes came the *nordanstigsväv* and bolster ticking, from Tuna, Idenor, Njutånger, and Enåker, coarse hemp or linen tabby, and from Delsbo, lining materials.

It was easy to imitate the striped and checked patterns fashionable in the Gustavian and Empire eras. The increased production of linen, the teaching of linen-weaving techniques, and the introduction of easily accessible cotton, which superseded linen from the 1820s, brought the Gustavian and Empire styles to all social classes and all parts of the country (fig. 192). They penetrated more thoroughly in Sweden than any other style has ever done.

Simple two- to four-shaft fabrics in linen, cotton, and hemp

Of all fabrics made from plant fibers, materials of linen and hemp have had the greatest importance for clothing and interior decoration. Up to the late 1800s, when industrial manufacture was firmly established, handcraft production in the home supplied the majority of linen products for household consumption as well as for sale. Two regions emerged as surplus producers, Hälsingland, starting in the Middle Ages, and western Sweden, in the seventeenth to eighteenth centuries.

The linen of Ångermanland was widely renowned for its exquisite quality (color fig. 10). This quality was generally attributed to the fact that early frost never allowed the flax to mature in this province, so that the fibers were finer and softer than those of fully matured flax. Furthermore, retting in streams and rivers with soft, lime-free water was considered to contribute to its special quality.

187. Two- to four-shaft weaves in tabby and twill. Top to bottom: bottom sheet of half-wool, Öland; bolster tick of tow cloth, Älvros, Härjedalen; and tick of spun garnetted wool, Kålland, Västergötland.

Weaving manufacture was concentrated in Nätra, Sidensjö, Anundsjö, Vibyggerå, Arnäs, and Själevad. Farm households in those localities would weave 100 to 300 ells of linen tabby per year. The linen weaving in Ångermanland reached a peak around the middle of the eighteenth century. Up to that time, very few knew how to weave superlative linen. One stimulus was provided by the director of the Flor textile workshop in Mo, Stephen Bennet, who organized spinning schools in western Norrland (figs. 169, 201). Deserving spinners were awarded prizes in the form of silver cups and medals. In addition, the linen of each parish was officially appraised in the weavers' homes by a jury, consisting of the local pastor and government representatives. To start with, the Ångermanland prize linen production was

quite small. In the years 1771–75 it averaged 36,400 ells, but by the peak year 1805 it had quadrupled. Ångermanland's southern administrative district (*fögderi, tingslag*), on the other hand, produced much flax and also coarse linens for sale.

In Västerbotten, the conditions were, on the whole, similar; in Medelpad and Gästrikland, though flax was cultivated, it was little more than sufficient for local consumption (figs. 13–15).

The trading of linen products was largely handled by the peasants themselves, by their own means of transportation. A small portion was handled by commissioned salesmen. Large shipments would be transported in the winter—land transport was easier at that time of year—to the fair on Frösö Island in Lake Storsjön in Jämtland, a fair which also attracted Norwegians, and to the big fairs in the towns of Bergslagen. However, although the market in Stockholm and the Disting Fair in Uppsala were much farther away, many peasants chose to make the trip. The prices that their linen could command in those markets made the trip worthwhile. In Stockholm at Hötorget (the hay market) and on board vessels anchored in the harbor, linen wares were offered for sale. Although peddling was prohibited, many salesmen would also go from door to door or through the streets to sell their wares. In these ways, peasants from Norrland would sell both prize linen and coarse linen fabrics. Merchants from Söderhamn, Hudiksvall, and Härnösand would also travel around the countryside to designated trading posts and to the markets, buying up flax and linen fabrics, which were then shipped along the coast down to Stockholm.

From the fairs in central Sweden and from Stockholm, flax and linen fabrics were distributed to areas of shortage. Linen production for household consumption in Bergslagen, the Mälaren valley, and even in western Sweden thus received raw materials from Norrland.

The linen production in Norrland remained a peasant industry, in spite of certain abortive attempts at a putting-out system, arranged between peasants of Hälsingland and merchants of Hudiksvall. This production represented a significant portion of the economic foundation for the peasant culture in Hälsingland and southern Norrland, a culture which received such magnificent expression in buildings and furnishings (figs. 75, 115). Some surplus from the linen production was converted into silver, and to this day, great prestige is added to these homes by the presence of this heirloom silver.

In the 1830s, flax growing and linen weaving started to decline because of pressure from the newly established cotton factories. These factories had developed in western Sweden, out of the handcraft production for sale, a production based on the putting-out system. Their increased capacity and the highly competitive cotton prices combined to undermine the flax and linen market.

188. The handcraft products of Västra Vingåker, Södermanland, were sold especially in Norrköping and Stockholm, where the Vingåker women were a familiar sight in streets and marketplaces.—Girl from Vingåker with a bolt of material under her arm and skeins of handspun yarn in her hand.

189. Fabric of scutching tow yarn in chevron twill, used in pants for the warm season. Harjager, Skåne.

Western Swedish linen production

Certain parts of Halland, Småland, and Västergötland were the centers of linen production in the western Swedish craft region with its putting-out system. As mentioned above, all districts imported their raw materials. The one exception was Mark.

Like woolen weaving, linen weaving apparently began some time in the seventeenth century, when woodcraft production could no longer continue as before because of indiscriminate deforestation. Since flax was cultivated in Mark, western Swedish linen weaving began there. Local tradition has it that diaper weav-

1. Apron materials of half-wool in tabby, twill, and satin weaves. Floda, Mora, and Sollerö, Dalarna.

2. Bottom sheet of rag weave and sheet of calf-skin. Rättvik, Dalarna, and Delsbo, Hälsingland.

3. Wadmal for men's coats: black from Filipstad mining region, Värmland; white from Västra Vingåker, Södermanland; blue from Torna, Skåne; and gray (in bolt) from Töcksfors, Värmland.

4. White woolen shift, Sveg, Härjedalen, and *bussarong*—work blouse with stand-up collar—in half-wool, Vännäs, Västerbotten.

5. Horse blanket of goat hair. Särna, Dalarna.

6. Apron materials of striped half-wool. Leksand, Dalarna.

7. Apron materials, top to bottom, of striped linen, Hälsingland, and striped half-wool, Skåne and Dalarna.

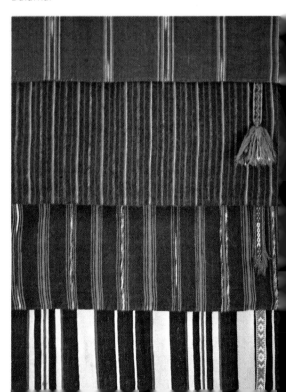

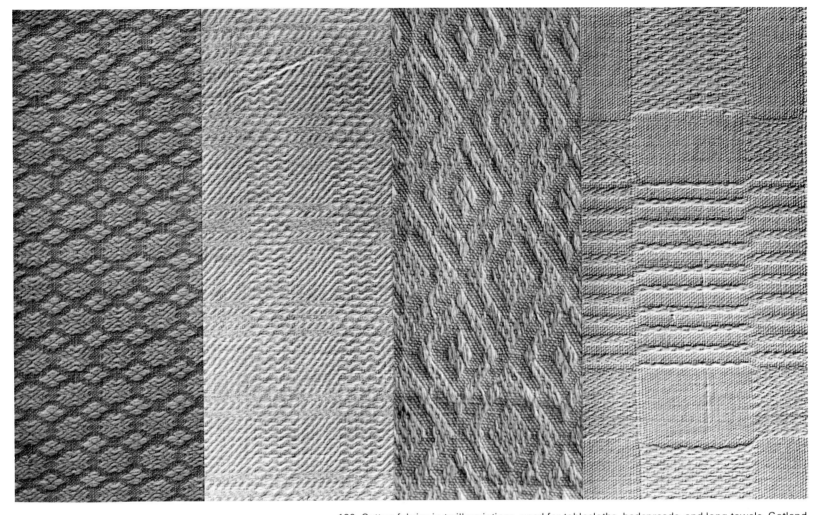

190. Cotton fabrics in twill variations, used for tablecloths, bedspreads, and long towels. Gotland.

ing was introduced by returning prisoners of war from Silesia during Karl XII's Polish War, 1700–08. How much basis in truth there may be for this tradition is not known. Istorp parish and Mark district were, however, the centers for all kinds of diaper weaves in the eighteenth century. In addition, all homes in the area, reports a source from 1773, produced coarse and fine linen tabby, bolster ticking, all kinds of cottons, handkerchiefs, and striped linen tabby. It is estimated that close to 12,100 people found their main livelihood in textile crafts. The work was carried on in families, not only by adults but also by children and old people (fig. 18). This description is equally applicable to other craft centers within the western Swedish craft region.

The big upswing in linen production came in the latter half of the eighteenth century, as a result of relaxed trade laws, protective tariffs benefiting the country's own production, and a favorable world market. In addition, the authorities made active propaganda for flax growing and linen production. At the expense of the state, a number of servant girls and men were sent from Dalarna to Ångermanland to be instructed in the preparation and spinning of flax. In Kronoberg county, an institute was founded in Gårdsby in 1811 for the same purpose. Kalmar and Blekinge county also benefited from the instructors who had come straight from Ångermanland to teach at Gårdsby. Alumni of the institute later worked in various places in southern

Sweden. Private individuals and the agricultural societies and other institutions vied with each other in awarding prizes and encouraging finer linen weaving. One could point out, with justifiable pride, that the Swedish wares were on a par with very fine foreign goods. Striped and checked indigenous linen fabrics were in general use. In Skaraborg county, linen weaving was one of the farmers' most important sources of income.

From flax to cotton
After the Napoleonic Wars, the importation of cotton was soon established, and western Swedish textile crafts quickly changed over from linen to cotton materials. Up to about

before. The new production centers were the districts of Bollebygd, Kind, and Ås, and, as before, Mark. Between 1830 and 1863, cotton weaving completely overtook linen weaving. Yardage, various cloths, and ribbons, all of cotton, were registered in Borås and Ulricehamn customs stations in ever-increasing quantities.

Craft production for sale decreases; production for household consumption increases

Government policy regarding the textile crafts in the middle of the nineteenth century was characterized by a willingness to support craft production for sale, which was having difficulty competing with industrial production. In spite of state support, craft production for sale continued to decline and could no longer hold its own against the ever-cheaper industrial products. This was the case in both the northern and the western Swedish craft regions. Craft production for household consumption, on the other hand, continued to increase in some localities. Generally it remained the most important form of production in rural areas.

On the basis of available statistics about the registered production for sale, it has been shown that the average annual industrial textile production around 1850 was no more than about thirteen feet of cotton fabric and about one foot of woolen per capita. Most textiles were thus still supplied by home production for private consumption.

From 1817 onward, the Board of Commerce gave an annual report on the total production of woven fabrics, based on the Crown bailiffs' data about the number of looms and the production of ells of linen, wool, or cotton fabrics. In certain parts of Skåne in 1817, one loom per household was reported. In one district in Småland, three looms per household were reported. On the basis of these reports and parish reports from the years 1847–55, Gustaf Utterström has made a survey of the position of craft production for household consumption. This survey is briefly summarized thus:

In Skåne, the southwestern plains were deficient in wool, whereas the forest region in the eastern parts had a surplus of wool. In the

191. Page from Maria Beata Siberg's sample book from the 1820s. Alongside each sample is a notation of the intended use of the fabric and, usually, the date of its weaving.

1820, linen production continued to increase, but when the influential merchant-employers in Göteborg started to hand out spun cotton yarn to the peasants for their weaving, flax growing was rapidly set back. In Göteborg and Älvsborg county, mechanized cotton-spinning mills were introduced, which increased the production of cotton yarn. Thus, the weaver

spent no time on the preparation of the yarn— a process which earlier had taken considerably more time than the weaving itself—and the total weaving output increased. Thus, although the labor force remained constant, the production of fabrics increased greatly. However, there was no change in the nature of the weaves, since the same looms were used as

latter region, handcraft production was extremely lively, the main products for sale being floor mats and horse blankets.

Halland, southern Småland, southern Gotland, and Fårö had a surplus of wool, whereas the plains of Västergötland and Östergötland had to buy wool. Manors in Götaland as well as Svealand often maintained sheep-breeding stations and produced wool. In Skåne, this wool was sold to the factories in Malmö; farther north, to the wool industry in Norrköping. Central Sweden was a generally deficient region. One exception was Västra Vingåker, where wadmal was manufactured, although the raw material was obtained elsewhere. On the whole, then, Svealand and Norr-

land were areas lacking in wool; here the Västergötland trade had its best markets.

In the 1840s, the wadmal production was reported to be declining because the factories had started to weave cheap coarse woolen cloth. The peasants in Östergötland, around Göteborg, and in parts of Småland, Blekinge, and Skåne were reported to have forsaken

192. Sample book with swatches of handwoven checked cottons. Mid-nineteenth century.

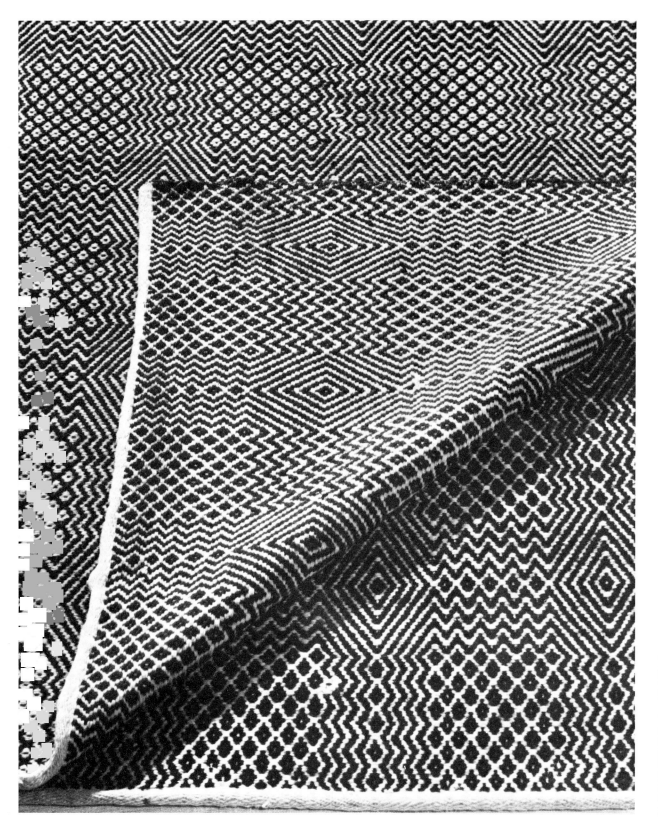

193. Coverlet, *åklä*, without fell, in broken lozenge twill variation. Uppland. (See also fig. 112.)

194. Coverlet of quilted diaper weave in black, white, red, and orange cotton. From a farmhand's bunk, Horn, Östergötland. Underneath, a coverlet in chevron twill variation with white cotton warp and black wool weft. Hycklinge, Östergötland.

wadmal in the 1850s for bought cloth. Farther north, factory goods were used to an even greater extent, mostly for holiday wear, while homemade coarse linen and woolen materials continued to be used for everyday wear. Even in northern Dalarna, conservative in dress and customs, homemade articles began to be displaced by factory merchandise, such as broadcloth, silk, and cotton. In Norrland the situation was much the same.

In some places, as in eastern Närke, the production of cottons was blamed for the phasing out of woolens.

Homemade linen goods, linen tabby and tow cloth for underwear and furnishings, were able to hold out longer than woolen fabrics in the competition with factory-made wares. Not only the flax surplus areas, but also the deficient areas, produced all linen needed for household consumption, the latter areas by working with purchased scutched flax or spun linen yarn.

Cottons were also woven in the home with bought yarn, which was woven into cotton tabby for everyday use, into checked and striped cotton dress materials, and into fabrics for neckerchiefs and fichus. In Östergötland, cotton and wool were woven into clothing materials for men and women. As late as the nineteenth century, some Stockholm factories had their cottons woven in Dalarna, where cotton spinning and weaving had been located since the previous century. Everywhere cotton yarn was much used, as warp in weaves with linen or woolen weft.

Multiple-shaft weaves in linen and cotton
As shown above, the simple weaves, tabby and twill, were used for everyday wear and furnishings in town and countryside (figs. 187, 189, 190, 195; color figs. 8–11). For other purposes, where aesthetic or prestige considerations predominated, more richly patterned many-shaft weaves were used, such as twill variations, diaper, and damask. Since the common hand-loom used for handcraft production was not capable of any more complicated variations (at least not before the eighteenth century), the above-mentioned patterned linens were

Fabrics

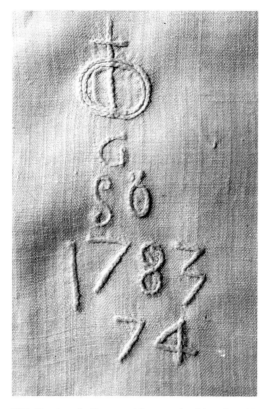

195. Sheet of linen tabby, embroidered with owner's mark, initials, date, and the number 74.

196. Linen in satin weave. Napkin monogrammed E.M. in satin stitch, outlined in red stem stitch. Gotland.

that, as a rule, similar conditions existed around all towns where there were professional linen weavers in the seventeenth and eighteenth centuries. As already noted, an intense pedagogical activity emanated from the Flor workshop in Mo, Hälsingland, so that the surrounding area produced many skilled spinners and weavers. It is highly probable that similar activities were associated also with the damask workshops in Vadstena, Örebro, and Jönköping. Ordinary handlooms offered limited possibilities for the weaving of *dräll* (twill or damask diaper) and damask. The adaptation of diaper and damask patterns for the simpler loom resulted in their simplification. Factory-owner J. E. Ekenmark and his family did much to adapt damask patterns for the simple handloom and to build out the loom with extra harnesses, making damask weaving in the homes a possibility.

Dräll (twill or damask diaper), simplified dräll (overshot damask), and damask
Dräll is woven in satin or twill binding in which the pattern is formed by the varying interlacing of warp and filling without the addition of a separate pattern weft. *Dräll* has been woven with four harnesses, but extra harnesses can be added so that a *dräll* of up to sixteen shafts or more could be woven on a handloom. The patterns used were therefore limited to ornaments based on square block pattern elements of filling on a ground of warp. Checkerboard patterns, stars, diagonal squares, and stripes have been combined in innumerable variations. The name *dräll* originally comes from the Latin *tri*, three, and *licium*, thread. From the German distortion *drillich* comes the Swedish *dräll*. It appears in the inventory of the royal collections in the sixteenth century. Originally, it was woven by professional weavers. The term *dräll* is common throughout the country from Skåne to Norrbotten. The technique and the pattern inventory are also universal, since these are limited by a certain restricted number of harnesses and a certain binding. In Östergötland, however, an unusually varied production of materials of wool on cotton or linen warp for

probably purchased. In the Middle Ages, linen patterns were limited to twill variations. The highly developed Dutch linen manufacture exported such twills under the name of *kruiswerk*. These patterns in twill variations have continued to play an important role in handcraft production on farms, in parsonages, and on manors. Although the technical equipment available could not compare with that of professional workshops, where these patterns had originated, the latter were copied with the simple tools available. The same was true about diaper weaves: professional weavers began to weave them in the sixteenth century but during the eighteenth century *bönhasar*, itinerant

weavers, and unguilded manorial craftsmen distributed them to the homes, where the women took over the production and the patterns. In his work *Linvävarämbetet i Malmö och det skånska linneväveriet* ("The Linen Weavers' Guild in Malmö and linen weaving in Skåne"), Ernst Fischer has shown the steps of this transfer. From the workshop milieu in Malmö, the weaving of not only twill and damask diaper but also damask was spread to large Skåne estates, with the aid of the above-mentioned groups. From there, the techniques reached the homes in the countryside and the towns by means of women permanently employed as weavers on the estates. One may safely assume

quilted coverlets evolved (figs. 193, 194). These coverlets were woven in *dräll* or multiple-shaft twill variations in strong colors: bright red, green, yellow, purple, and blue. Also in western Skåne, *dräll* in half-wool has been used for quilted coverlets.

Linen and half-linen *dräll,* woven on eight to ten shafts and used for tablecloths and napkins, was especially found in the southern Swedish linen surplus area. When cotton was introduced, *dräll* was woven also in this material. In Skåne peasant milieu can be found an enormous amount of *dräll,* transmitted by professional weavers working on larger farms and estates. These weavers also supplied the patterns which are still preserved in great numbers to this day, in the form of pattern drafts, threading drafts, and tie-up and treadling drafts. Generally these drafts come from manor or bourgeois milieu, but Ernst Fischer has noted some examples in peasant milieu. The patterns and their names in these various collections are so similar that a common origin must be presumed, namely the pattern repertory of the professional weavers. Fig. 198 shows a small selection of the amazing checks-and-stripes variations in this repertory. Most of these patterns were woven on a simple loom, although some of them required up to twenty shafts and thirty treadles. *Dräll* patterns often have fanciful names: "Lisbon Star," "Rosenborg Castle," "The French Rose," "Night and Day," and "The Little Wanderer." Some names are more prosaic: "Clover in Zigzag," "Cat's Paw," and "Reverse and Regular Cat's Paw." Collections of more complex linen patterns were also printed and published from the end of the eighteenth century. The most widespread collection, entitled *Afhandling om drällers och dubbla golfmattors tillverkning med begagnande af harnesk-utrustning* ("Dissertation on the weaving of *dräll* and runners in double weave with drawloom figure harness"), was written in 1828 by J. E. Ekenmark and his sisters. (For an example of such a runner, see fig. 208.)

The authors of these collections, to a large extent, took their material from already existing eighteenth-century standard pattern books, or from the latter's original sources.

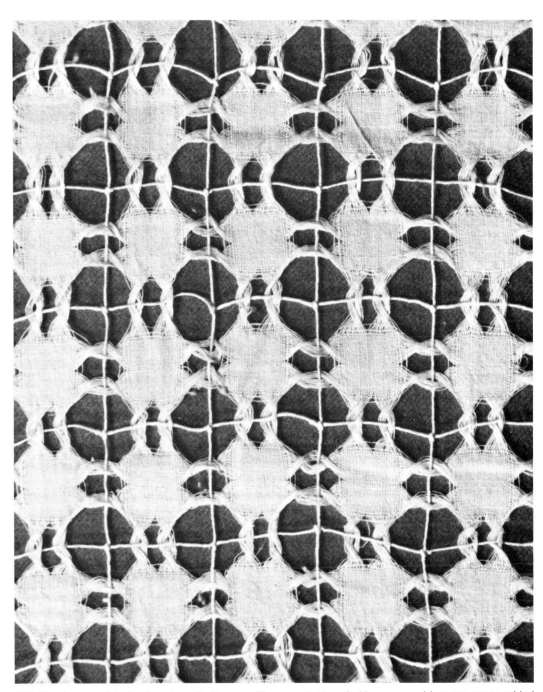

197. Curtain material of cotton, two-shaft weave. The warp is threaded in groups with cotton yarns added at intervals. The weft is similarly spaced, and the cotton yarns are knotted where they cross. Gladhammar, Småland.

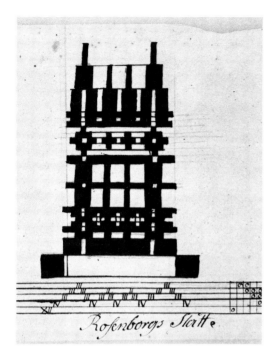

Rosenborgs Slott

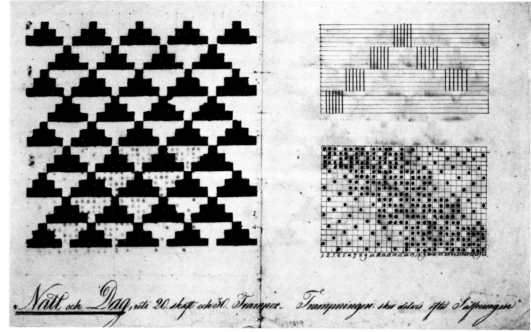

Natt och Dag, till 20 skaft och 31 Trampor. Trampningen skes delvis efter Söttningen

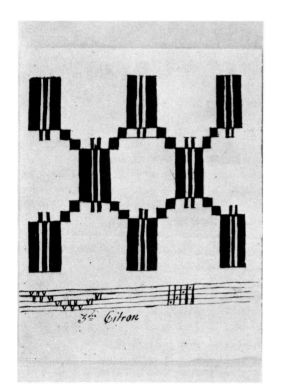

3te Citron

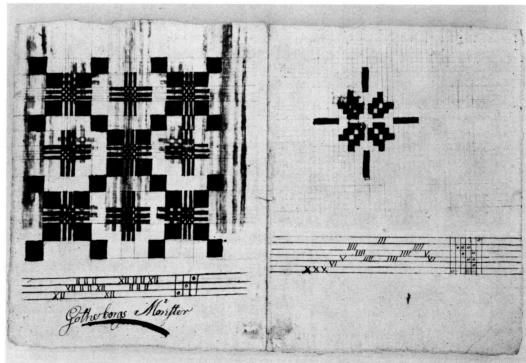

Gottherborgs Mönster

198. Patterns accompanied by threading and tie-up drafts for various diaper weaves. Drawings in India ink on paper. From personal pattern books.

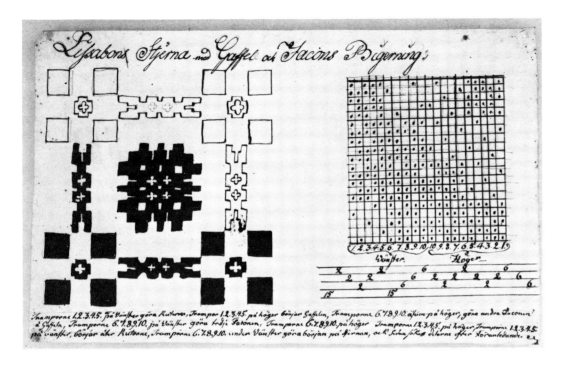

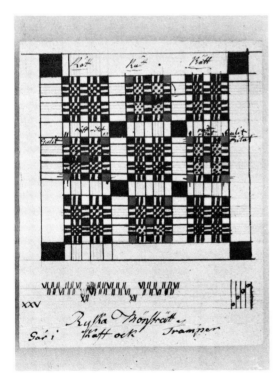

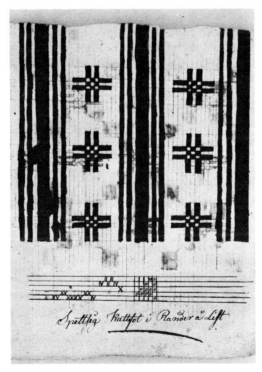

The symmetry of the more complex *dräll* patterns is dissolved when the pattern is transferred to a four-shaft handloom. The technical result of weaving an eight- or ten-harness weave with four shafts is that the pattern does not emerge in bound warp ends and filling picks but in a loosely floating pattern weft, which partly floats above or under the ground, and partly is bound into the plain ground fabric. A number of local names exist in Sweden for this simplified *dräll*, e.g., *daldräll* (*dräll* from Dalarna, the same as "overshot") (color fig. 11). During the first years of the Handcraft Movement, these variations had strong provincial associations, but later, a more thorough inventory has demonstrated their existence throughout the country. When cotton was introduced, simplified *dräll* was made also with colored pattern weft, especially with red on white ground. Damask in wool also occurred.

Because of its complex bindings, damask requires so many shafts that a special kind of draw system is necessary. Damask weaving therefore, as a rule, belonged in professional workshop production. However, in Skåne, damask was also woven in the homes. The weaving pattern book by Ekenmark meant much for the dissemination of patterns for simplified damask weaving, which enjoyed a certain popularity.

Professional manufacture
Regular import of especially fine linen fabrics has occurred since the fourteenth century. Professional manufacture of linen materials in Sweden does not seem to have developed until the sixteenth century (figs. 93, 199). During the years 1650–62 there were sixty-nine linen weaving workshops spread over twenty-one towns. Finland, then a Swedish province, had the greatest number of professional linen weavers. In the seventeenth century, there already were itinerant unguilded linen weavers working on large estates, where they would remain for some time weaving materials for the household's use and then move on. As an urban industry, linen weaving ceased during the second half of the eighteenth century. The workshop

199. Linen damask with Biblical motifs. From the life of Samson, e.g., Samson and Delilah (top). Holland, first half of the seventeenth century.

201. Linen damask with crowns and Sweden's national Great Coat of Arms. Woven at Flor damask workshop in Mo, Hälsingland.

200. Linen damask woven in Stockholm in 1701 for Queen Hedvig Eleonora. The pattern incorporates the royal insignia of three crowns and the Queen's crowned monogram.

202. Linen damask napkin, woven at the damask workshop in Vadstena in 1835. The central mirror monogram DE stands for Douglas Ehrenborg.

203. Towel of linen damask, woven at Stenberg's damask workshop, Jönköping, Småland.

204. Linen damask, woven at Almedahl factory after a design by Agnes Branting. The pattern is modeled on older napkins woven around Ystad, Skåne, in the 1860s. Marked G with red cotton yarn in stem stitch and satin stitch.

production found it difficult to compete with the unguilded professional craftsmen. In the craftsmen's workshops, mostly tabby and striped ticking were woven at first; but during the eighteenth century *dräll* and damask were also turned out, at least by the more skilled masters.

In the eighteenth century, when the state was trying to nurture a national industrial textile manufacture, there were also energetic attempts to start production of high-quality damask. From 1699 to 1706 there was a damask atelier in Stockholm, supplying the court with damask (fig. 200). This atelier was under the directorship of an "imported" German master, Georg Hoffman. In Mo, Hälsingland, the Flor damask workshop was founded in 1729 (fig. 201). It was headed by Stephen Bennet and his son Thomas. Flor ceased production in 1845. In Gävle, around the middle of the eighteenth century, a master named Halfvard Gäfverberg was active. Damask was

woven in Vadstena at Wadstena Fabrik (Vadstena Workshop) from 1778 to 1843 (fig. 202). The situation in Skåne has been studied by Ernst Fischer, who has made a table of Skåne linen weavers in the seventeenth century. The best-known weavers were four generations of the families Nyman and Lewanius.

In Norrköping, there were several workshops, e.g., C. G. Boberg's workshop, which was active until around 1800.

In Örebro, Gustaf Hellgren had a workshop from 1817 to 1886 and, in Jönköping, Ulla Stenberg's damask workshop carried on an important production from 1830 to 1883 (fig. 203). Sweden's first large cotton and linen factory, Almedahls, was founded in 1846 (fig. 204). However, the smaller Rydboholm Factory had already started to produce finer cotton weaves in 1836.

Double cloth

Double cloth has two layers of warp and weft, which are bound together at certain points. In other words, two complete widths of material are woven simultaneously. The pattern is formed by having the two layers trade places according to a predetermined system.

Pick-up double cloth is woven with four shafts and the pattern is picked up with a lease rod. Double cloth goes by different names in different parts of Sweden, e.g. *finskeväv* (Finnish weave) or *ryssväv* (Russian weave).

Double-cloth fabrics preserved from peasant milieu occur primarily in two regions: Halland-Bohuslän and Jämtland-Härjedalen. They date from the seventeenth century onward. There is, in addition, one double-cloth type which technically, and as far as pattern is concerned, is derived from the block-patterned *dräll*. It developed all over the country in the nineteenth century, transmitted by, among other things, J. E. Ekenmark's pattern book of 1828.

143

This book includes a type of double cloth (fig. 208).

The double-cloth examples in the two regions differ in two respects: first, those from the northern region are made completely of wool (fig. 209), whereas the southern group tends to have one layer of cotton or linen and the other of wool (figs. 206, 207, 210, 211). Second, double cloth from the southern region has a far richer pattern repertory.

Halland-Bohuslän
As a rule, the double-cloth fabrics in Halland and Bohuslän were executed in two, sometimes four, colors: clear red, blue, green, black, or brown, on natural linen ground. They were used mostly as coverlets of decorative nature, e.g., as table covers, bedspreads, or funeral palls.

These coverlets show a typical articulation of the surface in blocks of fixed, rhythmically repeated, motifs, and an edging of squares with repeating or alternating pattern (fig. 207). The pattern motifs in these weaves appear in many cases to be of medieval origin. Thus, one finds double-headed eagles within octagons, lily crosses, maidens, leopards, etc. There are also some patterns showing distinct Empire influence, taken from Ekenmark's pattern book. However, the latter patterns were only used for rugs, blankets, and table covers—all relatively late types of textile home furnishings.

Jämtland-Härjedalen
The northern region's double-cloth fabrics were, as a rule, used for coverlets of a distinctly formal nature. The earliest existing one is dated 1737; and they continued to be woven as late as the end of the nineteenth century.

Oldest in patterns and composition type is a group of coverlets with transverse bands across the surface and without borders. The ornamentation consists of diamonds, hearts, and stylized human and animal forms, lined up in rows and rhythmically filling the whole surface from selvage to selvage. Two, three, or four colors were used, whereby the bottom layer became striped or checked (fig. 209).

205. Characteristic pattern types in pick-up double cloth. Of medieval origin are numbers 1, 3, 5, 6, 7, and 8 (left). Of more recent origin are numbers 2, 4, and 8 (right).

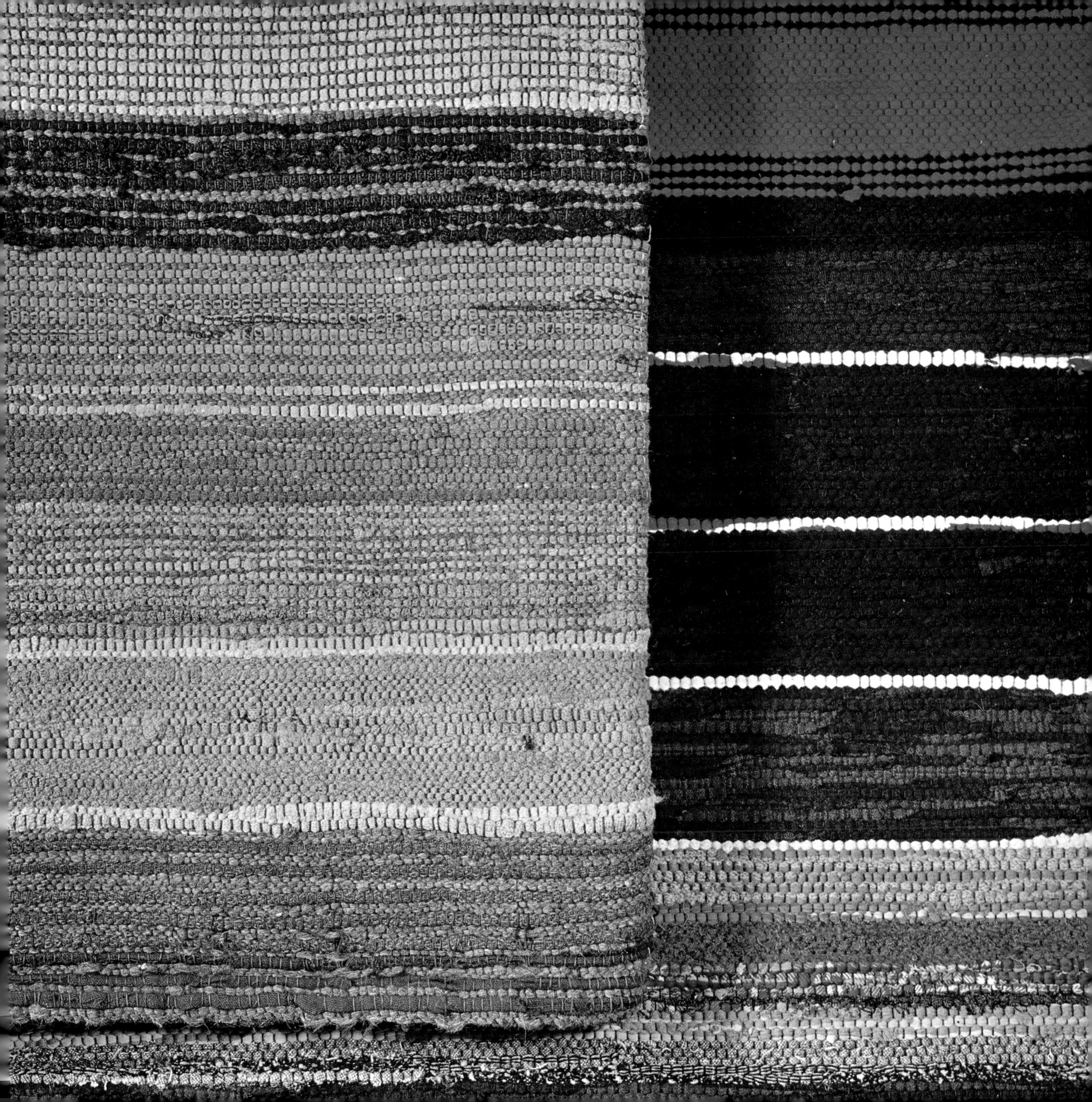

8. Rag coverlets. Left, old rug used at sea, black cotton warp with filling of hair yarn and rags. Right, recently woven coverlet inspired by the older one, black cotton warp and weft of rags. Hudiksvall, Hälsingland.

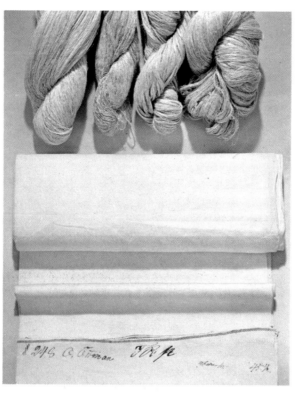

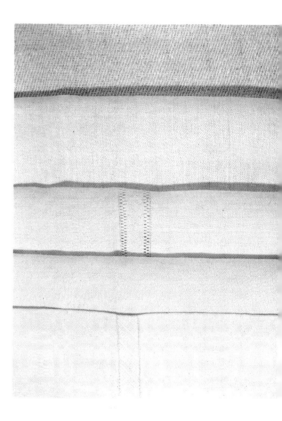

9. Shift or sark of scutching tow cloth, Järna, Dalarna; and skein of scutching tow yarn, Tingsryd, Småland.

10. Bolt of prize linen made in 1865 in Sidensjö, Ångermanland, and skeins of spun Ångermanland linen.

11. Tow-yarn twill, linen twill, two grades of linen tabby, and linen diaper weave. Dalarna.

12. Double cloth, one layer of linen yarn, the other of wool yarn. Thirteenth century, Kyrkås Church, Jämtland.

206. Double-cloth coverlet, one layer of white cotton yarn, the other of reddish brown wool yarn. Bohuslän.

207. Double-cloth coverlet, one layer of white cotton yarn, the other of green wool yarn. Initials EIS AMA woven into the bottom edge, the date into the top (not visible in picture). Jörlanda, Bohuslän, 1858.

208. Double-cloth carpet. Both layers are woven of reddish yellow and black wool yarn. Made in the 1820s in bourgeois milieu, Visby, Gotland.

209. Double-cloth coverlet. One layer has brownish black wool warp and weft of blue and lacquer red wool, the other layer has warp and weft of yellow wool. Älvros, Härjedalen.

210. Double-cloth coverlet, one layer of unbleached linen, the other of red wool. Initials and date, OPS BND 1787, are woven in (not visible in picture). Romelanda, Bohuslän.

211. Double-cloth coverlet, both layers of wool: one red, the other yellow in the panel but blue in the lengthwise borders. Initials and date, EDH 1676, in the bottom left hand corner (not visible in picture). Västergötland.

Fabrics

212. Wall hanging in double cloth from the fourteenth century. Both layers of wool in dark blue and grayish brown. Originally in Grödinge Church, Södermanland, now in Statens Historiska Museum, Stockholm.

Another group of coverlets from Revsund and Rätan in Jämtland and Sveg, Hede, and Tännäs in Härjedalen have pomegranate patterns, mostly in indigo and red, and panel-and-border composition. One of these coverlets is dated 1737, but the pattern type goes back to the Renaissance. Such coverlets have also been found in Hälsingland and Medelpad.

A third group has a characteristic coloring in red and black and a center panel with grape clusters diagonally framed or within a diagonal latticework of vines (fig. 205: 2). This group can be traced with certainty to the mid-nineteenth century, or later. It is very similar to double-cloth coverlets woven in Indalen, Stugudalen, and the Röros area in Norway. The latter were offered for sale in Härjedalen and were apparently also copied there. They often have numbers woven in, referring to the weaver's production number.

Double-cloth is also found in the adjacent provinces: Hälsingland, Dalarna, and Medelpad. It is not known whether these textiles were imported or whether the technique of double-cloth weaving was practiced here.

Double-cloth fabrics are relatively well represented in preserved textiles dating as far back as the Middle Ages. More recent samples of double-cloth preserved from peasant milieu reflect an earlier use of double weave in the most prestigious textiles in manors and castles. The social class for which the Västergötland coverlet in fig. 211 from 1676 was woven is difficult to ascertain.

The earliest examples of double-cloth that have been preserved all come from northern Sweden, namely, hangings from Överhogdal in Härjedalen and from Kyrkås, Revsund, and Marby in Jämtland. They date from around 1050–1200. Their motif repertory is definitely related to the figural motifs of late classical and early medieval silks made by Persian and Byzantine weavers and probably distributed by the international network of churches and religious orders. These early double-cloth hangings in Sweden were, in fact, all found in churches. The pattern motifs are stylized animals and horsemen. In the hanging from Kyrkås (color fig. 12), stylized birds and ships are framed by octagonal latticework, alternating with swas-

tikas and band motifs. One of the hangings from Överhogdal has similar pattern elements.

The material in these hangings is, in one layer, natural-colored linen, in the other, wool in two colors alternating in bands and stripes. When the two layers exchange places, a color scheme unrelated to the pattern emerges. The same method of striping one woven layer can be seen in double-cloth fabrics from the eighteenth and nineteenth centuries, a peculiarity which would indicate an unbroken tradition from the medieval hangings and later peasant double weaves in Jämtland-Härjedalen.

Another group of double-cloth fabrics, dating to the fifteenth and sixteenth centuries, is also associated with churches: hangings from the churches of Grödinge and Överenhörna in Södermanland and Södra Råda in Värmland. The ornamentation is romanesque, in spite of the dating, showing stylized lions and eagles on a stark checkerboard ground, surrounded by dragons (fig. 212). Both layers are of wool—of both linen and wool in the hanging from Södra Råda—and the two-color scheme is carried out throughout. In this respect, there is a certain similarity between this medieval group and the Halland-Bohuslän coverlets of double cloth. Thus, it seems that the division of preserved eighteenth- and nineteenth-century material from peasant milieu into one northern and one southern group extends back as far as the Middle Ages.

In sixteenth-century castle inventories, entries of "Finnish weave" and "Russian weave" occur regularly. The identification of these as double cloths has been made on the basis of these terms having survived until the present in Bohuslän. In this province, the terms can be traced in inventories back to the eighteenth century. It is believed that the names were first used for the quantity of double cloth imported from Finland and Russia in the sixteenth century, later also being applied to the indigenous product.

Tapestry, type "rölakan"

The term *rölakan* is derived from *rygglakan* (literally, "back cover"), i.e., a woven textile hung on the wall above a bench to protect one from drafts. Technically—though not in pattern—*rölakan* belongs among the simplest weaves known. It is a tapestry weave, consisting of warp and a discontinuous weft in tabby. The picks create the pattern: a different color pick is laid in, whenever the pattern so specifies, in the same shed, and connected to the first pick by interlooping. In the oldest examples a single weft is interlooped, i.e., two weft yarns, coming together from different directions, interloop around each other every other time they meet before starting their paths in opposite directions back across the warp (fig. 220: 3). In the later examples from peasant milieu the most common weave is double-weft interlooped tapestry, which means that the weft yarns are interlooped every time they meet, each weft being interlooped twice (figs. 213 and 220: 2). In Sweden, *rölakan* belongs above all in Skåne, where it has been used to create a wealth of patterns and motifs, many unequaled in the rest of Europe. Simple stars and checks are the most common motifs and appear, outside of Skåne, also in Blekinge, southern Småland, Halland, southwestern Väs-

213. *Rölakan* tapestry, reverse side showing the double-weft interlooped joints.

149

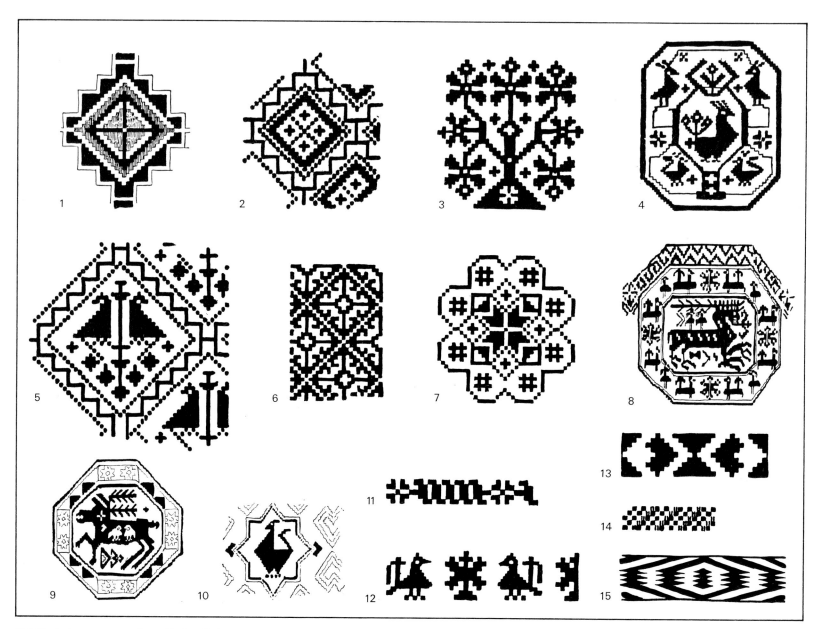

214. Typical patterns and motifs in *rölakan* technique. Geometric motifs, occurring throughout the country, are numbers 1, 2, 6, 7, 11, and 14. Animal and plant motifs of medieval type are numbers 3, 4, 8, 9, 10, and 12. The latter are, as a rule, found only in Skåne.

tergötland, and in Bohuslän. Isolated examples of *rölakan* fabrics have been found in central Sweden and Norrland. A magnificent coverlet in *rölakan* has also been found in Jämtland (fig. 219). In some parts of Norway, *rölakan* appears under the name *rutaväv* (checkered weave), often woven on a vertical loom. The existence of *rölakan* in southwestern Sweden as well as Norway, and the fact that some patterns are found in both regions, suggests the initial existence of one single area of distribution, directly connected with the Continent, where the technique has been known since prehistoric times. The eastern European variant of this weave, kilim, is found in Asia. Historically, the *rölakan* technique has also been used in the major ancient cultures of Egypt and the Near East. The existence of *rölakan* among the Mayas and Aztecs of Central America strengthens the impression that *rölakan* is one of the oldest weaving techniques known to man.

In Sweden, one can trace the *rölakan* technique back to the eighth and ninth centuries in fragments from the archaeological finds in the graves of Valsgärde and Birka. Agnes Geijer considers these fragments to be of indigenous origin. However, there are no *rölakan* textiles preserved from the Middle Ages in any of the Nordic countries, although a few German ones exist. The earliest example of *rölakan* in Sweden dated with a certainty is from 1710.

Because of the nature of *rölakan* patterns and their assimilation of period style elements, it is, however, generally believed that the *rölakan* technique has existed in unbroken tradition in Sweden from prehistoric times. Most common are the simple geometric patterns, consisting of squares, which form diagonal zigzag lines, or combine to form simple

215. *Rölakan* blanket, so-called thunderbolt blanket, with warp of wool and weft of roving, i.e., rolled, carded, but unspun wool, in brownish green and white. The width is 155 centimeters (about 5 feet). Sandvika, Harg, Uppland.

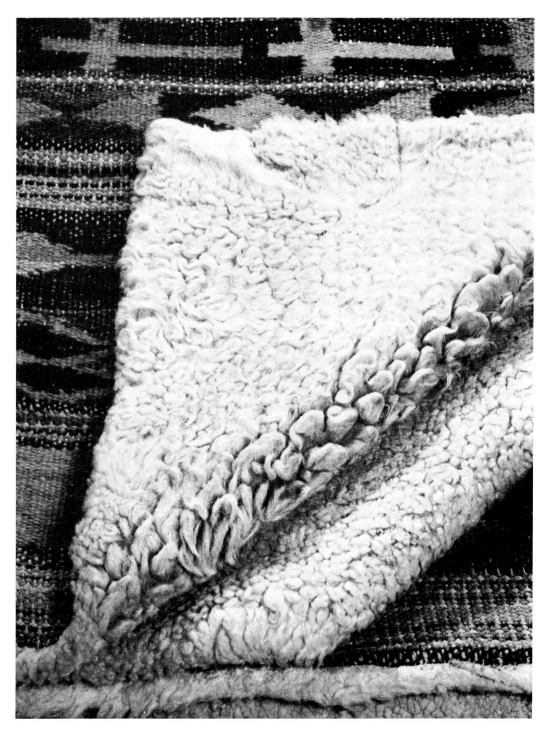

stars. These are ageless motifs, without identifiable origin, determined solely by the limitations of the two thread systems, the warp and the weft. Interlaced bands, the Solomonic knot motif, the eight-pointed star, the eight-pointed rose, and a double square also belong among the most frequently recurring motifs. Motifs of medieval origin are trees, with or without birds, various types of crosses, pomegranate patterns, the palmetto, the lily cross, and, of animal motifs, the double-headed eagle, the lion, the unicorn, the deer, and the bird inscribed in octagons (fig. 214). Andreas Lindblom has related these motifs to silk patterns from the eleventh and twelfth centuries, issuing from workshops in the Near East, Byzantium, and southern Italy. When woven in silk, these heraldic animals are inscribed in circles. Translated into a coarser material and a simpler technique, the circle becomes an octagon and the animals are further stylized. Apparently there is a Byzantine influence here, but when and where it made itself felt in Sweden cannot yet be determined. The transmission probably was effected by means of workshop traditions, which gradually reached peasant milieu. The more complex motifs with animal figures are mainly found in eastern Skåne. The exceptional coverlet from Jämtland has double-headed-eagle and tree motifs (figs. 148, 219). Aside from the basic geometric patterns, the only motifs occurring in the considerably coarser *rölakan* tapestries from Blekinge, Småland, Halland, Bohuslän, and southern Västergötland are the star, the eight-pointed rose, the Solomonic knot, and the lily cross.

216. Combination of fell and coverlet, the latter in *rölakan* with linen warp and with weft of wool yarn, hair yarn, and cotton yarn. Eringsboda, Blekinge.

217. Carriage cushion in *rölakan,* hemp warp and wool weft. Eljaröd, Skåne.

218. Coverlet in *rölakan,* warp of linen or hemp and weft of wool. Signed and dated twice, 1779 and 1818, along the bottom edge (reversed in picture). Skåne.

219. Coverlet in *rölakan,* linen warp and wool weft. Origin unknown; acquired in Jämtland.

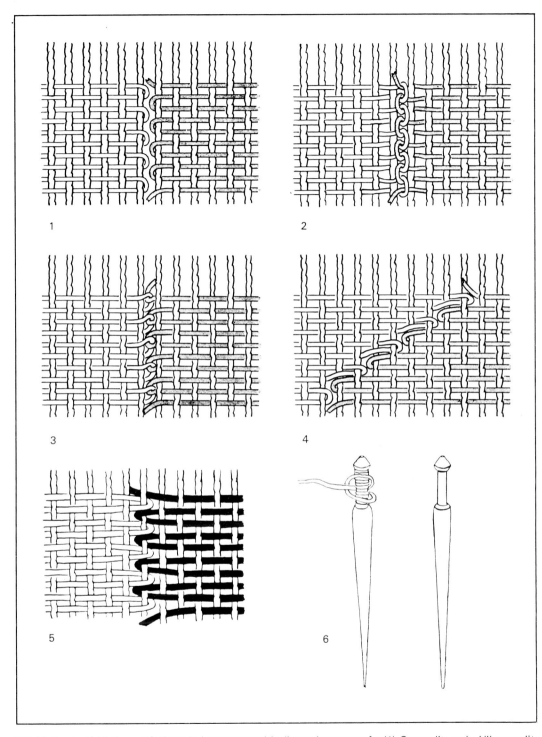

Tapestry, type "Flemish weaving"

Flemish weaving in Sweden has been thoroughly studied by Ernst Fischer, who has presented the results in a number of publications, the most comprehensive of which is *Flamskväv-nader i Skåne* ("Flemish weaving in Skåne"). The following discussion is based on his findings.

Flamskväv (Flemish weaving) is the Swedish term used for the type of tapestry that is made on a vertical loom which from the sixteenth century has been common in Sweden. "Gobelin" tapestry technique, as it is better known internationally, is a technique in which the weft is discontinuous and is inserted area by area, not across the full width of the warp. Thus, one pattern detail can be completed before another one is begun. Working one area after another allows for more curved lines along the direction of the weft. Hence, Flemish weaving patterns tend to be freer and more complex than the restricted geometric patterns of *rölakan*. Thus, this technique is used especially for pictorial representations. The Gobelin tapestries proper were named for the atelier created by Louis XIV in Paris in 1622, *Manufacture des Gobelins*. They were woven either on horizontal warp, *basse-lisse*, or on vertical warp, *haute-lisse*. In Sweden, tapestry weaving uses a vertical loom. When each pattern area is worked separately, vertical slits appear in the fabric. These may be left open (as in kilim) or stitched together after the weaving is completed. The pattern areas may also be joined during the weaving process by interlocking or interlooping. As in *rölakan*, this may be done in two ways: by interlooping alternate inlays (fig. 220: 3), or by interlooping each inlay (fig. 220: 2). The former is the most common in Swedish tapestries from peasant milieu. The inlays can also reverse direction without interlooping into another weft thread, but the kilim slits may be avoided by dovetailing the inlays, interlocking a single warp thread with one or several wefts (fig. 220: 4, 5). Thus, straight lines in the warp direction acquire the sawtooth appearance characteristic of Skåne tapestries.

The weft is, as a rule, of wool, the warp of linen. Other yarns have been used sparingly for effect. Flemish weaving is done from the

220. Methods of joining weft threads in weaves with discontinuous weft: (1) Open slit, as in kilim or slit tapestry. (2) Double-weft interlooping, in which the weft yarns are interlooped every time they meet, each weft being interlooped twice. The resulting joint is smooth on the front, raised on the back of the weave. (3) Single-weft interlooping, in which two weft yarns interloop every other time they meet, each weft being interlooped once. The resulting joint is smooth on both sides. (4) Diagonal multiple-warp interlocking, in which the wefts do not interloop. (5) Color joint in single-warp interlocked tapestry, toothed tapestry. The wefts do not interloop, but interlock the same warp thread. (6) Tapestry bobbin also used to beat in the weft in Flemish weaving.

221. Flemish weaving in progress. The weaver is Ida Larsson, Södra Sallerup, Skåne, 1962.

reverse side. The pattern or sketch is fastened behind the warp for reference during the progress of the work. The weft is wound on spool-shaped sticks, tapestry bobbins (fig. 220:6), with which the weft is also beaten down. For this latter purpose, a comb beater of iron with a handle in the middle has also been used.

Flemish weaving before the sixteenth century
No examples of Flemish weaving from the Middle Ages are preserved in Sweden. Whether any such tapestries did exist is doubtful. Admittedly, there are fragments of tapestries among the Birka finds, but it is not known whether they were made in Sweden or imported. In Norway, one part of a medieval tapestry has been preserved, the so-called Baldishol tapestry from the twelfth century, a spectacular work in pure romanesque style. It is believed to be indigenous, but may actually have been imported.

The weaving of tapestries first flourished in France, where the great masterpieces of the Middle Ages were created. At the court of the Duke of Burgundy this tradition was perpetuated. Because of political unrest in the Renaissance, tapestry weaving was moved to Brussels and Oudenarde in Flanders. Large workshops or ateliers supplied the princely and ducal palaces of Europe with the famous Flemish tapestries. The foremost artists of the day were commissioned to draw the cartoons. The weavers, in turn, succeeded marvelously in reproducing the Renaissance and baroque pictorial representations of large crowd scenes, in all their characteristic realism and energetic plasticity. These royal and princely ateliers were soon joined by smaller workshops, working in the same strongly illusionistic mode. Flemish weaving spread further to Holland, Germany, and Denmark.

Flemish weaving in Sweden
In 1515, some Flemish tapestries were mentioned in the inventory of a well-to-do Malmö home. In 1529, Flemish tapestry was listed in an inventory from Gripsholm Castle. And from the middle of the sixteenth century, the term

13. Table cover in *krabbasnår* and *halvkrabba*.
Linen and wool yarn. Vagnsbro, Västmanland.

14. Carriage cushion in *rölakan,* linen yarn warp and wool yarn weft. Färs, Skåne.

15. Coverlet in *rölakan.* Linen, wool, cotton, and hair yarn. Eringsboda, Blekinge.

16. Rug. Reversible diagonal *rölakan* without inter-looping, i.e., diagonal multiple-warp interlocked tapestry. Four-shaft chevron twill in wool, linen, cotton, and hair yarn. Woven 1850. Edebo, Uppland.

17. Hanging cloth in *krabbasnår* and *upphämta.* Pattern weft of linen and cotton yarn on linen tabby ground. Two of the Three Magi on horseback, Mary, and the Christchild. Nättraby, Blekinge. (See also fig. 236.)

18. Hanging cloth in *dukagång,* pattern weft of linen and cotton yarn. Blekinge.

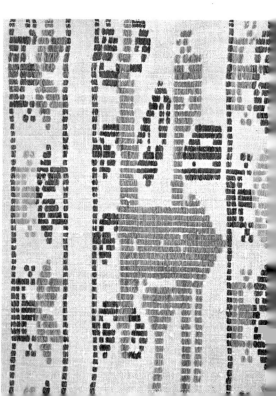

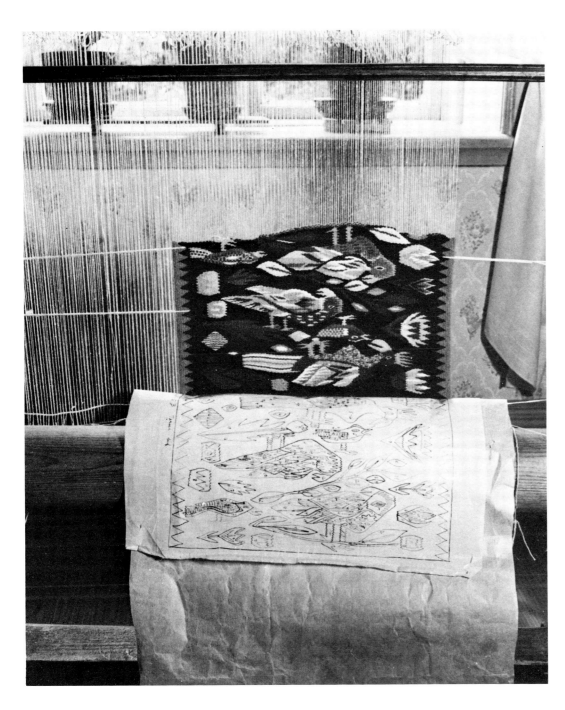

222. The pattern is fastened behind the warp, so that the work in progress can be easily checked against it. The weave is the same as that in fig. 221.

flamsk (Flemish), applied to various textiles, appears generally in royal and noble inventories. However, it is not known for a certainty whether all these textiles were indeed "Flemish" in the modern sense of the word, i.e., a type of tapestry. Some—or even all of them—may actually have been other kinds of fabrics imported from Flanders, hence "Flemish." Textiles were commonly named for their geographical origin at this time. In 1540, however, there was a weaver named Johan at Gripsholm Castle, who apparently was a Flemish tapestry weaver. To encourage tapestry weaving, King Gustav Vasa applied the same shrewd principles as in cloth manufacture. He requisitioned weavers from abroad —in this case, Flanders—partly to equip the royal residences with woven tapestries, partly to instruct and train Swedish weavers in the art of Flemish weaving. In 1544, the first Flemish weaver arrived. His name was Daniel van Santhro. He soon acquired a Swedish assistant, Nils Eskilsson, who later became the master of a tapestry workshop. During the reign of Gustav Vasa and his sons, fifty-three weavers—masters, journeymen, and apprentices—worked for the royal household. Most of them were foreigners, but, judging by their names, around twenty were Swedish. As in other crafts, journeymen stayed no more than two years with one master before they traveled on.

A certain decentralization of Flemish weaving and tapestry factories was already noticeable during the reign of Erik XIV, Gustav Vasa's eldest son. Karl XI, the youngest son, took an active interest in Flemish weaving and founded a workshop in Eskilstuna under the leadership of the Flemish weaver Jöran van der Heyde. Judging from the wealth of Flemish tapestries in noble castles and on estates, Flemish weavers must also have wandered from place to place, working to order for the noble households. These professional weavers undoubtedly helped spread the Flemish weaving technique to castles and manors, and from these, it spread further to parsonages and burgher homes. Karl XI's Queen, Ulrika Eleonora the Elder, founded an orphanage in 1688 at Karlsberg Castle in Stockholm, where girls

223. Wall hanging of Flemish weave from the sixteenth century. Linen warp and wool weft. When the hanging was discovered, it was serving as doormat in the bunkhouse on a Skåne estate.

224. Altar frontal of Flemish weave, detail. Linen warp and wool weft. Initials and date are woven in, MJS/SPD/A 1685. Probable origin, Skåne.

were instructed in Flemish weaving by three Finnish noblewomen. Characteristically, Flemish weaving developed from a male profession to a female home craft.

Judging from the frequency with which Flemish weaving was mentioned in ledgers and inventories, this type of patterned weave started to decline from the mid-seventeenth century. Bench runners, chair cushions, cushions, and wall hangings no longer occupied the same central position in interior decoration. It no longer paid to be a professional Flemish weaver, so Flemish weaving ceased to be a male profession and became a female avocation instead. However, in Stockholm, professional manufacture of wall hangings continued throughout the eighteenth century, in direct contact with contemporary French tapestry weaving. The tapestry production directed by the painter Pehr Hilleström during the latter part of the century had the same Continental ties. Apparently, this French-inspired manufacture had no influence on peasant tapestry weaving.

Patterns and production milieus
When Flemish weaving took the step from professional production to a handcraft practiced by women, the change of production milieu meant a continuous change in the design of the product. A craft provides its practitioners with technical training and access to patterns and models according to prevailing fashion. When the production is moved from a professional milieu, the organized supply of stylistic impulses is cut off.

In smaller workshops, the masters and journeymen had only their own sketches, collected during their years of study. At the stage when Flemish weaving moved from large ateliers to smaller workshops, a certain weeding out of patterns and motifs already had taken place, leaving only those within the capability of the less proficient weavers. Further weeding out occurred when Flemish weaving became a female home craft. Painterly aspects, perspective, and three-dimensionality disappeared from the scenes, whether landscapes or interiors. The difficulty of rendering human or

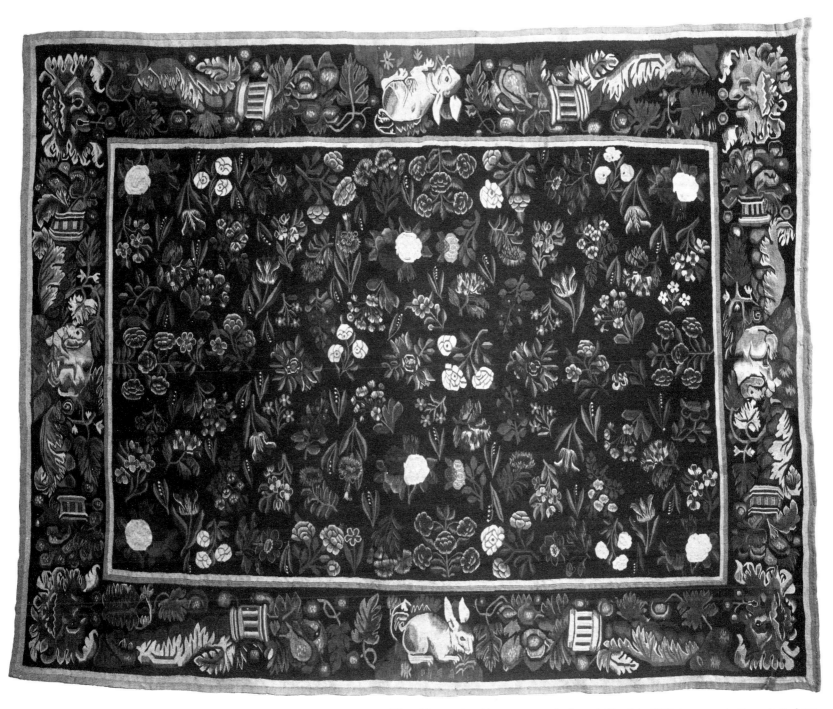

225. Table cover of Flemish weaving. Linen warp, weft of wool. The date, 1739, is woven in. Reportedly from Skåne.—This cover resembles in many ways a table cover from the Jönköping area in Småland, signed AF 1739.

Fabrics

animal forms made the female weavers avoid them. Instead, flowers and leaves took over, though no longer naturalistically rendered but more and more stylized and adapted to the now simplified technique. The careful shading which gave the objects plasticity in the workshop production disappeared in the peasant tapestries and was replaced by vertical lines (figs. 223, 226, 227).

Figure scenes were taken apart. The weavers would lift out single animals and figures and recombine them with flowers and leaves according to their own tastes (fig. 222). Hand-colored woodcuts of religius or patriotic motifs were at times used as patterns, as can be seen in one motif with a king on horseback and another with Gustaf III and his Queen, Sofia Magdalena. Embroidery samplers also served as a repository of motifs for Flemish weaving. Perhaps the women weavers had collected—as had Kerstina Jönsdotter during the second half of the nineteenth century—a store of isolated motifs drawn on paper, which could be combined in various ways. The original dramatic and story-telling representations were thus fragmented, their parts rearranged in completely different, more purely ornamental, composition schemes.

Table covers, bench runners, chair cushions, and cushions were generally decorated with a central scene, preferably with a scene from the Bible, surrounded by a lush wreath of flowers, leaves, fruits, birds, and quadrupeds. Especially popular motifs were Abraham's sacrifice of Isaac, Lot and his daughters, Samson and the lion, Solomon and the Queen of Sheba, the Annunciation (color fig. 19), the unicorn (fig. 224), the parrot (color fig. 21), flowers and birds (color fig. 22).

Skåne

In ledgers and protocols from Malmö around 1600, Ernst Fischer has found mention of women working as weavers in private households. Like seamstresses, they lived in their employer's home until the order was completed.

In Malmö, tapestries were used in interior decoration in affluent circles as late as the

226. Flemish weave, detail. Linen warp, wool weft. Initials and date woven in, A.P.A.W: MDD.S: ANNO : 1685 (not visible in picture). Stora Tuna, Dalarna.

227. Cushion or seat pad, detail. Flemish weave with linen warp and wool weft. Torna, Skåne.

seventeenth century and part of the eighteenth century. When this market disappeared around the middle of the eighteenth century, the weavers turned to more conservative peasant homes. They probably traveled from place to place with their pattern collections, which they had accumulated during the earlier years. From 1750 onward, Flemish weaving and upright looms became more and more common on Skåne farms. From this time, the technique, now a female handcraft, spread throughout rural Skåne. The oldest cushions in Flemish weave from this milieu date to 1750. Some of the about 700 preserved Flemish-weave tapestries from Skåne are signed and dated. Thus, it has been possible to distinguish two main regions with some distinctive traits. One of these two includes primarily Bara and Torna districts near Lund, the other the plains districts south of Malmö. The latter enjoyed a peak period of productivity in the middle of the eighteenth century, the former toward the close of the century.

The rest of Sweden
Although Flemish weaving as a Swedish folk art was nowhere so developed as in Skåne, it did flourish also in Småland parsonages (fig. 225). A group of tapestries were made by one Kristina Hellman, born in 1760 and married in 1796 to Johannes Haberg, vicar in Unnaryd parish, Västbo district. It is possible that her skill was learned in Skåne, as her father for a time was vicar in Kristianstad. Her three daughters, in turn, were all weavers. In Villstad parish, in the same district, women of the Krook family of clergymen were active weavers during the first part of the eighteenth century. Three Krook daughters married into peasant families and undoubtedly helped to bring Flemish weaving to peasant milieu. Some Flemish textiles attributed to parsonages feature

228. Table cover of Flemish weave. Linen warp and wool weft. Since the early nineteenth century at Berg, Moheda, Småland.

229. Bench runner of Flemish weave. Linen warp and wool weft. Långaryd, Småland.

230. Bench runner of Flemish weave. Linen warp, weft of wool. Woven-in cartouche with initials and date, LIS/AOD/MLD/1664. Mark district, Västergötland.

231. Wall hanging in soumak. Linen warp, ground weft and pattern weft of wool. Skog Church, Hälsingland, dated to about A.D. 1050–1200.

flowers, leaves, birds, and borders with flower and plant ornaments, all very skillfully drawn and resembling those on Dutch table covers. Some of these textiles may actually have been professional workshop products. For the rest, parsonage milieu in Småland mainly produced chair seat cushions with forest scenes and running stags. In peasant milieu, the same motifs were used—running stag, flowers and leaves, flower urn, and flowers and birds— though in a highly stylized form (figs. 228, 229).

From workshops in adjacent parts of Väster-götland and Halland, there are examples of Flemish weaving dating to the latter part of the seventeenth century, with birds among flowers (fig. 230), the Lamb with the banner of the cross in a circular frame with floral wreath, and, from the eighteenth century, a running stag of the same type as in Småland (color fig. 23).

From Västergötland comes a cushion from 1664 (fig. 230). It was probably a product of the professional weaving workshop in the neighborhood of Torpa Castle, family seat of the Stenbock family. In the seventeenth century, the Stenbocks commissioned a set of tapestries which still exist. These tapestries show a fairly direct influence from the royal ateliers of the Vasa era. (Gustaf Olofsson Stenbock of Torpa was related by marriage to Gustav Vasa.) For the rest, there are eighteenth-century cushions with a running stag within a laurel wreath, stylized flowers and leaves, and cushion covers with a bird among stylized flowers. They strongly resemble the Småland tapestries.

Gotland's widely branched-out trade connections with Denmark and northern Germany apparently stimulated an extensive Flemish weaving activity. A number of cushions from the middle and latter part of the seventeenth century hark back to patterns once common in these areas. They were apparently professionally woven. From the eighteenth century, there are Flemish-weave tapestries characterized by simplified, stylized patterns, much like those on the mainland.

Archival sources reveal that Flemish weaving was common on Öland in parsonages and on larger farms in the seventeenth century,

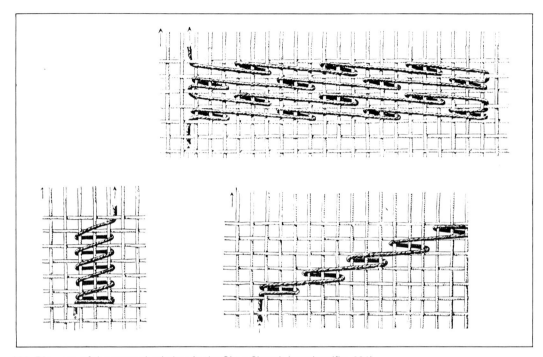

232. Diagram of the soumak stitches in the Skog Church hanging (fig. 231).

but whether the tapestries were imported or executed locally is not known.

In Blekinge, some Flemish tapestries have also been found, but they are probably of Skåne origin.

In Östergötland, a few such textiles exist, probably brought from Småland.

In central Sweden and Norrland, there are some Flemish tapestries from the eighteenth century. Their somewhat atypical patterns make it difficult to place them in any specific production milieu. It is not known whether their present location was also their place of origin.

Soumak

Soumak weaving is a technique which is used, like Flemish weaving, to create patterns in free forms, especially for figural representation. The technique is represented in Sweden by only a couple of examples, which, however, are of

special interest because of their age and their ties to prehistoric pictorial tapestries. The two examples are the famous hangings from Skog and Överhogdal churches in Jämtland (fig. 231).

The hanging from Skog extends 175 centimeters horizontally and 37 centimeters vertically (approximately 69 inches by 14 1/2 inches). It was originally longer. It is executed in soumak with an inlay of wool yarn on a ground of linen tabby. The hanging from Överhogdal consists of five pieces sewn together. Numbers 1 and 2 combine to form a complete hanging. Number 3 is part of another hanging, and number 4 is a hanging in double weave. Numbers 1–3 are executed in soumak with wool yarn on linen ground. The wrapping of the warp threads is done simultaneously with the weaving of the tabby ground and in the same shed, giving an effect resembling a stem stitch. The technique allows for free pattern design. It is similar to the

233. (a) Strip in soumak. Linen warp, ground weft and pattern weft of wool. Signed SIS 1850. Ingelstad, Skåne.
(b) Strip in double weave. Linen warps and woolen wefts. Revsund Church, Jämtland, medieval origin.

oriental soumak technique. Similar techniques were known also in Egypt from around 1000 B.C to around A.D. 1000.

The pictorial representation in the Skog hanging (fig. 231) consists of a crowd of animal figures, horsemen, standing human figures, and a cross section of a church with steeple. Generally, this representation has been interpreted as depicting the struggle between paganism and Christianity. It is dated to some time between A.D. 1050 and 1200. The hanging from Överhogdal, of roughly the same date, shows a more organized profusion of stylized animal figures, trees, ships, and horsemen. In both hangings, the content or subject matter of the representation is subordinated to purely ornamental interests.

Related to these two hangings is also a narrow strip in soumak from Dal Church in Ångermanland (fig. 233 a). It probably dates to the same era as the other two.

Technically, there is some correspondence between these three hangings and the pictorial hangings of the Oseberg textile collection in Norway. The latter hangings are executed in finer materials—colored wool yarns—in more varying stitches on a ground of linen tabby. But stylistically, and in overall composition, there are parallels between the medieval Jämtland soumak hangings and the Oseberg hangings, although the latter are superior in technique and design.

Brocaded tabby weaves, types "krabbasnår" and "halvkrabba"

Krabbasnår (figs. 234–39) is a dialectal term from Skåne for a brocaded tabby with the pattern weft floating across the whole pattern motif, tied down along its outline by the ground weft picks, one or several, which are shuttled in between the inlays.

In northern Sweden and some parts of central Sweden—Västergötland and northwestern Småland and, to some extent, Bohuslän and Halland—the same technique is known as *inplock* or *inplockning* (inlay, inlaying). Though technically identical, the weaves associated with these respective terms have different and distinct ornamentation. In both cases, the pat-

234. Characteristic motifs and patterns in *krabbasnår:* (1) Dentiled heart. (2) Heart rosette with diagonal cross. (3) Dentiled diamond. (4) Diagonal cross with inscribed hooks. (5) Double hooks. (6) Diagonal crosses and diamonds in diagonal latticework. (7) Bands made up of triangles, diamonds, and squares, found in coverlets with black ground.

235. Coverlet in *krabbasnår.* Ground weave of linen, pattern weft of wool. The border is partly in *upphämta.* Blekinge.

tern is created without technical aids on a tabby ground, often a weft-ribbed tabby. In the southern type, *krabbasnår,* the pattern weft almost completely covers the ground; in the northern type the pattern weft is comparatively thinly laid in. One variation of *krabbasnår* is *halvkrabba.* Whereas the pattern units in *krabbasnår* are diagonal in nature, the pattern units in *halvkrabba* (fig. 237) are small squares combined in a checkerboard pattern. The latter is usually found in combination with other techniques, used especially in coverlets, bench runners, and bed curtains. It is found in Skåne, Blekinge, Halland, Småland, Öland, and Västmanland.

The most ancient pattern types in *krabbasnår* are based on lozenges and diagonal lines, forming dentiled hearts, heart rosettes, dentiled diamonds, St. Andrew's crosses, stars, hooks, and zigzag patterns (fig. 235). The pattern areas stand out in relief above the ground, practically covering it. Highly stylized animal figures often form a border. This type of pattern is used for coverlets, cushions, bench

236. Hanging cloth in *krabbasnår.* Linen ground, pattern weft of cotton and linen. The horsemen on the cover of the book are taken from the center of this hanging, showing Mary and the Christchild with the Three Magi. Woven in are the words "Deta är de wise mennerna" (These are the [three] wise men) and the date, 1827. Nättraby, Blekinge. (See also color figure 17.)

237. Coverlet in *krabbasnår* and *halvkrabba*. Ground of linen warp and wool weft, pattern weft of wool. Augerum, Blekinge.

238. Coverlet, single width. *Krabbasnår* technique with ground of linen warp and wool weft, pattern weft of wool. Möklinta, Västmanland. Privately owned.

19. Chair cushion in Flemish weave, linen warp and wool weft. The Annunciation with Mary, the Angel, and, above them, the Holy Ghost in the shape of a dove. Marked IMS in cross-stitch. Brågarp, Bara, Skåne.

20. Altar frontal of Flemish weave. Linen warp, weft of wool yarn. The date, 1685, is woven in. Stora Tuna, Dalarna.

21. Bench cover in Flemish weaving. Linen warp, weft of fine plied wool yarn and white linen yarn. Skåne.

22. Flemish tapestry, linen warp and wool weft. Woven-in initials and date, PP HPD 1793. Skåne.

23. Chair cushion of Flemish weave, linen warp and weft of wool and linen. Källsjö, Halland.

24. Carriage cushion in Flemish weave. Linen warp, weft of wool and some silk. Woven-in initials and date, MOD 1750. The design features a stag within two floral wreaths; one is seen here. Höganäs, Skåne.

239. Coverlet. Linen warp with weft of colored rags, pattern weft of inserted wool and cotton yarn ends. Delsbo, Hälsingland.

runners, and, in combination with other weaving techniques, for wall hangings and hanging cloths and for cushion linings. It is found in Skåne, Blekinge, southern Småland, southern Halland, and on Öland.

In northern and central Sweden, the *inplock* was also used for coverlets. They are woven with wool or cow-hair yarn weft on a ribbed ground, or the same weft on white linen or hemp ground. Often, they have black ground and pattern weft in pastels (fig. 238; color fig. 13). They seem to have been a trade item, distributed by Västergötland salesmen. However, the technique and the patterns—sparse vertical ornaments, hourglasses, squares, and grain spikes—were taken up in various localities and given distinct local forms. Thus, there are distinguishable types from Västmanland, especially Västerfärnebo, from Floda, Dalarna, from Delsbo and Hälsingland, and from Ångermanland. The Floda type has a more robust and lush character and takes up motifs from embroidery and band weaving. The Floda coverlets were made for sale. Rag coverlets with inlaid pattern, woven in Gästrikland, Hälsingland, and a few parishes in Dalarna, also belong to this group. Rag weaving also occurred in northern Småland.

The inlay technique has been documented in the archaeological sites of Valsgärde and Birka. Inlay patterns of the southern type have a simple and timeless character conditioned by the technique itself, and are found in primitive patterns from all over the world.

Dukagång

Dukagång (swivel weave) is originally a Skåne dialectal term which has gained general acceptance through the efforts of the Handcraft Movement (figs. 240–45; color figs. 17, 18). The technique is on the whole found only in southern Sweden, with Skåne as its center. It has been executed in colored wool on wool ground or in linen on linen, in the latter cases usually in combination with *rölakan* and *krabbasnår*. The pattern is created by pattern-weft floats which are tied down at regular intervals and always by the same warp ends. This

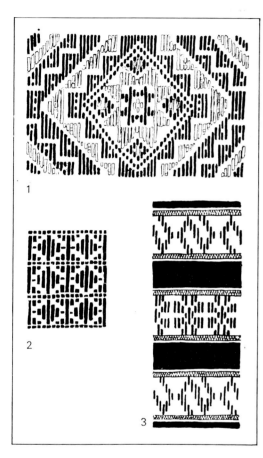

240. Characteristic patterns and motifs in *dukagång* (swivel weave): (1) Eight-pointed star in notched diamond. (2) Diamonds in rectangles. (3) Transverse borders with eight-pointed stars and double hooks (reverse S-shapes).

makes the patterned areas look as if they were composed of vertical stripes.

White linen wall hangings in *dukagång* with pattern in dark blue, red, and green occur only in eastern Skåne, the home of Sweden's largest and most magnificent peasant textiles (fig. 119). In many respects, *dukagång* used motifs similar to those in *rölakan* tapestries from the same region. Obvious comparisons are afforded by stylized animal figures—the lion, the double-headed eagle, the stag, the peacock, and tree with bird—in octagonal frames. Here, too, the models are to be found in the medieval motifs

241. Wall hanging in *dukagång*. Linen ground with pattern weft of wool yarn in dark blue, green, and two shades of red. Two widths with lion motif, joined across the middle with a seam. Marked END 1806 in cross-stitch. Skåne.

242. Wall hanging in *dukagång* (another section of hanging in fig. 241). Here the motif is castle, bordered by horsemen.

of stylized animal figures in round medallions. The *dukagång* hangings also used ships, horsemen, and palace architecture as striking pattern motifs. These motifs, however, were probably modeled on sixteenth- and seventeenth-century Dutch damask.

The way in which these patterns were transmitted is not known in detail, though it may be presumed that it happened via workshop production, in which the original model had already been simplified.

Medieval weaves in *dukagång* are preserved in the Birgittine Convent of Nådendal in Finland. Also of medieval origin is a small linen cloth from Bergshamra in Södermanland. These all help bridge the gap between the earliest known examples of *dukagång* in the Birka finds from the ninth and tenth centuries, and the later peasant works, the earliest dated

1734, and the majority made in the first half of the nineteenth century.

Dukagång occurs in southwestern Skåne in combination with *rölakan, upphämta,* and *krabbasnår* of wool, usually in coverlets, patterned with transverse bands of birds or trees or eight-pointed stars (fig. 243). In southeastern and northeastern Skåne, *dukagång* has been used only for bench runners and coverlets and as lining for cushions. Coverlets of white ribbed linen with bands in *dukagång* and *krabbasnår* also exist in this region. The striped cushion linings occur also in northern Skåne, southern Halland, southern Småland, and western Blekinge.

Simpler pattern forms, checks and lozenges, are more widely used as border patterns in all of Skåne, Blekinge, and Småland. In isolated cases, they are found as far north as Gästrik-

243. Bench runner in *dukagång.* Pattern weft of wool yarn in several colors on wool ground. The narrow bands between the pattern areas are woven in *upphämta.* Southeastern Skåne.

171

244. Detail of wall hanging in *dukagång* and *halvkrabba*. Blue wool pattern weft on linen ground. Skåne.

245. Hanging cloth in *dukagång*. Pattern weft of blue and light red linen and cotton yarn on linen ground. Blekinge.

land, Härjedalen, and Jämtland, in boldly patterned, coarse coverlets with black hair yarn ground (fig. 234: 7). They apparently belong to the commercial production distributed to central and northern Sweden by Västergötland salesmen. In Visseltofta, in Västra Göinge, Skåne, such coverlets were still being woven by a local woman in the 1920s and '30s.

Pile fabrics

Flossa is a southern Swedish dialectal term, originally meaning "fringe" or "loosely hanging threads" on a fabric. Today, the word is used to designate pile on fabrics, whether accomplished by teaseling—e.g., of wadmal—or by raising loops of warp or weft yarn above the surface of the fabric, as in terry cloth and velvet (warp loops) or bouclé (weft loops). The velvet can be cut or uncut, i.e., the loops can be cut or uncut (looped pile). Finally, pile can be formed by knotting the pile yarn into the warp while weaving. This can be done by alternately looping a continuous pile yarn over a flat wooden rod and knotting it around the warp threads. The rod is removed, and the resulting loops are then cut. The pile can also be knotted in by hand: one by one, measured and precut pile strands are knotted around two or more warp threads. Another type of weft-faced pile weave is chenille weave, made by using strips of ready-made pile, chenille, as weft.

Of the above-mentioned pile fabrics, those with raised nap, those with looped weft pile (bouclé), and those with knotted pile have existed as handcraft in Sweden.

There are two types of knotted pile weave: one, in which the knotted pile completely covers the ground (*helflossa*) (figs. 246, 249), one woven with areas of the flat background showing between the knotted pile (*halvflossa*) (fig. 257, color fig. 25). A variant of the latter is the Skåne *trensaflossa* (color fig. 30). *Helflossa* and *halvflossa* will be dealt with together, whereas bouclé will be discussed separately.

Knotted pile has been used, completely or partially covering the woven ground, partly for coverlets and rugs, partly for cushions and chair seat covers. The knotted pile rugs, ryas, and coverlets constitute, without comparison,

the largest and most important group. By its association with the bed, the rya has an ancient tradition. The use of knotted pile for seat pads and chair seat covering is, however, a considerably more recent phenomenon because of its connection with the chair, a relatively late addition to the gallery of interior furnishings.

Ryas (knotted pile rugs)

The word *rya* is related to words such as *ragg* (goat hair; shag), the English "rug," and the German *Rühe* (fur), indicating a very great age for both the word and the concept. In Blekinge, the rya is known by the name *kavring,* a southern Swedish dialectal word meaning coverlet (compare the English "covering").

As an object, the rya is nowadays used in interior decoration as floor covering or wall hanging with a purely decorative function. It is found throughout all strata of society and lacks local ties. One hundred or a hundred and fifty years ago, however, the situation was apparently completely different. As mentioned above, the rya was then a coverlet, part of the bedding. In some parts of the country it had a practical, warming function, in the coastal regions also being part of the personal equipment at sea. The rya was used with the pile or loop side facing down, for warmth. The pile side was, thus, the bottom or reverse side, while the plain side was the top or right side. To avoid confusion, the two sides will, in the following, be referred to respectively as, the pile side or pile face, and the ground side. In ryas used as warming covers, the ground side was, in other words, intended for view (fig. 250), and received all decoration. The generally accepted term for this type of rya is *slitrya* (literally, "wear-rya"), practical or functional rya. This is to distinguish it from the other type of rya, the decorative **rya** coverlet, appearing at the end of the seventeenth century as a purely decorative bed covering. In this latter type, the pile face became the show side, receiving all decoration.

Preserved ryas

The woven ground of a rya can be made of linen, hemp, wool, cotton, cow hair, or a mix-

172

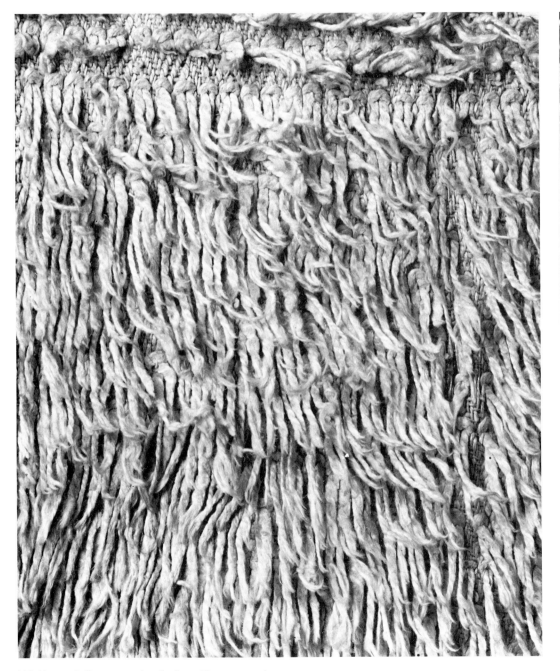

246. Knotted pile weave, detail of rya. Linen ground of 2/2 twill with pile of coarse wool yarn. Uppland. Privately owned.

247. Knotted pile weave, detail of ground side of a rya. The rows of knots are visible on the ground side, though flush with the surface of the ground weave. Bollnäs, Hälsingland.

ture of these materials. The pile is of the same type of yarn, or of rags, rabbit fur, foal hair, dog hair, or goat hair. The ground has been made in three different ways. The first type is found only on Öland, and is a narrowly striped weft-faced fabric with the pile knots visible on the ground side in strong relief. The second type, characteristic of Uppland, is a diagonal or goose-eye (lozenge) linen twill with the pile knots invisible on the ground side, and the pattern in colored stripes or checks (color fig. 27). The third type, occurring in other parts of the country, is made of the same materials mentioned above, in ribbed tabby. The knots are visible on the ground side though flush with the woven surface (fig. 247). In the first and third types, the knots partake of the design on the ground side, where they form lines, latticework, or figures. This is the case especially with the practical ryas, where the ground side is the displayed side. The woven ground can have a colored pattern made with two shuttles. This occurs in central and western Småland, in Ydre district in Östergötland, and in Närke. Rosepath patterns occur in ryas from northern Småland and Ydre. In Bohuslän, the ground has been woven in a ribbed binding, in twill, or in rosepath (fig. 257; color fig. 29).

The pile is made with a yarn that may be loosely spun or tightly twisted. The pile is knotted with a Smyrna or Ghiordes knot around two or more warp threads (fig. 248: 2). This knot has been used in all the Nordic countries and in rugs from Turkey and the Caucasus. The connection between the Asian and the Nordic pile knotting has not been explored.

The knotted-in tuft or loop of yarn is called *nocka*, in Skåne *noppa*. These tufts can be made either with premeasured strands of yarn or by knotting a continuous length of yarn over a rod, removing the rod, and cutting the loops. The loops in Swedish pile weaves are generally cut, though there are a few ryas from Blekinge and Småland with uncut pile, i.e., pile consisting of loops (color fig. 26). They are made of coarse cow hair and wool and knotted in a particular way. Some show similarities to Late Antique pile weaves from Egypt (A.D. 200–700). Certain other knotting variations occur, e.g., in one group of Bohuslän pile covers,

the knot is made with a looped pile strand, so that one "end" of the knot is a loop and the other "end" consists of two cut yarn ends.

As a rule, the pile is knotted on one side of the rya, but ryas with double pile, i.e., pile on both sides, do occur in Uppland and on Åland (fig. 254). Knotting with precut pile strands has been most common in these areas. In knotting a pile that is short and made of the outer hair of the sheep, the twist and ply of the yarn are easily lost. In such ryas, the pile has of necessity been formed over a rod and then cut open. Short, glossy, hairlike pile is characteristic especially of decorative coverlets (color fig. 28).

In Uppland (color fig. 27), Gästrikland, and to some extent in Småland and Blekinge, the pile was made of cut strips of rags and yarn waste. Linen and hemp were used for pile effects in Uppland, Småland, and Blekinge. In Bohuslän, cotton served the same purpose—quite naturally, in view of the importance of imported cotton in western Sweden.

The pile tufts may lie either closely together, evenly distributed over the surface, or in widely spaced rows, or in patterns partly revealing the woven ground. The latter is the case with ryas from central Sweden with patterned ground (see above), and the Norrland coverlets with pile of wool yarn in various colors, linen yarn, or cut rags (fig. 239).

Pattern and design
The knotted pile rugs or covers measure, as a rule, about five to seven feet by four to five feet. In exceptional cases they may be larger or smaller. Most practical ryas are woven in two lengths, while the decorative ryas are woven in one. This circumstance strengthens the impression that the decorative rya originated in a production milieu different from that of the practical rya. The decorative rya is also different with regard to patterns, and will therefore be dealt with separately.

The practical rya
Generally, one of the short ends of the practical rya, the head end, is marked with a border (figs. 249–51, 259). This border may consist of horizontal or vertical zigzag bands,

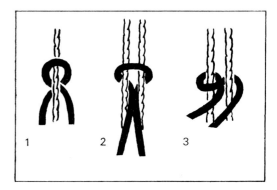

248. Pile weave knots: (1) Knot around one warp end, so-called Spanish knot. (2) Ghiordes knot, also known as Turkish knot or Smyrna knot. (3) Sehna knot or Persian knot.

checks, stars, crosses, diamonds, and chevrons. In addition, there may be—especially on the Öland ryas—initials or monograms and dates, framed or unframed, crowns, marks of ownership, or ornaments resembling coats of arms (fig. 249). Judging from descriptions in castle inventories from the Vasa era, these Öland ryas seem to echo earlier, more carefully executed practical ryas from upper-class milieu. Some practical ryas from Uppland have finer wool in the head-end border, which gives an insight into the use of the rya on the bed. Apparently, the head end was turned down, so that the border with its pattern of finer wool was seen. The decorated head end lived on even after another way of making the bed had become the custom, i.e., spreading the rya in its entire length on top of the bed, without turning down the head end. Practical ryas which lack any trace of marking on the head end are, as a rule, of a more recent type or have come from regions influenced by the decorative rya.

The border along the head end can be combined with a border along the two long sides and on the opposite short end, the latter ones quite different from the head border. Some practical ryas have a central panel and frame with lozenges or squares, stars, triangles, diamonds, Greek crosses, trees in a square, or simply a plain panel in contrasting color. The

249. Rya, knotted pile weave. Ground of linen *tvist,* extended tabby, knotted pile of wool yarn. The initials KPDL and the year 1864 are knotted in, to be read on the ground side. Note the center seam. Föra, Öland.

175

custom of marking the head end with a decorative border is, not surprisingly, found in those regions where the rya longest retained its original function.

The practical rya with the knots visible on the ground side has used the knots to decorative advantage. Since the ground side was also the show side, this practice was only natural. The decorative value of the knots was most consciously explored in Blekinge, on Öland, in Småland, and, to some extent, in Södermanland and Närke.

The decorative rya

The function of the decorative rya as an exclusively ornamental bedspread has helped determine its special overall design and patterns. The marking of the head end is gone. Overall designs treat the entire rya as one decorative surface. The rya is woven in one piece to avoid a center seam and the resulting difficulties in matching two separately woven halves (figs. 252–56). Unless woven by a master craftsman, these usually would not quite match (figs. 257, 258).

When one length is woven, the surface can more easily be treated as one centrally organized composition. In most cases, the pattern consists of a central panel with surrounding border. If there is no border, the surface is nevertheless tightly held together by a dominant central motif.

Decisive for the form and design of the decorative rya was the period in which it appeared. The predominant styles at the end of the seventeenth century and the beginning of the eighteenth century were the baroque and the Régence (the late baroque), corresponding to William and Mary and Queen Anne in English and American interior decoration. Patterned velvet, plush, shag, and the shaglike *trip* figured prominently in interior decoration of the time. Large amounts of these fabrics

250. Rya, ground side, knotted pile weave. Ground of linen *tvist* (extended tabby), knotted pile of wool yarn. The initials LOS/LPD and the date, ANO 1796, in cartouches, to be read on the ground side. Repplinge, Öland.

251. Rya, knotted pile weave. Ground of linen *tvist* (extended tabby), knotted pile of wool yarn. Decorated with the initials POD and the year 1808 in frames, to be read on the pile side. Föra, Öland.

252. Decorative rya, knotted pile weave. Ribbed ground fabric of linen, wool, and hair yarn, with knotted pile of wool yarn. Woven in one piece. Småland?

253. Decorative rya, knotted pile weave. Knotted wool pile on tabby ground of linen or hemp and wool. The ground side is quilted. Originally owned by the vicar Haqvin Bergenhem, Dalby, Värmland, who died in 1744.

were imported from Holland and England. As mentioned above, a Scotsman founded a factory in Sweden for the manufacture of, among other things, shags. England made a pile fabric modeled on oriental rugs. These rugs had figured in European (and Swedish) furnishings since the fifteenth and sixteenth centuries, used as floor and table coverings. The English pile fabric was called "turkey work," Turkish cloth, and was exported also to Sweden for use, above all, on chair seats and chair cushions.

Here, the rich oriental floral ornament merged, as in practically all textiles of the time, with the abstract western European escutcheon and band ornament of the Renaissance, the baroque, and the late baroque. Within the strict compositional schemes of these styles, the naturalistic flora of the Orient is "smartened up" and forced to fall into well-drilled formations towards the center (figs. 252–56). In the center, there is a flower in an urn, a tree, a cartouche, a bouquet of flowers,

or a candelabrum, surrounded by corner ornaments and a border with stylized flowers and leaves or geometric shapes: chevrons, crosses, checks, diamonds, or squares. It is highly probable that the patterns of the decorative rya covers were influenced by the padded and quilted coverlets in silk, cotton, and linen, with woven or embroidered decoration, which played such an important role in late seventeenth-century interior decoration with its ornate, prominently displayed, parade beds.

254. Rya, knotted pile weave with double pile. Ground of linen and wool tabby. The picture shows the underside with pile of white wool yarn. Woven in one piece. Reportedly of Swedish origin, though acquired in Finland.

255. The other side—the show side—of the rya in fig. 254. Knotted pile of wool. Woven-in date, 1778.

Aside from the general dependence of the decorative rya on the prevailing styles for pattern composition and motifs, there was one other source of inspiration for rya design. This rich and apparently frequently used source was the embroidery sampler. A large number of decorative ryas resemble samplers so much that they are actually called "sampler ryas." A large number of lettering and pattern samplers dating from the beginning of the eighteenth century on have been preserved in

Sweden. They supplied many of the motifs in the rya covers, e.g., the flower in urn, the floral wreath, the tree flanked by symmetrical birds, the running stag, and the reclining deer. Other frequently borrowed popular motifs were the patterned backgrounds with fish-scale pattern, braided bands, checks, diamonds, thunderbolts, checkerboard squares, etc. (figs. 311, 312). In many ryas there is a central panel in checkerboard pattern, surrounded by a framework of flowers and leaves.

The history of the knotted pile technique
Pile fragments have been recovered from Danish Bronze Age finds from around 1500 B.C., on one cloak and two woven caps. The pile on these garments is, however, sewn on, not knotted into the ground fabric. The idea seems to have been to make the garments warmer and, no doubt, also more striking. No weaves with knotted-in pile from that time are known in Scandinavia. The earliest knotted pile fabric, found in a grave at Valsgärde,

Fabrics

dates to around A.D. 750. Whether it was indigenous or imported is not known. There is one fragment from Birka, which may be of a pile fabric. The earliest definite proof that pile fabrics were made in Sweden dates from the Middle Ages. The first recorded rya is listed in an inventory from 1444 of the Archbishop's seat on the island of Arnö, Uppland.

In Vadstena Convent, pile covers were used as bedding in the fifteenth century, and in the sixteenth century a great number of pile bedcovers were listed in royal castles and on noble estates. For example, the 1554 inventory from Kägleholm Castle, Närke, lists forty-four ryas, most of them white, black, and gray, six with colored pile, and two white ones with red stripes. Gustav Vasa had pile rugs and covers made to order on Öland. In 1524 he granted the Öland farmers the right to export such covers to Germany. Up to 1816, a rya was part of the standard equipment of each enlisted man in the Royal Navy.

The practical rya disappears and the decorative rya arrives

In inventories from burgher homes during the seventeenth century, practical ryas were still listed, but after that time they occurred less frequently. This development began earlier among the upper classes. Geographically, the distribution area of the practical rya in peasant milieu was also shrinking. In Skåne, the practical rya disappeared during the course of the seventeenth century; on Gotland, during the eighteenth century. It was replaced by feather bolsters and quilted coverlets, as had happened in Denmark somewhat earlier. The development of the decorative rya was, thus, prepared for. From around 1700, ryas began to appear in middle-class home inventories, but now in the form of parade bed covers, decorative knotted pile spreads.

The manufacture and marketing of ryas

As mentioned above, the Öland ryas had a large market within the country and were even made for export. It is also known that ryas belonged to the merchandise of the Västergöt-land peddlers. Practical ryas were made in the production sphere of the Västergötland trade, i.e., Gotland, Öland, Småland, Halland, and the "Seven Hundreds." The ryas were spread as trade items. This circumstance is supported by the fact that it was precisely in the areas serviced by the Västergötland peddlers that the term "Västergötland rya" occurred in inventories. As early as 1622–23, pile rugs were listed in customs ledgers of goods brought into the cities from the countryside. In the seventeenth century, there were also records of export to Norway. From the eighteenth century, some such pile rugs and covers are preserved. A clear indication that they were a staple is the fact that they were part of the Västergötland peddlers' assortment. These pile covers apparently had a simple repeating pattern in several colors, possibly a regular zigzag pattern. One may suppose that these covers, like other trade items, went to the towns in the Mälaren valley and in central Sweden's mining region. From there, they would be distributed to more peripheral regions, i.e., to Värmland and Uppland, and also Gästrikland, Hälsingland, and other Norrland provinces. In these provinces the decorative rya appeared around the middle of the eighteenth century. To start with, it was offered for sale by Västergötland salesmen at fairs and town markets. Later, it was imitated by the local women. Whereas the rya disappeared in Värmland, other provinces—Gästrikland, Hälsingland, and the other Norrland provinces—created their own production with local, distinctive traits. Thus, the decorative rya took root in Norrland although the practical rya had never managed to replace the fell in these regions, the fell being especially suited to the climate. The decorative rya, with its ornamental and prestigious function, was taken up by the Norrland farmers who had grown affluent through linen production and, later, forest industries. To begin with, the decorative rya appeared in inventories from homes of simpler burghers, ironmakers, artisans, soldiers, workers, and other mobile rural groups, more often than in farm home inventories. The decorative rya was transmitted from the original social milieu—urban homes and manors in southern Sweden—to a rural milieu in various ways: by

256. Decorative rya, knotted pile weave. Knotted pile of wool yarn on ribbed linen ground. The rya is woven in one piece, reportedly by Anna Katharina Arvidsson of Källehult, after a model from Sandvik, Småland, where she had served in the early 19th century. Privately owned.

25. Coverlet of knotted pile weave, detail. Ground of linen or hemp warp and hair yarn weft. The knotted pile of plied wool yarn forms a checkerboard pattern; the ground side of the coverlet shows the transverse stripes of the ground. Åsenhöga, Småland. (See fig. 257 for a full view of the coverlet.)

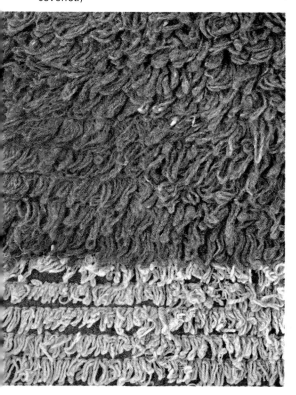

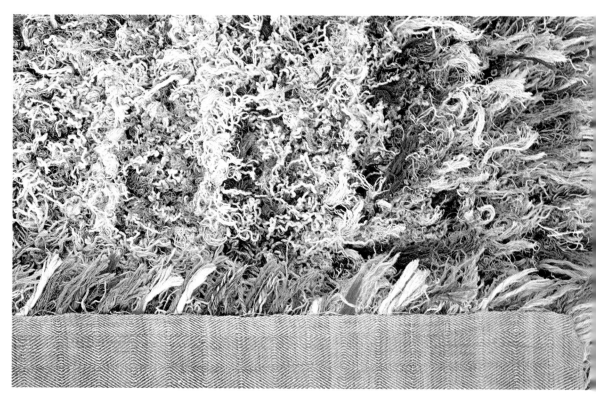

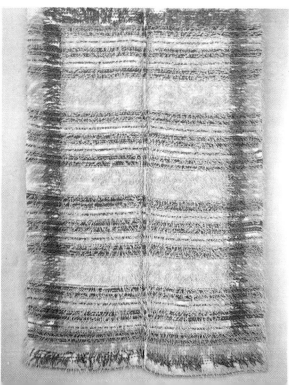

26. Coverlet of knotted pile weave, detail. Ground of linen or hemp warp and hair yarn weft. The knotted wool pile consists of uncut loops. Mjällby, Blekinge.

27. Coverlet of knotted pile weave. Ground of linen in "goose eye" or lozenge twill diaper, knotted pile of linen, wool, and cotton. Riala, Uppland.

28. Decorative rya, knotted pile weave. Ground warp of hemp, short knotted pile of glossy wool. Woven in one piece, with initials and date KPD AED 1803. Ådalsliden, Ångermanland.

29. Coverlet in knotted pile weave. Ground of hemp or linen warp and hair yarn weft. Long, sparsely knotted pile of plied wool yarn shimmers above the striped ground. Lidhult, Småland.

257. Rya, knotted pile weave. Sparsely knotted wool pile on striped ground weave of linen and hair yarn. Åsenhöga, Småland. (See also color figure 25.)

258. Rya, sparsely knotted pile weave. Pile of wool yarn on a ground of linen warp and mixed cow hair and wool weft. By, Dalarna.

estate auctions, by inheritance, by gift, sale, and as commissioned orders. There is concrete evidence that some clergymen's daughters wove bridal ryas to order for three well-to-do farmer's daughters from around Bollnäs, Hälsingland; also that ryas woven in parsonages or burgher homes entered peasant milieu in trousseaus. In Uppland there were female rya weavers who went from household to household, weaving whatever ryas were needed. In Vaksala and Bälinge districts, three weavers were active around the mid-1800s: Lisa Sköld, Lina Kindblom, and Lisa Persson. In Rengsjö, Hälsingland, around the middle of the eighteenth century, there was a clergyman's daughter weaving rug spreads to order, and toward the end of the eighteenth century, there was one Maria Åquist working in Luleå, Norrbotten.

The central region for the decorative rya in peasant milieu comprises the southern Norrland provinces, Uppland, and Bergslagen, and extends through part of Uppland and Bergslagen south into the Götaland provinces.

Bohuslän ryas

Bohuslän occupies a special position by virtue of its rich and varied knotted pile weaving. The province exhibits special pattern types and technical oddities, such as a looped-over pile strand. Practical ryas, solid gray or checked, were in use in the coastal districts until the end of the nineteenth century. Farther inland, where there was a tradition of professional rya weaving, the decorative rya could be found. The professional weavers were usually women, though one man, Börje i Björkebacka, born in 1786, is known to have woven ryas and pick-up double cloth. The Bohuslän rya derives its special character also from the prevalence of cotton pile instead of wool. Furthermore, the patterns point to a contact with sources of inspiration not available to other Swedish provinces. A few of the Bohuslän ryas used motifs offered by pattern books and samplers, but the majority apparently received impulses from oriental rugs (fig. 261). This suggestion is not as farfetched as it might seem. The near-by city of Göteborg was a major Swedish port

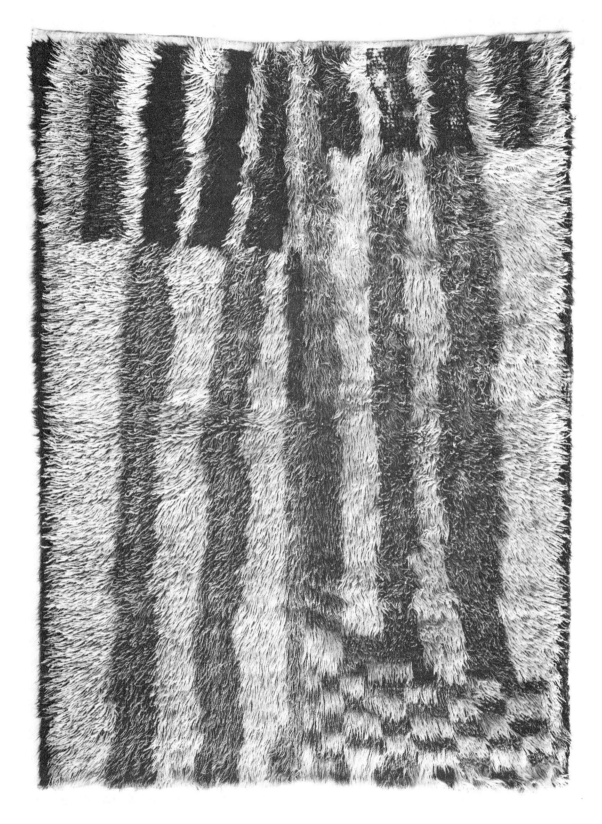

259. Rya, knotted pile weave. Pile of wool yarn on ground of linen warp and wool weft in chevron twill. Roslagsbro, Uppland.

1. Heart rosette
2. Eight-pointed star in diamond
3. Palmetto tree with birds
4. Double rose
5. Lily cross
6. Eight-pointed star in diagonal cross
7. Lozenge latticework
8. Vase with flowers
9. Triangles and diamonds in square panel

trading with the East Indies and Asia. It was the country's main port of entry for English and Dutch cultural influences, and the seat for resident English and Dutch merchants and industrialists. In other words, Göteborg offered a milieu in which oriental rugs played an important role in interior decoration. The presence in Bohuslän of cotton as a raw material also correlates with the intense textile activity emanating from Göteborg and the western Swedish craft region, and especially to the distribution of raw materials, instruction, and patterns by merchants' agents within the putting-out system.

Cushions and chair seat covers
Cushions woven completely in knotted pile are found, above all, in Jämtland and Härjedalen—where most of them have been used for pillions and carriage cushions—and in Västbo district in Småland. In the rest of the country, there are isolated examples in Bohuslän, Gästrikland, Halland, Hälsingland, Medelpad, Uppland, Västergötland, and Västmanland. They all have thick, short pile of the same pattern type as the decorative rya, and seem to be closely related to the English turkey-work cushions. Their sporadic occurrence indicates that they were not produced in peasant milieu. They may even have been imported. The pillions and carriage cushions of Jämtland and Härjedalen, however, must have been made locally, as they were made specifically for local traditional objects and holiday customs.

Trensaflossa
Trensaflossa is the Skåne dialectal term for a type of voided pile weave. It is knotted on a ribbed ground in the same way as regular knotted pile, but the pile tufts form patterns in low and distinct relief. The pile is short, and the pattern elements have a rounded cross section (fig. 262; color fig. 30).

260. Pattern types in *trensaflossa* (voided pile weave).

Trensaflossa is found only in Skåne, a fact which is no doubt related to the lack of regular knotted pile textiles in the province. Archival sources report that the rya existed in Skåne before and during the seventeenth century. But after that time, there is no mention of pile rugs; and no ryas from subsequent years have been found. Pile weaving in the form of *trensaflossa* has, however, been practiced since the end of the seventeenth century. It was used as pattern element on cushions (fig. 263) and seat pads only, never on coverlets or bedspreads. The central locality for *trensaflossa* was southwestern Skåne, extending north and northeast into the districts of Bara, Torna, Harjager, Onsjö, and Rönneberga, with occasional occurrences further north and east.

The patterns are familiar from *krabbasnår* and *rölakan*: palmetto trees with birds, lily crosses, hearts, heart rosettes, diamonds, diagonal stripes, and checks. The patterns stand out in vivid colors against an equally bright colored ground (color fig. 30). The strong color contrasts are most intense in a group of cushions with black pile on red, blue, or green ground. A group of cushions from Vemmenhög, northern Skytt, and southern Oxie districts combines *trensaflossa* with embroidery in wool yarn in a decorative scheme of unequaled sumptuousness.

Some other more complicated patterns with stylized flowers and leaves are clearly baroque in nature, reminiscent of the velvets and shags patterned with cut and uncut pile, so common during the latter part of the seventeenth and the first part of the eighteenth century. These velvets were especially used for chair seat covers and were probably instrumental in creating *trensaflossa*. Skåne *trensaflossa* is related to continental pile weaves, being an expression of western European influences, which so often can be identified in the rich Skåne textile art. The patterns used in *trensaflossa*, like those in

261. Rya, knotted pile weave. Ground of linen warp and wool weft, the initials ASD and the year 1812 knotted in. Ucklum, Bohuslän.

262. Cushion in *trensaflossa* (voided pile weave), detail. Wool pile on wool ground. Skåne.

Flemish weaving, were simplified and more or less set before reaching Skåne peasant milieu. The same forces and the same cultural currents brought *trensaflossa* and Flemish weaving to Scandinavia, as evidenced by the occurrence of both techniques in Norway as well.

Bouclé

Bouclé is a weave in which the pattern is formed by pattern weft loops pulled up between the warp ends (figs. 264, 265). During the nineteenth century, the technique was widely spread over Sweden in all social strata. It was used to make bedspreads for the bed in the separate bedroom or the extension sofa in the chamber. It appeared with the specializa-

tion of the dwelling house and its furnishings, and with the increased supply of available raw material in the form of inexpensive American cotton. Bouclé fabric was especially common in central Sweden, though it probably was not a local product. The lively western Swedish craft production in cotton made use of old patterns, stars and lily crosses, in bouclé. In Kind district, one such bouclé material was reportedly used as a canopy over the table at weddings. Colored bouclé is known from Gotland, central Sweden, and Västergötland; all-wool bouclé is known from Norrland.

Bouclé fabric was imported as late as the

263. Carriage cushion in *trensaflossa* (voided pile weave), wool pile on half-wool ribbed ground fabric. Torna, Skåne.

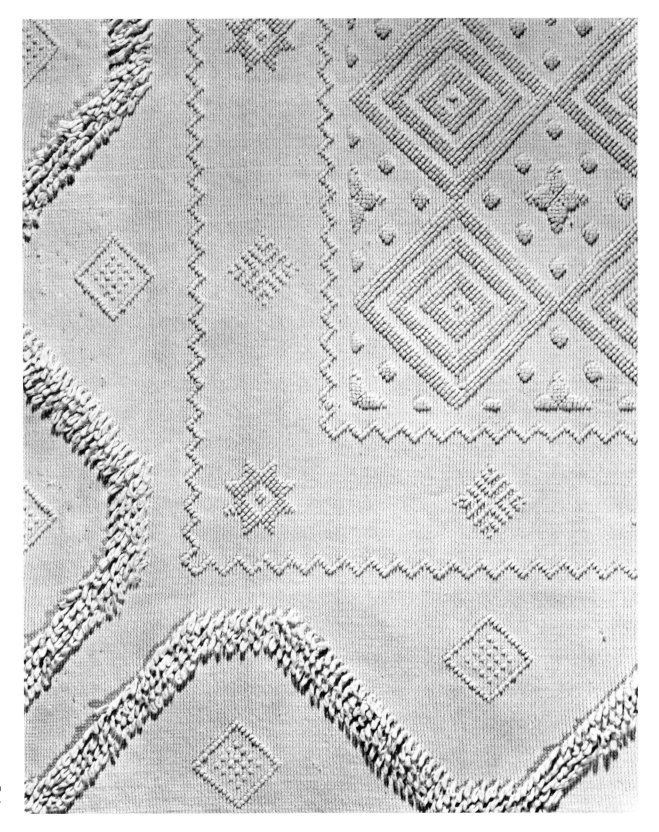

264. Bedspread in bouclé. Cotton weft pile loops on ground of cotton. Småland.

nineteenth century, although during that century it became a production item in peasant milieu for household consumption. Whether such fabrics were also made for sale is not known. It should, however, seem quite plausible that the western Swedish textile craft production with its early access to cotton would have found bouclé fabrics to be a marketable commodity.

Weft-patterned tabby, type "upphämta"
Upphämta is the generally accepted contemporary Swedish term for a weaving technique known to the whole country under various local terms, as *skälblad* (pick-up rod) and *sprötatäcke* (literally, "rod coverlet") (figs. 266–271; color figs. 17, 31).

The pattern is formed on a ground of linen or cotton by shuttling in pattern wefts, most often of wool, but also of linen or cotton, from selvage to selvage. *Upphämta* is, thus, a weave with shuttled weft thread, in which the pattern is formed by threads loosely floating over the surface and tied down by the warp according to a certain system. A pattern shed is obtained by inserting a pattern rod, a thin *spröt* (stick) or *blad* (blade), into the warp, hence the local names for this type of weave. The technique also allows the insertion of a pattern weft by hand. The pattern formations are simple: checks, diamonds, perpendicular and diagonal stripes, stars, and crosses, combined in a profusion of widely varied compositions.

Hangings
Distinct local variations in the use of *upphämta* developed especially in Skåne, where the custom of hanging the walls with textiles gave rise to the impressively patterned *upphämta* hangings, so-called *blådragningar* (blue hangings) (fig. 119). These hangings have star and check patterns arranged in wide bands in blue linen yarn on white ground. They are found

265. Bedspread in bouclé. Weft pile loops and ground of cotton. Umeå, Norrbotten, second half of the nineteenth century.

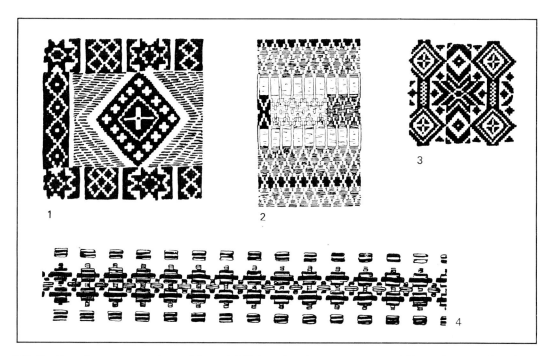

266. Motifs and pattern types in *upphämta:* (1) Eight-pointed stars, crosses, and diagonal crosses, inscribed in diamonds and squares. (2) Lozenge latticework and transverse bands. (3) Eight-pointed star and diamonds on lengthwise stripes. (4) Band of rectangles, diamonds, and crosses.

partly in northern Skåne, partly in southern Halland. Older examples from southern Småland and Blekinge show that they at one time were more widely distributed. Hanging cloths, clock cloths (decorative cloths hung over grandfather clocks), ceiling borders, shelf edgings, and other textiles belonging to the *dragning*—the textile decoration of ceiling and walls—of the house were woven in *upphämta,* alone or combined with *dukagång* and/or *krabbasnår* (figs. 9, 55, 60). The older hangings generally have blue patterns on white ground; the latter ones often light red and blue patterns on white (fig. 268; color fig. 17). The distribution area of these *upphämta* patterns—so strongly associated with the old custom of decorating the house with textiles—coincides with the area of the so-called Southern Götaland house type in Skåne, Blekinge, Halland, southwestern Småland, and —especially for hanging cloths—Västergötland (figs. 130–33).

Coverlets

The primary and most widespread use of *upphämta* was in coverlets. A certain local differentiation was noticeable also here. But the most interesting fact about this group of coverlets is the wide distribution of these so-called Västergötland coverlets all over the country and in parts of Norway and Finland. They were named for their distributors, the Västergötland salesmen. The manufacture probably took place in the putting-out areas of the western Swedish textile craft region, namely Västergötland, Halland, and Småland (figs. 24, 25). The coverlets have simple patterns, with checks, diamonds, and stars, in brown, red, gray, and sometimes green, on white ground, in characteristic and rather repetitive arrangements (figs. 112, 269).

The so-called *bunkatäcke* (vessel cover) of northwestern Skåne was used to wrap or cover the provisions basket brought to a communal

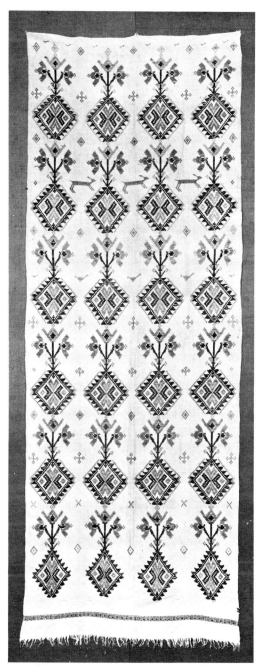

267. Hanging cloth in *upphämta* and *krabbasnår.* Pattern weft of blue linen and light red cotton yarn on linen ground. Jämshög, Blekinge. Privately owned.

189

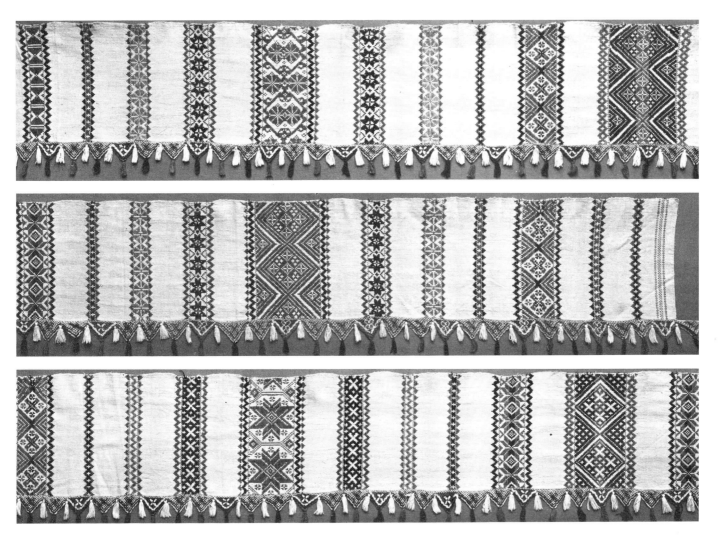

268. Hanging, horizontal wall runner, in *upphämta*. Pattern weft of blue and red cotton yarn on linen ground, cotton fringe of tassels and knotted net darned in red and blue. Breared, Halland. Privately owned.

celebration or party. These cloths used the same type of pattern as the Västergötland coverlets, but in other colors: black, blue, and red (fig. 271). Further, they were woven of wool yarn or cotton. The Bohuslän local type of *upphämta* coverlet, the *sprötatäcke,* used a repeating pattern of diamonds in red, green, or blue (fig. 270). In Västergötland, a similar pattern occurred, arranged in a central panel with border. In Skåne, Blekinge, and Halland there was a type of coverlet with shuttled-in or laid-in transverse bands on linen ground. *Upphämta* patterns were also used on smaller textile furnishings, such as cushions.

Munkabälte

Munkabälte (monk's belt) is a Skåne dialectal word for a four-shaft weave, in which two form the tabby ground and the other two the pattern. It resembles *upphämta* in that the pattern weft floats over the surface of the ground and in that both techniques were previously woven with pattern rods. The pattern, however, is simpler and consists exclusively of checks, diamonds, and stripes, which combine to form squares and stars (fig. 272). The pattern weft can be bound in two ways only: over and under two or six warp ends.

Monk's belt is found throughout the country.

In Dalarna it is called *förlåt* weave because in that province it was used only in bed curtains, *förlåtar* (figs. 69, 274; color fig. 32). Locally, the technique varied. Certain types had limited distribution, appearing, for example, in Skåne alone. In that province, primarily in the southwestern districts, a pattern of diamonds combined into stars and figures was woven on black wool ribbed coverlets. An-

269. Table cover in *upphämta,* detail. Pattern weft of colored wool yarn on linen ground. Rättvik, Dalarna.

270. Coverlet in *upphämta*. Pattern weft of wool on linen ground. Marked ASD 1850 H in cross-stitch with red cotton yarn. Ucklum, Bohuslän.

271. Coverlet in *upphämta*. Pattern weft of wool on linen ground, signed and dated with red cotton yarn in cross-stitch P×T×S 1648. The date is probably incorrect, a later addition based on a misleading family tradition. Skåne.

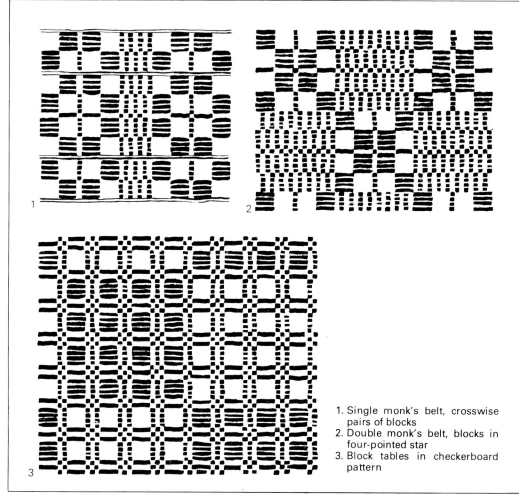

1. Single monk's belt, crosswise pairs of blocks
2. Double monk's belt, blocks in four-pointed star
3. Block tables in checkerboard pattern

272. Pattern types in monk's belt.

One variant of monk's belt was woven in a pattern of large checks, quite clearly influenced by block-patterned linen *dräll* (fig. 272: 3). This variant was especially common in central Sweden and Norrland, which would suggest connections with the commercial production of western Sweden.

In addition to these local variations of monk's belt, the pattern elements of stars, in allover patterns or bands, occur everywhere (fig. 273). The patterns and technique of monk's belt were undoubtedly related to patterned dressmaking and upholstery materials, which were brought in through import and through the fledgling Swedish weaving industry in the seventeenth and, especially, the eighteenth centuries. Workshop weaving also helped to spread the patterns of monk's belt.

Rosepath

As is the case with the terms for many Swedish weaving techniques, *rosengång,* rosepath, is also borrowed from dialectal Skåne vocabulary. There are two types of rosepath, regular rosepath and bound rosepath. Regular rosepath is a 2/2 twill woven on four shafts with the pattern weft floating on both sides of the fabric. Bound rosepath is a 2/1 or 3/1 twill with all weft picks bound on the surface, while they float under several warp threads on the reverse side. The result is a nonreversible fabric with a clear pattern on the face side and a floating, less distinct pattern on the reverse (fig. 275).

Regular rosepath occurred mainly in Norrland and northern Dalarna, Uppland, and Västmanland, with extensions into Värmland (figs. 277, 278; color fig. 33). Isolated instances of this technique have been found in Västergötland, Östergötland, Småland, Blekinge, and on Gotland.

Bound rosepath could be found all over the country, but with a marked concentration in Götaland (fig. 276).

Rosepath was, above all, used for coverlets and fell tops; in Skåne especially for cushion backings; in Skåne, Blekinge, Halland, Bohuslän, and Västergötland, for bench cushions; and in Dalarna, for bottom sheets of linen or hemp

other pattern of stars and laid-in ornament was woven in the same districts and also somewhat farther east.

In the area where Västergötland wares were usually sold, there was a kind of thin coverlet and bed curtain of hemp or linen ground with shuttled-in pattern weft of wool yarn in a monk's belt pattern, grouped in bands with shuttled-in broad stripes between. The colors were light reddish brown and golden brown, indigo and white (color fig. 32). These cover-

lets were probably originally commercial products distributed by the Västergötland trade, later copied and executed in the homes—as were also *upphämta* coverlets and ryas. The table covers in Västmanland and the bed curtains in Dalarna would then have been expressions of this imitative impulse.

Diagonally placed monk's belt stars, woven on eight shafts, so-called double monk's belt (fig. 272: 2), had a distinct distribution in eastern Götaland.

30. Cushion in voided pile weave. Pile of wool yarn loops on half-wool ribbed ground. Akarp, Skåne.

31. Hanging cloth, detail of patterned border in *upphämta.* Pattern weft of linen and cotton on linen tabby ground. Blekinge.

32. Coverlet in monk's belt. Wool pattern weft on cotton tabby. Norra Ny, Värmland.

33. Left, coverlet in rosepath with linen warp and wool weft, Sollerö, Dalarna. Right, carpet in rose-path, cotton warp and wool weft, woven around 1885. Hycklinge, Östergötland.

34. Woven bands, apron strings, of multicolored wool with wool pompons, and a black and white linen band with a large cotton pompon for a bride-groom's hat. Leksand, Dalarna.

35. Various woven bands used as binding and strings on aprons. Leksand, Dalarna.

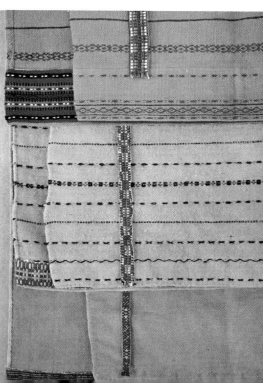

273. Hanging cloth in monk's belt, linen pattern weft inserted by hand on linen ground. Värö, Halland.

274. Bed curtain in monk's belt. Pattern weft of wool on wool ground. Rättvik, Dalarna.

and for coarse sacks of hair yarn or wool with warp of linen or cotton. The patterns in regular rosepath are derived from diagonal, pointed, or goose-eye twill. They differ from twill in that they are woven with two shuttles. The same pattern appears on both sides of the fabric, though in reverse colors. The pattern variation can be increased by broken threading or by increasing the number of shafts to six or eight.

The coverlets in regular rosepath may have a pattern covering the entire surface, either in a twill variation or in a broken twill variation with or without color separation into bands.

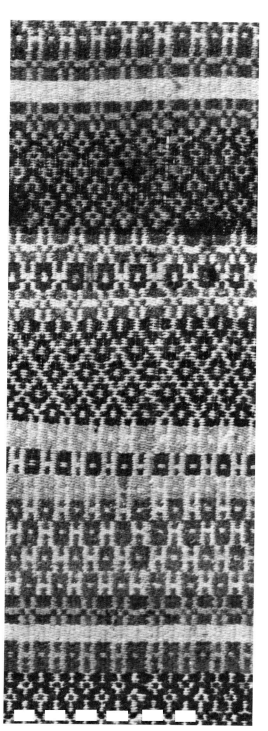

Double H

Star patte

Ring patte

Single H

Hemp pat

275. Typical patterns in rosepath. Numbers 1–5 appear in bound rosepath, numbers 6–8 in regular, or loose, rosepath.

276. Coverlet in rosepath, detail. Warp of fishnet yarn, weft of hair yarn and wool yarn. Obtained in 1929 from Beata of Braseröd, who also supplied the respective terms for the various pattern motifs. Woven by Beata's mother in the 1880s. Romelanda, Bohuslän.

Band patterns are also found in bound rosepath. Local variations have been cataloged by Emilie von Walterstorff in *Svenska vävnadstekniker och mönstertyper* ("Swedish weaving techniques and pattern types"). She coined the term *hampkrus* for what here is loosely referred to as regular rosepath. Her introduction of this term was met with some well-founded criticism by Ella Odstedt in "Namngivningen och dess principer i dalska textilier" ("The principles of naming Dalarna textiles"). Therefore, the term will not be used in this work.

Rosepath belongs among the basic techniques found wherever weaving is practiced.

Band weaving

For the weaving of bands, techniques identical to those used in all weaving have been used. Bands can be woven virtually without tools, simply by stretching a warp in the simplest fashion between two supports or between one support and the weaver's own body. With his fingers and/or the knife beater, the weaver forms a shed into which the weft is introduced and battened down with the beater. The possibilities for variations under these primitive conditions are legion. One basic element in all weaving is the forming of a shed. One shed-making device is the rigid heddle, widespread in the Nordic countries and also outside of Scandinavia. With the help of this simple tool alone, one may weave tabby bands, ribbed bands, twill bands, and tabby bands with picked-up warp floats in *upphämta* or rosepath patterns (fig. 281). A shedding device can also be fixed in a frame, combined with two warp beams—one for the warp and one for the finished band—and equipped with heddles and treadles. The result is a freestanding band loom (fig. 282).

In general, a wealth of bands was preserved until the latter part of the nineteenth century or longer in areas where older dress customs survived. Hence, the provinces of Dalarna, Hälsingland, Skåne, and the Lapp region especially stand out, by virtue of their particularly rich inventories of bands for various purposes and in varying techniques.

In traditional dress, bands had many functions: they served as boot laces, as garters, as edging and borders on skirts, jackets, and aprons. They were also used as neckbands, cuffs, and ties on shirts and shifts; for sashes, belts on fur coats, and neckcloths, on headwear, and as decoration on various parts of the dress. For each purpose, bands were designed to meet the specific demands of strength and elasticity. But the aesthetic effect of color,

277. Coverlet in regular rosepath, detail. Linen warp, wool and linen weft. Rättvik, Dalarna.

278. Coverlet in regular rosepath, detail. Linen or hemp warp, weft of wool and hair yarn. Rättvik, Dalarna.

279. Patterned woven bands of wool yarn, used as belts for fur coats. The middle band is tablet-woven and comes from Nederkalix, Norrbotten, the two outside bands are from Nås, Dalarna.

pattern, and texture was clearly also taken into consideration. As a decorative element, bands played a major role in local, traditional dress customs (figs. 287, 288; color figs. 6, 7, 34, 35).

Some kinds of bands were found all over the country. As a rule, they were probably made for sale and were spread by itinerant peddlers. Judging from customs lists, bands were one of their biggest sales items.

There were, however, also distinct local band types with regard to pattern and color. These were found precisely within the above-mentioned provinces of strongly traditional dress (fig. 283). Thus, Skåne stands out, with wide, magnificent sashes, which were wound twice around the waist and tied in great loops. These sashes as well as narrower bands—used as garters and apron strings—have a pick-up pattern and are finished with intricately braided fringe or tassels. The pattern elements—six-

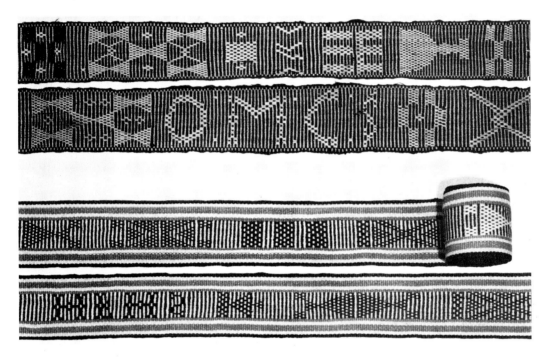

280. Patterned woven bands of wool, used as belts for fur coats, with woven-in initials. Nederkalix, Norrbotten (top), and Norra Degerfors, Västerbotten (bottom).

281. Band weaving with a "hole-and-slot" rigid heddle. Nössemark, Dalsland.

282. Band weaving on band loom. Rasbo, Uppland.

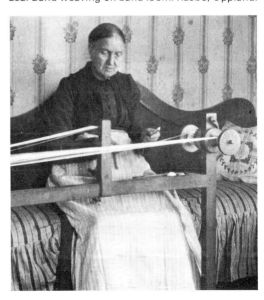

pointed stars, diamonds, hearts, ornate crosses, and dentiled triangles—are a natural outgrowth of the technique itself, and show considerable similarity to prehistoric bands. Aprons of linen and cotton with patterns dating them to the end of the eighteenth century and the beginning of the nineteenth century often have strings of ribbed cotton bands. These bands show a transversely striped ground with a sparse pattern of triangles—combined to form diamonds or hourglasses—crosses, and chevrons. There were also bands with simple patterns, such as stripes, dentiled stripes, or checks. Of these various band types, only the broad sash was indigenous to Skåne—as part of traditional dress, especially to eastern Skåne. All other above-mentioned pattern types were found throughout the country.

In Dalarna, bands of remarkable quality and in considerable quantities were made in several parishes. In Garsås village in Mora parish, manufacture for sale was extensive. The women sold patterned bands to other Dalarna parishes as well as outside the province. White linen and cotton bands were woven for hair ribbons. Wide patterned bands were made to bind shirt edges, to serve as men's garters and wrist bands in blue and white, and to decorate horse blankets, hats, and caps. Predominantly, the ground was linen and the pattern yarn red wool. In Leksand, white linen bands with patterns in black, sooted linen or silk were woven—remarkable bands, among the finest works of Swedish textile art. They were called "silk bands" or "soot-yarn bands," and were made for the woman's bonnet and the man's hat of the local costume (fig. 287). Those made for bride and bridegroom were naturally the finest. Up to the middle of the nineteenth century, they were relatively narrow, about 3/8

Band weaving

283. Sashes. Left to right: pattern warp of wool on linen ground, Ingelstad, Skåne; pattern warp of wool on cotton ground, Ore, Dalarna; and pattern warp of wool on cotton ground, Ål, Dalarna.

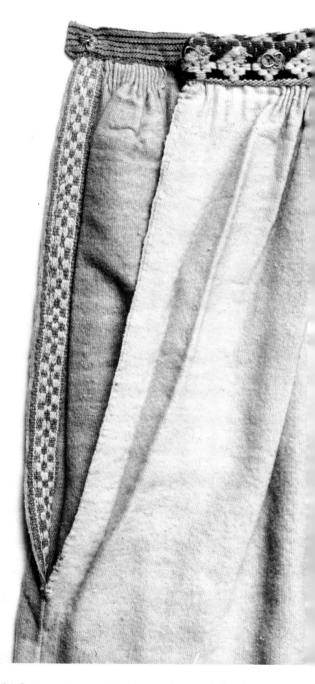

284. Patterned woven bands, used as waistband and placket on a skirt. Wool pattern warp on linen ground. Västra Vingåker, Södermanland.

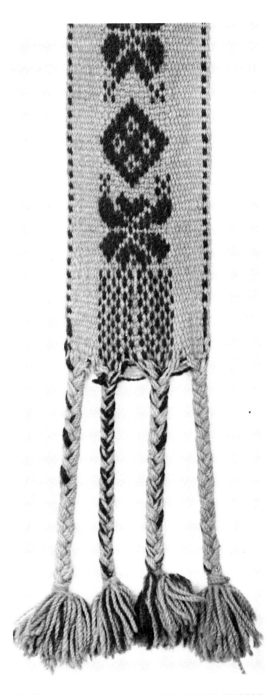

286. Typical band-weaving pattern. Knee garter from Herrestad, Skåne.

285. Woven band, warp and weft of wool, finished in braided tassels.

inch (fig. 289). The bands for men's hats were the narrowest—1/8 to 1/4 inch wide—but as much as ten feet long. They were wound around the crown of the hat and finished off with large tassels (fig. 288). The width was commonly given in the number of white pattern warp ends. After the middle of the nineteenth century, the bands for the woman's bonnet grew wider until, in the 1890s, they reached a peak with the "thirty-seven-end band." The patterns were based on the cross, the diagonal, and the post. These were combined in different ways, to form numerous variations, with different names and appearances. Thus, for example, the diagonal pattern existed in three variants. The older patterns were based completely on the diagonal line, forming triangles, chevrons, and dentiled motifs: crosses, triangles, diamonds, and hearts. The later patterns took up flower and foliage patterns from pattern books.

In the older bands, the linen was dyed with urine and soot. The soot was obtained from cobwebs impregnated with the soft, fine soot from burning splints of resinous pine, a common source of illumination. The resulting color was a brownish gray-black. Later, bands were woven with commercially dyed black silk. That black, obtained from chemical dyes, was hard and intense, and contrasted sharply with the white linen (fig. 287).

Linen bands with pattern threads of red or black wool yarn were similarly patterned. They were, however, not considered as fine as the silk bands. They were used for everyday women's hats of striped woolen fabric, for aprons, for waist bands, for skirt-bags (fig. 369)

and purses, and men's garters. As a rule, they were tasseled.

In Hälsingland, Gästrikland, Härjedalen, and Jämtland, band weaving was carried on much as in Dalarna, with pick-up patterns in wool yarn on a ground of linen or wool, later cotton. In Delsbo, apron strings and men's garters especially were wide and richly patterned.

The Lapps, who have retained their old way of life and form of dress, have also continued to weave bands for their costume, for sacks, pouches, and reins (figs. 84, 161, 290).

Band weaving among the Lapps is done with the aid of a rigid heddle of reindeer horn or bone with one or two holes in each slat. A heddle with two such holes can give greater pattern variation. The warp is tied at one end to, e.g., a *kåta* pole, at the other end to the weaver's belt. With her hands, the weaver picks up the appropriate warp threads and inserts the weft. Among some Lapps, the weaver battens the weft in a motion away from the body, as the heddle is closest to her and the band is being formed from the fixed point—the pole—in a direction toward her (fig. 290). Among other Lapps, the arrangement is reversed: the weaver beats the weave toward herself and the band is formed between her and the heddle. The bands are made with wool pattern warp on wool ground. The pattern motifs are the same as in the rest of Sweden: six-pointed stars, diamonds, triangles, diagonal crosses, dentiled diagonals, and chevrons. There is a certain preference for simpler patterns among the southern Lapps, who, on the whole, use fewer bands than the northern Lapps.

288. Bridegroom's hat, wound with narrow black and white bands and tasseled cords. Rättvik, Dalarna.

Tablet weaving

A shed-making device of a different kind consists of tablets or cards with holes into which warp ends are threaded. These tablets are generally square with a hole in each corner (figs. 291, 292). There are, however, tablets of varying shape—for example, circular, oval, hexagonal, or octagonal—and, depending on that shape, with varying numbers of holes through which the warp ends can be threaded in different ways, resulting in different weaves. The tablets may be made of wood, horn, bone, leather, cardboard, or some other stiff material.

To weave with tablets, the warp ends running through the tablet holes are tightened, the number of warp ends depending on the number of tablets. To obtain a shed, the tablets, which are stacked together, are turned all together in the direction of the warp, so that the threads in each tablet are twisted around each other. A shed is formed, into which the weft is introduced. After a given number of turns, the

287. In Leksand, Dalarna, married women wore black and white "soot-yarn bands" of linen on their bonnets.

direction is reversed. The weft is completely covered by the warp, so that the band seemingly consists of rows of cords lying side by side (fig. 291, bottom). By using different colors in the warp, a great variety of patterns can be created. In addition, it is possible to weave pick-up patterns as well as double weave by turning the tablets individually. In Sweden, however, the latter possibilities have not been fully explored. On the other hand, there are finds of four-hole tablets and bands woven with pick-up patterns from Nordic graves from the Age of Migrations and the Viking Age. These tablets were often used in weaving bands to serve as the third "selvage" in fabrics woven on the warp-weighted loom. The band's weft picks

were pulled out to one side into long loops, which formed the warp for the larger loom. Preserved bands from this time, woven with around 140 tablets in rich patterns, would seem to indicate that tablet weaving was more prominent in prehistoric times. In Iceland, the art of tablet weaving with individual manipulation of the tablets has been perpetuated and, consequently, more complex and varied patterns have also survived. Tablet weaving is a very old form of weaving, known almost all over the world, and practiced throughout Sweden.

Tablet-woven bands lack elasticity but are extraordinarily strong. They have therefore been used for reins, carrying straps, saddle girths, suspenders, sashes, etc.

290. Weaving of shoe laces. The warp is stretched from a pole in the *kåta*—the Lapp hut—to a strap attached to the weaver's belt. The weft is introduced between the heddle and the pole. Vittangi, (northern) Lappland.

291. Tablet weaving. Top, the weaving process; bottom, the result. Note that the finished weave sample is woven with ten tablets, whereas the process is demonstrated with only four tablets.

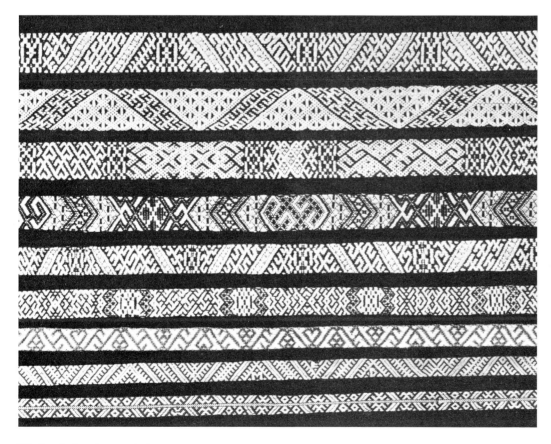

289. Bands for the married woman's bonnet. Pattern weft of soot-dyed linen on linen ground. Leksand, Dalarna.

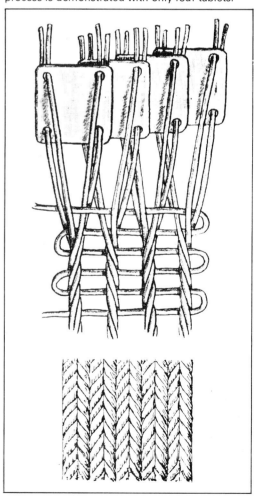

292. Tablet weaving. Wooden tablets with holes in each corner, linen warp, weft of wool yarn introduced with a netting needle or shuttle. Breared, Halland.

Needlework and embroidery

Sewing is a technique requiring a thread and one simple tool, a needle. These two, the thread and the needle, have existed as far back as human civilization can be traced. They are found among all peoples and at all stages of cultural development. The technique of sewing is not used only with textile materials. Skin and leather garments are stitched together with sinews; articles of clothing, household articles of birch bark, wood splints, and bark, and even boats of wood are sewn together with bast or root fibers. The simpler a tool is, the freer the hand that uses it, and the richer the variations possible. The more complicated the tool, the more inflexible and fixed the technique. In working with needle and thread, the possibilities for variation are indeed unlimited.

Material
Thread in the wider sense—a filament of animal or plant fiber or of metal—together with the material being sewn, influence the nature of the final product as much as the method by which the needle joins these two elements.

The development of raw materials and the introduction of new materials in threads and fabrics have continually provided new inspiration and creative impulses (fig. 293).

Stitches and seams
A stitch is the visible record of the needle's and thread's progress through and over the foundation material. Each stitch consists of two steps: the downward movement or "down stitch," from the right side or top side, and the upward movement or "up stitch," from the reverse side, or underside, through the fabric. Several stitches constitute a seam. A seam can consist of all the same stitches or stitches of several different kinds. Seams may be purely functional or purely decorative.

In the former case, the resulting work is called plain sewing, in the latter, decorative sewing or embroidery.[3] The terminology of stitches and stitch combinations is rich to the point of confusion. Some stitches and seams go by several names, and some names are applied to different stitches and seams. To avoid misunderstandings, the terms used in this text are, whenever possible, illustrated and

named in schematic drawings (e.g., figs. 296, 297).[4]

Basic stitches
The stitch, the smallest unit of needlework, can assume only a limited number of basic shapes. These might be called the basic stitches. The nature of the basic stitches is determined by the placement of the needle relative to the thread: if it is placed in front of the thread, the stitch is a running stitch; if behind, a backstitch; if through a loop, a chain stitch; if through a loop with a twist, a buttonhole stitch; if with the thread wound several times around the needle, a French knot; if through the thread, a split stitch; and if through loops and knotted loops, "in the air" or on a foundation, a lace stitch.

Combinations of stitches
By combining the basic stitches with each other in various ways, different decorative seams can be created. When talking about the basic stitches, it is possible to make clear distinctions on a purely technical basis. But when it comes to combinations of stitches used in decorative

93. Sewing and embroidery
materials from the eighteenth and
nineteenth centuries. Top to
bottom: silk on spools in a cardboard box, silk wound on strips of
paper, silk in skeins, silk in folded
rice paper with red Chinese
characters, linen yarn, DMC
embroidery cotton, pearl cotton
(*coton perlé*), mercerized cotton
yarn, wool yarn, package of beads
for beadwork, and various silk
winders—to the left, in the shape
of stars of mother-of-pearl, to the
right, of goose craw or gullet and
knucklebone.

294. Needlework accessories. Top to bottom: pin cushions; needle cases of leather, china, turned and carved bone; needle book; circular card with straight pins; thimbles and open-crown thimbles; and sewing wax in the shape of a hand.

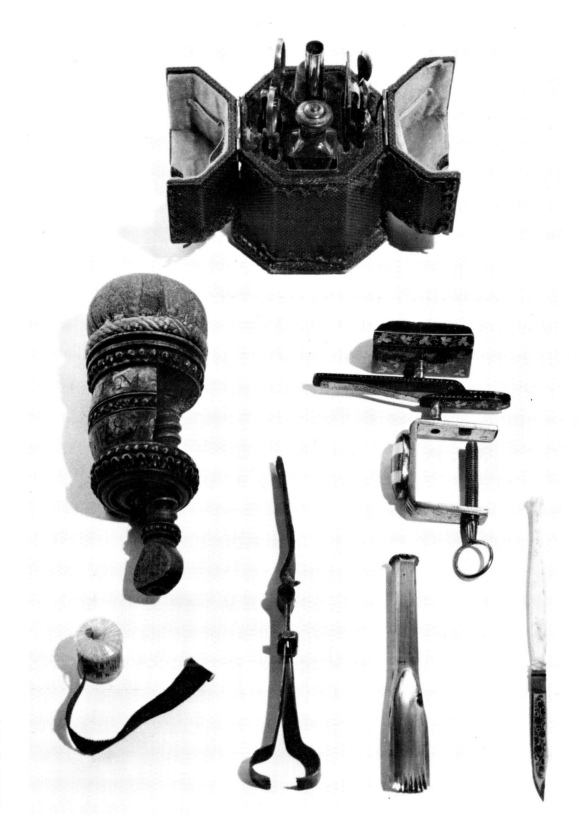

295. Implements for sewing and embroidery. Top to bottom: padded case holding scissors, ripper, needle case, thimble, and a bottle for eau de Cologne (to revive the faint seamstress); two needlework clamps, one from 1787, one, of engraved steel, from the second half of the nineteenth century; measuring tape, caliper-shaped needlework holder, hole punch, and ripper.

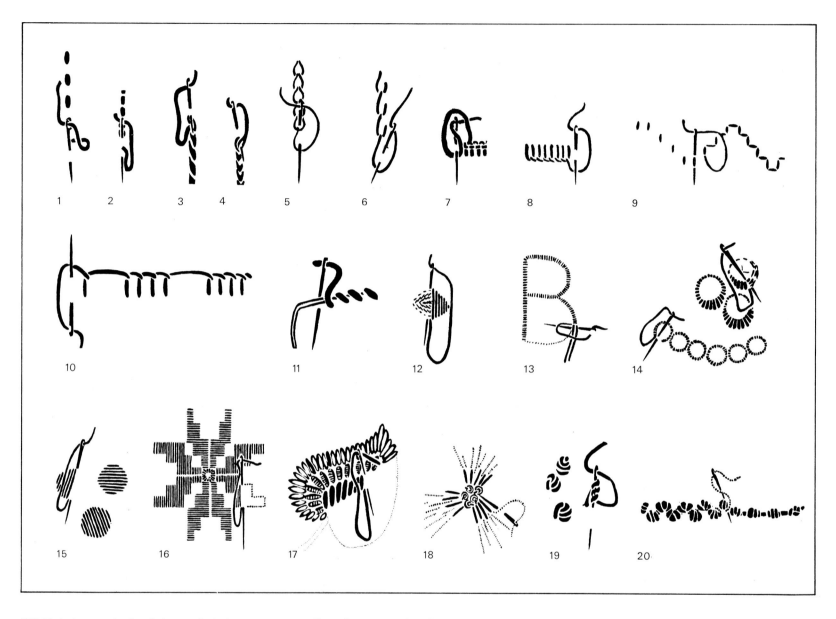

296. Variations on basic stitches and stitch combinations. (1) Running stitch. (2) Backstitch. (3) Stem stitch. (4) Split stitch. (5) Chain stitch. (6) Open chain stitch. (7) Tailor's buttonhole stitch. (8) Open buttonhole stitch (blanket stitch). (9) Diagonal line stitch or square stitch. (10) Spaced buttonhole stitch. (11) Whipped or overcast edges. (12) Padded satin stitch. (13) Couching satin stitch. (14) Padded satin stitch and overcast eyelet holes. (15) Satin stitch. (16) Geometrical satin stitch. (17) Shading stitch. (18) Shading stitch and French knots. (19) French knots. (20) Couched knotted string.

needlework, many other factors must be considered. The same basic stitches combine in a great many different ways to create patterns, thereby introducing a stylistic element which gives these stitch combinations their characteristic nature. In certain stitch combinations function and style are inextricably meshed. In some cases, they have specific local associations, which have named and helped establish them as conventional decorative seams, e.g., Blekinge work, Halland work, Delsbo work,

Skåne cut work, and Vingåker work. What created these stylistically distinct local types of embroidery was not technical differences, but differences in pattern and style. Style-making factors have therefore had a decisive influence on the development of decorative needlework.

Production milieus

As mentioned previously, tailors and shoemakers were the only craftsmen commonly

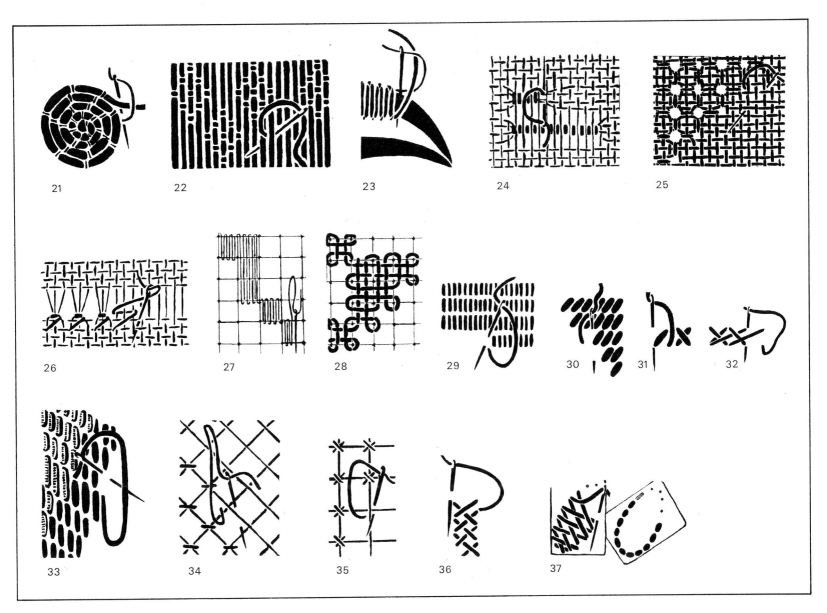

297. Variations on basic stitches and stitch combinations. (21) Couched thread in spiral. (22) Laid work with decorative couching. (23) Raised couching over cut-out "padding" of cardboard, parchment, etc. (24) Drawn-fabric work: vertical satin stitch drawn tight. (25) Drawn-fabric work: four-sided stitch. (26) One-directional drawn-thread work, antique hemstitch. (27) Embroidery on knotted netting or filet work: darning stitch (*point de reprise*). (28) Embroidery on knotted netting or filet work: linen stitch (*point de toile*). (29) Vertical Gobelin stitch. (30) Petit point, tent stitch. (31) Cross-stitch. (32) Long-armed cross-stitch. (33) Hungarian stitch. (34) Couched filling. (35) Couched filling, couching stitches crossed. (36) Herringbone stitch. (37) Shadow stitch, front and reverse side.

found in every parish and town. Tailor-made garments for men and women included breeches, coats, jackets, vests, coats of Inverness type, skirts, aprons, and bodices, of wool and skin and other materials requiring cutting. All linen and cotton articles that did not require cutting but only sewing were made by the women in the homes: shirts, shifts, *överdelar* (literally, "tops"; shirts), neckerchiefs, kerchiefs, and head scarves of linen or cotton; sheets, pillowcases, cushion ticks, bed curtains, and other accessories for the bed and interior furnishings. This division of sewing into two provinces—that of the professional tailor, and that of the housewife—was reflected in a division of labor, also, when it came to decorative stitching.

Tailors executed embroidery on coats, jackets, vests, bodices, aprons, and sashes of wool. Furriers and leatherworkers embroidered fur coats, breeches, bodices, and vests. Embroidery on gloves and mittens, which were bought ready-made in town or at fairs, was the responsibility of the glovemaker (fig. 350), embroidery on belts that of the beltmaker. The so-called *bindmössa*, a small, embroidered, lace-edged cap of the Mary Stuart type (fig. 79), which during the eighteenth century spread to most of the country, was made by professionals who also sold hat frames. Already embroidered material could also be purchased. Aside from above-mentioned professionally active groups of craftsmen, there were also those who supplemented their income by executing certain types of embroidery. These persons were, as previously noted, often unmarried women of good family or widows who were forced to make a living by their skill with the needle. The minutes of the parish council in Västra Vingåker mention that, aside from tailors, there were several groups—needleworkers of both sexes, cavalry men, and soldiers—doing silk embroidery in their homes on fur coats, aprons, coats, and caps.

Also needlework and embroidery on linen and cotton were done for a fee by highly skilled individuals (fig. 324). No doubt these needleworkers had access to new patterns and often served as transmitters of new impulses from one social group to another, and from one region to another. In the towns and in country manor houses, especially proficient women were employed as linen seamstresses. They must be considered to have been professional craftsmen, although their profession was not organized in guilds. It is also to be expected that the nonprofessional needlework carried on in the home by family members maintained a high standard, as clothing and textiles had to meet considerable functional and aesthetic demands (figs. 300, 305).

Professional activity

Guilded needleworkers existed throughout the Middle Ages and up to the middle of the nineteenth century. Up to the mid-1800s, embroidery played a role hardly imaginable today in formal dress and interior decoration. Embroiderers belonged to the guild of the "Broderers" and enjoyed a high social position, not least because they worked with the most precious and costly of materials: silks, pearls, gold, and silver. One famous "broderer" was Albertus Pictor, Sweden's best-known painter of the late Middle Ages and the artist responsible for the frescoes in a number of Mälaren valley churches. About twenty stitcheries are known to be by his hand or from his workshop in Stockholm, where he was active until the beginning of the sixteenth century. A remarkable number of specimens of medieval embroidery have survived to our time, mostly because the Church preserved ecclesiastical vestments and furnishings. In addition to secular craftsmen, guilded or in the employ of private noble houses, convents also contributed significantly. To "seam with silk and couch with gold" was an occupation often attributed to cloistered noble maidens in the old ballads. Thus, though much embroidery was imported, the convent in Vadstena produced a large number of excellent works, some of which are still in existence.

During the reigns of Gustav Vasa and his sons there was a broderer's atelier in Stockholm Castle. The salary ledger lists a considerable number of named artisans, among them gold-drawers and beadworkers, imported from France and Germany. They were required to provide the King and the Court with luxury items, and also to train Swedish craftsmen. There is reason to presume that these artisans were responsible for a good number of showpieces for use by members of the royal family, for ceremonial pomp, and for the interior decoration of the castle. From the accounts it can be seen that considerable quantities of pearls, gold and silver thread, and silk were receipted by the atelier. Some of these royal showpieces are preserved in the Royal Armory and the Royal Collections. In the seventeenth century, the workshop tradition at

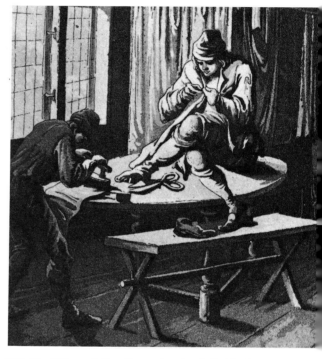

298. *The Village Tailor.* Engraving by J. F. Martin (1755–1816).

court continued. There were even Swedish embroiderers with their own ateliers, which shows that Gustav Vasa's efforts had paid off. However, the demand for orphrey was naturally limited by the very expensive materials used. During the first part of the seventeenth century, there were a number of competent embroiderers in Stockholm. They worked not only for the royal family and the Court, but also for private noble houses. During the first half and the middle of the seventeenth century, they executed a considerable number of decorative counterpanes, adorned with coats of arms and initials, for the nobility. Orders were also placed abroad. During the reign of Gustav Vasa and his sons, orders went to Hamburg and Augsburg; during the reign of Erik XIV, also to England and France. Queen Christina placed her orders in Paris, thereby shifting the orientation toward France, a focus which

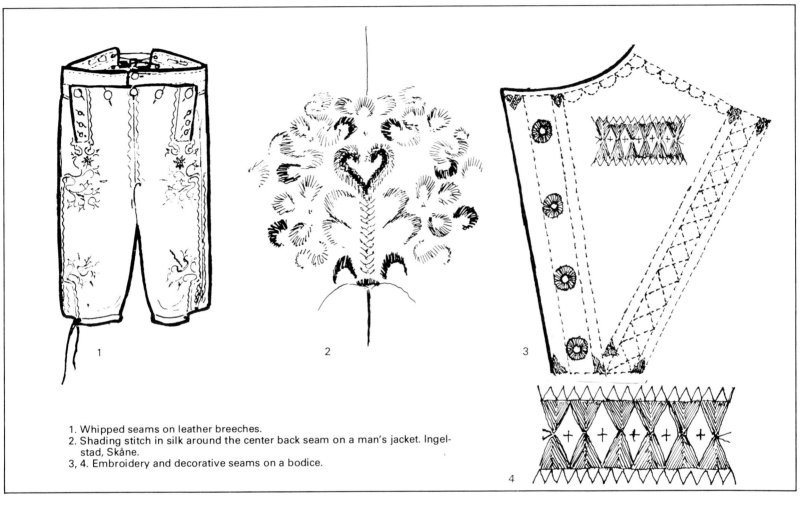

1. Whipped seams on leather breeches.
2. Shading stitch in silk around the center back seam on a man's jacket. Ingel-stad, Skåne.
3, 4. Embroidery and decorative seams on a bodice.

299. Decorative needlework, executed by tailor.

was to remain fairly constant for years to come. With the end of the seventeenth century, the importance of embroidery in dress and interior decoration steadily declined, although silk embroidery continued to be prominent on skirts, ladies' jackets, and vests, up to the 1760s. Instead, patterned brocades enjoyed an increasingly greater popularity. During the second half of the eighteenth century, the richly flowered patterns in fabrics and embroi-dery were replaced by prim, smaller, and con-siderably skimpier band patterns on single-color ground. Professional embroiderers, thus de-prived, found instead a rich outlet in military and civilian uniforms, which flourished from the end of the eighteenth century to the be-ginning of the twentieth century. The military's need for various insignia and rank symbols still keeps the profession alive, even though today's production is minimal.

Patterns and models
Though hardly available to the masses, the out-put of professional embroiderers has neverthe-less acted as transmitter of new patterns. Styles from the Continent have continually been brought into Sweden via the Court, then spread in ever-widening circles by trained journeymen, from embroidery workshops to noble estates, and from there to skilled pro-fessional seamstresses throughout the country.

300. All textile craft, especially embroidery, was considered a suitable occupation for young girls of good family.—War Councillor Wadenstierna's wife and daughters busying themselves with embroidery, filet work, and winding balls of yarn. Painting by Pehr Hilleström, 1760s.

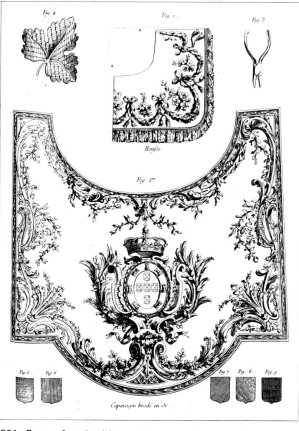

301. Page of embroidery patterns in C.-G. de St. Aubin, L'Art du Brodeur, Paris, 1770.

The development and dissemination of embroidery is largely a question of the mechanics and logistics of pattern distribution. Actual embroidered articles of course figured prominently as models, but there was also quite an extensive output of printed patterns, designs, and, not least, samplers. What roles these pattern transmitters may have played for handcraft in all strata of society is far from clear. So far, isolated data shed little light on the conditions at the time. Since each household produced most of its own textiles and, frequently, also some for sale, it is clear that the home before the mid-nineteenth century functioned as a school in various textile techniques. It is known that women especially skilled in Flemish weaving accepted pupils. It would seem probable that this was the case also with embroidery. To play the piano, to embroider, and to paint watercolors were acceptable and laudable occupations for young girls of good family in the nineteenth century. Thus, skill in these areas was proof of a certain social status. There is much to indicate that such was the case also earlier, as seen in the already mentioned medieval maidenly ideal reflected in folk songs and ballads. These songs give in a nutshell the then current ideal for young noblewomen's upbringing and education.

It is obvious that convents and monasteries played a significant role as centers for skills and learning of all kinds throughout the Middle Ages, and as long as they existed into the sixteenth century.[5] Furthermore, through their international organization, the monastic orders were able to transmit impulses from abroad to various parts of Sweden. We do not know precisely how patterns were transmitted from the internationally oriented, professionally active production milieus to the handcraft milieus up to the nineteenth century. We do know, however, that from this point on, printed models and instruction provided a regular supply of patterns.

It seems, on the whole, that those stitches

which are worked over counted threads—the so-called canvas stitches—make it possible for the needleworker to create to a certain extent his or her own patterns without the use of models. By combining certain simple motifs, such as squares, triangles, diamonds, crosses, stars, hearts, and zigzag lines—a basic repertory of ornament also in other textile techniques—a wealth of patterns can be created in decorative needlework too. This repertory is the basis for all counted thread work. To what extent these patterns may have been determined by technical and material conditions and how much they may have been based on older, previously spread patterns is difficult to determine before in-depth studies have been made.

Pattern books
As early as the sixteenth century, there existed pattern books. A hundred and sixty-five pattern books, dating from the sixteenth and seventeenth centuries, are known so far. They were published in a total of 400 editions, a large number of them in several editions. Their titles expressly state that they contain patterns for textile works, such as drawn-thread work, cut work, *reticella*, filet or darned netting, needlepoint lace, or bobbin lace (figs. 305–7). One pattern book from 1592 was intended for white embroidery worked over counted threads. This book alone was published in sixty editions.

Openwork on linen as well as embroidery on net ground have apparently existed for a long time in the eastern Mediterranean countries. It is no coincidence that these techniques spread to Europe during the sixteenth century. Though many other contributory reasons can no doubt be found, it is certain that one of the main reasons was the invention of the printing press with individual type, which made it possible to mass-produce patterns.

Openwork on linen, drawn-thread work, and cut openwork, often combined with geometrical satin stitch, embroidery on knotted net ground, and stitchery in wool or silk in ground-filling stitches were all widespread types of decorative needlework in the sixteenth and seventeenth centuries. They are still in use in certain areas. Later, they in turn influenced

302. Skåne peasant woman embroidering. Painting by A. Montan, 1883.

303. Small box covered with white satin, with relief embroidery in silver thread and shading stitch in silk. Initialed and dated AMN 1739.

and inspired patterns for the decorative embroidery over counted threads. Such is the case with, for example, Skåne cut work (figs. 330–32), Hardanger work, and Hedebo work, which have survived locally in Scandinavia. With the growing interest in handcraft toward the end of the nineteenth century, they regained popularity and again became fashionable.

There is of course one other factor to be counted with here: the basis for all ornament in stitches over counted threads, i.e., the weave of the ground. This ground provides a natural starting point for geometric shapes and figures: the square, the triangle, the circle and its sectors, the star, and the rhombus or diamond. Purely utilitarian sewing is always stimulated

toward a decorative usage of the fabric structure, because this practice also facilitates the sewing (figs. 325–37) (see "Weave-regulated needlework" on p. 226).

Certain of the patterns encountered in the apparently much-appreciated pattern books are found also in actual needlework specimens from the sixteenth and seventeenth centuries. In needlework from Swedish and European peasant milieu, they are found as late as the nineteenth century. It seems highly probable that pattern books were the foundation of this common European pattern inventory. Preserved copies of pattern books with missing pages, and loose pages with signs of use, together present a picture of a much-used pattern source. Moreover, it may be assumed that pat-

terns were copied and traced from the books onto paper and samplers, which might further have helped perpetuate individual patterns.

The profusion of purely textile pattern books diminished on the whole during the seventeenth century. During the eighteenth century, collections of engraved designs were published, intended for general ornamental decoration regardless of technique. Best known are those by the French engravers P. A. Ducerceau, D. Marot, and J. Bérain. These designers also published patterns specifically for needlework. In 1770, a number of patterns for professional production were published by C.-G. De Saint Aubin in his work *L'Art du Brodeur* ("The embroiderer's art"), part of the massive *Encyclopédie* by Diderot and D'Alembert (see

304. Coverlet of woolen twill. Blue central panel, red border, with embroidery in satin stitch, knot stitch, and couching stitch over white cording. In the center the initials EST in mirror monogram. First half of the eighteenth century.

306. Patterns from pattern book by Tagliente. Venice, 1530.

305. Title page of pattern book by Tagliente, published in Venice in 1530. The pictures show sewing, embroidery on a large frame and on a hand-held round frame, and weaving on a horizontal loom.

fig. 301). From the end of the eighteenth century and increasingly during the nineteenth century, pedagogical manuals of textile crafts were issued. Periodicals—a fact of Swedish life since the early 1800s—featured patterns and designs for various textile projects for the benefit of their readers (figs. 309, 310).

Samplers

Pattern books were directed not to male professionals, but to women. Vecellio dedicated his pattern book (1592) to "noble and skilled ladies." A pattern book by Schönsperger (1523–29), included blank pages of graph paper for the drawing of the reader's own

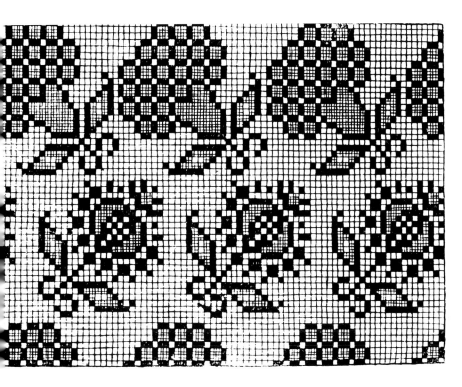

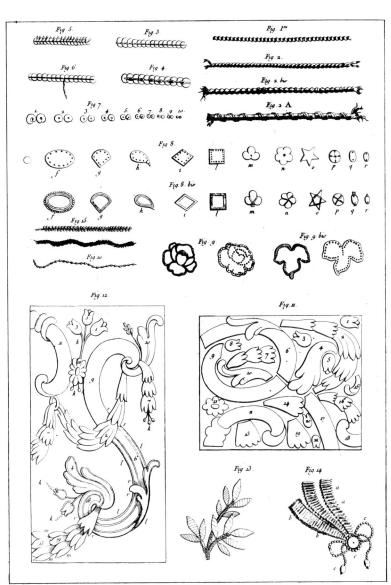

307. Pattern from *Neues Model-Buch* I, pattern book by Rosine Helene Fürsten.

308. Various loose sequins and paillettes, strings of sequins, and patterns for fancy spangle embroidery. From C.-G. de St. Aubin, *L'Art du Brodeur*, Paris, 1770.

patterns. Apprentices and journeymen in professional textile crafts used their years of apprenticeship to build up their own collections of patterns and motifs. A similar purposeful collecting of patterns must have been carried on in the homes. More or less systematically arranged collections of weaving patterns have been preserved in considerable numbers (fig. 198). From memoirs and correspondence we may glean a lively exchange of patterns and samples between friends and relatives. When it came to embroidery, one would often, in addition to drawn patterns, give samples of the stitches and—no less important—suitable motifs embroidered on a larger or smaller rectangular piece of fabric. This kind of stitched piece is commonly called a sampler (figs. 311–15).[5] Lettering samplers included the alphabet, numerals, often the name of the embroiderer, and the date, and a selection of motifs in a decorative, though often arbitrary, arrangement. It appears that some model existed for the "approved" layout and motifs of a sampler. The samplers were stitched in cross-stitch or

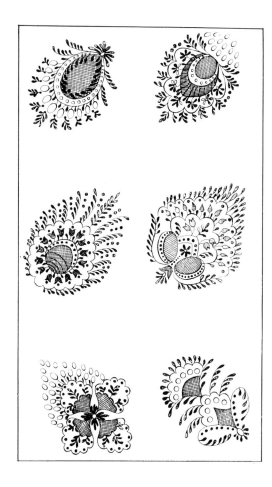

309. Embroidery patterns from *Konst och Nyhets-magasin,* 1822, ''intended to be employed in the corners of handkerchiefs or fichus, and certain to please our esteemed readers.''

310. Pattern for cross-stitch embroidery, printed and handcolored. Berlin work from the 1840s–50s.

petit point (tent stitch) in wool yarn. Before the middle of the nineteenth century, the ground was a loose wool tabby; later, canvas. Pattern samplers lack the alphabet and numerals. The whole surface is partitioned into squares or bands with samples of different stitches and stitch combinations. The earliest known samplers in Sweden date from the beginning of the eighteenth century. In England, there are samplers preserved from the sixteenth century. In the early Swedish samplers, filling stitches, cross-stitching, long-armed cross-stitching, and petit point predominate. They form richly patterned grounds in color, derivative of works and pattern books from the sixteenth and seventeenth centuries. Some of them have superbly drawn figure motifs and scenes. One may be almost certain that these patterns were created in a professional milieu, and that the embroidered fabrics possibly were sold already traced.

Around the middle of the eighteenth century, a large number of samplers were worked on fine white cotton or linen with samples of fillings or openwork grounds (fig. 313). During the nineteenth century, long, bandlike samplers dominated, with samples of drawn-thread work (fig. 314).

On the whole, samplers seem to have been limited to the middle-class, where they no doubt were of great importance for the maintenance of traditions in patterns from generation to generation. Motifs from samplers are found not only in embroidery but also in weaving. One example of this is offered by the so-called sampler rya (see above, p. 179).

311. Pattern sampler, worked on loose linen tabby, with several filling stitches. Dated 1733.

312. Lettering sampler of fine wool with silk embroidery in shading stitch, stem stitch, chain stitch, and cross-stitch. Dated 1801.

313. Pattern sampler with sixty-three different openwork grounds, worked on loose linen tabby. About 1800.

Pattern dissemination

There is evidence that there were a few professional pattern makers, who delivered patterns and designs primarily to upper- and middle-class milieu. In Nordiska Museet there is a collection of some fifty paper patterns, drawn, pricked out, and obviously used to transfer patterns onto some fabric. They were created during the first decades of the eigh-

teenth century up to around 1730, and belonged to a lady of the nobility, Baroness Beata Jacquette Ribbing. Who executed these patterns is not known; but they were made with extraordinary skill by someone trained and experienced in pattern drafting. From the end of the seventeenth century, archives provide evidence that paper patterns for needlework were imported. Distribution of patterns to customers

of yarn and thread occurred in the eighteenth century. In 1769, a painter named Wadstein reportedly drew and pricked out a pattern for the wife of Count Nils Adam Bielke, certainly not a unique occurrence. Fabrics with pretraced patterns for cross-stitching and petit point existed already in the early part of the eighteenth century (fig. 318), apparently sold ready made, much as they are today.

314. Pattern sampler of linen tabby strips, worked in various patterns of one-directional drawn-thread work. First half of the nineteenth century.

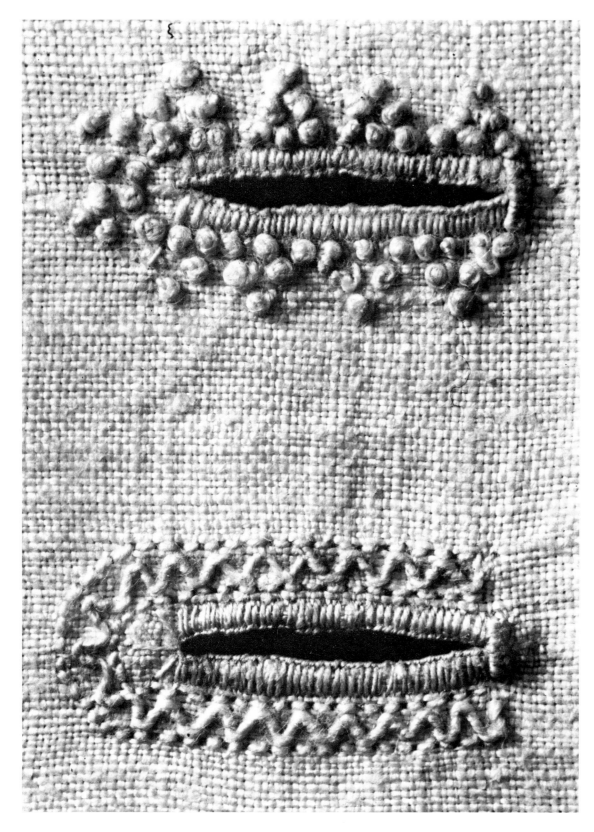

315. Sampler of linen tabby for buttonholes, signed MCD 1825. In addition to buttonhole stitch, the sampler shows French knots, backstitch, and whipped wave stitch.

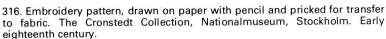

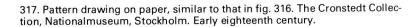

316. Embroidery pattern, drawn on paper with pencil and pricked for transfer to fabric. The Cronstedt Collection, Nationalmuseum, Stockholm. Early eighteenth century.

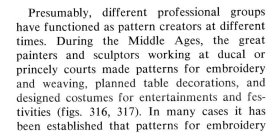

317. Pattern drawing on paper, similar to that in fig. 316. The Cronstedt Collection, Nationalmuseum, Stockholm. Early eighteenth century.

Presumably, different professional groups have functioned as pattern creators at different times. During the Middle Ages, the great painters and sculptors working at ducal or princely courts made patterns for embroidery and weaving, planned table decorations, and designed costumes for entertainments and festivities (figs. 316, 317). In many cases it has been established that patterns for embroidery from the sixteenth and seventeenth centuries were made with printing blocks, the same technique being used for the printing of woodcuts as for the printing of embroidery patterns.

There are also striking resemblances between, on one hand, certain embroideries in red and black silk on white linen in narrow double running stitch (Holbein stitch), and, on the other, hangings in white with printed red and black patterns (figs. 364, 365). As far back as handcraft production is documented, various milieus, primarily professional workshops, have created patterns which in different ways have been transmitted to the handcraft production milieu. Simpler patterns, based on the weave's right-angled network, one could devise oneself, just as one created simpler weaving patterns by certain tie-up and treadling systems. However, as soon as it came to design composition, motifs, or ornaments of more complicated nature, plant and animal motifs and figures—such as scenes with a certain narrative or dramatic content—one had to consult models. In Sweden, the Gustaf Adolf Bible—an illustrated edition of the Bible authorized by Gustav II Adolf in 1618—and other illustrated devotional literature frequently served in this capacity. One might also copy other textiles, pattern drawings, plates from pattern books, etc. As plates from pattern books were relatively rare until the end of the eighteenth century, one must always suspect quite special incentives when a certain type of embroidery became so widely spread as to reach peasant milieu.

In a limited number of cases the mechanics of this dissemination are fairly well known. Blekinge work has a quite distinct character. It is of continued popular appeal, still inspiring many to embroidery in a similar style. Two papers by Elisabeth Strömberg and Ingegerd Henschen Ingvar, "Broderade hängkläden från Blekinge" ("Embroidered hanging cloths from Blekinge") and "En grupp hängkläden från Nättraby" ("A group of hanging cloths from Nättraby"), respectively give interesting information about the creation and the transmission of the patterns of Blekinge work. Blekinge work was originally restricted to *hängkläden,* decorative hanging cloths for the Southern Götaland house type (fig. 320). As noted above, this is a type of house especially conducive to textile endeavor. Embroidered hanging cloths occurred in western Blekinge as early as the 1780s—one hanging is dated 1784—and reached a peak of popularity during the 1820s–'50s. Although there are four distinct groups, all Blekinge work features stylized flowers, foliage, bouquets, floral festoons, ribbons, birds, urns, and motifs in square frames (figs. 320–21).

The so-called Blekinge work clearly derived its inspiration from rococo flower ornamentation in multicolored silk or wool, preferably on white linen or cotton. This embroidery was the most appreciated decoration on skirts, bed curtains (fig. 321), bed coverlets, etc., around the middle of the eighteenth century.[7] It is apparent that one or several pattern draftsmen

318. Traced embroidery pattern on loose linen tabby. The pattern outlines are black, the colored areas stitched with wool yarn in several colors. First half of the eighteenth century.

from bourgeois milieu were active in western Blekinge during the first half of the nineteenth century. There are also references to one Mrs. Ådahl or Åmark, living in Asarum in the 1870s, who in her youth reportedly drew and stitched bed curtains to order. A textile craft instructor, Anna Månsdotter, born in 1846, used to go around to the households in the countryside embroidering hanging cloths. Her

patterns, however, were made up by a parson's daughter in Hällaryd. There are many similar references to poor, genteel spinsters and widows who supported themselves by sewing for peasants who could afford to pay for different and more fashionable embroidery on their linens, cushions, and coverlets. In Ovansjö, Gästrikland, there were seamstresses, especially skilled in embroidery, who embroidered the white "undercap" (fig. 426)—actually a lace-edged strip of cloth—worn under the *bindmössa*. In the nineteenth century, a sheriff's wife, Andriette Louise Pipping, her daughter Andriette, and her foster daughter Kristina Charlotta were active embroidering net undercaps to order.

The so-called Delsbo work (from Delsbo, Hälsingland) offers another example of the emergence of locally distinct embroidery and the solution to the problem of pattern drafting. A general inventory of Delsbo work in 1963 yielded—in addition to an overwhelming number of embroidered articles—a number of templates and stencils in the form of cut-out pieces of cardboard or birch bark in the shape of circles, semicircles, circle segments, leaves and arabesques, birds, etc. (fig. 322). These pattern elements were identified in the actual embroideries, where they had been combined in all possible ways in endless variation and with varying degrees of skill. Delsbo work gives an interesting insight into the creation of folk ornament, perhaps indicating the way in which the problem of pattern making may have been solved elsewhere. The type of decorative needlework known as Delsbo work is characterized by a pattern of flowers and leaves in satin stitch (figs. 322–24) and what is generally known as Järvsö work.[8] Delsbo work does not seem to be much older than the beginning of the nineteenth century. Drawn-thread work with geometric satin stitch, birch-bark work (fig. 333) (see below, p. 230), and cross-stitching (figs. 381, 382) are all older than Delsbo work. The latter techniques continue to use geometrical patterns over counted threads. The way in which the younger floral patterns entered the Delsbo repertory has not yet been determined. In the still living oral tradition surrounding Delsbo work and its origin, a Rudolphi family figures prominently. Locally,

319. Tablecloth of white linen tabby with red silk embroidery in stem stitch, detail. Most of the embroidery is gone, showing the traced pattern underneath. The cloth portrays the Annunciation surrounded by the four Evangelists; here, Matthew. Dated 1577.

320. Decorative hanging cloth of white linen tabby. Embroidery in shading stitch with cotton yarn in many colors. Blekinge, first half of the nineteenth century.

321. Bed curtains, hangings, canopy, and valance of white cotton tabby, embroidered with wool yarn in shading stitch, stem stitch, and chain stitch (crewel work). Dated 1740. Belonged to Governor Gustaf Abraham Piper, who reportedly helped embroider it himself.

the Rudolphis are given the credit for having created Delsbo work. To be sure, the templates and stencils were found in the possession of a member of this family. And in oral tradition there is often a grain of truth. However, the Rudolphis' efforts probably took root and flourished in an already well-prepared and rich soil. In any case, the Rudolphi family has played an interesting role in the history of embroidery in Delsbo, and also in the history of local lace making (figs. 435, 436).

In principle, it thus seems that all free pattern making requires some education or instruction, a model, or an aid of some kind. In the past, these demands were more easily met in bourgeois milieu. In peasant milieu special efforts have been necessary—a temporary association with a professional production milieu, or some other impetus of extraordinary kind—to set in motion the working of free-form embroidery.

Neither bourgeois nor peasant embroidery has been researched to the point that a reasonably comprehensive survey can be made at the present time. My findings are the result of personal experience, gained mainly in the course of my work with the collections at Nordiska Museet, which I have had reason to study, especially in connection with an exhibition of embroidery in 1942. Ingegerd Henschen-Ingvar's *Svenska broderier* ("Swedish embroideries"), published in 1950, is the only recent survey of embroidery in Sweden.

The focus in the following discussion of decorative needlework is the general stylistic development. However, not even in bourgeois milieu can this development be said to strictly reflect the chronological phases of art history. And in peasant milieu, there are always displacements and skipped stages in the development, style blends and additions, all jumbled together, which makes a survey extremely difficult. I have chosen to discuss the weave-regulated embroidery techniques and the free embroidery techniques separately. The reason for this division is that the former techniques, by and large, used the same pattern types, whereas the latter techniques have developed their patterns from other sources and under other conditions.

322. Cardboard stencils and templates for Delsbo work, satin stitch, and stem stitch. Formerly in the possession of Karin Svensk, Delsbo, Hälsingland.

323. Embroidery with red cotton yarn in Delsbo work, using motifs from stencils and templates such as those in fig. 322. Delsbo, Hälsingland, 1850–1900.

324. Mrs. Karin Andersson (1864–1948), living in Delsbo, embroidered to order for people in the parish and for the Handcraft Society in Hudiksvall. She drew up her patterns freehand, penciling in the curved stem of the vine as far as she could reach. She then stitched the drawn lines while they were still clearly visible, drew some more, stitched these, and so on. The flowers were drawn with the help of stencils and templates, of which she had a sizable collection.

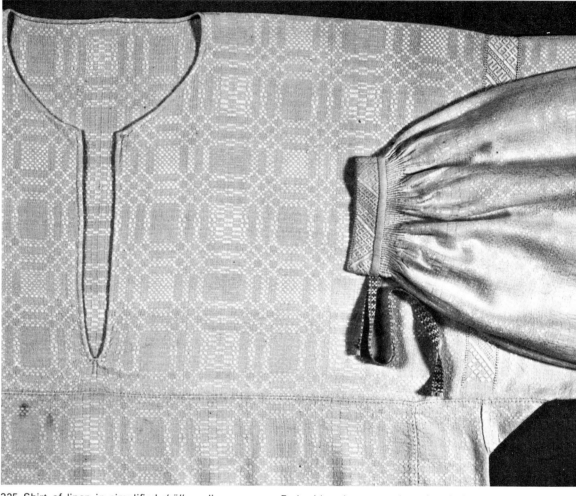

325. Shirt of linen in simplified *dräll* or diaper weave. Embroidery in geometric satin stitch along the shoulder seams and on the wristbands. Leksand, Dalarna.

Weave-regulated needlework

Plain sewing

It has been emphasized above that garment-making requiring cutting was the province of the tailor, thus belonging, on the whole, to a professional milieu (figs. 298, 299). Seaming and embroidery on linen were carried on in the home, almost exclusively by women (fig. 302). Before plentiful supplies of linen fabrics allowed for a more general use of linen articles, the latter were luxury items and treated accordingly.

The most elementary function of a seam is to join two or more pieces of material. The stitch most used for seams of this kind was backstitching. Running stitch and whipstitch, open buttonhole stitch (blanket stitch), and tailor's buttonhole stitch all had their special uses. The great care lavished on plain utilitarian sewing often gave a strong decorative touch to the work.

Exquisitely stitched seams in backstitch made fine, distinct, dotted lines. Sometimes the stitches were extremely small and done with a fairly thick thread, so that a pearl-like effect was achieved (fig. 326). Hems were secured with very fine whipstitch or backstitch. In shirt-front slits and around collars and wristbands, whipping and backstitching were combined with plain hemstitching. The desire to make all visible edges very straight helped develop drawn-thread work. By pulling out one or a couple of threads from the weave, one can make a straight hem or edge and, in addition, achieve a decorative effect by plain hemstitching. Folding the fabric on the line of the hemstitching, e.g., along the edge of a collar or wristband, and then overcasting the folded edge with its protruding thread groups with buttonhole stitches, gives a line of picots. In Dalarna, where this technique was frequently used to finish wristbands, the picots were called "*nuggor*" (fig. 327). In paintings and engravings from the sixteenth and seventeenth centuries these picots can be seen; their gradual evolution from a practical detail into needle-made, richly ornamented lace edgings is also apparent. The various parts of a garment could also be joined along two hemmed sides by oblique topstitching, so that a narrow gap was left between the two hems. By strengthening the threads with buttonhole stitching, the result would be something like a lace insertion. Other practical necessities, such as slit reinforcements on shirts and shifts, were similarly elaborated (fig. 328). A garment's decorative motifs were generally derived from the garment's function and from needlework solutions to related problems. The extra material at neck, armhole, and wristband was not cut away but gathered into fine pleats, which were secured with one catch stitch per gather. This could be done on the reverse side of the garment or on the outer side. When done on the reverse side, the fabric forms neatly laid groups of gathers contrasting beautifully with the softly billowing part where the gathers stop. If alternate pairs of folds are joined by catch stitching in alternate rows, smocking results. This decorative gathering has never been especially common in Swedish dress. On the Continent, during the Renaissance, it seems to have been a well-liked decorative element on shirts, shifts, and women's headdresses. In certain regions of Europe, this stitching has survived in the shirts of the folk costume, especially in a type of blouse worn in England, called a smock; hence the name of this ornamental gathering.

326. Shirt of white linen tabby with embroidery in backstitch, whipped wave stitch, and geometric satin stitch. Västra Vingåker, Södermanland.

White embroidery

White embroidery developed naturally out of plain sewing. It first flourished in the sixteenth and seventeenth centuries, when it was the dominant form of decoration on bedding and dress linen. Borders along necklines and slits, wristbands, the edges of pillowcases, sheets, and tablecloths were worked in one-directional drawn-thread work such as hemstitching, or two-directional drawn-thread work combined with geometrical satin stitch (figs. 330, 331).

One-directional drawn-thread work (*punto tirato*)—based on threads drawn out of the fabric in one direction—is very old. Textiles adorned with small areas worked in hemstitching and drawn-fabric work have been found in Egyptian tombs from 300–200 B.C. Peruvian articles from the pre-Columbian era were executed in the same techniques. During the Middle Ages, drawn-fabric work with colored thread on loose weave was executed in much the same fashion. Borders of this type on shifts and shirts can be seen in portraits from the late Middle Ages.

During the fifteenth and sixteenth centuries, white embroidery reached a very high level of excellence, especially in Italy. A number of variants of drawn-thread work were developed. Particularly highly developed was the two-directional drawn-thread work, in which both warp and weft threads are drawn out to form open squares. In these squares, threads are strung and overcast with buttonhole stitch. Geometric ornamentation is characteristic of the early patterns in this decorative work, employing stars and circles inscribed in squares (fig. 334). This is the so-called *reticella* pattern. *Reticella*, from the Italian meaning "small net," refers to the square holes in the fabric resulting from the drawing out of warp and weft threads. Later, the squares were widened, and diagonal threads were added. Instead of draw-

327. Wristband, detail, showing embroidery in geometric satin stitch and row of *nuggor*, whipped-over picots. Dalarna.

328. Slit reinforcements and red monograms on shirts and shifts. Sorunda, Södermanland. Privately owned.

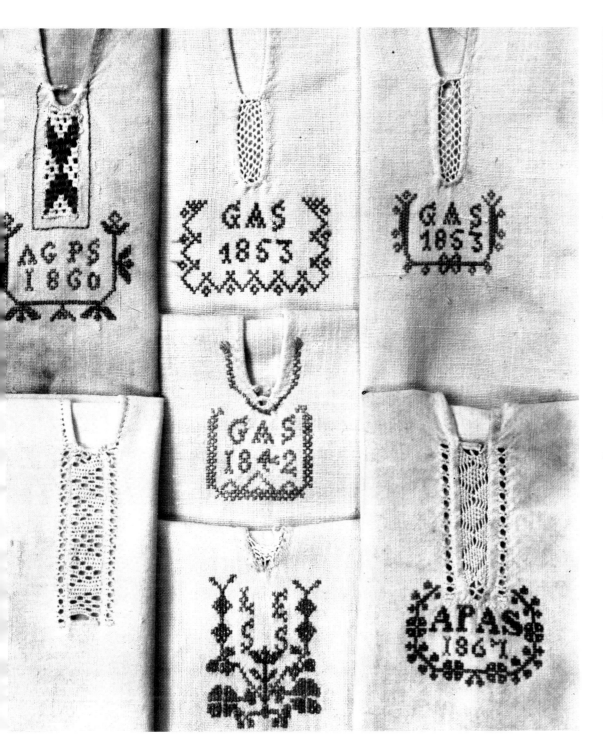

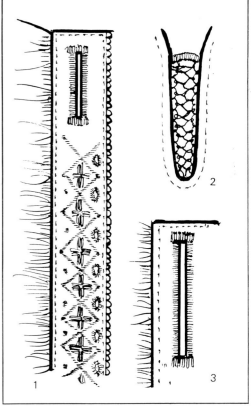

329. Needlework details on shirt: (1) Wristband. (2) Front slit reinforcement. (3) Buttonhole. Jörlanda, Bohuslän.

ing out warp and weft threads, large portions of the fabric were simply cut away and the holes filled with a great variety of *reticella* patterns, resulting in so-called cut work (*punto tagliato*).[9] Softly curving forms were introduced: vines, animals, and other figures. At this point, baroque forms began to supplant the completely geometrical forms of the Renaissance.

However, Renaissance ornament was to have a greater impact than baroque ornament, because the former was compatible with the right-angled structure of the ground fabric, and also, it should be added, because the period of Renaissance ornament coincided with the

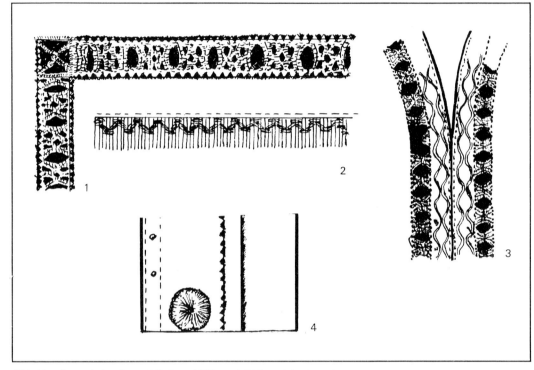

330. Needlework detail on shift from Hällestad, Skåne: (1) Edge of collar with one-directional drawn-thread work. (2) Small pleats, secured by backstitching. (3) Neck-opening slit with one-directional drawn-thread work. (4) Wristband with webbed button and rows of backstitching and knot stitches.

invention of the printing press. Duplication of texts and pictures opened up unlimited possibilities, and the distribution of patterns was facilitated accordingly.

In Sweden, one-directional drawn-thread work with colored thread is found on the shirts worn by the members of the Sture house when they were assassinated in 1567.[10] These shirts are now exhibited in the Vestment Chambers in Uppsala Cathedral.

In the latter part of the sixteenth century and throughout the seventeenth century, *reticella* work dominated ornamental needlework, especially on sheets and pillowcases, where it was the accepted decoration in southern and western Europe. Even today, in various parts of Europe, can be found examples strongly reminiscent of this decorative work in peasant

milieu. It takes the form of one- and two-directional drawn-thread work, usually in combination with geometrical satin stitch. In Sweden, there is an unbroken tradition of openwork in certain parts of Skåne, in the form of both drawn-thread work and cut work. It flourished on the collars of shirts and shifts, along shirt-front slits and on wristbands, on headcloths, decorative handkerchiefs, cloths to cover provisions baskets, sheets, and pillowcases (figs. 328–32)—all the articles that had been decorated with openwork for the aristocracy in the sixteenth and seventeenth centuries. However, among the upper classes, *reticella* started to disappear in the latter part of the seventeenth century, whereas among the peasants of Skåne it remained as a fixed form for the decoration of dress and bed linen. This

tradition continued up to the middle of the nineteenth century also in Blekinge, Småland, Hälsingland, Dalarna, and to a certain extent in Västra Vingåker, Österåker, and Sorunda—all in Södermanland—and in certain parts of Värmland.

The birch-bark work of Hälsingland—actually a two-directional drawn-thread work—is so called because it was sewn on linen tabby stretched over birch bark or on threads strung across the bark (fig. 333). One could also use a very loose tabby, and pull together groups of threads with stitches (drawn-fabric work). The basic pattern motif was the diamond or rhombus, created by drawing the fabric together in various ways, creating contrasting areas of light and shadow. Dalarna white embroidery was dominated by the geometrical satin stitch, and drawn-thread work was generally limited to one or a couple of threads drawn out along the edges (fig. 336). The *reticella* proper, i.e., squares in two-directional drawn-thread work, was thus missing here. Typical patterns of this province consisted of crosses, diamonds, diagonal crosses, diagonal half-crosses, zigzag lines, dentiled chevrons, and dentiled crosses—all traditional ornaments traceable to prehistoric times. To a certain extent, what has been said about the white embroidery of Dalarna was true also for the embroidery of Värmland, Blekinge, Södermanland (fig. 327) (Sorunda and Västra Vingåker), and Hälsingland—though the "white" embroidery of Hälsingland was done also in red or red and white. Only in Skåne was the *reticella* pattern so strongly anchored in peasant milieu that it has continued in unbroken tradition to the present.

In all peripheral regions of Europe, *reticella* —sometimes quite extensively transformed— has survived in peasant needlework, for example, on the Greek islands, in the Balkan States, in Spain, and in Italy. In Denmark it survived in the so-called Hedebo work, which was popularized at the end of the nineteenth century and became quite prominent in bourgeois needlework. Skåne cut work and the Norwegian Hardanger work, likewise preserving the *reticella* work of the Renaissance, became fashionable around the same time. *Reti-*

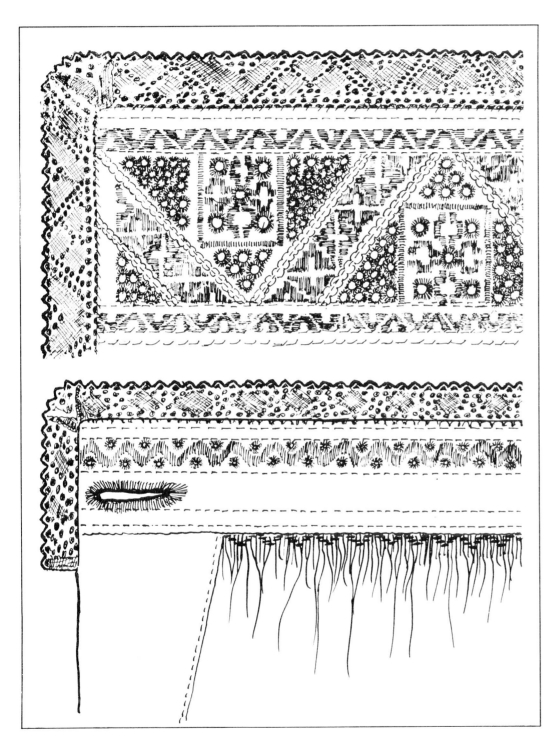

cella embroidery is characterized by the order and linear clarity typical of Renaissance ornament. Although *reticella* lived on in upper-class milieu far into the seventeenth century, certain pattern changes crept in from around 1600 and were to have far-reaching consequences. Stylistically, the baroque era—in Sweden, in the latter part of the seventeenth century—demanded massive, rounded, and spatially developed forms. The somewhat dry linearity of *reticella* yielded to flowers, foliage, animal and human figures. To begin with, these were embroidered with the help of the interlaced thread systems of the ground fabric. But fairly soon a decisive change took place. White embroidery was freed from the structure of the fabric, and during the latter part of the seventeenth century, patterns were allowed to extend freely over the surface.

Embroidery on knotted net

Another technique well suited to the linear ornament of the Renaissance, with its sharp contrasts between ground and ornamentation, is embroidery on knotted net (darned netting or filet work).

The art of knotting nets was known in the Stone Age. As mentioned above, fishnets of bast were among the earliest textile products known. The knotting of the filet—the knotted net ground for embroidery—is done either with the fingers alone, as in bast knotting, or with the aid of a netting needle over a mesh pin, as in knotting fishnets, or with a special filet needle. The netting needle and the filet needle were already known in prehistoric times. The filet needle (figs. 392–94) was introduced in Sweden towards the end of the eighteenth century, when netting and filet work of various kinds were very much in vogue—part of a general revival of interest around 1800 in classical antiquity. In the same way, embroidery on knotted net had spread from the

331. Embroidery on shirt of linen tabby from Hörby, Skåne. Collar, geometric satin stitch, overcast holes, and drawn-fabric work. Cuff, geometric satin stitch, overcast holes, rows of backstitching, and decoratively secured gathers (smocking).

232

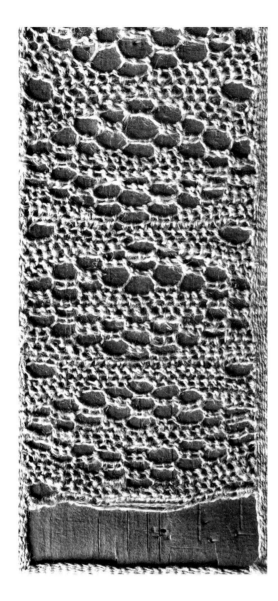

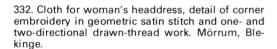

332. Cloth for woman's headdress, detail of corner embroidery in geometric satin stitch and one- and two-directional drawn-thread work. Mörrum, Blekinge.

333. Birch-bark work. Birch bark was used as a foundation for the working of needlepoint lace. Delsbo, Hälsingland.

334. Cloth, consisting of squares of linen tabby embroidered in two-directional drawn-thread work, alternating with squares of needlepoint lace. The patterns of embroidery as well as lace squares are of *reticella* type, typical of the Renaissance. First half of the seventeenth century.

335. Bed with two pillows, both in pillowcases with "caps." The "cap" on top is embroidered in a red star pattern, the bottom "cap" with stars in geometric satin stitch in red cotton. The top sheet has an insertion of bobbin lace. Gräsbo *fäbod*, Hälsingland.

Mediterranean countries with the general cultural currents during the sixteenth and seventeenth centuries, which also looked back to ancient Greece and Rome for inspiration.

Filet embroidery is an art with a long tradition, occurring in the ancient civilizations around the Mediterranean, in Coptic Egypt, and in medieval Europe. In Sweden, knotted silk net with loops of varying sizes is preserved from the Middle Ages as part of a canopy, now in Statens Historiska Museum, Stockholm (The Museum of National Antiquities). From the

sixteenth and seventeenth centuries, there are numerous examples of knotted net work with pattern created by weaving a thread back and forth in straight stitches over bars of the netting (darning stitch or *point de reprise*) (figs. 339, 341, 402), or weaving it vertically and horizontally, forming a kind of loose tabby (linen stitch or *point de toile*) (figs. 338, 400), or by looping the thread in soft loops around the net bars (loop stitch or *point d'esprit*).

It is probably no coincidence that no less than three throne and table canopies as well

as bed curtains, preserved from the sixteenth and seventeenth centuries, were made in embroidery on knotted net. Furthermore, filet work was often used for borders on bed valances, and as insertions in sheets and pillowcases; in other words, as a substitute for lace. The great popularity enjoyed by bobbin lace and needlepoint lace at this time was a strong stimulus to the production of lacelike needlework, such as filet work.

Above all, in those parts of the country where older traditions lived on in the textile

336. Decorative handkerchief of white linen tabby, embroidered in geometric satin stitch, whipped wave stitch, and one-directional drawn-thread work. Leksand, Dalarna.

235

338. Knotted net of red silk, consisting of four squares with different motifs, embroidered with blue, green, and yellow yarn in linen stitch (*point de toile*) sewn together. Fifteenth century.

decoration of the house, embroidery on knotted net achieved such importance in peasant milieu that it survived there long after its heyday. As pointed out above, one especially conservative region was that of the Southern Götaland house type in southwestern Småland and adjacent parts of Västergötland. Especially in Västergötland, net work achieved monumental expression in ceiling cloths of considerable size and quality. Nordiska Museet possesses two

337. Decorative handkerchief of white linen tabby, embroidered in geometric satin stitch, one-directional drawn-thread work (hemstitching), and Holbein stitch. Västra Vingåker, Södermanland.

such ceiling cloths in linen, so-called *språng-sparrlakan.*[11] They consist of widths of linen alternating with rectangular panels of darned knotted net with pattern in linen stitch. To darn, sew, or embroider on net has in this region been called "[to] *språnga,*" and each darned panel has also been known as a *språnga.* The design is, in part, a diagonal check pattern with lily crosses or stars, and, in part, a pattern divided into transverse bands with three stylized female figures alternating with two such figures flanking a tree. The pattern type is medieval and the function of the hanging is also of medieval origin. Ceiling cloths have retained their function as inner roof linings in Västergötland. They are fixed by their upper end to the ridge pole and hung under the sloping roof down to the top of the wall, where they are finished off with a braided fringe (figs. 55, 400).

In Småland and Halland, also in the region of the Southern Götaland house type, there are canopies (figs. 401, 402) with inserted panels of knotted net, darned or embroidered in darning stitch and loop stitch in red and white. The pattern here also draws on old motifs: stars, diamonds, stylized trees, and checks. Decorative hangings on walls or ceiling, ceiling cloths, hanging cloths, and bed curtains were often finished off with borders (fig. 268). Borders were also hung on shelves, beams, purlins, indeed, from all projecting edges (e.g., fig. 133). They were called *taklister* (ceiling borders), *hyllkanter* (shelf edgings), and *opphängen* (hangings), and were done in net work. These knotted net strips were decorated with tassels and fringe, or with darning stitch in white or white and red linen or—in the nineteenth century—in cotton (see fig. 341). The patterns were in part of the above-mentioned medieval type, in part of unmistakable Renaissance type with Solomonic knot motifs, stylized vines, and pairs of confronting stylized lions

339. Canopy composed of twenty-eight square panels of knotted green silk net, embroidered with the ancestral coats of arms of Nils Lilliehöök and Virginia Hand in darning stitch (*point de reprise*). Dated 1654.

340. Bed curtain. Shading stitch embroidery in silk on knotted net of linen. Mid-seventeenth century.

and birds—motifs which demanded a model, indicating a contact with another production milieu. Embroidered net work is found only in southwestern Sweden, just as is white embroidery in the form of drawn-thread work and cut work with geometric satin stitch in patterns of *reticella* type. Both white embroidery and embroidered net were apparently brought by western European cultural waves, which reached Sweden from the south via Denmark, and were felt especially in the former Danish provinces of Skåne, Halland, and Blekinge, and

in adjoining parts of Småland and Västergötland.

Canvas work
Like the weave-regulated white embroidery, canvas work is dependent on the structure of the ground weave, the right-angled net work of the weft and warp threads. Precisely because of this similarity, these two types of embroidery also made use of similar patterns, which facilitated a wide pattern distribution. Filling stitches

are: cross-stitch, petit point (or tent stitch), long-armed cross-stitch (i.e., cross-stitch with one cross arm extended), oblique Gobelin stitch, and Hungarian stitch (fig. 343). The ground weave is usually a coarse tabby of hemp or jute; in finer work, it is cotton or linen tabby. In the nineteenth century, a special loose canvas came into use. This type of embroidery was therefore often called canvas work, or, in French, *broderie en tapisserie*. The Swedish term for long-armed cross-stitch, *tvistsöm,* was derived from the ground on

341. Border or edging of knotted cotton net with pattern of white and red cotton yarn in darning stitch (*point de reprise*). Knotted fringe of finer cotton yarn with tassels in red and white. Västbo, Småland.

342. Wall hanging in canvas stitches; cross-stitch and long-armed cross-stitch in wool on loose linen tabby. Ramsele Church, Ångermanland.

which it was commonly worked, *tvist* weave (an extended tabby, resembling Penelope canvas).

The earliest known example of cross-stitching in Sweden is a hanging from Fogdö Church in Södermanland, dated to around 1500. It is now in Strängnäs Cathedral Museum. Two other early examples are an altar frontal from Marieby Church in Jämtland and a hanging

from Ramsele in Ångermanland (fig. 342), stitched in cross-stitch and long-armed cross-stitch. The use of *tvist* weave for ground in canvas work is confirmed by archival data from the sixteenth century. There are great similarities between the patterns of these cross-stitched works and the patterns on graph paper published in the sixteenth and seventeenth centuries, on one hand, and white embroidery over

counted threads, on the other (figs. 306, 332, 345, 400). No doubt these pattern books were used for all the counted thread work which flourished in the Renaissance. Judging from a few preserved objects decorated with different kinds of counted-thread work, this type of pattern on textiles was already known to some extent in the Middle Ages. It is quite certain that a medieval ornamental heritage was pre-

343. Table cover, silk embroidery in Hungarian stitch and petit point on loose linen tabby. The central motif is the combined coats of arms of the houses Trauttmannsdorf and Kirchberg. First half of the seventeenth century.

344. Carriage cushion, long-armed cross-stitch in wool yarn on coarse *tvist* weave, an extended tabby resembling Penelope canvas. Initialed and dated GHLS 1788. Hörby, Skåne.

345. Cushion in long-armed cross-stitch in wool yarn on coarse *tvist* weave, an extended tabby resembling Penelope canvas. Embroidered with the date 1833. Veberöd, Skåne.

served in the geometric diaper patterns in the pattern books, and also in the samplers worked over counted threads. Here, as at earlier stages of pattern development and in all simpler pattern design, there are simply zigzag lines, stars, squares, and diamonds. At times, the similarity between star or check patterns embroidered in weave-like stitches and the same patterns in discontinuous brocade—e.g., *krabbasnår* (fig. 236), with the pattern weft laid in by hand with a needle in a kind of geometric satin stitch—is so great that only careful scrutiny can tell them apart. Geometric stem stitch, forming zigzag lines or diagonal checks, is found, like cross-stitch and long-armed cross-stitch, all over the country in motifs taken from samplers. In Skåne there is, however, a very high frequency of sixteenth- and seventeenth-century patterns in cross-stitch and long-armed cross-stitch (figs. 344–46). In spite of intensive collecting and analyzing activity on the part of museums, this pattern treasure is not yet fully cataloged. In practically every home, the products of generations remain, in the form of bench runners and cushions in cross-stitch and long-armed cross-stitch. As late as the nineteenth century, needleworkers faithfully copied sixteenth- and seventeenth-century pattern models. The patterns were predominantly of a repeating type, covering the surface with lozenges, stars, and zigzag motifs. The Skåne long-armed cross-stitch work also shows a rich development of floral motifs, palmettos and tulips, and proportioned compositions with central panel, borders, central motif, and corner motifs, all in Renaissance style. The borders generally include Solomonic knot motifs, diamonds, squares, stars, etc., or stylized foliage. The corner and central motifs are stylized trees and flowers.

Some of these textiles may have used additional pattern elements on the undecorated surfaces, in the form of initials, crowns, flower urns, chairs, and dates—motifs taken directly from samplers and strewn over the existing

346. Cushion, long-armed cross-stitch in wool on coarse *tvist* weave, an extended tabby resembling Penelope canvas. Skåne.

composition in a kind of *horror vacui*. It was characteristic of canvas work in the eighteenth century that it demanded more patience and persistence than skill. Hence it was not considered the province of professional embroiderers.

Free embroidery
Wool and silk
Embroidery with silk, gold, and silver thread has always been a genre demanding considerable economic resources. In the Middle Ages, it was the Church and the king and his circle that had need for the ostentation in which embroidery played such an important role. Professionally trained embroiderers, aided by the best and most style-conscious pattern drafters available, created and maintained a standard for orphrey—silk, gold, and silver embroidery —which, aesthetically and technically, was comparable to, and possibly even surpassed, painting. Medieval figure embroidery was called *peinture à l'aiguille* or "painting with a needle." The gold- and silver-embroidered ornaments framing these "paintings" can be compared to goldsmith work. The Renaissance with its predilection for solid forms and clear outlines attached greater importance to overall composition than did the Middle Ages. The medieval diaper patterns were replaced during the Renaissance by compositions specifically designed for the surface to be decorated (fig. 367). A distinct expression of the latter tendency is the use of the cartouche and the division of the surface into borders and panel with richly developed central and corner motifs (figs. 304, 317).

During the seventeenth century and the first half of the eighteenth century, metal embroidery played a significant role, perhaps mostly in combination with silk embroidery (figs. 301, 303, 348). The intensive use of metallic materials declined markedly from the mid-eighteenth century. One chronicler writes that, in the 1750s and '60s, metal embroidery was used only in liturgical textiles and costumes for theatrical entertainments and masquerades. With this decline, professional embroidery as a whole started to lose ground. Considerable

349. Cushion for bridal kneeler. Blue wadmal, embroidered with wool yarn in shading stitch, stem stitch, and couched filling stitches. Marked KPD 1806. First used at the wedding of Kerstin Bengtsdotter in 1806. Vä, Skåne.

350. Fine leather gloves with silk embroidery in shading stitch. The gauntlets are embroidered with the date 1798.

351. Bridal sash of red wadmal with silk embroidery in shading stitch. Monogrammed and dated OIS 1804 and KID 1804. Loshult, Skåne.

and were probably manufactured centrally and distributed through salesmen. The embroidered fabric was sold ready for mounting on hat frames. At Nordiska Museet there is a coverlet made entirely from such unmounted cap materials. As a rule, these materials date to the beginning of the eighteenth century. Ready-made embroideries are also found on neckerchiefs embroidered in colored wool.

The transition from silk to wool in peasant embroidery was facilitated by the fact that it had already taken place in bourgeois milieu.

Lavish shading stitch work in colored wool, with baroque and rococo floral motifs and lingering elements of Renaissance composition, was done in varying frequency throughout the country. Above all, chair cushions of wool featured this type of embroidery. As the chair was a relatively late addition in peasant milieu, the existence of chair cushions and of shaded crewel work in peasant homes is generally attributed to a direct influence from bourgeois milieu in the form of purchases, gifts, inheritances, or orders from professional workshops.

In the provinces along the Norwegian border, these cushions show a clear rococo influence—typical of Norwegian peasant milieu (color fig. 38), but not generally found in Sweden.

In other provinces, especially Småland and Halland (fig. 352), certain Renaissance features have lived on in overall composition: a proportioned design with well-developed corner motifs, sometimes also a central motif, combined with floral patterns of baroque or rococo type. In Skåne, free embroidery in colored wool yarn on wool was remarkably

247

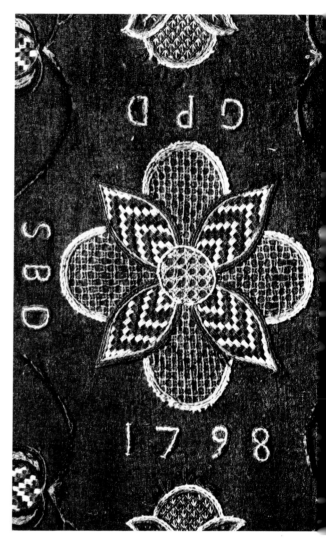

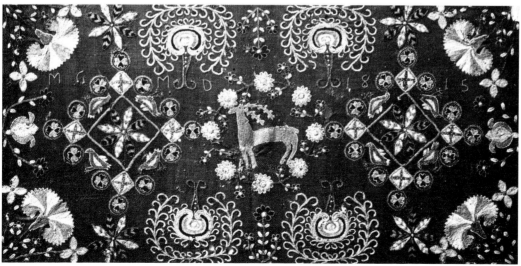

352. Cushion of wadmal, embroidered in shading stitch, stem stitch, and chain stitch. Halland.

353. Cushion of red wadmal, embroidered in satin stitch, various filling stitches, and stem stitch. Marked BNS/ CPD/ SBD/ 1798. Skåne.

354. Cushion of wool twill, embroidered in satin stitch, shading stitch, and chain stitch. Marked MG MD 1815. Skåne.

355. Coverlet of red wadmal, wool embroidery worked in shading stitch, stem stitch, French knots, and various filling stitches. Marked ANS/ HND/ 1827. Skåne; now in Kulturhistoriska Museet, Lund, Skåne.

well developed in chair and carriage cushions, pillows, coverlets, and carpets (figs. 349, 353–61). Side by side, one would use more formal compositions with corner ornaments, central wreath, crown, and initials, as well as echoes of the same motifs in freer floral compositions, distributed evenly over the surface. Embroideries of figural compositions, Adam and Eve and the Serpent in Paradise, horsemen, men and women, deer, parrots, birds, lions, and various other actual or mythical beasts are strikingly reminiscent of some Flemish weaving designs, and have probably been created in the same way—i.e., certain motifs have been taken out of their context and combined with others (color figs. 36, 37, 39, 40). New combinations of traditional elements have been made by every succeeding generation. The free-form

356. Cushion of wool, detail showing embroidery with wool yarn in shading stitch, satin stitch, and stem stitch. Dated ANO 1787. Önnestad, Skåne.

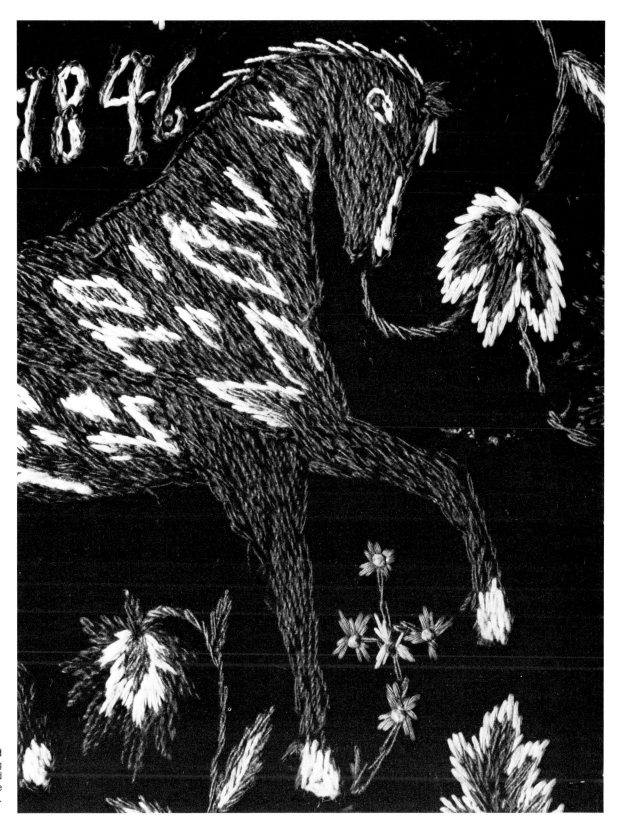

357. Cushion of black wool, embroidered with wool and cotton yarn in shading stitch, stem stitch, chain stitch, and French knots. Detail of central horse motif. Signed and dated ONS 1846. Skåne.

358. The cushion in fig. 357, detail of bird.

36. Carriage cushion of black half-wool in satin weave, embroidered in chain stitch, double stem stitch, and knot stitches with wool and white cotton yarn. In the center is the Fall of Man, flanked by, right, the Creation of Eve and, left, the Expulsion from Paradise. Marked NIS IBD ANO 1814. Åkarp, Skåne.

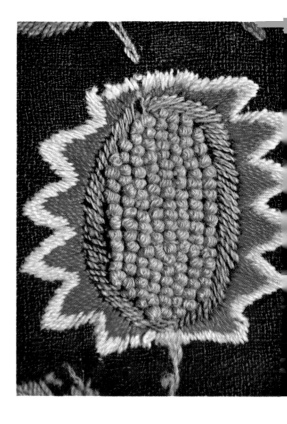

37. Carriage cushion, completely covered with wool and silk embroidery in satin stitch, stem stitch, and knot stitch. Detail of the central motif, a unicorn. Svedala, Skåne.

38. Chair cushion of wadmal, detail showing floral motif of wool embroidery in shading stitch, marked in stem stitch FFS 1763. Härjedalen.

39. Cushion of black wool tabby, embroidered with wool yarn in stem stitch, French knots, filling stitches, and shading stitch. Detail, showing flower worked in shading stitch, stem stitch, and French knots. Signed and dated ANO 1787 NPS in stem stitch. Önnestad, Skåne.

40. Chair cushion of green wadmal, detail showing wool embroidery in shading stitch, satin stitch, and stem stitch. Signed EOD 1832. Skåne.

41. Jacket of woolen cloth, detail showing wool embroidery in shading stitch, satin stitch, and stem stitch. Floda, Dalarna.

359. Chair cushion of black wool, embroidered with wool yarn in shading stitch, stem stitch, filling stitch, satin stitch, etc. Detail of central motif with bird. Signed and dated MND 1820. Bara, Skåne.

360. Chair cushion of wool, with wool embroidery in shading stitch, stem stitch, and filling stitch. Dated in stem stitch 1780 D 16 M. Norra Åsbo, Skåne.

embroideries of this type in the Nordiska Museet date from 1750 to 1850.

Free-form embroidery as well as Flemish weaving were stimulated by favorable economic conditions and their influence on the living and housing standards. Particularly in the affluent northeastern parts of Skåne, a number of large coverlets were created with rich floral decoration in shading stitch and filling stitches in colored wool on red, blue, or green wool (fig. 355).

These coverlets show a certain similarity to the embroidered Blekinge hanging cloths and crewel embroidered cushions in floral patterns (figs. 320, 321, 362). There is obviously a connection in that the same style, rococo floral ornament, had a great impact on both Skåne and Blekinge. The penetration of this style was undoubtedly aided by improved economic conditions—perhaps caused by the financial gains from the lively seafaring trade along the Baltic coast in the eighteenth century—which made possible a higher living standard. One could afford to consult pattern drafters from bourgeois milieu.

Double running stitch (Holbein stitch)
There are a number of works preserved from the sixteenth and the first part of the seventeenth centuries, predominantly in red silk on white linen (fig. 364), mostly employing stem stitch and also diagonal line stitch (square stitch), cross-stitch, and drawn-fabric work. A major part of the preserved works in double running stitch (Holbein stitch) consists of narrow strips, which probably decorated neckbands, wristbands, and collars on shirts and shifts. This stitch is seen in portraits from the first part of the sixteenth century as an important detail in fashionable dress. In Germany this type of embroidery is called Holbein work because it can be seen on the linen in most of the portraits by Hans Holbein the Elder. In England it is called blackwork, quite naturally, as it was most often stitched with black thread on white. It is also known as Spanish work, possibly indicating the way in which the technique reached England. As in many other

cases, Spain, like Italy, had probably, in turn, received the inspiration for this kind of embroidery in colored silk on white linen from the Orient. Similar stitchery can be found today in the textile traditions in Asia Minor, Syria, Greece, and North Africa. A wealth of oriental patterns and motifs was transmitted by Arabs, along with silk, cotton, and other textile materials, as part of the growing trade between the Mediterranean countries and the Orient in the Middle Ages. Supply permitting, silk became a highly appreciated replacement for wool and linen yarn.

Colored running stitch in silk was a relatively short-lived fashion phenomenon. The practical difficulties of using silk for bed and dress linen—by repeated washings the silk would wear away or disintegrate—probably helped hasten its decline in favor of white embroidery with linen yarn. Patterns of silk in double running stitch on large tablecloths have with time been largely obliterated, except for the traced outlines (fig. 319). By stylistic elements, it can be determined that they were made in the sixteenth century or the first part of the seventeenth century. They appear to be traceable to southern Sweden. The close relationship between these tablecloths and cloths from northern Germany or Denmark is apparent. The cloths preserved in Sweden are therefore either imported goods from Danish or German territory, or, possibly, copies of such models. The figures and ornaments in certain of these tablecloths show clear stylistic influences from fifteenth- and sixteenth-century woodcuts illustrating the Bible. They mark a transition between Gothic and Renaissance design, incorporating calligraphic, ornamental folds in the costumes of the figures portrayed, and the lush Renaissance acanthus in the border. As has already been pointed out, embroidery of this linear kind shows a close relationship to the graphic arts in general.

There is a good reason for discussing in some detail a group of embroideries which obviously were products of professional pattern drafters. The situation was very similar to that of canvas work: the execution did not demand much technical skill, provided one had a pattern. It is not known whether drawn-up and ready-

made patterns were offered for sale, nor is it known how the contact between pattern sources and embroiderers was made.

There is evidence that Holbein work was produced in the homes. It was used in bedding—sheet borders (fig. 364), pillowcase caps, bed valances—and in dress linen in simpler patterns, which were more accessible for poorer and socially less prominent milieus.

The peasant class accepted this type of decorative stitchery. With regard to material (white linen and colored yarn) and technique (double running stitch with stem stitch, diagonal line stitch, cross-stitch, and geometric satin stitch), two types of Swedish peasant embroidery immediately come to mind. These are the so-called *svartstick* (literally, "black stitch") work of Leksand, Dalarna (figs. 365, 366), and the Vingåker work from Södermanland (fig. 337). Leksand blackwork was used in fichus for women's formal wear, so-called *svartsticks-kläden* (black-stitch cloths). It was executed in black silk or linen in cross-stitch, whipstitch, and geometric satin stitch on white linen or cotton fabric (figs. 365, 366). The oldest dated specimen is from 1809, the latest from the 1890s. In the earlier one, the thread is brownish black, almost sepia in color. Not until after the middle of the century, with the more general use of chemical dyes, could the thread be dyed completely black. The pattern is concentrated in one corner of the square cloth, as these cloths were worn folded on the diagonal. There are borders along the two sides joining to form the pattern corner, and smaller motifs in the two corners which are divided diagonally by the fold. The central motif is either one or three squares and a diagonally placed motif, resembling a stylized tree or candelabrum composed of crosses, hearts, and diamonds (fig. 365). The ornamentation of the corner squares is related to canvas-work motifs on samplers: diamonds, chevrons, and dentiled crosses. There is one Leksand blackwork fichu from the mid-1700s which has only the candelabrum motif and none of the later common checks of geometric satin stitch. There are no older embroideries preserved which might help connect Leksand blackwork to the Holbein work of the Vasa era, but the

361. The *sal,* drawing room, with area rugs embroidered in shading stitch by Mrs. Else Christensdotter in 1900 for her son's newly built home.

362. Hanging cloth of white linen tabby, embroidered with linen yarn in shading stitch, filling stitch, and stem stitch. Dated 1840. Åryd, Blekinge.

363. Hanging cloth, detail showing the Fall of Man, embroidered in shading stitch, satin stitch, and stem stitch. Legend: A=Adam, E=Eve, LO=*Lede Ormen* (The Evil Serpent). Blekinge.

latter is the only type of embroidery to which it shows any greater stylistic similarities.

In this context the decorative handkerchiefs of Västra Vingåker also deserve to be mentioned. They are decorated with diagonal line stitch and geometric satin stitch in red, green, and yellow silk. The pattern elements, which form squares in all four corners, are checks, diamonds, and hearts.

Appliqué, inlaid appliqué, and patchwork

Appliqué, inlaid appliqué, and patchwork are techniques in which pieces of cloth, or sometimes leather, are cut out in various shapes or figures and attached with various stitches to another fabric, either on top of, under, or edge to edge with the other fabric. Usually a cord, a strip of skin, or one or more threads are sewn down along the edges with couching stitches (figs. 367–70). The cut-out shapes are of a different color from the background, so that the patterns stand out in bold reliefs. Just as drawn-thread work and cut work have developed out of linen needlework, so have these techniques probably developed out of the tailoring of cloth, wadmal, and leather. As mentioned above, the sewing and decoration of all woolen articles and the decoration of fells and skin sheets were the responsibility of the tailor. By fulling and shearing, woolens became so felted that they could be cut or punched out in elaborate shapes without fear of the weft picks coming loose and pulling out

257

of the warp. In the late Middle Ages, these cutouts were a featured motif in fashionable dress. The same was true of the joining of different colored fabrics. One might, for example, join a red hose leg to a green hose leg, or make one half of a tabard blue and the other half yellow, or divide it into four panels with diagonally corresponding colors. One might cut out round, square, or star-shaped holes and lay a contrasting fabric under the holes. Piping and cording—strips of cloth or leather inserted in seams, bindings, edges, bands, etc.—were also made of contrasting color. The entire feudal system with its ceremonial apparatus created a considerable demand for decorative, heraldic textiles easily readable at some distance. Thus, banners, garments, canopies, wall hangings, and other articles were appliquéd with the family's coat of arms, and other signs of ancestry and family ties. Some artifacts of this type have been preserved, but they are primarily known through archival sources. Heraldic beasts—lions, deer, eagles, and double-headed eagles—and other symbols were important secular design elements. A few examples have survived from the Middle Ages. The ecclesiastical milieu also put appliqué to good use. Some altar frontals and other church furnishings using appliqué are preserved from that era. During the sixteenth and seventeenth centuries, the genre enjoyed great popularity. The stylistic ideal of the Renaissance dovetailed with the linearity and clear color combinations inherent in appliqué work. It is comparable to marquetry and stone mosaic, both of which were admired forms of decoration during the Renaissance. A number of large coverlets and also some smaller objects in appliqué, such as cushions, are preserved from the seventeenth century. They were apparently the work of professionals, being made either by the royal workshop or individual embroiderers attached to the court, or artisans trained at court and working for members of the Swedish aristocracy (fig. 367).

Hardly any of this work is found in peasant milieu. From Småland and Halland come some cushions and coverlets in appliqué, but they were probably the work of tailors or others with professional contacts (color fig. 44). Two

364. Sheet of white linen tabby, embroidered in red silk with the coats of arms and initials of Erik Olofsson Stake and Ingeborg Posse worked in stem stitch and satin stitch. 1590s.

signed works are known by one Maria Krook, a parson's daughter mentioned above in connection with Flemish weaving.

In northern Sweden, however, there was a development of appliqué work which probably went back to the Vasa era, possibly to the Middle Ages. Appliqué was used to decorate skirt-bags and purses (figs. 369, 370), which

365. Corner of *svartsticksklädé* (black-stitch cloth), fichu for woman's formal wear, from Leksand, Dalarna. Embroidery in geometric satin stitch, cross-stitch, and diagonal line stitch (square stitch). Marked BOD 1821.

366. Detail of embroidered corner of *svartsticksklädé* (black-stitch cloth) in geometric satin stitch and herringbone stitch on white linen tabby. Gagnef, Dalarna.

259

367. Chair cushion of red wadmal, appliquéd with black velvet outlined with blue linen cording. The design incorporates the coats of arms and initials of Mathias Soop and Elisabeth Oxenstierna and the date 1644.

of purse which was worn in full view, attached to the costume, flourished in the Middle Ages. In Dalarna, Hälsingland, Gästrikland, Jämtland, Härjedalen, Medelpad, and Ångermanland, and in certain conservative parts of Svealand and Götaland, the peasantry continued to wear the medieval type of purse; since it was intended to be worn in full view, it was trimmed accordingly. The most widespread and uniform of these decorative purses was the appliquéd purse. It was made of dark blue or black wadmal with appliquéd shapes in red and green, rarely any other color. The shapes were outlined with pewter thread. In Dalarna similar appliqué work was done also without the outlining pewter thread (fig. 370). The designs show different degrees of stylization, but can generally be traced to the medieval ornamental vocabulary—trees, crosses, dentiled squares, and hearts—with an addition of the later floral-urn motif.

The purses were often edged and backed with skin. Some were made entirely of skin with appliquéd pieces of wadmal, skin strips, and diverse other things—buttons, scraps of material, ribbons—and in some cases also with a mosaic of skin pieces (fig. 369). It is not known whether these purses represent older traditions, like those in birch-bark craft work, or whether they were made professionally and sold in Hälsingland and adjoining provinces. The standardization of design and technique indicates, however, the existence of some kind of centralized production. The relation of Lapp pewter embroidery to these appliquéd purses has been debated in various contexts. The consensus seems to be that Lapp pewter work has its own traditional forms, materials, and techniques.

Free embroidery in linen and cotton
As mentioned earlier, softer and freer patterns in white embroidery developed during the seventeenth century. To produce these patterns, other techniques were needed. Instead of stitches regulated by the weave, free stitches were used. Satin stitch, stem stitch, shading stitch, French knots, and couched filling stitches imparted a more painterly character

were worn to church as a decorative and formal touch to the costume. The custom of tying loose bags of pockets around the waist or to the belt is a practical and universal solution to the problem of where to carry small personal items. In the Middle Ages, decorated bags and purses were an important part of the

well-dressed man's and woman's attire. During the sixteenth century, the purse disappeared from the male costume, which instead acquired pockets; however, it figured prominently in bourgeois female dress as late as the eighteenth century and in peasant dress up to the latter part of the nineteenth century. Thus, the type

368. Embroidery on silk, appliqué with plain and patterned silk cutouts, outlined in silk couching. French knots, filling stitches, and back-stitching help articulate the pattern elements. Dated 1720.

369. Purses of skirt-bag type, skin with buttons and appliquéd red and green wadmal stitched with silk thread in back stitch, satin stitch, etc. Rättvik, Dalarna.

370. Decorative purse proper—with metal purse frame—in appliqué, blue wadmal with couched pewter thread outlining the red wadmal cutouts. Härjedalen.

to white embroidery in accord with baroque ideals. Special attention was paid to the contrast between the surface of the fabric and that of the embroidery. The resulting patterns combined solid shapes and clear outlines with interesting surface texture. The latter element was especially cultivated and reached a flowering, in more than one sense of the word, at the end of the seventeenth century and the beginning of the eighteenth century. The patterns lost their earlier order; the pattern drafter

seems to have given way to the virtuoso embroiderer or embroideress. Their ability to give life to the surfaces, to vary the fillings, to create new and surprising effects with the help of imaginative uses of the basic stitches, seems to have been unlimited (fig. 371).

The development of dress customs and house furnishings also created new uses for white embroidery. In the costume, embroidered decoration on decorative handkerchiefs, shirts, and shifts was, as a rule, replaced with laces, just

as was decorative trim on sheets and tablecloths (fig. 372). The use of lace as edging dominated completely and gave rise to lively export industries in Italy, France, and Flanders (pages 298 ff.).

Lace was so expensive that its importation was considered detrimental to state finances. There is a wealth of evidence testifying to the incredible extravagance of these fashionable laces. Ordinances were enacted to prevent the importing of lace, which was draining gold out of the country. Fashion, however, which made such lavish use of lace, demanded a replacement. White embroidery on batiste, which circumvented the sumptuary laws, made an excellent substitute (fig. 373). Embroidery on the finest linen batiste grew into a home industry in Germany with customers all over Europe. It was spread under the name of "Saxon embroidery." The skill attained here marked a high point in the development of white embroidery. It was clearly an exclusive decorative art form, which required near-professional training. The costly materials helped restrict these products to a fairly narrow circle. Technically, it meant a further enrichment of white embroidery. The thin material allowed extensive use of drawn-fabric work in a variety of grounds. There are samplers from the mid- and late-eighteenth century with close to a hundred different such grounds and filling stitches (fig. 313). Shadow work, with either appliqué or stitching on the reverse side, gives an exquisite, soft effect.

Batiste embroidery was a result of the encounter between white embroidery and the sheer white fabric which was first produced in Europe in the eighteenth century. Little wonder that people, charmed by its sheerness and delicacy, sought to cultivate its subtle interplay of light and shadow. This type of embroidery was taken up in Swedish peasant milieu only in the province of Blekinge. A number of preserved shifts with free linen embroidery testify that the materials of batiste embroidery were translated into local terms—more robust linen tabby and sturdy linen thread (figs. 374, 375). This circumstance is of interest because, among other things, it confirms the existence of intimate contacts of this region with bourgeois milieu since the latter part of the eighteenth century.

Cotton fabrics of all kinds, not least the thin, transparent fabrics like lawn, cambric, and batiste, completely dominated fashion around the year 1800. This vogue, spurred by the

371. Decoratively quilted coverlet of linen tabby, detail. Embroidery in geometric satin stitch, French knots, couching, and a wide variety of filling stitches. About 1750.

372. White embroidery, probably for pillowcase, in linen thread on fine, white linen tabby. The stitches include stem stitch, satin stitch, knot stitches, and filling stitches. Detail, showing Adam and Eve in Paradise, flanking the Tree of Knowledge. Middle of the seventeenth century. Nationalmuseum, Stockholm.

42. Tucker, embroidered with colored beads on waxed woolen shalloon and wadmal. Initials and date, HID 1845, in beadwork. Ingelstad, Skåne.

43. Bobbin laces of linen thread. Top to bottom: lace for shirt collar (pattern identical to that of drawn-thread work on the collar), Ingelstad, Skåne; Skåne lace; lace for linen hood, Leksand, Dalarna; lace in light red and white, Delsbo, Hälsingland; sheer hood lace from Rättvik, Dalarna; and lace for lace-edged cap, Floda, Dalarna.

44. Chair cushion of wadmal patchwork with overcast piping covering the joins. Åsenhöga, Småland.

45. Needle-looped wool mittens. Left, embroidered with wool yarn in shading stitch, Dalby, Värmland; right, embroidered with wool yarn in chain stitch, Sorunda, Södermanland. (See also fig. 441.)

46. Jacket sleeves, detail. Knitting of wool yarn in carnation pattern. Alfta, Hälsingland. (See also fig. 456.)

47. Knitted wool jackets. The dates 1854 and 1877, respectively, are knitted into their fronts (not visible in picture). Delsbo, Hälsingland. (See also figs. 457 and 458.)

availability of cotton, opened up new avenues for white embroidery. The thin, almost transparent, white cotton fabrics were often stitched with fairly thick, white, somewhat flossed or fuzzy cotton yarn (fig. 377). The effect was one of pure white on a shimmer of gray. Distinct, three-dimensional forms were also striven for (figs. 376, 379). It is with good reason that the padded or raised satin stitch now became the leitmotif in white embroidery. It appeared on dresses, shifts, vests, handkerchiefs, underwear, and the novel pantalettes for ladies. The latter were adorned with rows of wide, embroidered ruffles, which in the 1820s and '30s were worn showing below the hem of the skirt. This embroidery was also used on sheets and pillowcases, for large decorative monograms (fig. 379) on tablecloths, napkins, and towels—everywhere the padded satin stitch was to be found, usually combined with overcast eyelets. This particular combination was known as English embroidery—*brodérie Anglaise*—and became so popular that it was soon copied in a machine-made version. It can still be bought as yardage, so-called eyelet, which today has regained some of its past popularity. In Sweden it is commonly referred to as *tårtpapper* (literally, "cake paper"; paper doily), which actually is a reversal of cause and effect, as it is the paper doilies with stamped pattern which are an imitation of eyelet embroidery, and not vice versa.

Through a technical invention, white embroidery was given yet another expressive medium. Until 1818, all very fine netting had been made by hand, either on a lace pillow with bobbins, by knotting, or by looping with a needle. It was a tedious and laborious process, as a rule carried out only in conjunction with the making of laces. The French town of Tulle had specialized in net production—hence the name of the product. When tulle overnight could be produced by machine, embroidery on net experienced a tremendous upswing, espe-

373. White embroidery, probably for vanity table, of linen batiste embroidered in stem stitch, satin stitch, knot stitches, filling stitches, etc. Middle of the eighteenth century.

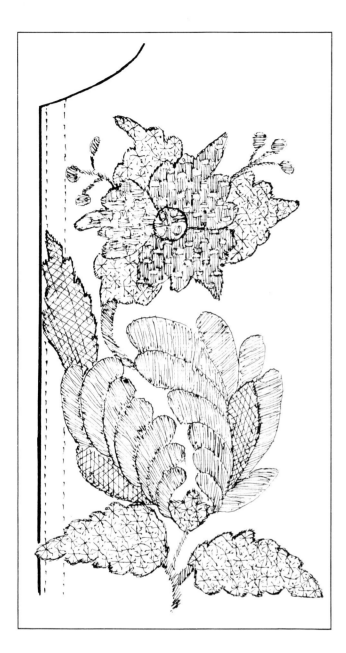

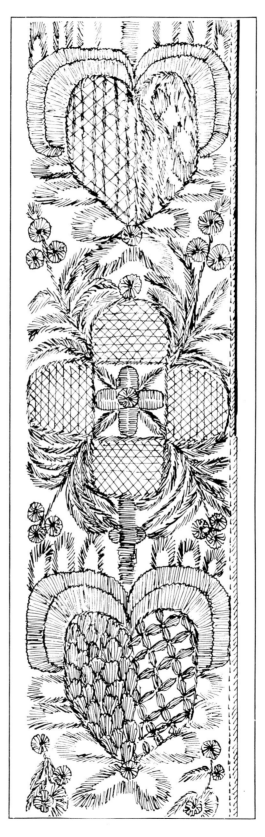

374. Woman's shirt of white linen tabby, detail;
embroidered with white linen thread in satin stitch,
stem stitch, and filling stitches. Hällaryd, Blekinge.

375. Sark or shift of white linen tabby, detail;
embroidered with white linen thread in satin stitch,
filling stitches, and overcast holes. Blekinge.

376. Vest of white cotton tabby, detail; embroidered with white cotton yarn in satin stitch, padded satin stitch, and tambour stitch. About 1800.

cially as it was decorative and easy to do. Embroidery on tulle thus also became most fashionable. It was used above all for shawls, collars, fichus, hair ornaments, hats, and was also inserted into other more sturdy weaves, e.g., thin cotton and linen tabby, linen and batiste (fig. 380). Simultaneously, an older form of net work experienced a renaissance, namely embroidery, threading, or darning on knotted net (filet). Embroidery on tulle and on knotted net have played an important part in peasant costume as well as interior decoration. To what extent these related techniques were commonly practiced or were the province of professionals is, however, not clear. During the Renaissance filet work was completely in accordance with prevailing stylistic ideals. Like *reticella* work, filet work has linearity and clarity of outline, is based on the construction of the ground, and relies for its pattern effects on sharp contrasts between light and shadow. During the nineteenth century, filet work returned in large tablecloths and curtains.

During the latter part of the nineteenth century, white embroidery as well as other decorative art forms deliberately sought inspiration in older period styles with which they were felt to have a kind of affinity. Thus, the *reticella* of the Renaissance returned, taken up from folk embroidery in which the techniques had lived on. Hardanger work, Hedebo work, Skåne cut work and drawn-thread work were taken up during the nineteenth century (fig. 314), and have continued to play a major role in home needlework also in the twentieth century.

The origin of certain other groups of decorative needlework—having in common that they are worked in red on white linen or cotton, in cross-stitch, stem stitch, and geometric satin stitch, etc.—is far more complex and unclear. This decorative work is found in distinctly separate parts of the country; there is, for example, one intensely productive region in Hälsingland-Gästrikland (figs. 381, 382), another

377. Fichu of sheer cotton muslin, embroidered with white cotton yarn in tambour stitch. Beginning of the nineteenth century.

378. Christening dress of sheer white cotton, detail; embroidered with white cotton yarn in tambour stitch and French knots, and with fillings of drawn-fabric work. Beginning of the nineteenth century.

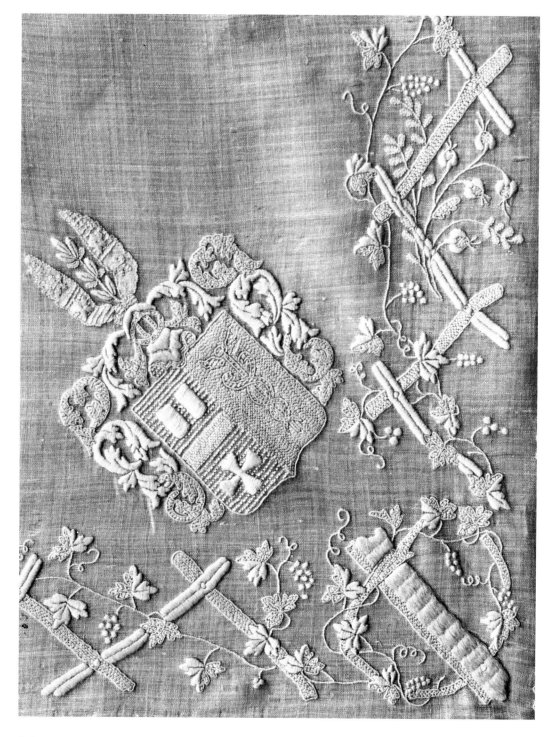

379. Handkerchief of linen batiste with embroidery in padded satin stitch, knot stitch, shadow stitch, buttonhole stitch, etc. Privately owned.

380. Hat net of white cotton tulle, embroidered with cotton thread in darning stitch and openwork grounds.

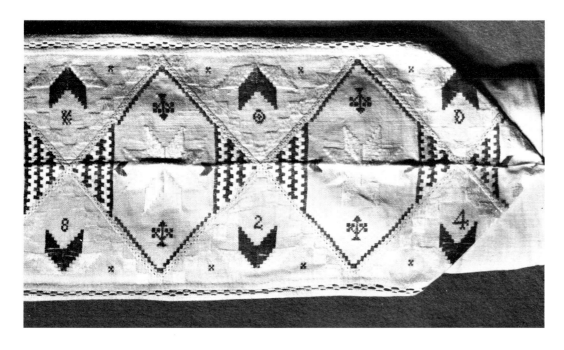

in Halland. It has also occurred in certain parts of Småland and Blekinge (fig. 383). These are clearly phenomena of highly mixed and diverse origin. The common denominator seems to be partly the effect—colored pattern on white linen ground—and partly a conservative pattern inventory, consisting of geometric ornament: diamonds, checks, chevrons, crosses, and triangles. These geometric elements are combined to form stars, hearts, trees, candelabrum motifs, or squares. There is no reason to discount a close relationship between all types of needlework over counted threads. A closer look reveales that the same basic ornament appears in white embroidery, in embroidery on canvas, and in darned netting (filet work). In Hälsingland, white embroidery, as well as embroidery in red on white, have been practiced. As pointed out above (page 223), a surfeit of such material has been preserved especially in Delsbo and Järvsö, offering an unusually nuanced picture of the development of a local embroidery specialty. Since the early Middle Ages the supply of flax and linen in this region has been greater than the domestic demand, encouraging a production of luxury bed and dress linens comparable only to that of Skåne. Here are found traditional techniques and patterns going back to the Middle Ages. The drawn-thread work and cut work of the Renaissance have been taken up here, in white and also in red. It cannot yet be determined when the red was introduced, but it is found in specimens from the eighteenth century. Since the embroidery was done with linen thread, the red color is today very washed out, at times almost white. Cotton is easier to dye and more colorfast. Thus, the introduction of cotton probably gave a big boost to embroidery in red (figs.

381. Pillowcase of white linen tabby, folded to show the "cap" embroidery: linen and cotton yarn in geometric satin stitch, cross-stitch, drawn-fabric work, and needle-made lace. Date and initials in red cross-stitch IKOD 1824. Delsbo, Hälsingland. Privately owned.

382. Hanging sheet of white cotton tabby. Red cotton yarn embroidery in cross-stitch, bobbin lace and fringe of white and red cotton yarn. Delsbo, Hälsingland.

381–85). On the whole, because of its lower price, cotton made it possible for everyone to acquire the bedding which for so long had been prized as a symbol of prestige and prosperity. It seems likely that embroidery in red cross-stitch became most highly developed when cotton yarn and cotton tabby were easily available. Also, it is probable that patterns from free white embroidery and from canvas work were used—in any case, the pattern motifs and the way in which they were combined were the same. The creation of patterns in connection with the later development of embroidery has already been touched upon, as has the relationship of pattern making to locally distinct types.

Sprang

Språngning[12] is the accepted contemporary Swedish term for a technique which at the end of the nineteenth century was known in Sweden only in Jämtland, where it was known as *"pinnbandsflätning"* (braiding with shed sticks).[13] Works in this technique were known as *språngning* in southern Swedish dialects. In other parts of Sweden, the dialectal words *språng, spranghuva,* and *språngsparrlakan* designated various kinds of openwork. It is not known for certain whether the medieval terms *sprang* and *språng* referred to the same kind of work that today is known as *språngning*. It is clear, however, that they were used about some kind of openwork. In Norway, the term *sprang* refers only to works in what is now called *språngning*.

Thus, there is some justification for the use in English of the term *sprang* to signify that textile nonweaving structural process which is carried out on a frame with an even number of threads stretched vertically between two horizontal bars or wires. Starting at the top, the threads are crossed over or under, or twisted around adjacent threads, according to a certain system. A shed stick is slipped into the shed that is formed at the upper end of the work, and the shed is opened and cleared through the warp to the bottom of the work. Another shed stick is inserted at the bottom of the shed. In

383. Wall runner of white linen tabby. Red linen yarn embroidery in geometric satin stitch, filling stitches, and cross-stitch. Knotted-on tasseled fringe in red and white. Fjärås, Halland.

384. Wall runner, same as in fig. 383, showing the two motifs which alternate along the entire length of the runner.

385. Hanging sheet. The center strip is of white cotton tabby, embroidered with red cotton yarn in surface satin stitch, stem stitch, closed herringbone stitch, and satin stitch. Privately owned.

386. Frame for *sprang* and the basic technique of *sprang* (knotless netting on frame).

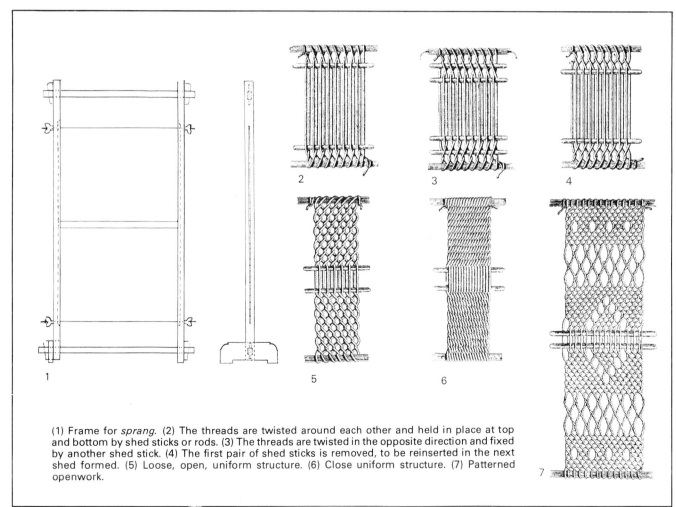

(1) Frame for *sprang*. (2) The threads are twisted around each other and held in place at top and bottom by shed sticks or rods. (3) The threads are twisted in the opposite direction and fixed by another shed stick. (4) The first pair of shed sticks is removed, to be reinserted in the next shed formed. (5) Loose, open, uniform structure. (6) Close uniform structure. (7) Patterned openwork.

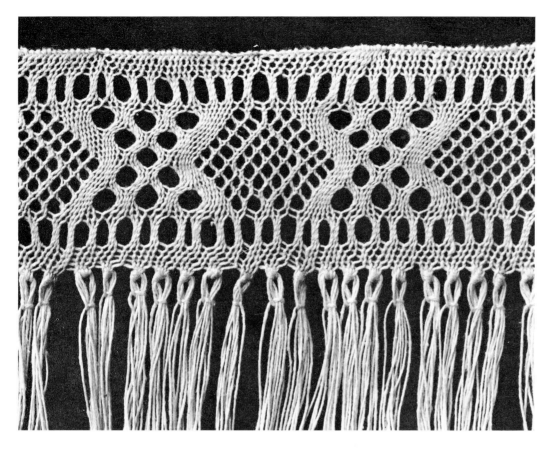

this fashion, identical patterns are created at the top and at the bottom, until the two parts meet at the middle of the warp, where a thread is introduced to bind the whole work (fig. 386). The pattern is made up of areas of open mesh alternating with areas of close mesh, creating a diagonal meshwork with variously combined pattern holes.

No implements for the making of *sprang* from before the twentieth century are known in Sweden today. Those now existing are reconstructions based on descriptions by old women in Jämtland, who knew the technique as late as the beginning of the twentieth century. Since that time, the handcraft society in Jämtland has encouraged a renaissance of *sprang*. At times the resulting output has been quite extensive, and highly complicated patterns have been executed in this technique (fig. 387).

A fairly limited number of older articles in this technique have been preserved in peasant milieu, namely in the provinces of Skåne, Småland, Halland, Östergötland, and Jämtland.

Objects in *sprang,* or decorated with this type of meshwork, were generally made to serve traditional, now outdated, functions. The most magnificent example is a canopy from Ydre district, Östergötland (fig. 388). It has an eight- to ten-inch-wide fringed meshwork strip inserted in white linen tabby. This canopy was in use up to 1840 at festive occasions, when it was suspended under the roof of the ceilingless house above the banquet table. From Halland comes another example: a bonnet or hood, probably from the eighteenth century, with the crown executed in richly patterned meshwork. In Skåne, as in Jämtland, *sprang* was similarly used: on hanging cloths and wall and ceiling hangings, i.e., on older types of textile furnishings. It has also been used in the costume. Bands which needed to be somewhat elastic, such as garters, were worked in a simple form of *sprang*. They are found in various parts of the country under different names (fig. 389).

Historically, *sprang* was one of the textile techniques used in Scandinavia as early as the Bronze Age. The first known examples come from Danish Bronze Age graves: a hood of wool in such tight *sprang* that it has lost its

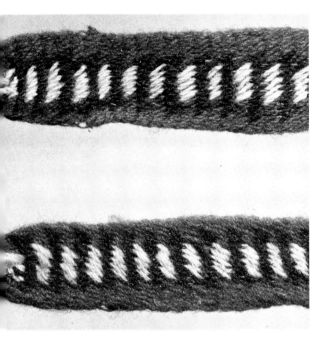

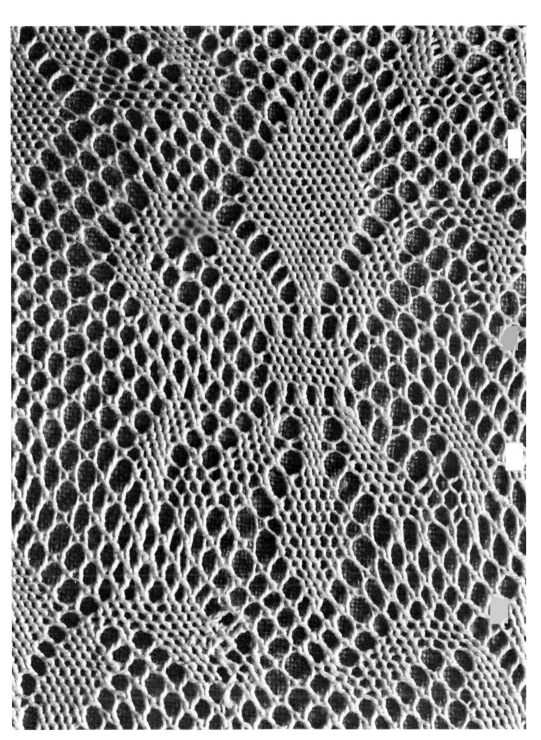

387. Linen yarn fringe in *sprang*, made by the Jämtslöjd Handcraft Society after an older model from Norderö, Jämtland.

388. Canopy of white linen tabby with inserted panels and borders of *sprang* in white linen yarn. Ydre, Östergötland.

389. Band of wool yarn in *pinnbandsflätning* (literally, "braiding with shed sticks"), i.e., *sprang*. Västra Vingåker, Södermanland.

390. Pillowcase cap in *sprang* of linen yarn. Voxtorp, Småland.

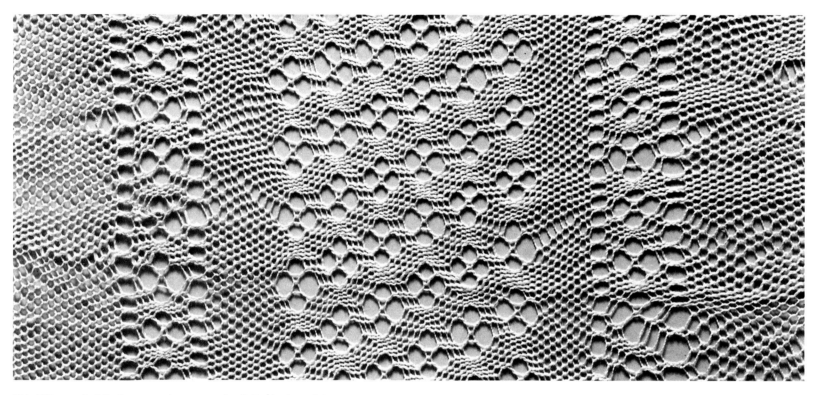

391. Mittens of white linen yarn in *sprang,* detail. Beginning of the nineteenth century.

netlike character, and a hair net of horse hair. Articles in *sprang* also occur in finds from the early and late Iron Age. Linguistically, it is documented by the frequent occurrence of the word "sprang" in various forms and compounds during the Middle Ages and the sixteenth century.

Only one textile work with *sprang* is known from upper-class milieu before the year 1800: a piece of material, dated 1707, in Svalsö Church in Denmark.

Examples of *sprang* have been discovered in archaeological finds from Ancient Egypt dated around 2000 B.C. Later, *sprang* was practiced in the Mediterranean countries and in western Europe. In the beginning of the nineteenth century, a particular type of *sprang* was introduced into Sweden from the Mediterranean, along with certain other techniques. It was introduced as a fashionable handcraft, suitable for the making of diverse personal costume accessories, such as mittens (fig. 391), handbags, and purses of different kinds. Belts in *sprang* were used with certain military uniforms. However, like so many other fads, the technique soon vanished without leaving any trace in the form of continued production.

Knot work

Knot work belongs among the techniques used to create openwork patterns or a net ground for embroidery. The latter use is dealt with under the heading of "Needlework and embroidery." However, the making of the net will be briefly discussed here.

Netting

To date there has been no investigation of netting in Sweden. Indeed, a study of all types of net work—regardless of tools and materials used—is needed, along with a detailed analysis of the techniques (fig. 392). Netting has such interesting historical aspects, however, that it deserves to be discussed in spite of incomplete data.

On the whole, two types of netting can be distinguished. In one type—the warp-knotted net—free-hanging threads, usually warp threads of a weave, were knotted together without a tool into a net, often finished off with tassels or fringe. In the other type—the weft-knotted net—the net was knotted with the help of a tool, in some cases, a lath or mesh pin of bone or wood. The width of the mesh pin determined the size of the mesh (fig. 396).

392. Implements for knot work:
filet needles, cases for needles
and mesh pins, netting needle,
mesh pin and net, knotting forks,
tatting shuttles, handkerchief with
tatting, and macramé work. (The
handkerchief can also be seen in
fig. 407.)

Knot work

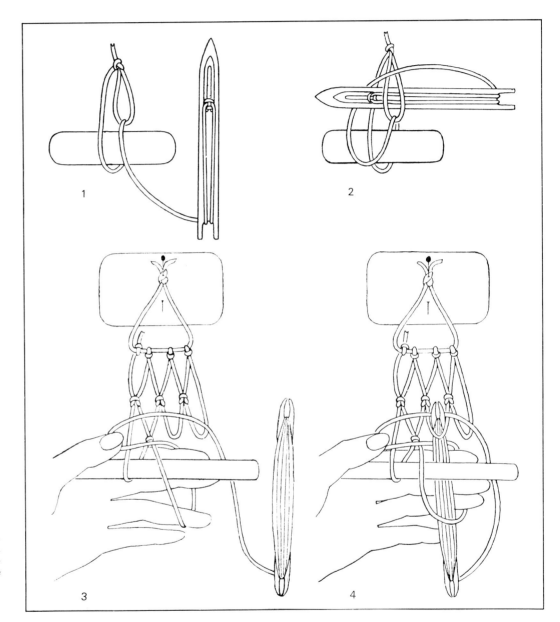

393. Woman knotting fishnets. Oil painting by Hanna Winge (1838–96). Second half of the nineteenth century.

394. Knotting of netting (filet), the foundation for embroidery or darning on netting (filet work). Ida Larsson, Södra Sallerup, Skåne.

395. Tatting. Oil painting by Pehr Hilleström, 1760s.

396. Knotting of net and filet. (1, 2) The thread is fastened at one end, and a loop is made. The thread is looped around the mesh pin and the netting needle is threaded through the loop, which is pulled up to a knot. The first knot is now on the mesh pin. (3, 4) In knotting with a filet needle the same principle is involved.

The mesh can be either square or diamond-shaped. Both types have been used as a foundation for embroidery. Net made exclusively of white linen thread or linen threads in white, pink, or blue has been used especially as edgings on tablecloths, canopies, and borders for bed curtains. Net occurs with greatest fre-

quency in the maritime provinces of Norrland, but also occasionally in southern Sweden. Several stylistic impulses have undoubtedly influenced this work, but they have not yet been sufficiently studied for a clear local distinction to be made.

In its simplest form, netting is used especially

in fishnets, the oldest known textile product. Fishnets of knotted bast fiber are known from the early Stone Age. Decorative knot work figured prominently in the cultures around the Mediterranean and in the Orient. In the Middle Ages, there were knotted nets, with or without embroidery in linen or silk. During the

Knot work

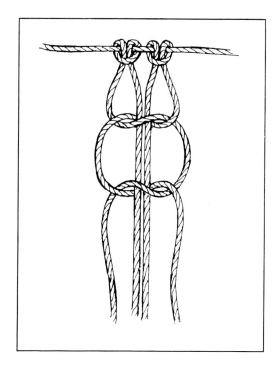

397. Macramé knots. Two cords, attached to the head cord with reversed double half-hitches or lark's head knots, form a square knot.

398. Tatting, first half-hitch or over knot. (1) Starting position, the thread held taut over three fingers. (2) The shuttle is passed, with the thread held taut, from below over the thread in the left hand and under the thread in the right hand. (3) The half-hitch is completed.

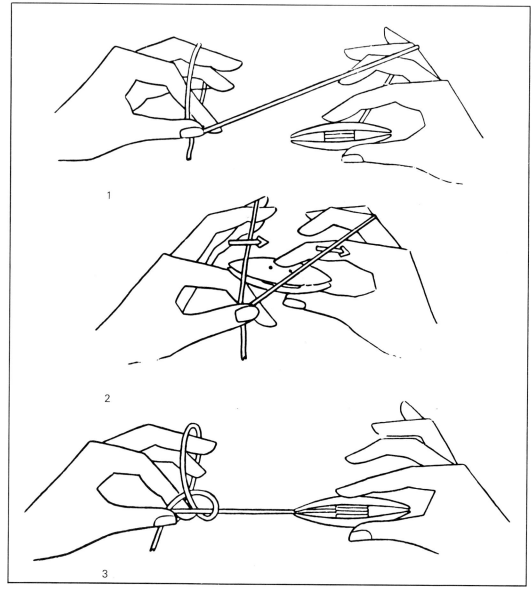

Renaissance, the baroque era, and, above all, the nineteenth century, so-called filet work enjoyed great popularity.

Knotted netting with square mesh was the ideal foundation for the geometric ornament of the early Renaissance, as the ornament was seen in sharp relief against the square mesh. The heavier baroque ornaments with their greater plasticity were also often placed on a net ground. Net knotting enjoyed a second peak period toward the end of the eighteenth century and the beginning of the nineteenth century (fig. 404). At that time, close contact with the Near East introduced a number of techniques into Europe, some of which were new to that part of the world, whereas others, previously known in prehistoric times, were reintroduced. It became fashionable to knot decorative bed curtains (fig. 403), purses, narrow shawls or scarves, mittens, aprons, and other dress accessories. Darning stitches on knotted net (filet work) in white cotton were used in tablecloths, curtains, and other furnishings.

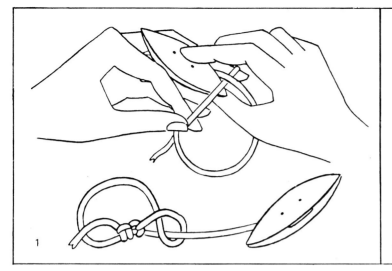
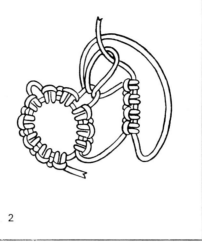

399. Tatting, second half-hitch or under knot, completing the reversed double half-hitch or double stitch. (1) Movement of shuttle after the position in fig. 398:3. (2) A number of tatting knots pulled together into a ring. A ring in progress is joined to a completed ring by means of a picot.

400. Ceiling cloth of white half-linen tabby with inserted widths of knotted netting, embroidered in linen stitch (*point de toile*) with white linen yarn. Västergötland.

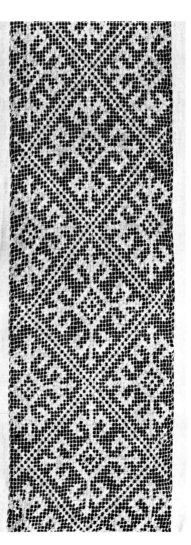

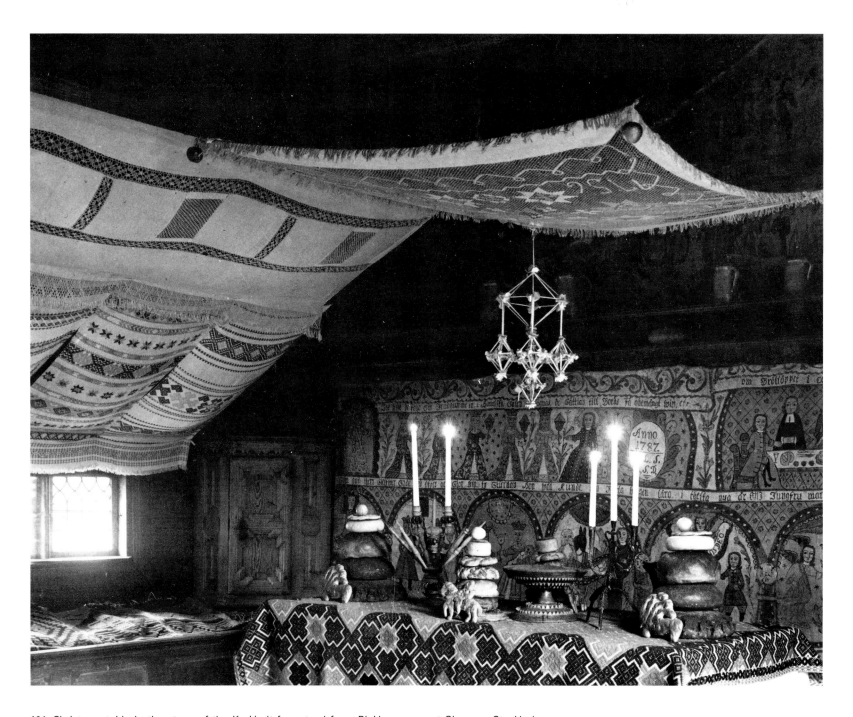

401. Christmas table in the *stuga* of the Kyrkhult farmstead from Blekinge, now at Skansen, Stockholm.
Ceiling hangings and, above the table, a table canopy of darned netting.

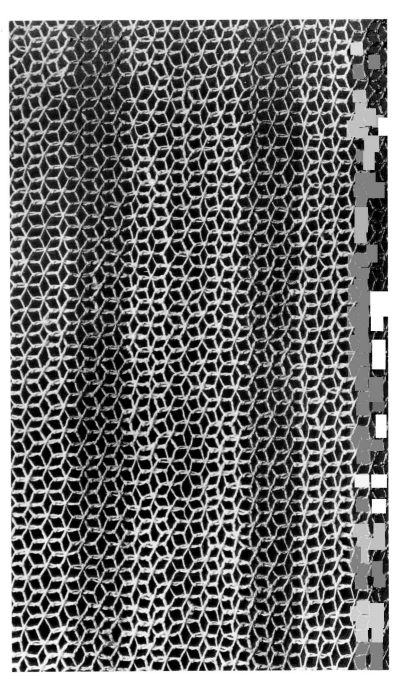

402. Ceiling cloth of knotted netting, darned with blue, red, and white cotton yarn. Knotted fringe around the central panel and the edges. Härlunda, Småland.

403. Bed curtain in knot work of white, pale blue, and dark blue cotton yarn. Beginning of the nineteenth century.

Knot work

404. Count Claes Julius Ekeblad knotting fishnets while his wife reads aloud. Drawing by Lars Sparrgren from Stola Manor, Västergötland, 1783.

405. Sewing bag of silk with macramé trim of cotton yarn. 1870.

Macramé

Around the beginning of the nineteenth century, the form of decorative knot work known as macramé spread from the Mediterranean countries to the rest of Europe. In its more intricate forms, it was professionally practiced. Forms of decorative knotting made by the "lacemakers"—an independent guild already in the Middle Ages—flourished throughout the Renaissance and the baroque period (fig. 406), and, later, in the late 1800s. Decorative knotting, occurring in various social milieus as a

handcraft, was probably stimulated, to a greater or lesser extent, by professional prototypes.
The lavishly tasseled knotted fringe from peasant milieu was, thus, probably inspired by the
prominent passementerie of the Renaissance
and the baroque era. But an influence from
still older traditions is not unlikely. The Renaissance interest in macramé provided the
basis for some embroidered net work. The bulk
of embroidered net work, however, dates from
the beginning and first half of the nineteenth
century (fig. 405).

Macramé is worked on a hard pillow, preferably using cotton cord with a strong twist.
For finer work, other materials may be used,
such as linen, silk, and fine cotton threads.
The knotting is done with the hands without
any tools. The cords to be knotted are attached
to the cushion with pins or looped around a
tightly stretched holding cord. Some knots used
are half knot, square knot (fig. 397), and
double half hitch. The cords should measure
seven times the length of the finished work.

Tatting

Tatting[14] is yet another form of knot work
which became fashionable in the nineteenth
century. Tatting is done by means of a small
spool or shuttle, on which the thread—generally, thin white cotton or linen thread—is wound.
The tatting shuttle is composed of two blades,
joined by a bar in the middle and drawn out
to a point at the ends, where the two blades
come closer together, somewhat like the forked
ends of a filet needle. The thread is laid in a
loop, through which the shuttle is passed. The
result is a loop with a reversed double half
hitch, somewhat like a buttonhole stitch (figs.
398, 399). Tatting has been used especially in
laces and other openwork (fig. 407). Nordiska
Museet has a collection of shuttles of bone,
wood, mother-of-pearl, tortoise shell, and
metal, varying in length from two inches to

406. Fringe of green silk. Tradition has it that it was
knotted by Queen Ulrika Eleonora during military
maneuvers at Edsköldsmoar in 1722. Probably
professional work. Privately owned.

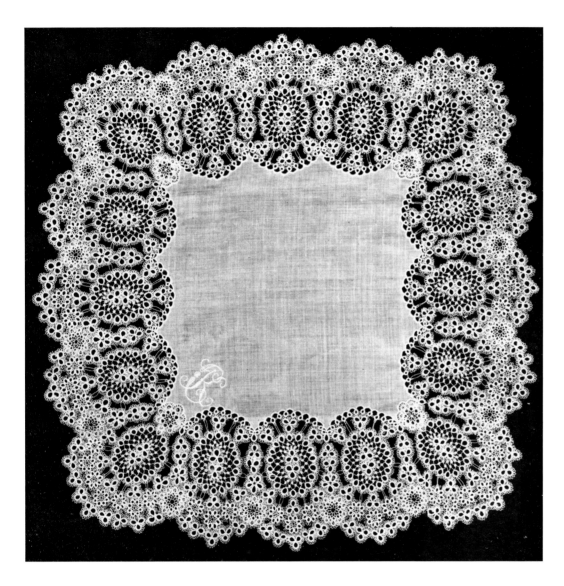

407. Handkerchief of lawn with tatted lace. Monogram CK of linen thread worked in padded satin stitch. Middle of the nineteenth century.

about six inches. Of special interest are a couple of shuttles of gold on mother-of-pearl, exquisitely ornamented in rococo style. A painting by Pehr Hilleström from the 1760s (fig. 395) shows a lady tatting. However, no textile works from that time or earlier have been positively identified as products of what is now known as tatting. It is possible that other knot work may have been executed with these "tatting" shuttles.

Crochet

Crocheting is done with a needle with a hook at one end, hence the name of the technique. The hook may be made of wood, bone, or metal. Its length and thickness vary, depending upon the thread. For coarse yarn, wool yarn, thick cotton yarn, or bast fiber, sturdy wood or bone hooks are used. For silk and thin cotton or linen yarn, there are more slender hooks of metal, which, because of their fineness, are set in a handle of wood, bone, cork, etc. (fig. 408). In addition to the above-mentioned materials, crocheting can also make use of rick-rack and bands of narrow ornamental braid for effect and variety. The crochet hook forms loops of the thread, which are pulled through each other—chain stitch—or through previously made loops. In the latter case, a single crochet stitch is formed; this can be joined to already existing stitches in various ways. The method of alternating chain stitches and single crochet stitches gives crochet its distinctive character. A great many variations are possible, each with many names, differing from place to place and time to time. A systematic survey of these variations must wait until some special research has been done on crochet. A couple of types can, however, be mentioned here. One is Tunisian crochet, which is made with a long straight hook without a handle. The loops are all taken up on the needle going in one direction, then chain stitched off the needle in the reverse direction, whereupon new loops are taken up, and so on. Another important variant is crochet lace. Crochet lace can be made either lengthwise or crosswise, in the former case often directly on to the fabric edge to be decorated.

Crochet came to Sweden with cotton, along with certain other textile techniques imported from the Mediterranean countries, around 1800. It has, however, been known in the Orient for a long time. It was possibly also known in Europe in the Middle Ages. During the nineteenth century, crochet work was very much in fashion. Time and again, interest in crocheting has revived.

Crochet (figs. 409–11) has been made both as openwork, especially in laces, and as a solid

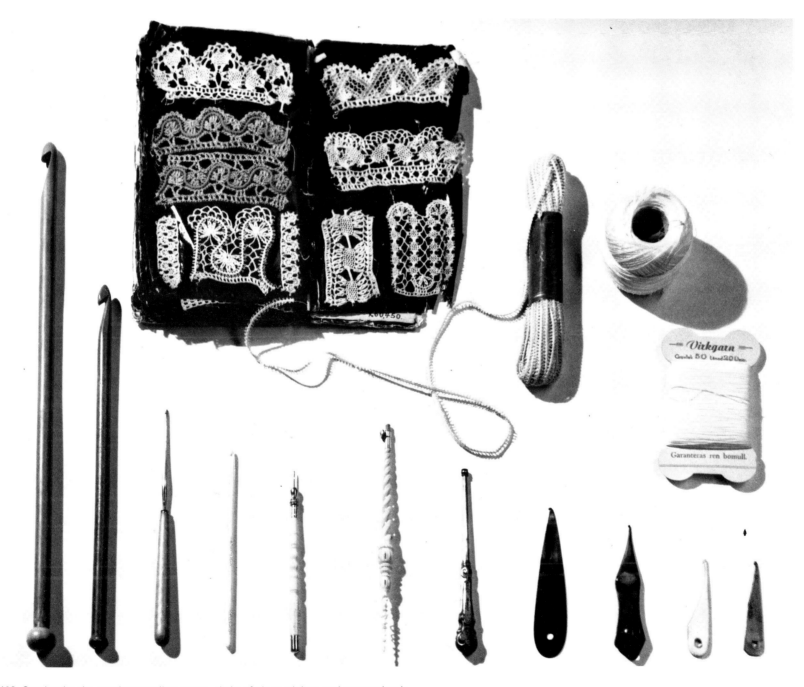

408. Crochet hooks, crochet needles, yarns, skein of picot edging, and pattern book.

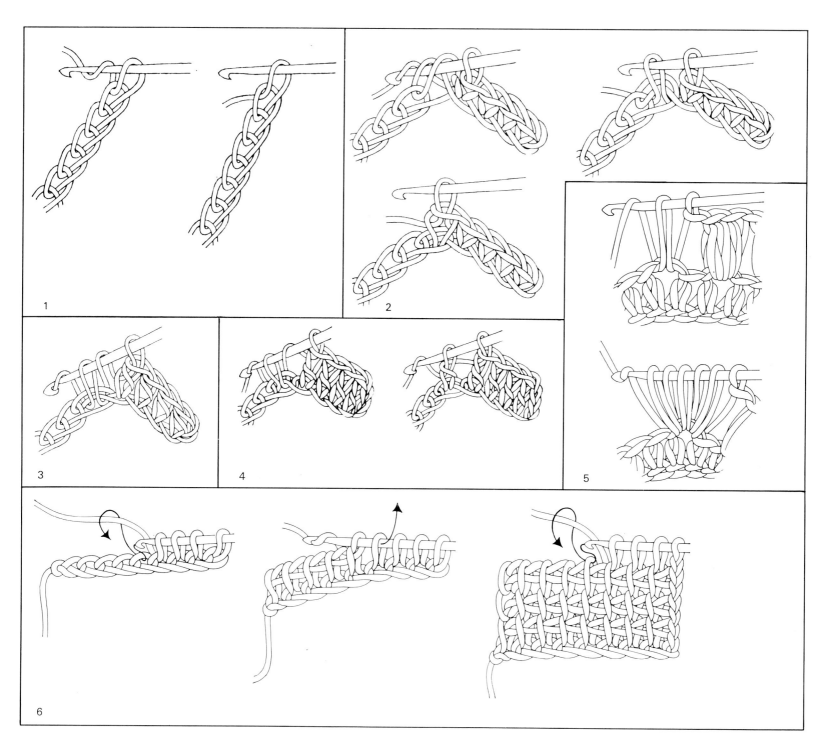

1

2

3

4

5

6

409. Chain stitches and single crochet stitch in various combinations: (1) Chain stitch; (2) Single crochet stitch, plain, or close stitch; (3) Half double crochet; (4) Plain double crochet; (5) Cluster or pineapple stitch; (6) Plain Tunisian, or afghan, crochet.

410. Bedspread, crocheted of white cotton yarn in hexagons. Beginning of the twentieth century, Högsby, Småland.

411. Collection of pattern samplers, so-called stars, crocheted of white cotton thread. Middle of the nineteenth century.

fabric, widely used in domestic furnishings and articles of clothing.

Crochet was first introduced in Sweden in bourgeois milieu, but spread very quickly to peasant milieu. From the middle of the nineteenth century, there were local variants of crochet, used for garments of traditional character, e.g., women's fichus in Floda, Dalarna. It was also used in many places to make lace edgings on the strip of white fabric worn under the *bindmössa*, on shifts and shirts, and as laces for sheets, pillowcases, and tablecloths.

The first Swedish crochet manual was published in 1844, although the first Swedish fashion magazine, founded in 1818, had printed some crochet patterns earlier. Such patterns have continued to be featured in weeklies, fashion magazines, needlework books, and loose pattern leaves.

Braiding

A simple and natural way of finishing a textile is to braid together the loose hanging warp ends, which are left when the fabric is taken down from the loom. At an early stage, man understood how to create both simple and intricate patterns in this way. Braiding is also generally known in all parts of the world. Originally part of the weave, the braid work was eventually separated from the fabric and made in long strips, which were sewn onto ceiling and wall hangings, tablecloths, hanging cloths, etc.

Braiding has been done either with the fingers, or, in exceptional cases, as in Blekinge, with bobbins. There are two kinds of warp-end braiding, four-end braiding and three-end braiding. Braiding has also been used for the

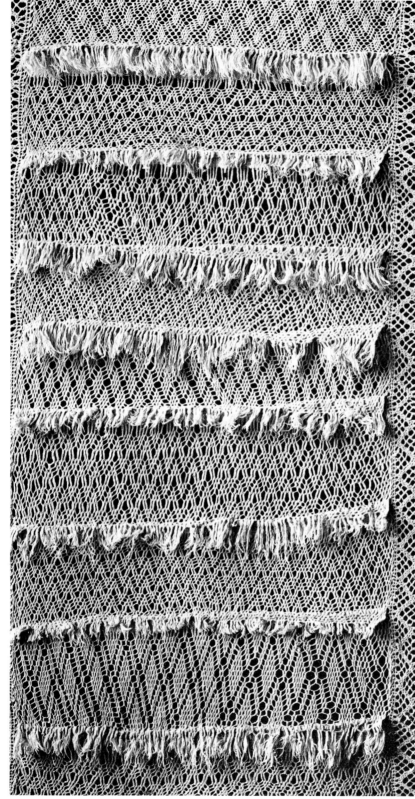

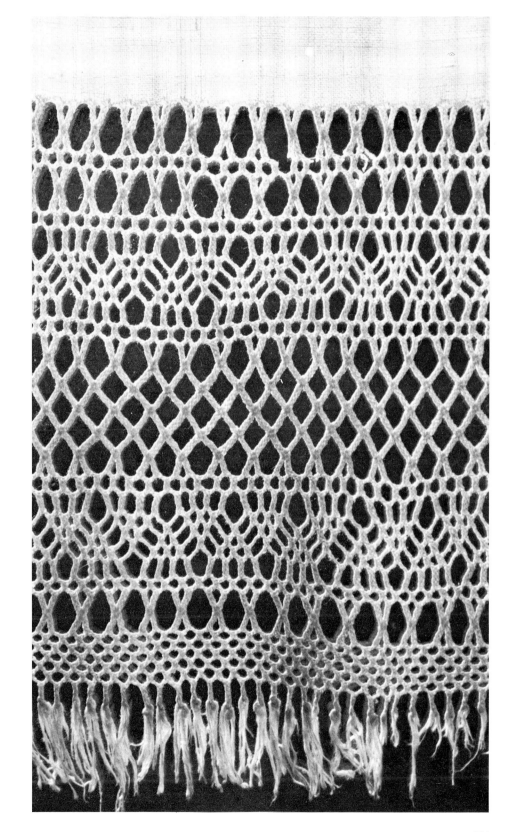

412. Wall hanging of white linen tabby with insertion of braiding and bobbin lace. (See fig. 121.) The photograph shows a detail of the insertion. The vertical band is bobbin lace. Ore, Dalarna.

413. Groups of eight warp threads on a hanging cloth of linen tabby worked into a fringe of four-end braiding. Mora, Dalarna.

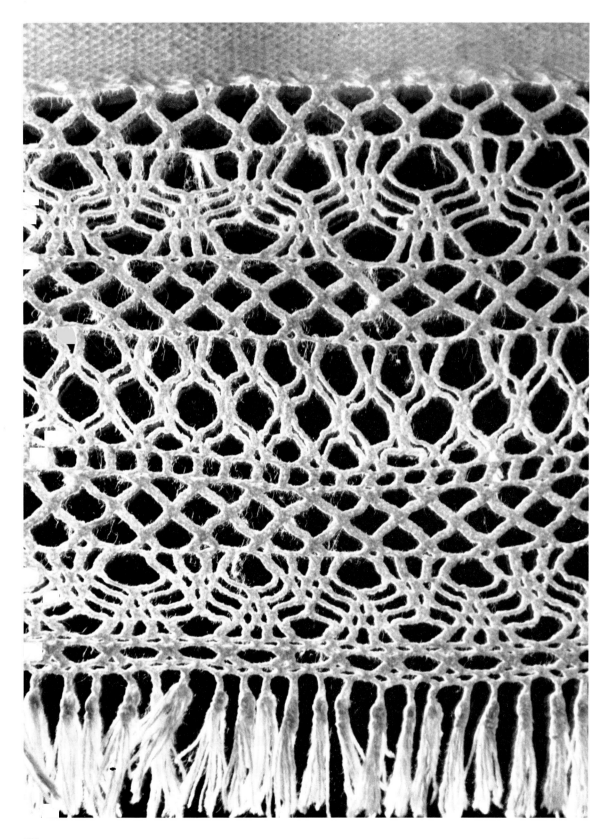

414. Half-linen tabby with fringe of four warp threads in four-end braiding. Dalarna.

415. Fringe of six warp threads in three-end braiding on weave with linen warp. Sunnerbo, Småland.

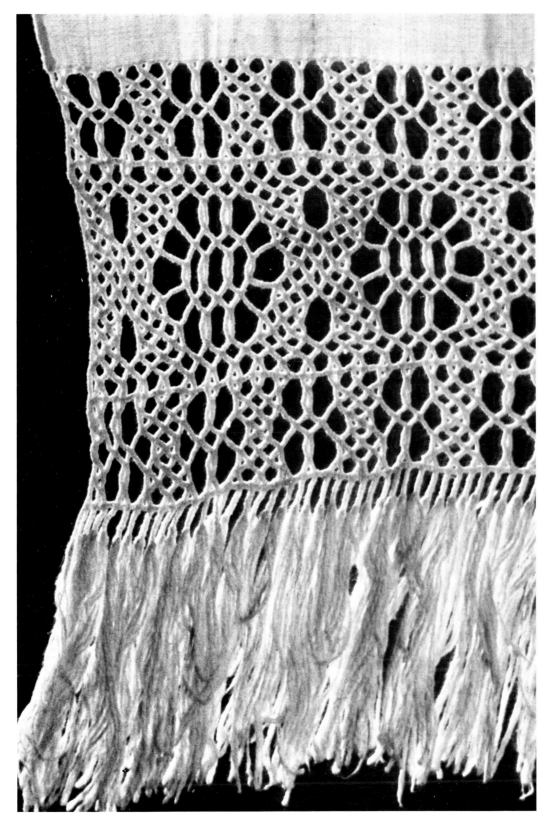

making of bands, by laying warp ends, which are secured at one end, over and under each other, working from the edges towards the center (figs. 416, 417).

Four-end braiding

Four-end braiding consists of braiding together the warp threads of a fabric in groups of four (figs. 413, 414). These tiny braids can be split into two pairs of two threads, recombining with adjacent thread pairs to form new braids. The thread pairs are twisted between each diagonal crossing. This creates a pattern based on alternating loosely and closely braided parts. Four-end braiding is found primarily in more conservative regions such as Dalarna, Gästrikland, Hälsingland, Härjedalen, and Jämtland, and the Småland relic area with adjoining parts of Västergötland and Östergötland. Four-end braiding appears also in Värmland, Dalsland, Västmanland, Uppland, and Södermanland.

Three-end braiding

Three-end braiding is made with three warp threads in each braid. Thus, it is not possible to divide the braids evenly, which results in a different pattern structure (fig. 415). Similarities between this type of braiding and Italian braided lace from the sixteenth century are striking. Three-end braiding is found mostly in southern Sweden, i.e., Skåne, Blekinge, Halland, Öland, and parts of Småland. The geographic distribution of the two types of braiding is by no means strict. On the whole, however, the four-end braiding is found in northern and central Sweden, whereas the three-end braiding dominates in southern Sweden. Detailed investigations of braiding still remain to be made.

Braiding

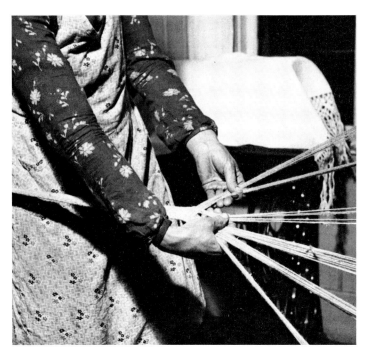

416 a. Braiding of shoulder straps for rucksack. (Continued in fig. 416 b.)

416 b. Warp threads of goat hair are secured at one end; at the other end they extend in long loops around the fingers of the seated braiders. These loops are moved from finger to finger in the same sequence as in regular braiding. For a wide band with many warp loops several braiders are required: one to pull the threads tight, and the rest to exchange loops. Sollerö, Dalarna.

417. Garter, braided of woolen yarn. Ljusdal, Hälsingland.

Bobbin lace

Laces of different types

Spets, the Swedish word for lace, covers a variety of technically quite different ornamental openwork fabrics. A lace can be sewn with a needle and a single thread, or made with bobbins by which threads are twisted, crossed, and braided. It can be braided, knotted, made with *sprang,* woven, knitted, or crocheted. It can be made of silk, linen, wool, cotton, or synthetic fiber. This variety of methods and materials has, however, been employed toward the same end: to create an ornamental openwork fabric, suitable and aesthetically pleasing as edging or for insertion in another fabric. Lace, in a more narrow sense, refers to bobbin lace (pillow lace) and needle-

418. Venetian needlepoint lace, *punto grosso,* detail. Second half of the seventeenth century.

point lace, the so-called true laces. Before these were developed, however, lacelike fabrics were created in other techniques—embroidery, *sprang,* knotting, and braiding—which all more or less contributed to the creation of the pedi-

295

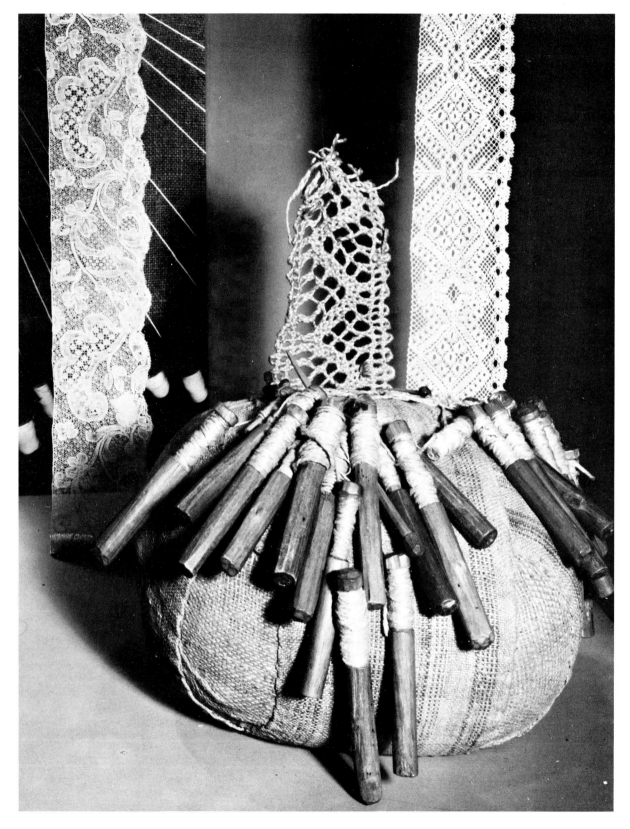

419. Pillow for making bobbin lace
without pricked pattern and pins.
Ore, Dalarna.

grees of bobbin and needlepoint laces. Qualitatively and quantitatively, the true laces are at the center of the development of the art of lace making. Crocheted, knitted, and woven laces are secondary to bobbin lace and needlepoint lace, as the former were used as less expensive substitutes for the true laces.

In Sweden, the only true lace with a relatively unbroken tradition and a fairly wide geographic distribution is bobbin lace. Needlepoint lace was made for a short period, from the middle of the nineteenth century to the beginning of the twentieth century, but aside from this brief appearance, it is not known to have been produced in Sweden. The secondary laces are further discussed under their respective techniques.

Two things distinguish the making of bobbin lace from general braiding or intertwining of threads: in lace making, continuous threads are used, and the threads have to be wound on spools, called bobbins, for the lace maker to be able to twist or braid them in the intricate patterns required. To easily execute the steps in the braiding process, the threads, with the bobbins hanging on them, are attached to or hung on a round pillow or cushion, which in its most sophisticated form is equipped with a cylindrical roller. This roller, which rotates around its own axis, is set into a wooden box and surrounded by a padded semicircular board, the pillow, on which the bobbins rest (fig. 146). Older types of pillow lace were worked without a pattern, whereas more developed types cannot be made without them. The desired pattern is affixed to the roller (fig. 435). A pattern is drawn on a so-called parchment, a strip of paper or parchment, and holes are pricked in this strip to indicate where pins will be inserted to keep the threads in position while the lace is being made (fig. 421). Nowadays the parchments are usually made of strong and flexible cardboard, but, as the name indicates, earlier patterns were pricked on parchment or vellum. As the work progresses, the threads are fixed with pins. When a pattern element or a part of it has been completed, the pins are transferred to the next set of prepricked holes.

The particular movements, or "passings," of

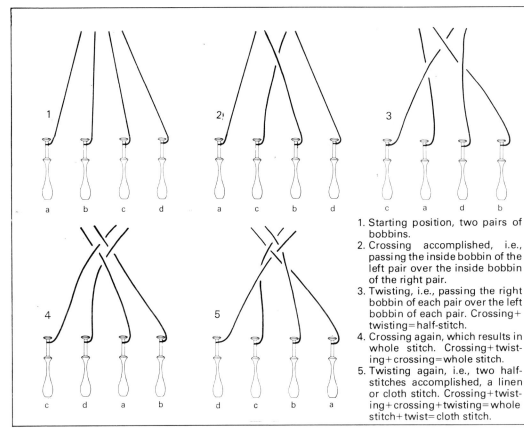

1. Starting position, two pairs of bobbins.
2. Crossing accomplished, i.e., passing the inside bobbin of the left pair over the inside bobbin of the right pair.
3. Twisting, i.e., passing the right bobbin of each pair over the left bobbin of each pair. Crossing+twisting=half-stitch.
4. Crossing again, which results in whole stitch. Crossing+twisting+crossing=whole stitch.
5. Twisting again, i.e., two half-stitches accomplished, a linen or cloth stitch. Crossing+twisting+crossing+twisting=whole stitch+twist=cloth stitch.

420. Basic passings in bobbin-lace making.

the hands which produce the web of bobbin lace are crossing and twisting, done with four bobbins in two groups of two (fig. 420). Crossing signifies passing the inside bobbin of the left pair over the inside bobbin of the right pair, while the outside bobbins remain passive. Twisting is the movement of simultaneously passing the right bobbin of each pair over the left bobbin of each pair. Crossing and twisting once make a single or half-stitch. Crossing, twisting, and crossing again give a whole stitch.[15] Two half-stitches—whole stitch and twist—constitute a linen or cloth stitch. From these three basic stitches, innumerable different patterns can be created.

The main types of bobbin lace

Certain laces are made exclusively or predominantly with four-end braids. This kind of lace is called plaited or braided lace. Early Italian and Flemish laces of the sixteenth century are almost exclusively plaited laces (fig. 422). In certain of these laces, the braid or plait was combined with so-called tallies—wheat-grain or leaf motifs—made by a variation of the cloth stitch. These two elements, the braid and the tally, almost exclusively made up seventeenth-century Genoese laces and the so-called Maltese lace—a variety especially appreciated around the turn of the twentieth century.

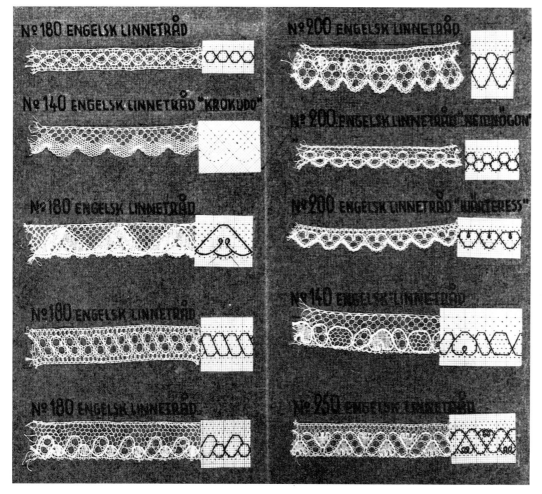

421. Samples of bobbin laces with their respective names, drawn and pricked patterns, and notes about recommended thread gauges. Vadstena bobbin-lace schools.

The clothwork lace is dominated by areas in which threads cross each other at right angles, making parts of the lace look like a fabric woven in tabby. The earliest Dutch and Flemish laces employ clothwork more than any other type of lace (fig. 422, middle). At times, the web of these laces is so close that the pattern is visible only as a series of adjacent holes. To a certain extent, this tendency is found also in some Skåne peasant laces (fig. 431).

Toward the end of the seventeenth century, the figures in lace design were connected by means of one continuous ground. This ground has been variously developed and named, as is exemplified in fig. 424 and the accompanying caption. The ground will here be called by the common term *réseau,* or net ground, in spite of the fact that this is also the name of one of the particular grounds used in modern bobbin lace. As shall be seen, the net ground completely changed the nature of lace. It was to completely dominate lace making, leading to a further differentiation of lace types.

Bobbin lace up to around 1700

The development from braid work and embroidery, respectively, to lace took place during the first part of the sixteenth century. Bobbin laces did exist, judging from pictures and contemporary sources, around the middle of the sixteenth century. These bobbin laces were narrow and braided—plaited lace—resembling picot edging. During this earliest period they were often made with colored thread or metal thread, and were called *passement*[16] (fig. 422, bottom). Bobbin lace thus betrays its relationship to braid work in more than one way. It cannot be ascertained where bobbin lace was first fully developed. However, Italy and Flanders stand out from the very beginning as the foremost producers of bobbin lace.

Judging from preserved specimens and contemporary references, pure plaited lace reached its fullest development in Italy in the seventeenth century. Whereas Venice is known in the history of lace above all for her magnificent needlepoint laces (fig. 418), bobbin lace was traditionally associated with Genoa and Milan. It is not absolutely certain whether all laces today known as Genoese or Milanese were actually manufactured in these cities. "Genoese lace" and "Milanese lace" must rather be regarded as generic terms, and these laces have probably also been made elsewhere in Italy.

Genoese laces were in great demand and were exported in considerable amounts to the rest of Europe. Their great popularity was perhaps mainly due to the effects that could be achieved by converting patterns for Venetian needlepoint lace, especially *reticella* lace, into patterns for bobbin lace. The bobbin laces could, in addition, be produced at a lower price. The lace makers in Genoa could easily reproduce the clear and stringent compositions of contemporary needlepoint lace, at the same time as the technique made a finer and more graceful design possible. Through lavish use of braids and tallies this effect was achieved. The lace in fig. 423 is almost completely composed of single braids or plaits, whereas it has no tallies. Thus, this lace acquired a transparent sheerness. It certainly deserves its name, *rosoni*

422. Bobbin laces without *réseau*. Top to bottom: Genoese lace, straight lace from the mid-seventeenth century; lace of early Flemish type, free lace from the mid-seventeenth century; and plaited lace of gold thread, straight lace from around 1600.

Bobbin lace

genovesi (Italian, "Genoese rose windows"), referring to its likeness to the large Gothic rose windows (see also fig. 422, top).

Under the name of *point de Gênes,* the lace from Genoa spread all over Europe, appearing also in Sweden. Not until the year 1650 is there, however, any documentary evidence of its existence in Sweden. Genoa lace is listed in a bill for various laces "for collars and sarks." However, numerous portraits of Swedish nobles and, especially, many portraits of Gustav II Adolf show that Genoese lace had already found a receptive market in Sweden at an earlier time (fig. 423).

Later Genoese laces from around 1650 sought to adjust pattern and technique to the more lavish and massive foliage scrolls consistent with baroque aesthetic ideals. Lavish use of the more solid and three-dimensional tally marks this stage. But it does seem as if the popularity of the Genoa laces was so firmly associated with the *reticella* pattern type and the light and airy braids that lace production in Genoa was unable to adjust to the new demands and therefore experienced a decline. Lace manufacture did, however, continue as a vital folk expression in Italy as late as the nineteenth century.

The second Italian bobbin lace of importance, Milanese lace, can stylistically be characterized as a baroque lace. This type was suited, technically, to achieve the effects so well loved by this era, especially chiaroscuro. The assertive and solid floral patterns were designed to project over a certain distance. The massive forms favored the use of clothwork in large floral vines, standing out in their solid whiteness against the surrounding "air." Braiding was only used in the brides—connecting threads —joining the floral ornaments into a continuous whole. The floral and foliage ornament, especially cultivated in Milanese lace,

423. Collar of Genoese lace on dress from the 1640s. Worn by Margareta Grip, married to Hermann Wrangel. Oil painting, Svenska Porträttarkivet.

300

sometimes had a definitely bandlike character. The vines and scrolls were formed by fairly even bands of bobbin lace (fig. 424, top), or, in simpler laces, by actual woven bands or tape. These were laid out in a foliage pattern and joined by brides. In Sweden, this type of lace is known as *guipure*. The term *guipure* is also used for other laces, in which added threads and braids impart greater plasticity. The intention was to produce, by simple and inexpensive means, a lace resembling the Venetian needlepoint lace as closely as possible. On the whole, at this stage in the development of lace, bobbin lace was a substitute for the costly needlepoint lace.

Ornamentally, the Milanese lace is related to Venetian baroque needlepoint lace with its massive floral and foliage scrolls. At a later date, probably not until after 1700, Milanese lace developed into a *réseau* lace. This development was not an isolated phenomenon; rather, it was a reflection of the general change in the laces of France and Flanders, taking place around the same time.

The development of réseau lace after 1700

By the end of the seventeenth century, French lacemakers were beginning to make lace on a *réseau,* a net ground, against which patterns of stylized flowers and leaves are seen with great clarity and precision—a characteristic late baroque stylistic ideal. During the first half of the eighteenth century, rococo lace developed in France, featuring graceful flower and vine patterns and rocailles, partly along the bottom edge of the lace, partly filling the surface above the edge in a light and airy pattern. Also, needlepoint lace from Brussels quickly came

424. *Réseau* laces developed during the end of the seventeenth and the beginning of the eighteenth century. Top to bottom: Milanese lace, end of seventeenth century; Flemish lace, end of seventeenth century; two Flemish laces from the first half of the eighteenth century; and Point d'Alençon, a needlepoint lace, first half of the eighteenth century.

to play an important role in the development of new forms. Brussels produced needlepoint as well as bobbin laces—certain laces even combined the two techniques—and Brussels laces became the epitome of fashion and quality around the middle of the eighteenth century.

In Flanders, superb raw materials and the incomparable fineness of its linen thread—Flanders was renowned for having the finest thread in Europe—laid the foundation for a lace manufacture, which in the eighteenth century rapidly grew into the most productive in Europe. This manufacture had already been quite extensive in the middle of the seventeenth century, producing its own type of lace with a main market in northern Europe. Nevertheless, through the end of the century, Venetian and French laces dominated lace production in Europe. But with the taking up of *réseau* lace in Brussels—and shortly thereafter, also in other Flemish lace centers—the laces produced in Flanders were soon in great demand and distributed to all parts of Europe.

Bobbin-lace manufacture enjoyed a period of expansion in the eighteenth century, thanks to the influence of the Flemish laces. Flemish bobbin laces and their lace patterns were spread along with Flemish flax. Flax merchants also distributed pricked patterns for lace making. In Sweden, the authorities imported Flemish bobbin-lace makers to serve as instructors.

Bobbin lace in Sweden
Réseau lace

The center for *réseau* lace in Sweden is Vadstena in Östergötland. As far as is known, it is the only place in Sweden where bobbin laces of Flemish type have been made extensively, reaching out to different social strata and different parts of the country. The Vadstena lace corresponds, on the whole, with the *réseau* lace developed at the end of the seventeenth century. Through the distribution of Vadstena laces to various parts of the country, the technique and patterns of this lace became especially influential. More will be said about this influence below. First, it might be helpful to briefly give some data about lace making in Vadstena.

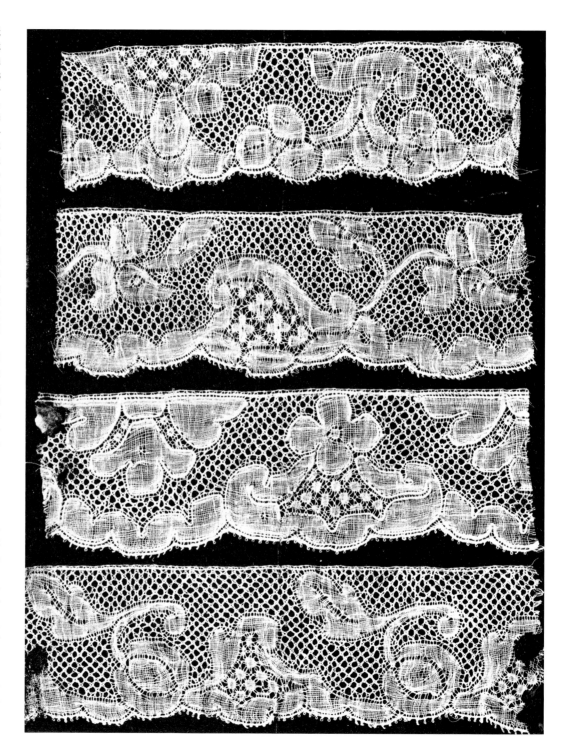

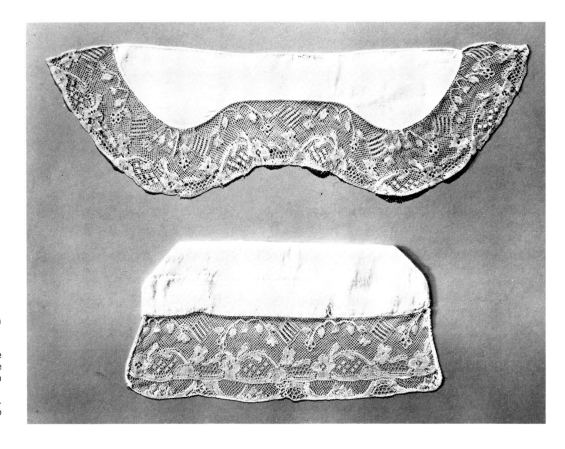

425. Vadstena laces of Flemish type, 1750s. From the Berch Collection, Nordiska Museet.

426. Vadstena laces of Flemish type became coarser, looser, and more angular in design in the peripheral production milieus. Top, lace of Flemish type on strip to be worn under the *bindmössa,* a small, embroidered lace-edged cap. Östergötland. Bottom, woman's cap with two laces combined to form a suitable lace edging. Mockfjärd, Dalarna.

Vadstena lace making

In the sixteenth century, Sweden already imported white linen laces in considerable amounts. In the 1630s, customs ledgers report, pillows, bobbins, and pins for the making of bobbin lace were being imported. This must be considered proof that the making of bobbin lace on pillows with pricked pattern and pins had been introduced in Sweden. It is not known where this production might have been centered. However, it is known that in the year 1757, Vadstena and surrounding areas were carrying on such an extensive lace production that women in practically every household busied themselves with this manufacture. These laces were *réseau* laces of Flemish type (fig. 425), as can be seen from the samples from Vadstena in the collection of Nordiska Museet. It is also known that the authorities at the same time sent skilled lace makers to Vadstena to further improve the skill of the local women.

Vadstena laces were sold partly through salesmen in the town of Vadstena, partly by Västergötland peddlers on their country-wide tours. The laces were used especially on the *bindmössor,* which were decorated with a strip of lace, the so-called *stycke* (literally, "piece"). By means of these caps, Vadstena lace making was spread throughout the country (fig. 426).

In regions where the older type of bobbin lace, without pricked pattern and pins, was being made, Vadstena laces apparently gave new impulses with regard to technique and patterns. Thus, they gave rise to local variations of *réseau* lace. The home production was largely intended for household consumption or local sale. The Vadstena manufacture, on the other hand, was organized as a putting-out system—those who traded in lace "put out" or supplied the material to their lace makers, who were paid in cash for their work. The laces were distributed widely: partly sold in shops, partly peddled by traveling salesmen, and partly made to order for customers all over the country.

Although Vadstena lace making, like all lace manufacture, declined markedly in the nineteenth century when laces were no longer fashionable, the volume of lace making in Vadstena remained sizable as late as the 1870s. At that time, more than 800 lacemakers were still active in Vadstena and its surrounding areas.

At the beginning of the twentieth century, the activity in Vadstena had, however, practically ceased. Bobbin-lace making, on the verge of dying out, made a remarkable recovery with

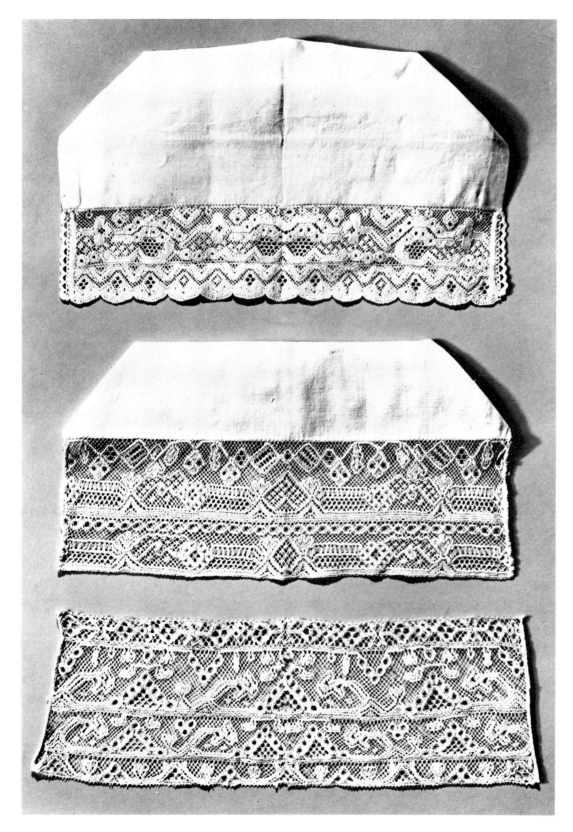

427. Top to bottom: Cap of cotton tabby with bobbin lace of linen thread, Floda, Dalarna; cap with lace, and cap lace, both from Gagnef, Dalarna. The model, Vadstena lace of Flemish type, has here become stylized and angular.

428. *The Lace Vendor*. Painting by Gabriel Gresley (1710–56). Art Museum, Dijon.

the help of the last few practitioners of the old art. A continuous instruction in the making of bobbin lace was organized in Vadstena in 1903 on the initiative of *Föreningen för Svensk Hemslöjd* (The Society for Swedish Handcraft), under the direction of Mrs. Ingeborg Petrelli. This instruction created a corps of skilled lace makers in the traditional lace making parishes, and laid the foundation for a considerable lace production in this century. This production utilizes traditional Vadstena patterns as well as modern patterns, created by noted designers.

In the case of bobbin lace, it is perfectly clear from where and along what routes it was introduced into central and northern Sweden. It has been established that it was spread from the center, Vadstena, primarily by itinerant peddlers. Quite likely, some laces of Flemish type also reached Sweden from Raumo, the Finnish lace center, in western Finland. Raumo laces were sold on both sides of the Baltic. They may, along with the Vadstena laces, have provided the impetus for some of the local *réseau* variations (fig. 147). In southern Sweden, local bobbin lace was inspired by other sources.

Before turning to local variations of *réseau* lace, we might first look at the occurrence of lace without *réseau*.

Lace without réseau

It has been noted above that an older type of bobbin lace survived in Sweden as late as the end of the nineteenth century. This is a type that had existed long before the introduction of the fully developed bobbin lace with its paraphernalia—pillow with cylinder, bobbins, and pricked pattern. This older type of bobbin lace seems to have been made without pattern and pins. It is closely related to the early Italian and Flemish bobbin laces from the sixteenth century, a time before lace making had become a large, commercially organized industry. The origin of this older bobbin lace and the time and place at which it came to Sweden cannot be clearly established, but a number of circumstances seem to indicate the Birgittine Convent in Vadstena as one of the points of entry.

Bobbin lace

Vadstena Convent and bobbin-lace making
Vadstena Convent was founded in 1370. The rules of the Order stated that the sisters should do textile work, among other things, "sömgerning och sprangade gerning" (needlework and *sprang*). The term *sprangade gerning* has been interpreted—probably rightly so—as a collective term for all kinds of openwork, not necessarily limited to or even including what is now known as *sprang*. There are records of bobbin lace being made in Nådendal, a daughter institution of Vadstena in western Finland. When the monasteries in Sweden were dissolved in 1527, the nuns of Vadstena Convent were granted the right to remain until their death. At the end of the sixteenth century, a few nuns were still living there. In 1757, an extensive lace production reportedly existed in Vadstena. It was considered to be a direct descendant of the lace production in the Convent. It seems likely that bobbin laces were made in Vadstena Convent as early as the Renaissance. This is a reasonable supposition, considering the extent to which its activity was consistently characterized by precisely this type of production. Vadstena's intimate connections with four daughter institutions in Flanders and the Netherlands and three in Italy are confirmed in numerous ways, e.g., by preserved correspondence. Vadstena owned its own ships, which sailed, probably from Söderköping, across the Baltic to outposts along the southern Baltic shore. From there, the Order's own horses would carry travelers on to the two Birgittine convents in Rome and Florence. Against this general background, it certainly seems natural to view Vadstena as one—perhaps the most important—bridgehead in central and northern Sweden for bobbin-lace making, as well as for a number of other textile techniques.

429. Laces of linen thread, the top five from Leksand, Dalarna, the bottom one from Almundsryd, Småland.

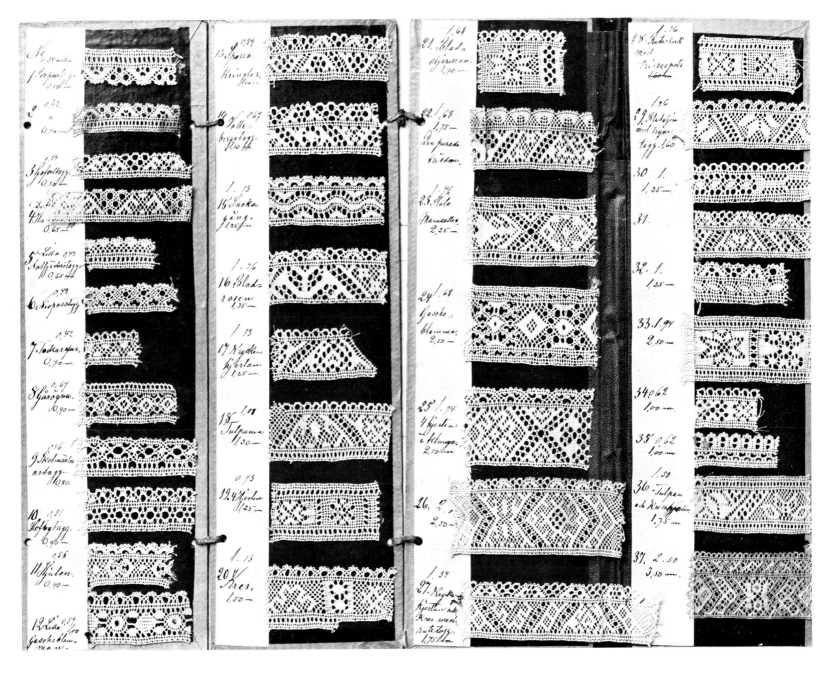

430. Skåne lace. Samples of bobbin laces made in Ingelstad district with notations of pattern names, widths, and prices.

Local types of bobbin lace without réseau
The two main groups distinguishable among bobbin laces are laces without *réseau*—belonging to an earlier stage of the development, before the use of pins and pricked patterns—and laces with *réseau*, technically more developed forms, worked on a pricked pattern with pins on a pillow. Both types are found as handcraft in defined local areas, sometimes existing side by side.

The older type, bobbin lace without *réseau*, must have existed before the more developed bobbin lace appeared. It is likely that the lace with *réseau* more easily gained entrance in those areas where the older type of bobbin lace was already known.

The occurrence of bobbin laces made without patterns has not been mapped. It is obviously most documented in those localities where such a manufacture still existed at the

Bobbin lace

end of the nineteenth century, above all in Ore, Dalarna, and Ovanåker and Delsbo in Hälsingland. A nationwide inventory would probably reveal several other locales where the older type of bobbin lace was once made.

Bobbin laces of the older type are preserved on older textiles from separate parts of the country. These older textiles—sheets, pillowcases, ceiling cloths, etc.—can be dated to the sixteenth and seventeenth centuries. Whether these laces are of indigenous manufacture or imported is not known. In Skåne, Blekinge, and Halland, laces from a later date of apparent domestic origin have been found. They closely emulate Italian sixteenth-century laces. The technique probably spread from western European and northern German centers, directly or via Denmark, to the then Danish provinces in southern Sweden. Many other textile techniques traveled this way: *reticella,* embroidery, filet work, weaving, and knitting.

Characteristic of the older bobbin-lace type was the material: homespun, sturdy, fairly loosely plied yarn. It clearly differed from the fine, tightly twisted thread of bobbin lace with *réseau.* Older bobbin-lace pillows, preserved in Ore, Dalarna, consisted of a padded cylinder covered with fabric, placed in a basket or box. To this type of pillow belonged whittled bobbins of juniper wood, and thinner sticks of wood to fix the edges of the lace (fig. 419). Pattern and pins were not used.

In her paper "Knyppling utan fast mönster" ("Bobbin-lace making without pricked pattern"), Gertrud Rodhe distinguishes between three basic types of bobbin lace without pattern. The first type is a plaited lace—each line in the design consisting of a four-end braid—with lozenges of clothwork as "spine" (fig. 429, bottom). The edges lack firmness, which was no problem, as these laces were generally used as insertions in woven fabric. The second type features a diagonal latticework, with the lines intersecting at right angles (fig. 430, numbers 6

431. Edging of woman's headdress. Linen tabby with drawn-thread work and darning stitch in white and gray linen yarn. Made by Bengta Andersdotter, Ingelstad, Skåne, in the 1840s.

308

and 9). There are several simpler variants of the latticed lace, with wavy, loose lines. Though generally double-edged and used for insertions, latticed lace occurs also as edging. The third type has a certain number of threads traversing the lace from edge to edge at right angles, pulled tight between the sticks fixing the edges, and running like the weft in a weave, i.e., clothwork (see, for example, fig. 430, numbers 21 and 28). These types represent laces made without pattern pins but nevertheless with a certain firmness. The types, of course, also occur mixed. Thus, a common combination is a lace with latticework and supporting braided bars, from which yet another variant has developed, the "latticed square."

The bobbin laces without *réseau* mentioned here can be found in pattern books from the sixteenth and seventeenth centuries and in preserved textile specimens from southern and western Europe. They occurred generally, not only in Sweden, but wherever the impact of period styles was felt. The simple technique did not allow for any greater pattern variation. Because of the dearth of material, it is hardly possible, at this time, to determine whether any local differentiation existed. However, it has been established that simplified latticed laces with clothwork bands were especially common among peasant laces from northern Skåne, and that the third type, with its cloth-like structure, shows interesting technical similarities to the peasant laces of southern Skåne. The plaited lace with clothwork lozenges and the lace with latticed bands occur, in pure form or in combination, in older preserved material from Småland, central and northern Sweden, and, in simplified forms, in a well-documented peasant production in Ore, Dalarna, and Ovanåker and Delsbo, Hälsingland.

Delsbo textiles with older types of embroidery, geometrical satin stitch, and drawn-thread work were often decorated with these early, simpler types of bobbin lace. The later bobbin lace with *réseau* adorned especially the so-called *svartluva* (black hood) (fig. 436), the black velvet hood worn locally by older women for churchgoing, etc. Local records confirm that the old women in Delsbo could make bobbin lace without a pattern, but that they did not know lace making with pins and pricked pattern.

Delsbo laces were also made with colored thread, used as a pattern element in the predominantly white lace (fig. 434; color fig. 43). An inventory of embroidered textiles in Delsbo in 1963 yielded many articles of bedding decorated with narrow, plain laces with a simple checkered pattern or with square panels and continuous colored threads. Before this material has been studied in greater depth, the historical position of the material is open to discussion.

Also in Blekinge and Småland, simplified forms of latticework lace were made in peasant milieu, as well as latticed laces with colored threads.

The most remarkable offshoot of the older bobbin lace was the particular lace developed in the southeastern districts of Skåne. As late as the beginning of the nineteenth century, it was executed by peasant women; from the 1830s onward, this unique lace was energetically supported by the Ehrenswärd family in Tosterup, later by the province's handcraft societies.

The lace from southeastern Skåne has, to a great extent, come to be regarded as the typical Skåne lace. From what is now known, it must be characterized as a distinctly local phenomenon (fig. 430). There is no other type of lace that can be pointed out as its direct model or inspiration. It is true that some of its patterns, to some extent, go back to European common patterns from the sixteenth century—latticework or latticework with four-end braids—and, in a few instances, to eighteenth-century Flemish pattern types. But, on the whole, the origin of the particular designs of this Skåne lace is more easily understood in the light of the rich patterns of Skåne drawn-thread and cut work, woven fabrics, and bands.

Technically, the southeastern Skåne lace was simple enough not to need a pricked parchment, although its pattern was worked to some extent on a net ground. Ornamentally, it was characterized by a rhythmical division of the lace surface by means of vertical and diagonal bars in clothwork. In "Den textila hemslöjden" ("Textile handcraft"), Ingegerd Henschen

Ingvar sees in this phenomenon a unique trait of the Skåne lace, which helps link it to the typical Skåne embroidery in drawn-thread and cut work of *reticella* type (fig. 431). Actually, in this area the patterns of bobbin lace are often identical to the patterns of embroidery on, for example, the bands on the female dress. Ingegerd Henschen Ingvar is of the opinion that this correspondence demonstrates the dependency of early bobbin lace on the models provided by needlepoint lace and its precursors, before bobbin lace had started to develop in its own direction. She does, however, also point out that these patterns possibly represent a simplification and stylization of more complex patterns, somewhat like the simplification of Flemish floral motifs seen in the bobbin laces of Dalarna and simpler Vadstena laces.

The ornamental inventory of Skåne lace consists, on the whole, of the same simple patterns noted in weaving, band weaving, embroidery, and knitting: stars, hearts, diamonds, and other geometric figures not requiring patterns for their execution on right-angled thread systems. It may also be added that in Skåne lace making, the bobbins are hung on the lace pillow in a vertical line, straight across the cylinder, whereas Vadstena lace bobbins are hung on diagonally.

It is not known for how long Skåne peasantry has been making bobbin laces. However, from 1749 there is a description by Carl von Linné (Linnaeus)—not only a great naturalist but also a sharp-eyed observer—of a woman's headdress, a shirt, and a decorative handkerchief, all trimmed with lace. The lace type, derived from sixteenth-century lace, and its *reticella*-related patterns, seems to indicate that bobbin-lace production might have started in the sixteenth century or at least in the seventeenth century. In any case, the manufacture was based on models of *reticella* type.

Motifs other than the purely geometric also occur in Skåne lace. Horsemen, deer, swans, roosters, flowers in urn, old women, etc., are combined with stars and diamonds in the older rhythmic compositional schemes. The figures are taken from the old Skåne hangings. They are executed in clothwork on a net ground. The figures do not occur in the older Skåne lace types. It is not known to what extent the lacemakers themselves thought of imitating weaves in lace or whether they were influenced to do so by such bobbin-lace enthusiasts as the members of the Ehrenswärd family of Toste-rup, Skåne. It is, however, quite clear that some bobbin lace was made after the models of fabrics, bands, and embroideries with geometric patterns. *Réseau* was used to a certain extent in this type of Skåne lace, however, not as a ground but as a pattern element. Also, as it was executed without a pricked pattern and pins, it is clear that the makers of this lace never adopted the new technique associated with *réseau*.

Local types of bobbin lace with réseau

The distribution of bobbin lace of Flemish eighteenth-century type from the neighborhood of Vadstena is well documented. Judging from preserved specimens, the quality varied. There are samples preserved of coarse as well as fine bobbin lace. Some patterns closely resemble those of the Flemish prototypes, others are highly simplified versions of the latter. The eighteenth-century Berch collection in Nordiska Museet includes lace samples that look exactly like contemporary Flemish laces (fig. 425). It is also possible that these samples are indeed foreign laces, imported to serve as models for the fledgling Swedish bobbin-lace manufacture which the authorities so wished to encourage.

During the latter part of the eighteenth century, bobbin lace lost much of its prominence in fashionable dress. But among the peasants, lace continued to play an important role. It was used above all on the *stycke* under the *bindmössa* (fig. 426). It seems likely that it was precisely this lace-edged strip of linen or cotton which created the great demand for lace and, particularly, for lace with *réseau*. The lace-edged cap was used throughout Sweden with the exception of Dalarna, Blekinge, Skåne, southern Småland, and Halland. In Dalarna the women of most parishes still used the older form of linen hood, also edged with lace (fig. 432). The lace-edged cap was generally spread throughout the country around the mid-1700s

and remained in use up to about 1850. In other words, there was a great demand for lace, lasting longest in peasant milieu.

As in many other contexts, certain localities took up purchased lace patterns and copied them to the best of their ability in an already mastered and familiar textile technique. Older techniques and older patterns therefore came to live on as decorations on older furnishings, such as bedding, wall hangings, dress linen—especially collar and wristband lace—decorative handkerchiefs, and *förningsdukar,* cloths used to wrap around the decorated vessel holding food for communal feasts or special treats brought to women in childbed. Newer patterns were instead associated with the relatively newly arrived lace-edged cap strip.

Dalarna is one of Sweden's foremost bobbin-lace provinces, with a well-documented production up to the beginning of this century, when it was taken over by the Handcraft Movement. In the parishes of Boda, Bjursås, Floda, Gagnef, Leksand, Mockfjärd, Orsa, Rättvik, and Ål, bobbin-lace making developed under the influence of eighteenth-century *réseau* lace. The artist Ottilia Adelborg, who founded a school for bobbin-lace making in Gagnef in 1903, tells that older women from Vadstena wandered around the country selling laces. These women would pay for their lodgings on the farms by teaching the local women the technique of Vadstena, "store-bought" lace (fig. 426), which was considered finer than one's own "everyday" lace. Without pins and pattern, and with thick homespun thread, the result was such that only a study of transitional forms reveals the Flemish origins of the homemade Dalarna lace patterns (fig. 427). Even the simpler laces from Vadstena itself failed to reproduce the fine floral and foliage patterns of the Flemish originals, with their softly curved rococo scrolls following the edge of the lace against the sheer net ground. Flemish laces of this type are found all over the country, especially in Dalarna, where they apparently gave a vital impetus to the local development. As the lace makers in the province did not use pricked patterns, the results were extraordinarily varied; i.e., local types with distinct characteristics developed.

In Dalarna the process of making bobbin

lace as well as the lace itself are referred to as *knytning* (literally, "tying"; netting). The lace was used primarily to edge the woman's linen hood or cap. In Gagnef, Floda, Mockfjärd, and Ål parishes, it was of generous width—preserved specimens measure six inches—and consisted of two or three lace strips sewn together (fig. 427). It was not possible to maneuver all the threads required for a six-inch-wide lace without the aid of pattern and pins. In Leksand and Orsa, the lace edging was narrow, and was used also on other parts of the costume, e.g., the fichu, decorative handkerchief, and shirt.

In Mockfjärd are found the most clearly Vadstena-inspired laces. Simple as well as more complicated patterns were used as models. The curvilinear patterns of Flemish rococo lace have become stylized to angular "curved" lines with geometrical forms, replacing the flowers and leaves. For the wide cap lace, two or three lace strips were sewn together, all of the same motif, but of different widths (figs. 426, 427, center and bottom). The patterns are seen against a diagonal net ground. The figures are formed by areas in clothwork with holes, surrounded by a thicker contour thread or gimp. The older tradition survives in patterns formed by diamonds and diagonal bars. However, most varied are the types inspired by Vadstena's floral patterns, types given fanciful names like "German Crown," "Tulip Rose," and "Highway Lace."

Also in Ål, laces have a net ground made of quite fine thread. The gimp is considerably thinner than that of Mockfjärd laces. The pattern elements are diamonds and triangles, combined to form a kind of hourglass shape outlined by gimp. These shapes are seen against more closely interlaced areas of the fabric with diamond-shaped holes in diamond formations.

Gagnef laces are closely related to Ål laces in their use of certain patterns of diamonds and hourglass shapes. The thread is, however, coarser. The finest lace, used on the very best Sunday cap, closely resembled Vadstena lace. It was called *bottenknytning* (ground lace) (fig. 427). It adorned the articles of clothing given by the bridegroom to his bride. Without a hood with Vadstena-like lace, the married woman could not possibly attend a wedding. Patterns were named after their predominant motifs, e.g., "A" lace for an A-shaped motif, etc. Bobbin-lace making ceased in Gagnef earlier than in Mockfjärd, where Gagnef women from then on would buy their hood lace.

Floda lace used patterns similar to those in Mockfjärd, though the thread and gimp are coarser. The lace for the hood is wide, consisting of two wide laces and one narrow edging all joined together (fig. 427, top).

Together with Boda and Bjursås laces, the laces of Rättvik form a separate group of laces with sparse, open structure. The thread is extremely fine. The net ground is open, with long brides, in which the threads have been twisted around each other a couple of times. Rättvik laces are the sheerest, having only two threads twisted around each other in the very long brides between the pattern elements (figs. 432, 433). On closer scrutiny, the pattern is found to comprise diamond shapes, triangles, diagonal bars, and chevron bands, i.e., pattern elements recognizable from other laces of closer and firmer structure.

Some old women living at the beginning of the twentieth century recalled conditions around the middle of the nineteenth century. Laces used to be made more narrow and closer in structure. They used to be made with fewer bobbin pairs and without picots, a practice retained in Boda longer than in Rättvik. The laces of the hood were made in suitably adjusted lengths and patterns. Laces sold in Orsa were, however, sold by the yard, as they were not used for the woman's hood in this parish. One of the transmitters of tradition in Rättvik, an old woman who was still making lace at the age of 80 in 1907, had learned the art from her aunt in 1840. The aunt had learned it during the first years of the nineteenth century. Lace making was not a craft practiced by everyone—"it demanded a knack and you sort of inherited it."

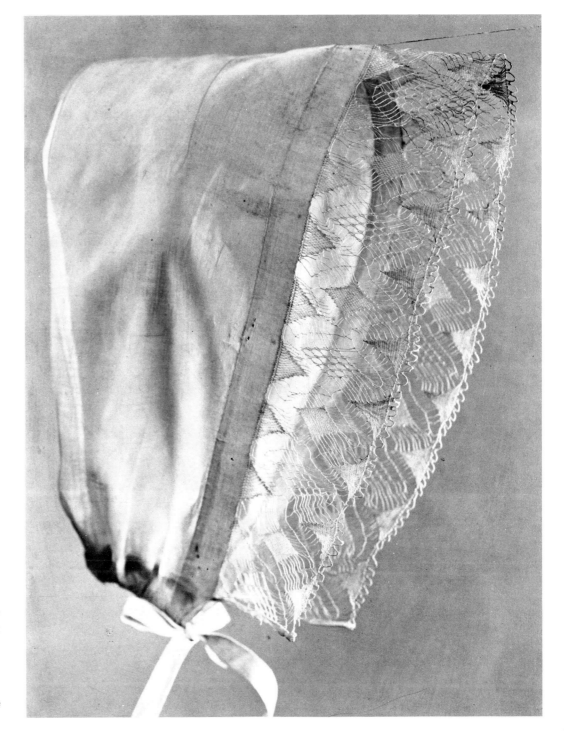

432. Woman's hood of linen tabby with bobbin-lace edging. Rättvik, Dalarna.

Bobbin lace

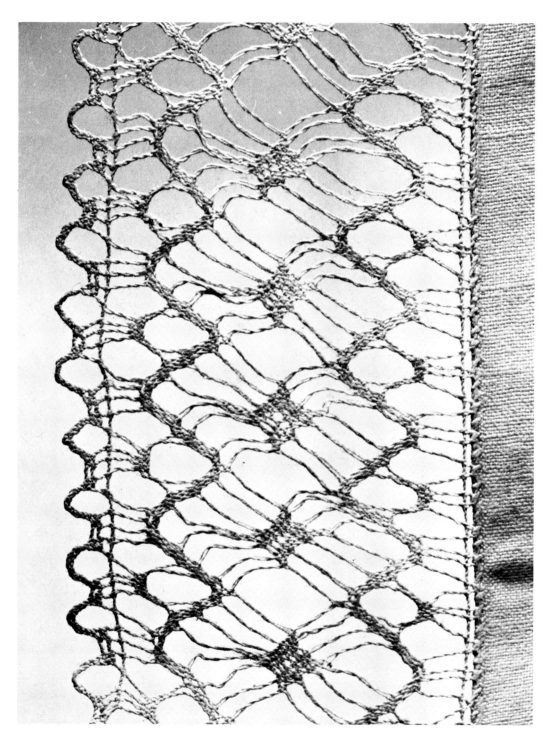

In the 1870s, some new patterns were introduced. Lace making with cotton thread had begun. However, in the 1880s and 1890s, lace making for sale stopped. Apparently the typical, sheer Rättvik lace was a late development, probably dating from some time between 1850 and 1880.

In Orsa, narrow laces were made of gray-white linen which was not washed, in order to retain its natural color. The patterns consisted, for the most part, of diamonds, triangles, and crosses, seen against a net ground. The ground could also be minimal or practically nonexistent, in which case the lace closely resembled bobbin lace without *réseau*.

In Nås, laces were made with, as well as without, a net ground.

In the lace-making parishes of Dalarna, three types of bobbin lace may be found: (1) the oldest type without *réseau*, (2) the diamond-triangle-diagonal bar type, and (3) the simplified Flemish lace. But whether all three type existed everywhere as a result of local lace-making activity is not quite clear. It is nowadays fairly difficult to establish what might have been brought in from other provinces, by Västergötland peddlers or lace makers from Vadstena, or purchased from other Dalarna parishes. Where primary source documentation exists, it clearly shows that local lace production has undergone significant changes in the last few generations. Apparently the *bindmössor* with their lace edging have meant a great deal for the distribution of the Flemish type of lace with *réseau*. Even as conservative a province as Dalarna took up the wide lace edging, however, not on the *bindmössa* but as decoration on the old hood. The *bindmössa* itself did not gain a foothold.

Ovanåker and Delsbo, both in Hälsingland, have already been mentioned as locations for the old type of bobbin lace without pattern and pins. This lace continued to be made for so long that it has been possible to obtain first-

433. Bobbin lace of linen thread for woman's hood. Rättvik, Dalarna.

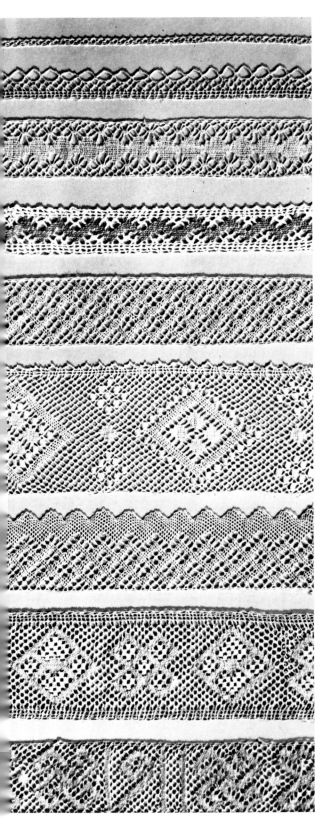

hand information about it and about those who made it.

These older, narrow laces (fig. 434) were used to decorate certain objects of older type, such as wall hangings, bedding textiles, and funerary cloths.[17]

In Delsbo, lace with *réseau* was the special decoration on the black velvet church hood. It was made with white thread, then dyed black and starched. The church-hood lace differed from other bobbin laces of Delsbo in pattern elements, ground, and color. Other laces use the common motifs: diamonds, triangles, and diagonal bars, combined into hearts or S-shapes, whereas the black-lace patterns consist of larger and smaller diamonds and wheat-grain motifs, tallies, combined to larger diamonds. In other laces, the pattern elements are seen against a sparse ground, or joined only by loosely twisted brides; in black lace, the pattern elements are outlined against a net ground, a *réseau*. Other local laces often include figures in red or red and blue, sometimes other colors as well; the hood lace is uniformly black. Local tradition asserts that the Rudolphi family introduced to Delsbo not only free embroidery in red—Delsbo work—but also bobbin-lace making. On closer scrutiny, one is first tempted to view the Rudolphi contribution with regard to bobbin lace with some skepticism. The Rudolphis cannot have been the first to make bobbin lace in Delsbo, for there are textiles with bobbin lace preserved which antedate the Rudolphis. These bobbin laces are of the older type, made without pricked pattern and pins. This older type seems to have been generally entrenched and made by many women in the province, who did not learn the "new" way of lace making until the twentieth century.

However, when it comes to church-hood lace and bobbin lace made with pricked pattern and pins in general, there may be reason to heed the local tradition.

In the middle of the eighteenth century, an army surgeon named Carl Friedrich Rudolphi came from Barth in Pomerania and settled in Delsbo parish. According to local tradition, he and his male descendants made bobbin laces for two generations (see fig. 436 and accompanying caption). Thereafter, lace making was taken over by the women in the family, who ever since have been known as expert lace makers. Female members of the Rudolphi family are still making laces.

One member of the family still possesses an early lace pillow, covered with vellum and equipped with a cylinder fitted with a strip of birch bark (fig. 435). This bark has diagonal perforations, into which pins were stuck during the making of the lace. No other pattern was used. The pillow appears to date from the eighteenth century. It would seem likely that the Rudolphis did, in fact, introduce the pattern characteristic for the church-hood lace, as well as bobbin-lace making with pins and pricked roller. The use of birch bark to fit around the roller may of course have been a local adaptation: birch bark was used locally also in the so-called birch-bark work, *näversöm,* a kind of two-directional drawn-thread work (fig. 333). And data confirm the use of birch-bark strips for bobbin-lace making in Dalarna, as well. However, black-dyed lace was found primarily in the Netherlands and parts of Germany.

Ovanåker parish has been discussed above in connection with the older bobbin-lace type. Flemish-type laces were used on the lace-edged strip under the *bindmössa.* It is reported that these laces were sold by Finnish peddlers. In other words, these laces were probably from Raumo, not from Vadstena.

In a number of publications, bobbin-lace specialist Sally Johanson reports on technical peculiarities in the Hälsingland laces of Flemish type, which would tie them to the Finnish lace production rather than to the Swedish. This tie is far from unlikely; rather it would be quite natural in Norrland, where trading of goods across the Gulf of Bothnia (the upper part of the Baltic) has long been active.

In conclusion, it should be pointed out that there is a certain resemblance between the bobbin laces of older type in widely separated

434. Laces of all white or white and light red linen yarn. Delsbo, Hälsingland.

parts of the country. Such is the case with the simple patterns of diagonal bars, which are encountered in Leksand lace in Dalarna as well as in southeastern Skåne lace. A group of simple, coarse laces from Floda, Dalarna, have a rhythmic partitioning by vertical bars like that of the Skåne lace. In Delsbo, Hälsingland, and in Blekinge is found a type of lace with extremely sparse decor of squares or interlaced wavy bands accented with colored thread. There are also the universal patterns with diamonds and triangles, which seem to appear everywhere. Apparently, only one clearly documented center of lace distribution, namely Vadstena, has been identified so far; and even for that center, the documentation is substantial only after the middle of the eighteenth century. Surely there must have existed other centers, but these still remain to be identified and researched. Presently, the field of geographical distribution of techniques and patterns is spottily illuminated at best.

There are bobbin laces preserved throughout virtually the entire country. They decorate dress linen, bed linen, and hangings. Technically, some of these laces are of the older type with patterns from the sixteenth century. Others are laces of Flemish type or imitations of it. A third, transitional, group has simple geometric figures, diamonds, triangles, and diagonal bars, on a plain net ground. Laces of this third type appear all over Europe. Their relationship to the older, patternless bobbin lace, on one hand, and the later *réseau* lace, on the other, is not clear. To what extent particular laces were made within the locality where they have been found is not known for the bulk of the preserved material. A general cataloging of this material and a collecting of data about local manufacture still remain to be done. Laces of localities where lace making was still practiced when the Handcraft Movement began have, however, been studied in greater or lesser detail. The results of these studies have been presented in a number of publications.

435. Bobbin-lace pillow. The roller is covered with diagonally pricked birch bark, in which the pins are stuck in lace making. Delsbo, Hälsingland. Privately owned by a member of the Rudolphi family.

436. Black *réseau* lace of linen thread, used on the church hood of black velvet. Made in 1879 by the churchwarden Isak Rudolphi, grandson of Carl Friedrich Rudolphi (1735–1814), who immigrated to Sweden from Pomerania in the mid-seventeenth century.

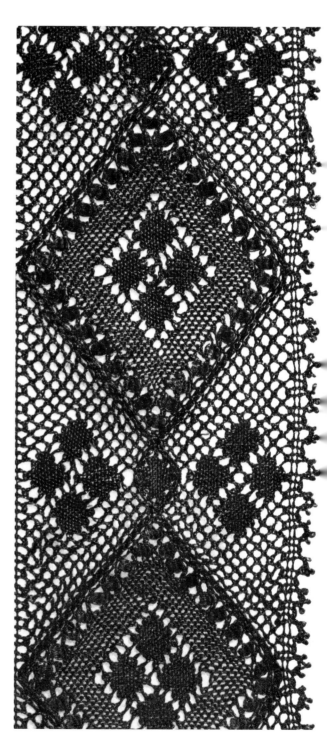

Needle looping

Needle looping is an ancient technique of producing a fabric with a nonwoven structure. At one time, it was known throughout Sweden; today it survives in only a few places. It appears to have been in some way bound up with knitting, in that wherever knitting gained an early foothold, needle looping disappeared.

Different provinces have different local terms for needle looping. In Värmland, Dalarna, Jämtland, and Uppland it is variously called *nålbindning* (sewing with needle), *binda med nål* ([to] sew with a needle), *nåla* ([to] needle), and *sömma* ([to] seam). The term *påta* ([to] poke) has also been reported but it has been used also to designate a type of crochet or all looping work done with simple tools or the fingers alone. *Nålbindning* (the noun) and *binda med nål* (the verb) are today the generally accepted terms in Sweden for needle looping.[18] In needle looping only a coarse bone needle was used, with an eye either in one end or near the middle of the needle (fig 139, top). Preserved looped articles show that the preferred materials were wool yarn, horse hair, cow's tail bristles, goat hair, and human hair.

The technique consists of forming and interlocking circular loops. The loops are formed when the thread is pulled tight around the left thumb, which functions as a mesh pin. Simultaneously, the needle is guided through one or several loops in the preceding row of loops (fig. 438). The work is, as a rule, done from left to right. In spite of the technique's simplicity, a great number of variations are possible, depending on how many of the previously made loops in the same or preceding row are included by the needle in each stitch. The needle can, furthermore, go above one and under one loop, or above one and under two, three, or several loops. This produces fabrics of varying density, with more tightly bound loops and a certain texture on the right or outer side and floating threads on the reverse or inner side. Depending on the material, the technique can also produce widely varying results. Needle looping with horse hair, cow's tail bristles, goat hair, cow hair, and human hair gives a loose elastic fabric (fig. 437). This structure was

437. Mitten, sock, and insole with toe cap, all in needle looping. Cow's-tail bristles and cow hair.

315

Needle looping

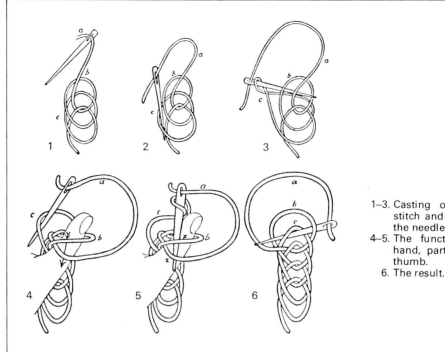

1–3. Casting on the first stitch and the path of the needle.
4–5. The function of the hand, particularly the thumb.
6. The result.

especially suited for milk strainers—circular looped mats used to strain fresh milk (fig. 166)—for work mittens, for stocking feet, for cuffless socks, and for insoles with toe caps designed to be worn in the shoes in severe cold. While the insoles were usually made with hair yarn and goat shag, cow's tail bristles were used for milk strainers and stocking feet, and wool for mittens. For looping mittens, between four and six loops were picked up on the needle; for other articles, fewer.

Needle looping in these materials was also used for items as large as horse blankets. Loose, elastic fabrics were made also of wool, but, as a rule, wool items in needle looping are fairly firm and made more so by fulling. Articles made with needle looping were mostly mittens and strainers (figs. 438–41). A few hoods have also been preserved.

Needle looping is carried on today to some extent in northern Värmland and certain parts of Dalarna, in Hälsingland, and in Härjedalen. Preserved objects and recorded traditions testify that, in the nineteenth century, the technique was used largely in central and northern Sweden. In Norway and Finland today, needle looping is practiced on a limited scale, but it was at one time far more widespread. During the Viking age, men from Gotland sold wool mittens in Russia and the Baltic states. Apparently, these mittens enjoyed great popularity, as they were presented as official gifts to magistrates in Novgorod. There is, of course, no way of determining whether these mittens were made of cloth or by needle looping, but it is quite possible that they were looped. In any event, needle looping did exist in western and southern Europe as late as the Middle Ages; and furthermore, it did and still does exist in cultural fringe areas on all continents.

This world-wide distribution—a characteristic of other equally basic techniques—indicates an extremely ancient origin. The earliest find in Sweden of a needle-looped article is a mitten from the Åsle peat bog in Västergötland. By pollen analysis it has been dated to the late Iron Age, probably A.D. 200–300. Danish Bronze Age finds include needle-looped socks. Needle looping is one of the oldest, most primitive techniques known to man, definitely going

438. Needle looping, tools and execution.

439. Needle-looped mittens of wool yarn with wool embroidery in shading stitch and chain stitch. Dalby, Värmland.

440. Mittens of wool yarn with sewn-on pile trim. Left to right: in knit stitch with cut voided pile on the cuff, Toarp, Västergötland; in needle looping with long cut pile, Uppland; knitted with two ends, cut pile weave (locally, *fax*) on the cuff, Värmland.

Needle looping

back to a stage in development when articles of clothing, textiles in general, and baskets were all made by the same techniques—at that time possibly the only technique known for the making of a fabric.

Decoration

Milk strainers and insoles contributed nothing to the formal equipment of the household, nor to personal appearance. They were rather a kind of plain consumer goods. The mittens, on the other hand, had two functions. In addition to the purely practical function of protecting the hands against cold and damp in fishing, working in the forest, etc., mittens also had a purely decorative function. Mittens for formal wear especially were decorated with extraordinary care. The dense structure of needle-looped mittens lent itself to embroidered patterns. Best known were the Dalby mittens and Floda mittens, which are still made today (fig. 439). They were ornamented with naturalistic flowers and leaves on the back side of the mitten, flowers and leaf scrolls on the cuff, and a small motif on the thumb. The material was wool yarn in many colors. The pattern was executed in shading stitch, with strong stylistic influences from the mid-1800s and later. In isolated specimens, the embroidery is based on older traditions from the beginning of the nineteenth century. One group of mittens from northern Värmland has embroidered cuffs in a yet older style: the pattern elements are squares, diamonds, circles, and crosses, sewn in stem stitch, cross-stitch, satin stitch, and spaced buttonhole stitch, etc., with predominantly red, blue, and green wool yarn.

The very oldest decorative element on mittens is sewn-on fringe or pile strip—chenille—in different colors, *fax*, as it is called in Värmland. It is found on some Värmland mittens, also on a mitten from Uppland in natural brown wool, and on the Åsle mitten.

441. Wool mittens of needle looping. Left to right: fulled and embroidered in chain stitch, with pile edging, Sorunda, Södermanland; embroidered in backstitch and cross-stitch; and embroidered in cross-stitch, chain stitch, and buttonhole stitch, Dalby, Värmland. (See color figure 45.)

318

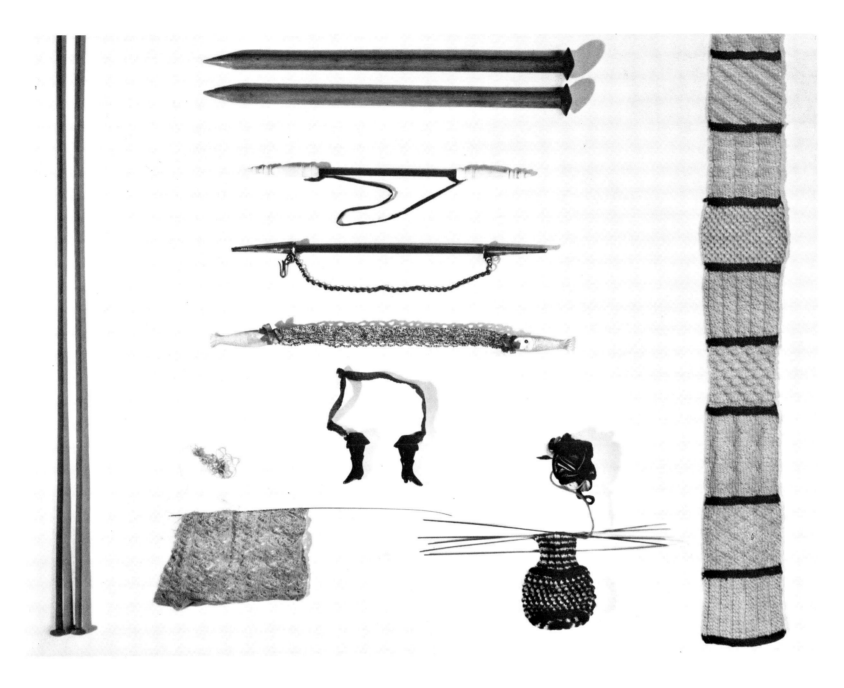

Knitting

Today there is a commonly accepted term for knitting in Swedish, *stickning,* although several dialectal terms are still used locally.

Technically, knitting is a technique based on a single, continuous element—the thread—which by manipulation with two to five needles forms an elastic fabric. Only two needles are used at a time. For circular knitting of, for example, stockings, five needles are required. With one needle a loop is formed, the stitch, which is transferred to the other needle. These stitches are of two kinds, purl stitches and knit stitches, depending upon from which side the thread is pulled through the loop. Viewed from one side of the fabric, a particular stitch will be a purl stitch, viewed from the other side, a knit stitch. At the outset of the work, a number of stitches are cast on to one needle

442. Knitting tools and patterns: knitting needles of different sizes, sets of knitting needles with stoppers on the ends, one pair of stoppers in the shape of a pair of shoes, and sampler of eighteen different knitting patterns.

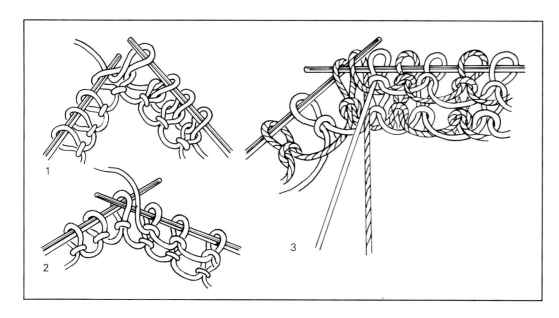

443. (1) Knit stitch. (2) Purl stitch. (3) Knitting with two yarns, reverse side. (See also fig. 460.) For clarity, one yarn is shaded.

444. Knit jacket, detail. Knit stitch and purl stitch in red wool yarn. Halland.

and then knit on to the other. This is called one row. The purl stitch and the knit stitch are the basis for all knitting, and with them all kinds of knitting can be done.

In northern Sweden, knitting was often done "with two ends." In this kind of knitting, two balls of the same yarn are used, or two ends from the same ball. The knitting is done, alternating yarn on every stitch. The result is a thick and dense fabric with a characteristically structured reverse side (figs. 139, 443:3, 460). The right side, however, looks like ordinary knitting.

The preferred material was wool yarn, but linen and cotton yarns also were used to a certain extent. Yarns made of horse hair, cow hair, and woman's hair were used in certain articles with specific functions, e.g., in mittens used in wintertime to work in the forest, or to pull in fishnets, or in any other occupation where the water-repellent nature of the material was important. Rabbit wool was also used for special pattern effects.

Patterns and motifs

Patterns in knitting are created either by alternating yarn of different colors in the same stitches (fig. 458), by alternating purl and knit stitches with yarn of the same color (fig. 444), by a combination of these two methods, or by decreasing or increasing the number of stitches, whereby an openwork pattern is created (fig. 466).

Pattern motifs in Swedish knitting were, on the whole, borrowed from other textile techniques: weaving (fig. 444), embroidery (fig. 466), band weaving (fig. 465), and lacelike fabrics such as crochet (fig. 442), *sprang*, and braiding. The technical characteristics of knitting tended to restrict the choice of patterns (fig. 451). A sharp local differentiation shows that local textile tradition in general put its stamp on each area's knitting patterns. On each article of knitting, the particular placement of the pattern motifs also points to an influence from older traditions established for articles of woven fabrics (fig. 445).

Patterns created by either alternating yarn color or by alternating purl and knit stitches were common all over the country. Color effects, however, completely dominated northern Swedish knitting, whereas stitch alternation was prevalent in the south. Openwork patterns were found primarily in southern Sweden and in the coastal provinces of Norrland.

Practical uses

Knitting was used throughout the country for stockings, mittens, and caps. Knitted jackets and other larger articles of clothing were found less generally in peasant milieu. Thus, the use of knit jackets since the seventeenth century is documented in certain southwestern provinces, namely Skåne, Halland, Blekinge, and parts of Småland and Bohuslän. In central and northern Sweden, knitted jackets were found in certain parishes in Dalarna and Hälsingland, in southeastern Härjedalen, and, to some extent, in Medelpad. In northern Sweden, the use of knit jackets cannot be traced farther back than the end of the eighteenth and the beginning of the nineteenth centuries.

History

Knitting is today one of the most commonly practiced household crafts. It was given a strong impetus by fashions in the 1920s, and has since increased in popularity and, on the whole, retained its appeal until the present. Modern knitting, whether handmade or machine-made, is still inspired by continuous contact with older knitting in peasant milieu. The latter was, in turn, the product of two earlier stylistic currents. To properly understand the geographic differentiation (see below for further discussion), knitting must be seen in historical perspective.

Some knit articles from Coptic Egypt have been preserved. The technique was apparently widely spread around the Mediterranean. From

445. Knit jacket. Detail, showing the side "seam" and border around the sleeve cuff. Knit stitch and purl stitch in wool yarn. Halland.

the fifth and sixth centuries, knitted liturgical mittens are preserved in Europe. But not until the fifteenth century was knitting generally spread on the Continent (fig. 447). If the sources are correctly interpreted, hose knitting was practiced by Birgittine nuns in Nådendal Convent in Finland in the fifteenth century. If knitting was done in Nådendal, then why not also in Vadstena Convent, the mother institution? Whatever the case may have been, the earliest preserved knitted garments in Scandinavia were found in Denmark. During the seventeenth century a flourishing hose manufacture for sale developed in Denmark. In Sweden, King Erik XIV secured a pair of silk hose from England in the 1560s. These must have been a rarity, since the King paid a price for them equal to a valet's annual salary. The first stocking-knitting machine was invented in England in 1589, at approximately the same time as hand knitting started to spread in Sweden. From the middle of the seventeenth century, two knit tunics of silk are preserved in Sweden. One, in white and gold with a floral pattern, is now in the collections of Nordiska Museet (fig. 448). The other is of red silk with a star pattern and embroideries in silver thread. It belongs to Göteborgs Museum. Both are luxury garments. Portraits from the same time show that knit tunics of this type were worn as a sort of undershirt. Judging from preserved material, it was a widespread fashion in western Europe.

The oldest preserved Swedish knitting from peasant milieu is a group of knit jackets from Halland. At least one of them can be traced back to the middle of the eighteenth century. They closely resemble the above-mentioned seventeenth-century tunics in form and pattern. Local tradition in Halland relates that knitting was introduced into Halland by a Dutch-born lady, later married to Governor Durell in Kristianstad, who owned the Wallen residential estate in Våxtorp parish. She started the women on the estate knitting with wool yarn. In this way, then, the art of knitting supposedly spread. There is reason to believe that it may have happened in just this way, not only in Halland but also elsewhere in the old Danish provinces. In the seventeenth century, Den-

446. Knit jacket, detail. Knit and purl stitch in red wool yarn. Oxie district, Skåne.

447. The Virgin Mary knitting a jacket for her son Jesus. Painting, part of the Buxtehude altar by Meister Bertram (1340–1415). Originally in Buxtehude Church, now in Kunsthalle, Hamburg.

448. Tunic, knitted of white silk and gold thread in knit stitch from the middle of the seventeenth century. Stamped with the official customs seal, indicating that it was imported. Probably of British origin.

mark already had a flourishing handcraft production of stockings for sale, and it seems quite natural that knitting should have come to southern Sweden from Denmark.

However, it is obvious that knitting was not commonly practiced until some time in the eighteenth century. In bourgeois milieu, cloth stockings were worn throughout the seventeenth century, and not until the eighteenth century did stockings of wadmal and broadcloth disappear from this social stratum.

As late as the latter part of the 1860s, cloth stockings were still worn in a few places in peasant milieu, e.g., in the parishes north of Lake Siljan in Dalarna, in certain parts of Hälsingland, and in Västra Vingåker and Östra Vingåker in Södermanland.

Around the end of the eighteenth century and the beginning of the nineteenth century, knitting again became fashionable. Strong impulses from the Mediterranean countries reached Sweden, among them a renewed interest in knitting. Cotton was now generally available, and white, therefore, became the fashionable Empire color. White stockings and white mittens were imperative in fashionable dress. Moreover, a new pattern type was also introduced at this time, namely openwork created by decreasing and increasing the number of stitches. This patterning technique and the cotton material were the nineteenth century's contributions to the development of pattern knitting (fig. 466). Aside from stockings and mittens, there were also knitted coverlets, pillowcase caps, laces (figs. 469, 470), etc. The knitted coverlets especially became prestige items—an ostentatious part of the bedding in the late nineteenth century. This development was linked with the appearance of the separate bedroom and the new type of bed frequently placed there.

Local characteristics
Local differentiation in knitting in peasant milieu may be discussed on the basis of this historical overview.

449. Wherever knitting was used to manufacture goods for sale, men as well as women would knit. Such was the case above all in Halland, though Öland also had male knitters.—Interior from Halland with knitting men and women. Oil painting from the middle of the nineteenth century.

Halland
In Halland, seventeenth-century patterns in their purest form are found in knit jackets with long peplum. They exhibit a star pattern in purl and knit stitch or a carnation pattern in alternating colors (fig. 142). The star pattern shows great similarity to the corresponding pattern in weaving, the former in Denmark even known by a linen-weave term, *damask* (figs. 444–46).

The carnation pattern was known also in northern Sweden (fig. 457). The seventeenth-

century traditions lived on in Halland, as late as the nineteenth century, in the knit jackets which were such a characteristic part of local peasant dress. In Halland, as in Skåne, where knit jackets played an even greater role in female dress until the end of the nineteenth century, these jackets testify to the strong influence of Renaissance fashions on Swedish peasants especially in the southern provinces.

Halland is the one Swedish province where knitting has played a major role as a domestic craft for sale.

450. Man knitting. Gräsgård, Öland.

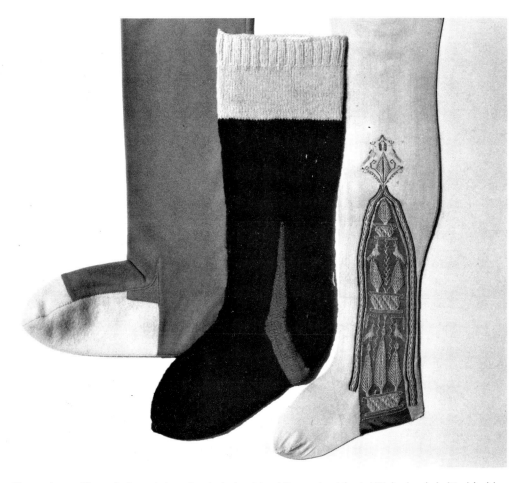

451. Women's stockings. Left to right: of red cloth with white wadmal foot, Hälsingland; knitted in blue wool yarn with red wedge or gusset, Halland; and in yellow silk with patterned gusset and embroideries, machine knit, from the 1770s–80s. Note the fashionable gusset, the model for gussets in plainer homemade stockings.

The importance of Halland knitting for the putting-out system in Västergötland has been mentioned above (page 21). From the middle of the eighteenth century, a large production of knitted goods was the main livelihood for the people in the district of Hök. Hasslöv and Våxtorp parishes specialized in stockings and nightcaps (figs. 449, 451). In the year 1771, the peasantry in the districts of Halmstad, Hök, and Tönnersjö asserted in parliament that the manufacture of coarse wool stockings was their main livelihood, and so extensive that they

could make deliveries to entire regiments. In the 1770s, the population in southern Halland specialized in knitting women's stockings with colorful gussets, whereas other parts of Halland manufactured men's stockings. A large stocking fair took place in the little village of Våxtorp every year, from October to around Christmas, and again in the spring. Stockings from several parishes were sold there, and Borås merchants bought them up in bulk.

Jackets were also knit to be sold. Like the stockings, these were not as fine or as carefully

made as those for domestic use. The object was of course to knit as much as possible in as short a time as possible. Men, women, and children were all occupied with this craft. Specific working customs developed: in certain designated houses, people would get together in the evenings to stimulate each other with frenetic knitting activity. Two persons knitting on the same garment was another common way of stepping up production. The so-called Halland jackets were made of coarse yarn, often patterned in rows of red and

Knitting

blue rectangles. They were made by circular knitting, then cut up for fashioning, and finally sewn together along the sides and the underside of the sleeves (fig. 452).

It is difficult to state with any certainty what knitting was practiced in Halland generally, and what may have been a localized specialty. The knitting that exists today in the various parts of Halland was no doubt created in response to and inspired by the Västergötland peddlers' distribution of knit goods in the province. As with weaving, knitting was also spread with the aid of Västergötland peddlers. But when, where, and in what way it happened is not yet known. It must, in any event, have happened at such an early stage that local variations and separate developments have since had time to establish themselves. Considering that the expansion of the Västergötland trade occurred in the latter part of the eighteenth century, this docs give a general idea of the time span within which knitting probably gained a foothold and spread within the country.

Bohuslän
The jackets found in Bohuslän have much in common with the Halland jackets as far as pattern is concerned. However, the Bohuslän jackets were custom-made and not cut up the sides (fig. 453). They have a carefully executed repeating pattern on the front and back pieces, finely knitted and patterned sleeve and neck gussets, and knitted side "seams" of four rows in contrasting stitch.

452. Man's sweater in white, red, and blue wool yarn, made by circular knitting, then cut up and sewn together along the sides, the shoulder seams, and the undersides of the sleeves. Årstad, Halland.

453. Man's cardigan of white wool yarn in knit and purl stitch, pattern knitting on the shoulders, around the bottom, and around the wrists. Knitted around 1890 by Beata Olsdotter, Jörlanda, Bohuslän, who supported herself by knitting to order locally.

Skåne

As mentioned above, jackets were an important part of female dress in Skåne, especially in the western parts, where they were used at an early date and from where they spread eastward. These jackets differed completely from those of Halland. They were made in knit stitch of uniform black, green, or red wool yarn. Through fulling they became so thickly felted that the stitches were practically invisible. Only a closer look would reveal that the garments were indeed knitted and not made of wadmal. The jackets were often decorated around the bottom edge, along the sides, and on the shoulders with some small knitted pattern of a few rows of purl stitch. For the rest, the decoration consisted of sewn-on patterned bands and borders around neck openings and sleeves, exactly as on cloth garments. The consistency of this knit fabric was very much like that of a woolen fabric, for through fulling the knit lost all its elasticity.

Men's stockings in white, usually bridegroom's stockings (fig. 459, right), displayed spectacular pattern knitting in knit and purl stitch. They were made of wool yarn. There were also stockings with openwork patterns, often of cotton. Women's stockings from southern Skåne were generally plain and knit of black wool yarn. Openwork patterns were lavished on cotton mittens, belonging to church or holiday dress.

Knitting in Skåne was geared toward production for household consumption. It was often done by poor women, since knitting was considered a less prestigious occupation than weaving. Knitting was also done by women from Halland, who would wander south into Skåne in the fall to help with the harvest and threshing.

The remainder of southern Sweden

In Belkinge, Småland, Västergötland, Östergötland, and on Öland and Gotland, the same forms of mittens and stockings were found as in Halland and Skåne. Thus, there were three strata of knitting: one stratum of older eighteenth-century traditions, one stratum of Gustavian and Empire openwork in cotton, and

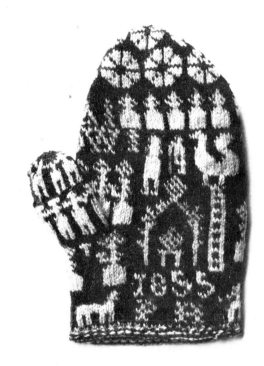

454. Mittens, knitted with natural black and white wool yarn in intricate pattern. The date, 1855, is knitted in as part of the composition. Dalsland.

one in nineteenth-century patterns in color, preferably red, probably inspired by imported machine-knit stockings and caps which were found everywhere (fig. 459, left and middle). On Gotland and Öland, the situation was somewhat unusual: from written sources it is known that there was once a large local production of mittens, stockings, and jackets; but there is very little preserved material that can give any idea of what these may have looked like (fig. 450). As in the case of Halland, the area once supported a lively craft production for sale, the products of which were distributed throughout the market area of the Västergötland trade. The Gotland peasants reportedly sold knitted articles, among them jackets and sweaters, on their sailing trips in the Baltic. It is possible, then, that knitted goods from Gotland were spread throughout the entire Baltic region. In his travel diary from Gotland in 1741, the

naturalist Carl von Linné mentions, in fact, that Gotland peasants were wearing knitted jackets.

Central and northern Sweden

In central Sweden, no knitting of locally distinct nature has been preserved. Neither is there any indication that such knitting ever existed. It would seem probable that central Sweden was instead one of the large market areas for Halland knitting.

Farther north, in Värmland, northern Dalarna, Gästrikland, Hälsingland, and Jämtland, knitting was, on the other hand, greatly differentiated. It showed locally distinct types of pattern as well as of technique. Most of it was carried out for home consumption, with the exception of a flourishing production for sale in Västerbotten during the nineteenth century.

As previously mentioned, knitting with two yarn ends and patterning by color alternation were characteristic of northern Swedish knitting. This pattern type had local variants, one of which had a decidedly western distribution and was closely tied in with a Norwegian area of intensive knitting, Selbu district in southern Tröndelag. In Sweden, this type occurred in Dalsland, Värmland, Härjedalen, and Jämtland. The pattern was formed by alternating two colors, natural black and natural white. This choice of colors is ancient, as it includes only the wool's own natural colors (fig. 454). Some of the patterns were also of a simple and ageless nature.

A further characteristic of knitting in northern Sweden was that, as a rule, the whole article was dyed, not the yarn, a procedure followed especially for articles of uniform color. Stockings, for example, were dyed either red or blue, though the feet were generally not lowered into the dye bath. Supposedly this was done for reasons of economy, but it also was justified by the fact that the wool retained its warming properties better when undyed. Whole jackets and sleeves of a highly decorative nature were also dyed in the same way—as finished garments (fig. 455).

The particular form of cattle raising practiced in the *fäbod* region necessitated an active outdoor life for men and women alike. Working in the forest, or with the cattle, exposed particularly hands and feet to cold and damp, which made warm socks and mittens imperative. The same working conditions favored knitting as a technique, as it required no cumbersome or heavy implements and could be done also while walking. Knitting was, as a matter of fact, the particular handcraft of the cattle tenders in the *fäbod* region (fig. 138).

455. Man's green wadmal jacket with knit sleeves. The sleeves were knitted with two yarns in black and white wool and then dyed red. Gagnef, Dalarna.

456. Woman's jacket of dark blue wadmal with knit sleeves. The sleeves are in knit stitch, patterned in green and red wool yarn and white cotton yarn. Alfta, Hälsingland. (See also color figure 46.)

457. Woman's knit jacket. Knit stitch in red, black, and green wool yarn and white cotton yarn. Initials and date IBHD 1840 are knitted in, partly visible in the picture. Delsbo, Hälsingland.

458. Woman's knit jacket, detail of fig. 457. The typical color combination can be seen in color figure 47.

Jackets

In northern Sweden, the jacket developed as a part of holiday dress in the provinces of Dalarna, Hälsingland, Härjedalen, and Värmland. The role of the simple working sweater—known as the Gotland sweater—knitted in natural white or gray is not known. The working sweater was far more exposed to the wear and tear of everyday life, and is so rarely mentioned that its existence might be doubted were it not for certain documentation of a large manufacture of such sweaters for sale. In addi-

tion, one does get the impression that the superb technical quality, design, and patterns of the knit holiday jackets cannot have appeared out of nowhere.

Jackets with knitted sleeves were used by men and women in Floda and Gagnef parishes in Dalarna. They were knitted with two yarn ends in white and black, respectively. After completion, they were dyed red, resulting in a black pattern on red ground. The patterns were made up of stars, crosses, and narrow, stylized leaves (fig. 455). There was also a type with

thick vines with foliage forming a pattern of square shapes, which seems to have been directly inspired by pattern books.

Also in Alfta and Ovanåker in Hälsingland, jackets with knitted sleeves were used. However, here the entire shoulder and the very top of the front piece were also knitted (fig. 456). In Nordiska Museet there are four such garments from Alfta and Ovanåker. They are attached to cloth: in one case, calamanco, in another, grosgrain. In material and cut they are of eighteenth-century type. The patterns and the

329

knitting technique are especially worth noting. The patterns consist of stars and carnations, which were noted above in Halland jackets of seventeenth-century type. The ornament is seen in color and white, alternately, against white or colored ground in square panels. The jackets were made of cotton and wool. They were undoubtedly regarded as particularly sumptuous pieces of clothing. The similarity between these jackets and seventeenth-century fashion should also be noted. Seventeenth-century knit tunics were worn under a bodice, which gave the same effect that was later approximated by the Hälsingland jackets with knit sleeves and shoulders. It is possible that knit jackets had already been brought to northern Sweden in the seventeenth century by Västergötland traders, whereupon they were copied.

Jackets completely made of knit material were used above all in the parishes of Delsbo, Ovanåker, and Ljusdal in Hälsingland, from where they spread to southeastern Härjedalen. In Delsbo and Ljusdal, they were used by men as well as women. From Alfta and Ovanåker only jackets for women have been preserved. The preserved material represents, of course, only a fraction of the original output. But a careful study even of existing inventories would surely offer a more nuanced picture. Until that is undertaken, however, one must rely on the fragmentary data available. In Delsbo parish, locally distinctive dress customs survived as late as the second half of the nineteenth century. Therefore, conditions for collecting material have been more favorable there than in most other localities, both with regard to artifacts and to data. Nordiska Museet owns twenty-five women's jackets, dated 1840 to 1881. From Delsbo parish alone, there are sixteen women's jackets and eleven men's jackets. They are knit of wool yarn in knit stitch with a colorful and assertive pattern (figs. 457, 458; color fig. 47). Certain parts of the pattern are knitted with white cotton yarn. The sleeves are knitted separately and sewn in, the shoulder seams bound off together on the reverse side, and there is a narrow border of purl stitch around the bottom of the jacket and the cuffs. From the earliest example, dated 1834, to the latest, dated 1898—i.e., for almost

seven decades—the basic pattern retained its original character. This constancy was probably due to the fact that the manufacture was centralized, carried out in the home by two or three generations of knitters. According to data from the parish, there were always two or three Delsbo housewives who knitted jackets for a living.

How the pattern was created and distributed is not known. But certain similarities of this knitting to the knitting in Halland would seem to indicate that the original impetus might have been introduced by the Västergötland trade. In Järvsö and Delsbo, white, simple sweaters were called "fishermen's sweaters" or "Gotland sweaters." Knitting may, in other words, also have come across the Baltic from Gotland. There may at times even have been regular importation of knitted goods from Gotland.

The Delsbo type of knitting was also distributed in Härjedalen. Some women of Härjedalen walked every year to Hälsingland with their spinning wheels to spin and earn enough to buy a little flax. These women must surely have helped transmit Delsbo knitting to their home province.

Leggings and footgear

The need to protect feet and legs against cold and damp has given rise to an extraordinary variety of articles in northern Sweden. Modern terminology lacks names for many of these articles. The stocking, a single covering for leg and foot, was a fairly late addition to the dress in central and northern Sweden. The material for leg coverings was, until late in the nineteenth century, wadmal or linen weave—in the latter case in the shape of a tube without a foot. On the foot itself, one would wear a sock, shoe hay, foot wrap, and an insole with toe cap. In severe cold, one would also wear "long socks," long stockings reminiscent of medieval hose. In addition, the men might wear "snow socks," which were pulled on over the shoes. Inside the shoes one might also wear cuffless socks and a kind of stocking with knit-on feet or toe caps, which were also used indoors as slippers.

For everyday wear, one would wear leggings and footgear of needle-looped yarn or of wadmal or linen. The latter were made by the village tailor like all other garments of broadcloth or wadmal. From Ovansjö parish in Gästrikland reports indicate that, as late as the middle of the nineteenth century, all knitted stockings were purchased. In inventories knitted stockings were called "Västergötland stockings." Conditions in Ovansjö were very likely typical of northern Sweden as a whole.

At the very earliest in the beginning of the

459. Men's stockings. Left, natural black and white wool in richly patterned knit stitch, Jämtland. Center, knit stitch in elaborate pattern of dark purple and sharp magenta wool yarn, Tuna, Medelpad. Right, bridegroom's stocking, patterned in knit and purl stitch of white wool yarn, Ingelstad, Skåne.

460. Stocking, knitted with two yarns in wool. The top of the stocking is turned down to show the reverse side. Purl stitches form the "seam" or [hair] "part." Dalarna.

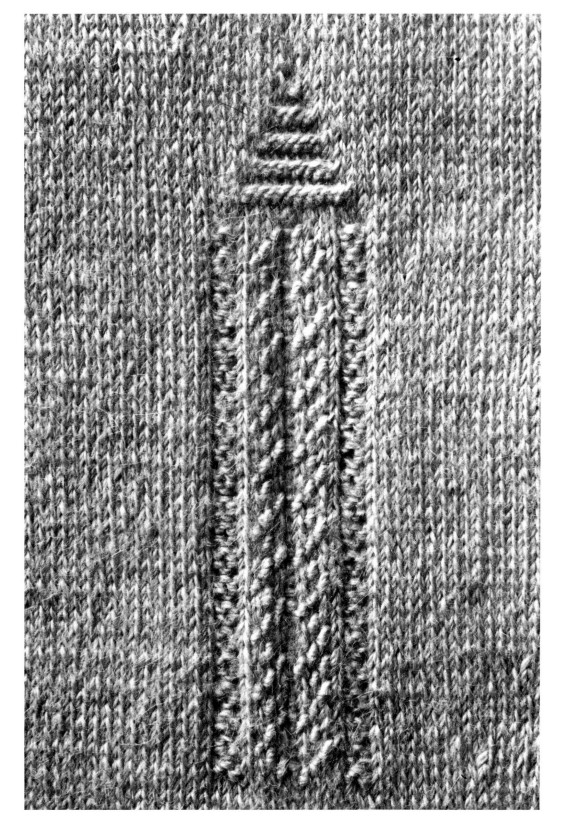

nineteenth century, stockings were commonly knitted by local women. Northern Swedish stockings were, as a rule, knitted in knit stitch with two separate yarns and dyed in one piece when finished. The foot, as mentioned above, was generally left undyed. The top of the stocking had a "seam" of one or two purl stitches. In Floda, Dalarna, this "seam" was called the "[hair] part" (fig. 460). In addition, the stocking may have sported gussets or "darts" from the beginning of the heel intake and part way up the calf (fig. 461). Above all in Dalarna and Hälsingland, stockings were given a particular shape: they were wide and loosely fitting. In Rättvik, they were especially baggy and wide around the ankles, resembling cloth stockings. It must be remembered that stockings of sewn wadmal and linen fabric continued to be used alongside knitted stockings during the entire nineteenth century. Thus, the sewn-stocking tradition greatly influenced the design and pattern of the knitted stockings. This influence helps explain the presence in knit stockings of a center "seam" and side "dart" as well as the practice of fulling and napping the knit surface until it resembled that of wadmal. Most preserved stockings are colored, which would indicate that they were intended for special occasions. Not until later did knitted stockings become everyday wear; then, they were knitted of natural wool.

In Jämtland, Härjedalen, and certain coastal parishes in Norrland, stockings in pattern stitch have been found. Those from Jämtland and Härjedalen are in natural black and white, in accordance with the Norwegian traditional lengthwise striping (fig. 459, left). Fashionable stockings were also copied. Thus, there were stockings with stripes in chiné imitation, and white cotton stockings with lengthwise patterned stripes, made by increasing or decreasing the number of stitches. Stockings with horizontal colored stripes, preferably in red and inspired by current fashion, occurred sparingly around 1850 on the southern periphery of the northern Swedish craft region.

461. Detail of stocking in fig. 460, showing the pattern detail, the "dart," on the outside of the ankle.

Mittens

In Sweden's northerly latitudes there has always been a need for protection of the hands against cold. Mittens existed as early as the Bronze Age, their shape, in principle, the same as today. They were made of skin, cloth, or needle-looped yarn. A more primitive type of

462. Knit gloves and mittens. Left to right: knit glove in knit stitch with patterned border and fringe, Baltic States; chamois glove with shading stitch embroidery in silk, Gotland; patterned knit glove in red and white, Gotland; knit glove in white cotton yarn, patterned by decreasing and in-

creasing, Skåne; patterned knit mitten in brown and white, Gotland; knit glove in knit stitch with two yarns of white wool, Dalarna; and knit glove of natural black wool yarn embroidered in chain stitch and shading stitch in wool and decorated with sewn-on pile trim, Värmland.

463. Mitten, knitted with two yarns of black and red wool. Initials and date HKED 1874 are knitted into the mitten (not visible in picture). Sveg, Härjedalen.

464. Mittens of wool, knitted in knit stitch with two yarns. Purl stitches decorate the cuff edge and mark the "seams" at cuff and thumb. Ore, Dalarna.

hand protection survived until the eleventh century in the form of fabric strips wound around the hands. The principle was the same as that of the foot wrappings, a Bronze Age article long surviving in military footwear. Under the heading of "Needle looping" above some older traditions are discussed, which later influenced mittens in other techniques. Mittens of cloth or skin played an important role, especially in formal wear. This fact is reflected in the wealth of surviving mittens which are pure luxury items, embroidered and otherwise decorated, and in the intense development of customs around this article of clothing and its symbolic significance (figs. 350, 439–41, 462–66).

There are several different forms of mittens: ordinary mittens; knit gloves; mitts, which protect only the hand, leaving the fingers free; mittens with a slit across the palm for sticking out the fingers; knit gauntlets; wrist guards

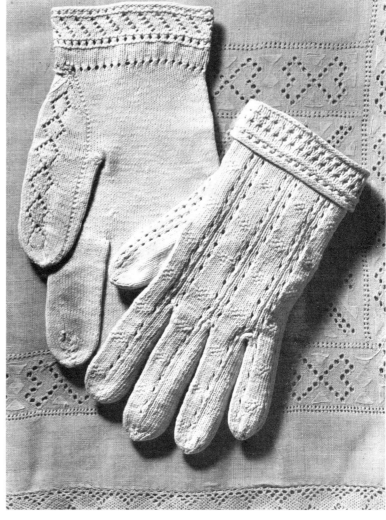

465. Mitts in knit stitch, knitted with two yarns in white wool. The cuffs are patterned in red wool yarn and a thinner white wool yarn. Boda, Dalarna.

466. Knit gloves of white cotton yarn. The pattern is formed by decreasing. Compare the pattern with that on the underlying decorative handkerchief, embroidered in hemstitching and geometric satin stitch and with drawn-fabric work. (The bottom of the picture shows the bobbin-lace edging of the handkerchief.) Skåne.

protecting only the wrists; and mitten liners designed to be worn inside another pair of mittens. Handwear was a prestigious accessory in all social strata. The glove maker belonged to a flourishing profession which greatly influenced the shape and design of handwear, not only in the towns or among the most affluent, but also among the peasantry. From the Middle Ages, embroidered skin gloves were part of the standard wedding gifts, as were embroidered mittens of broadcloth or wadmal and, from the end of the eighteenth century, white knitted cotton mittens. To a large extent, these luxury items were made by professional craftsmen, who sold their products at fairs and of course also in shops in town. Most of the preserved dress gloves in peasant milieu are, as a matter of fact, the work of professionals. However, a certain limited provincial manufacture of mittens can be distinguished as well as some home production for domestic consumption.

467. Left, man's pillbox cap, *tallriksluva* (plate cap), in knit stitch with purled pattern. The same kind of cap turned inside-out, right, shows wool yarn floats added for warmth. Torna, Skåne.

Their products were, however, highly influenced by the professionally made mittens. Only a few of the most prominent, locally distinctive groups will be mentioned here.

In Dalarna, Värmland, and, generally, in all of northern Sweden, needle-looping traditions were especially tenacious in mitten making. The rich, embroidered decor clearly indicates the existence of a highly developed pattern tradition at an early stage. First, the design is in part quite primitive in style; second, the embroidery presupposes a fulled fabric ground. Fabrics in needle looping are usually fulled to provide a firm ground for embroidery stitches, as embroidery on an elastic material—knitted or looped—is not particularly permanent. In the above-mentioned province, knitted mittens were also fulled, and then often decorated with embroidery like that on the needle-looped mittens (figs. 439, 462). Ornamentation of needle-looped mittens with pile of sewn-on threads

as fringe or in tufts was likewise transferred to knitted mittens. This particular type of decoration was used already on the Åsle mitten, but in the preserved material it turns up on knitted mittens only in Värmland, Uppland, and Dalarna. On mittens of a later type, the pile fringe and tufts were knotted separately and sewn on with thread, whereas the older type had a pile of individually sewn-in threads like the needle-looped mitten from Uppland. Of particular interest is a mitten from Värmland, with knitted fingers and hand, but with a four-inch-wide cuff of needle looping with decorative stitchery. Equally interesting is the fact that a mitten from Ås district in Västergötland has knitted fingers and hand and a four-inch-wide needle-looped cuff with a separately made chenille strip stitched on in a pattern. It might be added that this latter mitten is knitted with two yarns, the only one of this technique discovered south of the line Värmland-Dalarna-

Gästrikland. It would appear as if decoration with knotted pile was especially associated with the technique of needle looping. For this reason, and because of its occurrence in Danish Bronze Age finds, it seems clear that knotted pile is an extremely ancient form of decoration.

In Dalarna, mittens had a decor in pattern stitch, also used on the edges of stockings, namely rows of purling breaking up the knit stitch (figs. 464, 465). They resemble the backstitch rows and herringbone-stitch borders on Dalarna linen embroidery (fig. 336). The close relationship between patterns for knitting, embroidery, and band weaving is obvious in Dalarna. It is quite clear that the patterns of the two latter served as the source of inspiration.

Diverse articles of clothing
One sales item of great popularity and extensive distribution was the knitted cap. Through

468. Knitted men's caps. Back to front: Two double stocking caps with pile brim, Jämtland and Dalarna; brimless cap in red and black, Norrbotten; machine-knit cap of thin white cotton yarn with red decorative border and pile brim, Småland; and *tallriksluva* (plate cap) or pillbox, Skåne.

ever, in Leksand and Rättvik, specific local forms of stocking caps developed. These caps were made in stockinette knit of wool yarn, with transverse colored stripes in stylized chiné pattern. They were used on festive occasions. Whether they were products of local knitting traditions is not quite clear. The fact that they were not knitted with two yarn ends would seem to indicate that they were made elsewhere.

In Nås, Dalarna, wool scarves were knitted with rich patterns in black on red ground. The knitting was done in black and white and then dyed red. Of the two scarves preserved in Nordiska Museet, one is dated 1872, the other 1875. The pattern in one consists of lily crosses, stars, diamonds, triangles, hearts, and a panel with lily crosses and small stars in squares. The other one has the same pattern elements, but lacks the division into squares; this element is replaced by two rows of something very much resembling herringbone stitch. On the whole, embroidery is generally believed to have been the source of inspiration for these knitted scarves.

Knitting with cotton and linen yarn

The great surge of interest in knitting at the beginning of the nineteenth century, combined with a more ample supply of cotton, gave rise to new uses for knitting. Because of its greater firmness, cotton yarn offered possibilities for new types of patterns. Openwork patterns came to dominate the style-conscious knitting in upper-class milieu, and also had a certain influence on peasant knitting. Openwork patterns were also, to a limited extent, used in knitting with wool yarn. In Hälsingland, above all, linen yarn began to be used for stockings and mittens and cotton yarn was taken up as a pattern element in wool knitting. The red border on mittens from Rättvik was also inlaid with a narrow white cotton thread, which gave the mittens a distinctive look (fig. 465). In the jackets from Delsbo, the white pattern elements were also knitted with cotton yarn (fig. 457). However, most of all, white cotton yarn was used for textile furnishings, knitted bedspreads, pillowcase caps, knitted lace on hang-

the ages, Swedish knitted caps have retained the shape of that perennial favorite, the stocking cap (fig. 468). As mentioned above, this cap type was executed also in needle looping. Whether this means that the form was as ancient as the technique in Sweden is not known. It is a fact that it already existed in the countries around the Mediterranean in prehistoric times. It is none other than the so-called Phrygian cap, depicted in ancient Greek and Roman works of art. During the French Revolution, it acquired great significance as a symbol of liberty and as the special sign of recognition among the revolutionaries. By the eighteenth century and probably earlier, a considerable number of stocking caps were exported from Germany. A significant portion of these reached Sweden via Norway with the Norrland traders who visited Norwegian towns and fairs. They brought these so-called Nor-

wegian caps back to Jämtland, Härjedalen, and Hälsingland. Since the caps arrived with traders from Jämtland, they came to be known south of Jämtland under the name of "Jämtland caps." They did occur, however, throughout northern Sweden. They were knitted of red wool yarn in the shape of a long, wide tube, closed at both ends. The tube was turned up inside itself, thus creating a two-layered cap. In some cases, the inside was lined with pile of pulled-up loops or knitted-in threads, showing on the outside on the turned-up brim. On others, only the brim had knotted pile, often in a contrasting color, e.g., green. In some cases the brim had a wavy edge, and the cap was thoroughly fulled and napped so that it stood straight up and lacked the characteristic softer shape of the stocking cap. The bought caps came to serve as models for a widespread and undifferentiated household production. How-

Knitting

ing cloths, show towels, tablecloths, and a number of other small decorative textile items. It was also used in mittens, caps, etc. which were knitted in openwork patterns with the finest cotton thread and knitting needles the gauge of sewing needles (fig. 442). These openwork patterns belonged in upper-class milieu, particularly in the first half of the nineteenth century. However, with the introduction of the thin, machine-spun thread available to anyone and everyone, the types and designs of knitted articles, as well as particular techniques, became less and less provincially and socially differentiated. Patterns, designs, and models were spread through newspapers, magazines, pattern books, and textile-craft instruction. Through manufactories, cotton knitting and its characteristic patterns spread in the eighteenth century. Flor textile workshop in Mo, Hälsingland, probably made important contributions to knitting in all the coastal provinces of southern Norrland by its manufacture of stockings and mittens.

470. Pattern book for knitted lace, assembled in 1844 by Mathilda Leufenmark, age 12.

469. Bedspread of white cotton yarn, in knit patterned hexagons, from the 1880s. Ala, Gotland. Privately owned.

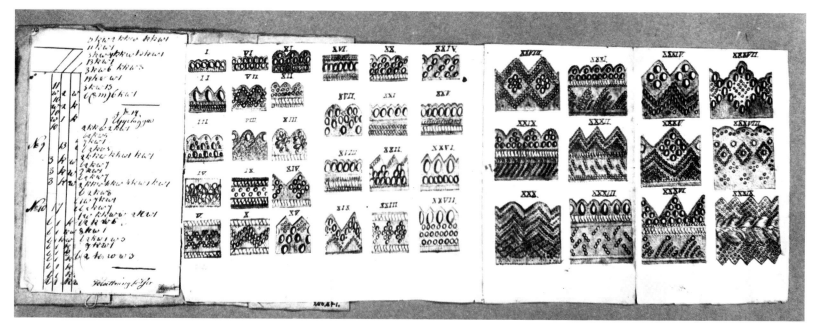

Woodcrafts

Background

The rhythm of the agricultural year allowed plenty of time for crafts during the winter season. In rural areas, construction work and the making of tools, vehicles, simple utensils, and furniture were all part of a man's normal work. In fact, all woodcraft, with the exception of basketry, was the exclusive province of the man, just as textile crafts were the woman's. In many localities the household's production grew beyond its own needs and laid the foundation for a craft production for sale, as has been noted above.

Woodcraft products are, as a rule, bulky and therefore best suited for distribution to nearby markets. A craftsman would often work where both raw material and demand existed, since his tools were easily transported there. The craftsman's skill was what he was paid for, whereas his raw material, wood, could be had practically everywhere at little or no cost.

Woodcrafts in Sweden were highly differentiated. Specialization was essential in the more professional craft production. Home craft skills were the basis for the emergence of provincial craftsmen, working within distinctly local traditions, as well as the emergence of entire craft regions, specializing in one or two main products for sale.

Governors' Reports between 1822 and 1905 give a picture of the occurrence and extent of craft production as it was in the provinces before it started to taper off and disappear, or became absorbed by industrial enterprise. These reports usually indicate whether the craft production in question was intended only for household consumption or whether it was also intended for sale. In addition, the reports give some idea of the quantity of commercial craft products. On the other hand, these various products are rarely described. However, it is likely—and preserved material seems to bear this out—that commercial craft products usually were standardized items without a noticeable local stamp. This standardization must have been a condition for selling to a wide circle of customers. The more individual and locally varied production, which can be grouped under

the label "manufacture for household consumption," has probably been suited to its own original milieu with its particular customs and holiday traditions. This production particularly includes wooing and wedding gifts, made with great care and often extraordinary skill; also tack and vehicles for formal occasions, furniture and household utensils, serving vessels for the festive table, and other symbolic ceremonial objects.

Supply of raw materials

Natural conditions within each region have obviously determined the supply of raw material. In areas of mixed forestation, the choosing of wood was a highly selective process. Different woods were used for different types

471. Supplies of rough lumber stored for future use. The man is sitting at the entrance to his wood shed, where materials for runners, scythe snaths, and tools are piled together with birch bark, bundles of twigs, withes, and roots for various woodcrafts. Mangskog, Värmland, 1911.

of objects, sometimes different woods for different parts of the same object.

In northern and central Sweden, spruce, pine, and birch have been used. In the southern hardwood regions, beech and oak have been more important. Birch, which is a hardwood, has been used for implements, vehicles, boxes, ladles, hay rakes, and turned wood items. Pine and spruce have been used in staved vessels in northern and central Sweden; in the south, oak and beech have been used instead. Other woods have found a certain limited use: rowan tree

472. The spinning-wheel maker E. O. Berglund from Malå, Västerbotten, on his way to the woods to look for suitable raw material. 1928.

down a wagon load. Burls and abnormal growths on birch trees were used for burl bowls. These various rough forms would be brought home from the forest and laid to dry out or season in the wood shed, storage shed, or up under the beams in the *stuga*. There they might stay for years, ready for use whenever needed.

For certain purposes logs and commercially prepared boards were obviously required, but for smaller-scale woodcraft, the procurement of raw material was characterized by the hoarding, selectivity, and experience of the woodworker himself (figs. 471, 472).

Shape and surface decoration

To shape the raw material, woodworkers have always used relatively simple tools. Ax and saw are used to cut the wood into suitable lengths and blocks. For planing and hollowing, different types of axes are used, the broadax and the hollow adze; for thinning and smoothing, different types of shaves. All types of finer woodwork require knives of a highly specialized nature.

Specialized tools are also required by the various woodcrafts: carpentry, cabinetry, wood carving and whittling, turning, coopering, wood molding, birch-bark craft, and basketry. As a rule, contacts with professional craft milieus have been of major importance in the development of these techniques and tools.

Most techniques used in Sweden for decorative treatment of wood have been surface oriented: different types of carving and engraving, wood burning, relief work, and painting. There has been very little sculpture in the round. On the other hand, contour carving combined with surface ornament was the preferred decoration for details such as knops and projecting moldings on permanent furnishings, furniture, household utensils, and implements. In the creation of smaller items, an imaginative and self-assured wood carving has developed, in the form of rich moldings and latticework. Geometric ornament dominates. Botanical forms occur relatively sparingly, whereas the animal world has provided rich and varied inspiration.

473. Notched corner construction. The upper log is hewn to fit into the notch in the bottom log. Leksand, Dalarna.

Carpentry and cabinetry

Building customs in central and southern Sweden have been dominated by groove-and-tenon plank wall construction and cross-lap corner-joint construction or by the groove-and-tenon plank wall construction alone (fig. 52). In northern Sweden, cross-lap corner joints were the rule. Groove-and-tenon construction has been found in remnants of buildings from the Iron Age; the use of notched corner joints is considered to date back to the ninth to tenth centuries. In Sweden, a few buildings with corner joints are preserved from the late Middle Ages. In the parishes north of Lake Siljan in Dalarna, many buildings are dated by inscription. A considerable number date from the sixteenth and seventeenth centuries, although most of the buildings existing today

was used for spoons and ladles; maple, bird cherry, and alder for rake handles and rake tines; juniper for tankards and milk bottles; aspen for troughs and bowls; and naturally curved spruce and willow for hoops on coopers' ware.

Typically, the raw material was obtained by selecting wood suggestive in its natural state of the forms of farm and household implements and articles. A skilled woodcraftsman had to have keen eyes for the potential of a tree's natural shape. Curved trunks might be the raw material for runners and skis. A trunk with strategically placed branches could become a scythe snathe, a suitably curved branch an ax handle. Distinctively shaped tree forms had to be found for wooden plows, harrows, and hooks or loops securing the ropes fastening

474. Corner joint between the doors on the bottom floor of a storehouse, dated 1646. All logs are chamfered towards the corner notch. The square corners of the logs to the left are also chamfered. Grangärde, Dalarna.

were built in the eighteenth and nineteenth centuries (fig. 47).

Two main periods may be distinguished in the treatment of the felled log. In the earlier period, the log was shaped into rough lumber, not only by emphasizing the naturally round shape of the log, but also by planing it until it had a perfectly circular or oval cross section. The log ends could be left round, or given a hexagonal shape (fig. 474). Log ends with square cross section first appeared in western Sweden. The projecting log ends in cross-lap joints constituted a decorative as well as functional element. The decorative effect was reinforced by planing the lapped log ends and trimming the log ends butting on door jambs, or by chamfering the logs (fig. 476). This decorative treatment can be found not only

475. Two-story storehouse on posts with gallery. The bargeboards end in animal heads. The corner construction dates the building to the first half of the sixteenth century. Carved posts support the gallery. The building was used for storing provisions and valuables and for defense purposes. Fragments of arrowheads of wood, iron, or bone can still be seen in the logs around the wall apertures. From Älvros, Härjedalen; now at Skansen, Stockholm.

Woodcrafts

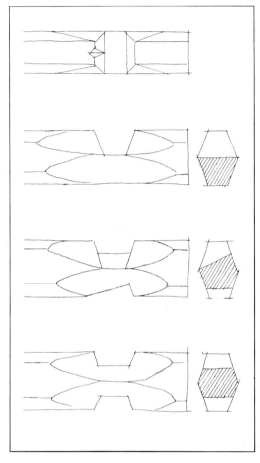

476. Various types of corner joints: saddle-notch joint, Rättvik joint, and *underhalsknut* or double saddle-notch joint. Orsa, Dalarna.

in Dalarna but also in Uppland, Halland, and Småland. During the later period, square-hewn logs were used (fig. 473). These have been common in Götaland and southern Svealand since the late Middle Ages. In later years, they came to dominate, also, northern Sweden's corner-jointed log building architecture. The eventual victory of the square form over the round one is one expression of the victory of the saw over the broadax.

The first step towards a more rational utilization of the forest was the setting up of water-driven sawmills. The first mills were founded

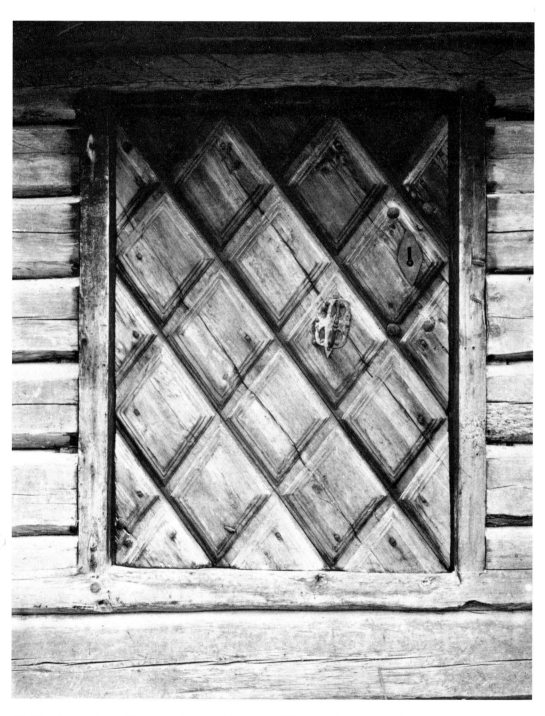

477. Storehouse door with diagonally placed boards and diamond faceted paneling. Djura, Dalarna.

342

478. Profiled bargeboards and molding on paneled house. Brännkyrka, Södermanland.

479. Stoop, roofed by projecting pediment, supported by slender columns, with dentils and carved decoration. Marked with initials and date OJS EJD 1845. Alfta, Hälsingland.

by the fifteenth century. They were equipped with only a wooden frame with one single thick saw blade, which laboriously ate its way through a log. However, they saved much labor, which would otherwise have gone into splitting, planing, and two-handed sawing. Improved frame saws with several blades were introduced in 1742, resulting in a considerable increase in building activity. House construction, however, lost a unique characteristic in the process. The earlier hand-shaped logs had tended to give a house a distinctive and aesthetically expressive character (fig. 475). The carpenter continued to contribute to the ornamentation of houses, however. He would add various decorative elements, such as molded bargeboards in the shape of animal heads, extending above the ridge; also, ornamental cutout gable crests, door and window frames, arc-shaped carvings on supporting posts and beams of outdoor galleries, and incised carvings in the form of vines, interlaced bands, and palmettos (figs. 478, 479). The oldest corner-jointed houses in Sweden, dating from the late Middle Ages up to the seventeenth century, are found in the Dalarna parishes of Mora, Älvdalen, Malung, and Venjan. In these localities, Viking and romanesque features have survived to a surprising extent.

Carpenter-made furniture

The carpenter also made furniture. The manufacture of furniture for the home had, on the whole, the character of carpenter's work so long as much of that furniture was built in (figs. 53, 55, 60, 69–72, 79, 81, 106). Carpentry techniques were used in making beds and benches built into the walls, simple backless seats with mortised legs, stools of naturally formed tree trunks, chests of hollowed-out tree trunks, and joined chests with mortised corner posts (fig. 103; color fig. 55) and sides of nailed or butt-jointed planks.

In the *stuga,* where the members of the household slept in the wintertime, the furnishing was dominated by built-in bedsteads and closet-beds, bedsteads with doors and shutters, often combined with cupboards and stools, which were built into a corner or between two walls. They could not exist freestanding, being dependent on the walls and ceiling for their support. Any piece of furniture constructed of tenoned planks or boards fitted into mortised or grooved corner posts and walls belongs to this category. Freestanding bedsteads were similarly joined: mortised or grooved posts were fitted with tenoned planks.

These carpenter's construction methods are also found in benches and seats attached to a gable wall, a side wall, or both. The same holds true for the frame of the characteristic seatless benches, filled with dirt or straw, found in the region of the Southern Götaland house type (fig. 53). These methods were also used in freestanding chest-bench combinations with lid, and joined chests with or without lid, which had sides of tenoned or tongued planks fitted in the mortised or grooved corner posts. There were also built-in cupboards and shelves (fig. 51). These more or less permanent furnishings were given different kinds of ornamentation.

480. Kors Per Persson selling his own handmade unfinished chairs of Windsor type. Siljansnäs, Dalarna.

The older kinds were executed on unpainted wood—they are found more frequently north of Lake Siljan—while the later kinds were worked on a painted surface (fig. 81).

Built-in, carpenter-made interiors characterized Swedish building customs throughout the sixteenth and far into the seventeenth centuries in rural, as well as urban and upper-class milieus. In rural peasant milieu, however, this interior type remained the norm much longer —in some areas, e.g., northern Sweden and certain conservative regions in southern Sweden, well into the nineteenth century.

Furniture made by the cabinetmaker

Buildings and furniture of the late Renaissance and the baroque eras are characterized by a definite freeing of the furniture from the support of the walls. The condition for this was a technical development towards lighter, more efficient constructions. Furniture was no longer made by the carpenter, but by the cabinetmaker. A structural framework filled in with panels and moldings was used. This new technique was to long dominate furniture making and its aesthetic aims, in rural milieu up to the latter part of the seventeenth century. Especially in Bergslagen, built-in bedsteads, benches and chests utilized this technique. Sculpted and painted decoration is a characteristic element of Renaissance and baroque furniture types, especially cupboards and chests (figs. 76, 96, 104). Renaissance cupboard types from northern Germany and the Netherlands gained entry into Sweden during the seventeenth century, especially in upper-class milieu, and spread from there into the provinces. These types of cupboard, the box, and the chest in various forms became the most characteristic pieces of Swedish furnishing. Their wide acceptance gave rise to local manufacture, distinguished by richly carved and painted decor (figs. 58, 59, 69). Although the new techniques of cabinetry were not always mastered by the local craftsmen, the latter were quick to adopt the decorative schemes of Renaissance and baroque furniture.

When the cabinetmaker's technique became a necessity for furniture making, handcraft production for sale was forced to become highly specialized, handled by men with some professional training. A few such provincial cabinetmakers are known by name; and it is known that they received their training from professionals. In so far as their products were strongly anchored in local traditional function and design, they must, however, be classified as handcraftsmen rather than professionals. The furniture manufacture in Lindome, near Göteborg, can to a certain extent be considered to have been a rural workshop production with full-time workers. From the middle of the 1740s, its products were modeled on the fashionable styles of the day and were exported to both England and Germany. In Östervåla, Uppland, a furniture manufacture grew up during the nineteenth century (fig. 481). Its labor force included farmers doing carpentry on the side, and unpropertied poor for whom carpentry was the main source of income. This manufacture was geared to the Stockholm market with its contemporary tastes. The cabinetmakers and woodworkers of Norrland have, on the other hand, continued to work in local traditions (fig. 480), in spite of having had some professional training and exposure to contemporary ornament and design in printed builder's guides and design plates.

Wood carving and turning

The overwhelming importance of wood as a material for tools and utensils of all kinds is emphasized above in the chapter about milieu and function. From prehistoric times until to-

481. Illustrated catalog of chairs offered for sale by E. Petterson, Östervåla, Uppland, towards the end of the nineteenth century.

Woodcrafts

482. Lapp at work, gouging out a tree burl intended for a bowl. Tännäs, Härjedalen.

483. Man carving wooden spoons and woman binding whisks. Bollebygd, Västergötland, 1943.

484. Woodturner making rolling pins. Malå, Västerbotten, 1928.

day, a large share of these household articles has been produced in the home by shaping massive logs with different edged implements, mainly axes, shaves, and knives of various kinds. In this fashion, troughs and tubs of impressive size as well as the tiniest objects were made, some of them for household consumption, others for sale. The overview of craft regions above shows that certain highly specialized production milieus supplied the majority of wooden ware in spite of a widespread household production of simpler utensils. Within these specialized craft regions an increased demand brought about a certain mechanization by the introduction of simple turning techniques.

Turning is based on bringing a cutting tool into contact in various positions with an evenly rotating object. Turning with a bow lathe is known from the ancient Mediterranean civili-

485. Turned treen from various provinces; among other things, bowls, pedestal stands, plates, four-tipped bowls, serving vessel with spout (*tappskål*), tankards, pots with lids, and rolling pins.

zations of Egypt, Greece, and Rome. In western Europe, simple turning lathes have existed since the Middle Ages, and more complicated versions capable of continuous rotation since

347

around 1500. In the seventeenth and eighteenth centuries, wood turning became a fashionable craft and hobby. It was practiced by professionals and high-born amateurs. Among others, Adolf Fredrik, king of Sweden from 1751 to 1771, was a passionate amateur wood-turner.

Guilded wood-turners were responsible for an extensive mass production in response to the great popular demand. They also made exquisitely turned masterpieces in wood and bone. In the sixteenth and seventeenth centuries, turned household utensils were the most common in all classes of society, in everyday use and at festive occasions. Preserved accounts document that the Danish court during the sixteenth century ordered enormous amounts of turned serving vessels, hundreds of tankards, and barrelfuls of wooden beakers. Some of the turned household utensils from upper-class milieu are still preserved: beakers, bowls, and tankards, painted red or with other painted decor, and tankards and other drinking vessels of curly birch, often finished with a turned bone knop (fig. 485). During the course of the seventeenth and eighteenth centuries, dinnerware of turned wood was replaced by pieces of pewter, silver, earthenware, and china (fig. 92). Professional wood turning gradually declined. However, it continued to find a certain market, at least for a time, in peasant milieu, where wood remained the most important material (figs. 18, 484).

Simple turning techniques had, however, presumably been taken up locally at an early stage in the more commercial handcraft regions. In the sixteenth century, the districts of Mark and Bollebygd in Västergötland were already known for their manufacture of turned wood vessels. The majority of these vessels were of simple and standardized design, suited for distribution to widely varying consumer groups (fig. 140). Thus, peasant inventories all over the country include plates, bowls, beakers, and boxes of turned hardwood. For this widespread

486. Turned "butter-sticks," on which a cone of butter was impaled for the festive table. Bjuråker, Hälsingland; Ingelstad, Skåne; Gagnef, Dalarna; and Ångermanland.

48. Mangling board with floral design, carved in sunken relief, edged with single-triangle-cut chip carving. Carved date and initials ANO 1756 AAS MED. Estuna, Uppland.

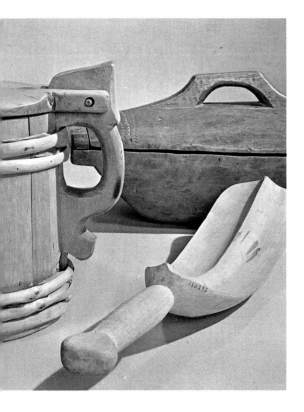

49. Staved tankard of oak and beech, incised ANO 1832 SLS, Rackeby, Väster-götland; covered dish for carrying food, of hardwood, carved NNS ANO 1866, Uppland; and washing beater or beetle of spruce, Grava, Värmland.

50. Small chest with painted decoration. Dated and initialed 1844 KOD.

51. Toy horses. One horse is from Väst-manland, one—the gray and white saddled horse on wheels—from Osby, Skåne. The rest are *dalahästar* (Dalarna horses) from various places in Dalarna.

52. Staved tankard of oak and beech with boldly profiled handle, Unnaryd, Små-land; wooden drinking cup, the bands completely covering the staves for decorative effect, Visingsö, Östergöt-land; and *kåsa* with bold relief carving, the bottom inscribed IIS 1692. Orsa, Dalarna.

53. Molded wooden box with scratch carved and pierced design and decora-tively shaped lappers, secured with chain stitching. Vemdalen, Härjedalen. (See also fig. 535.)

487. Turned and painted *tappskål* (tap bowl), serving vessel with short spout, signed and dated BAS 1818. Stenkyrka, Bohuslän.

distribution, at least in northern Sweden, the Västergötland peddler was undoubtedly responsible. The more elaborate forms of drinking vessels—serving platters or stands on pedestal base, butter sticks (fig. 486), butter chalices, ornate storage boxes—are found in the Götaland provinces. They are of medieval or Renaissance type, which might have to do with the fact that craft production for sale was already centered in Västergötland in the six-

teenth century. It is quite clear that in the southern and central parts of Sweden, wood turning became generally widespread, bringing with it a number of continental vessel types, fashionable in the fifteenth and sixteenth centuries. In northern Sweden, on the other hand, wood carving with its more individualized technique played a leading role far longer, thereby preserving and perpetuating an older inventory of forms (fig. 496).

Sculpture in the round

Three-dimensional representations of animal and human forms were not commonly made in handcraft production milieu. Sculpture in the round has mostly been used for baked bread in symbolic forms, food sculpture for display purposes, toys, boxes, and candleholders. The toy horse from Mora, Dalarna (fig. 488), is a world-renowned animal sculpture (color fig. 51). It has many relatives, not only in Dalarna, but also in other parts of the country. In Östra Göinge, Skåne, a spindly Appaloosa horse with reins was made, which was distributed widely at fairs and by itinerant peddlers. Roosters, pigs, and some wild animals have also been the woodcarver's subjects. But hardly any of these others enjoyed the wide distribution and appreciation given the *dalahäst* (Dalarna horse). Its popularity was not merely due to the recognized sales skill of people from Dalarna. The toy horse is one of those nonutilitarian objects which through their universal appeal have become standard articles of commercial craft production. This remarkable development merits further discussion.

The making of toy horses in Mora can be traced back about three hundred years. In the nineteenth century it was a complement to, or a by-product of, cabinetry. The horses were whittled from left-over wood pieces. Wooden horse manufacture existed sporadically in several other Dalarna parishes, though nowhere permanently. In Mora parish, however, the making of toy horses grew from being a sideline into a manufacture in its own right. Toward the end of the nineteenth century, the production had reached such extensive proportions that practically every farm in the village of Bergkarlås was making horses. The villages Risa, Vattnäs, and Nusnäs have also been widely known for their Dalarna horse production. A certain specialization developed in the nineteenth century, so that some would carve and others would paint the horses. These two steps could even be done in different villages. In the latter part of the nineteenth century, Stikå Erik of Risa was famous for his painting skill. In the 1930s, Mother Nisser of Vattnäs was generally considered the foremost painter (fig. 488). She was probably an heir to the tradition of Stikå Erik of Risa. In a wider and more general context, the painting of Dalarna horses should be seen as an outgrowth of the decorative painting of furniture and wall hangings.

The early trade of toy horses was handled by those who accompanied wagonloads of staved

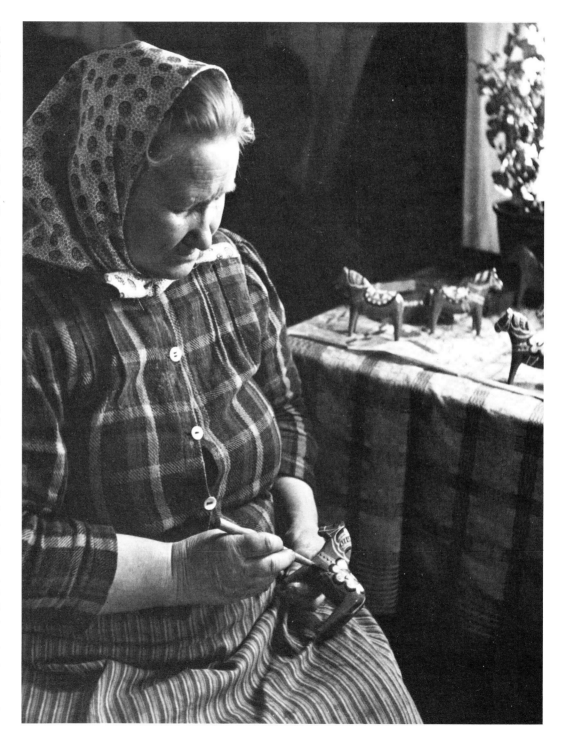

488. Mother Nisser painting wooden horses. Vattnäs, Mora, Dalarna, 1940.

vessels and splint baskets to market. The horses were often given away as payment for lodgings, thus becoming a kind of currency. From the 1890s, however, the toy-horse output was bought up by middlemen for further distribution.

Another sculpture-in-the-round tradition is connected with dolls. Dolls were turned and painted or carved with a knife. In Nås, a new manufacture of birch-bark dolls was started as late as World War I. Dolls have, of course, always been among those occasional toys made by parents for their children, but this doll manufacture grew, like that of the Dalarna horses, in response to market demands.

From Urshult, in Småland, come a number of figures carved in the round, thinly disguised as candleholders (like those in figs. 489, 490). Apparently these sculptures were the work of a local artist who evolved a somewhat stiff, naïvely realistic style inspired by local tales and legendary figures. It brings to mind another latter-day artist rooted in the Småland wood-carving tradition, i.e., the wood-carver A. R. Petersson, also known as "Döderhultaren" (The Man from Döderhult) (1868–1925).

Spoons and knives were standard table accessories and, as a rule, were the peasants' only eating utensils as late as the nineteenth century. Spoons were generally part of each diner's personal belongings. For festive occasions as well as for everyday use, spoons were shaped with extraordinary care. The simple spoons for everyday meals were very specifically designed for particular eating techniques and table customs. For example, eating from a communal porridge bowl entailed its own special technique and etiquette. One had to help oneself in a considerate manner in one's own sector of the bowl, not encroach on the neighbor's territory, nor sneak too much of the central butter pat. If milk was served with the porridge, one was not supposed to slosh it around and make the bowl unappetizing for the others. The spoon for porridge eating was short-handled

489. Carved and painted candle holders in the shapes of a man and a woman. Mjölby, Östergötland.

490. Candle holders, man and woman, carved and painted by an enlisted soldier named Ek of Jösse Company. Brunskog, Värmland.

491. Carved wooden spoon, designed to be inserted tip first into the mouth. The curved end of the handle is the thumb grip. Norrala, Hälsingland.— Spoons like this one were left with the girls at the *fäbod* by their visiting callers.

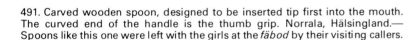
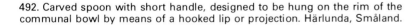

492. Carved spoon with short handle, designed to be hung on the rim of the communal bowl by means of a hooked lip or projection. Härlunda, Småland.

and held vertically when dipped into the bowl and then put into the mouth, narrow end first. The handle on this type of spoon was shaped accordingly, with a well-defined thumb grip (figs. 491, 492).

Thus, the spoon was a highly personal item, often given as a christening gift and, especially, as a courtship present (figs. 493, right, and 516). In Jämtland and Härjedalen the spoon figured prominently as a wooing or wedding

gift. Beautifully carved spoons with elaborate, sometimes overly ornate, decor—completely negating any practical function—were made especially in the parishes of Hammersdal and Ström for the general market. A group of wooing spoons from Härjedalen, characterized more by enthusiasm than any actual artistic skill, features a handle carved in the shape of a naked female figure.

As already pointed out, figure sculpture in

the round was, on the whole, an exception. For what little there was, courtship and wedding gifts provided the strongest incentives. The desire to woo and display virility and self-assurance, sometimes also a dash of sympathetic magic, raised the carver's aesthetic ambitions to a higher pitch in these gifts than in any other type of objects. Here is found a profusion of brilliant colors and intricate forms, a constant striving to surpass previous efforts,

493. Back to front: candleholder, Blekinge; washing beaters or beetles, Närke and Bohuslän; wooden spoons, Härjedalen; two bobbin winders, band reed, shuttle, and distaff peg (for securing the roving on the distaff), all from Dalarna; and distaff, Uppland.

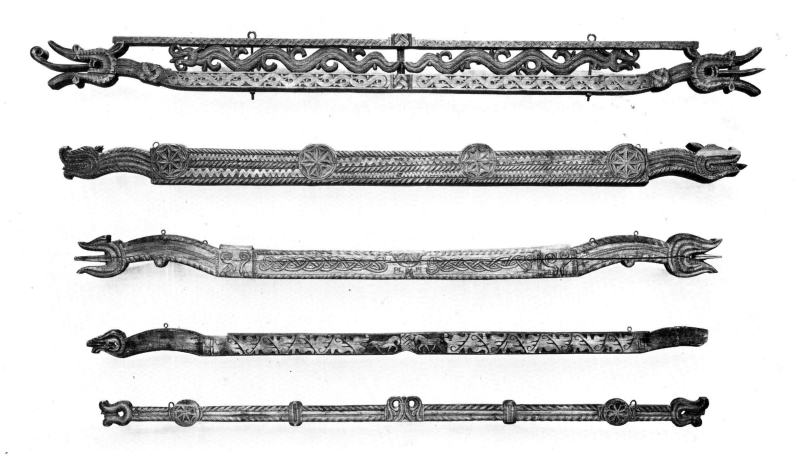

494. Crown rails. Sollerö, Dalarna.

resulting in outstanding works of great virtuosity (figs. 493, 503, 504). Obviously, it was not for every man to carve these showpieces. Undoubtedly they were made by specialized craftsmen with more or less professional training, either to order or as part of a regular line for sale. The latter production was designed to meet a traditional demand for articles which, besides their purely practical function, also figured prominently in the rituals of courtship and marriage, christenings, and funerals. On these special occasions, one could also find a less permanent type of sculpture in the round, namely sculpted and molded food. There were

"sculptures" of butter and bread, and decoratively molded porridges, cheeses, and puddings. Molded dishes were shaped in wooden molds, carved in imitation of the not yet commonly available metal molds (figs. 517, 518).

Contour carving
The most notable products of contour carving (flat freestanding sculpture)—and examples of a remarkable conservatism as well—are the magnificently stylized dragons' heads at either end of the so-called *kronstänger* (crown rails), found, above all, in northern Dalarna (figs.

494, 495). Artfully and expertly carved, these rails are concrete embodiments of prehistoric zoomorphic ornament, boldly rendered on a large scale. As a rule, these rails served as hangers to hold clothing, lumber, and other household articles (figs. 61, 81). However, it has been suggested that they originally had a more formal function: their top sides are equipped with holes, possibly for holding candles, in the manner of the so-called candle planks of traditional Norwegian peasant milieu. In addition to the dragons' heads, the crown rails are also decorated with low-relief vines, chip carving, and scratch-carved designs.

355

Around fifteen such rails are known at present. They come from a number of parishes in Dalarna and one parish in Värmland. The oldest ones probably date from the Middle Ages, the rest from the sixteenth and seventeenth centuries.

Before the nineteenth century, the chair had the character of a seat of honor. This formal function was especially emphasized by the decorative carving of animal, human, or abstract forms on the chair backs, the ends of armrests, and the armrests themselves. Stools and simple seats were made of tree trunks, whose natural shapes often suggested animal or human forms (figs. 60, 71). Judicious carving would further emphasize the likeness.

Several types of drinking vessels belonging to the traditional table, especially dippers float-

495. Detail of crown rails in fig. 494. Contour carving, modeled and two-plane low-relief carving, and single-triangle-cut chip carving. Both rails terminate in dragon's heads. The top rail has interlaced bands on the "neck," running vine on the "body," and pierced carving, echoing the dragon motif, on its "back."

496. Carved bowls and bird-shaped vessels, so-called ale geese. The latter, "swimming" in a large ale bowl, were used as drinking cups or dippers. Jämtland, Dalarna, Hälsingland, Värmland, and Ångermanland.

497. Bowl in the shape of two birds, cut from a single block of wood. Offerdal, Jämtland.

ing on the surface of the ale-filled bowl, were shaped like birds with head and tail (figs. 496–98). Natural irregular forms, resembling horned animals or fantastic beings, were further emphasized in the carving of bowls, cane handles, nutcrackers, dipper handles, etc. (color figs. 54, 56).

Animal motifs, a vital element in free artistic creation, have been highly developed through the influence of the medieval bestiary. In this category belong the whittled splint birds, created under influence from Christian symbolism (figs. 499–502). There are the Holy Ghost in the form of a dove and Christ as the pelican, pecking its breast bloody to feed its young. Similar forms of splint birds are found on the Continent also; and there is reason to suppose that this type of wooden sculpture originated there. Secular birds, such as the black grouse, capercaillie, and rooster, have obviously also served as models. Technically, the conditions for splint-bird manufacture were especially favorable wherever there was manufacture of molded, or bentwood, boxes, as well as white coopering. Thus, splint-bird making was more widespread in woodworking centers, such as northern Skåne and Småland, which have produced several splint-bird carvers. An exceptionally beautiful variant of the splint bird was created in the twentieth century by Carl Thyrstedt, who died in 1959 (figs. 500–2). He based his creation on paper-thin wood splints in a fanlike arrangement, and on the traditions of the old woodcraft region in southern Östergötland. Contour-carved horse figures have been frequently used on candlesticks found especially in Småland and Östergötland.

Existing somewhere between sculpture in the round and freestanding contour carving are certain decorative horse figures serving as handles on mangling boards (fig. 503). The mangling board was first introduced into Swedish burgher homes, probably from Germany, no earlier than the sixteenth century. The decoration on early mangling boards is of pure Renaissance type with rich carvings in

498. Staved *kåsa,* two-handled drinking vessel, with animal heads for handles. Mora, Dalarna.

499. Splint birds. Skåne.

54. Bowls carved out of wood. The shape of each bowl has been determined by the natural properties of the wood, whereby animal and human forms have been "found" in nature's own forms. Lima and Mora, Dalarna, dated 1806; Offerdal, Jämtland; Hede, Härjedalen, with the incised date 1816; and Krokstad, Bohuslän.

55. Prehistoric and medieval interlaced band ornament has long survived in more conservative parts of central and northern Sweden. It was used to decorate wood surfaces as late as the nineteenth century.—Joined chest with the sides mortised to the corner posts. The front is decorated with interlaced bands in two-plane low relief, stylistically datable to the twelfth century. Bjuråker, Hälsingland. In the foreground, small boarded chest of pine with incised ornament on lid and sides. Handle, bands, and escutcheon of iron. Lillhärdal, Härjedalen.

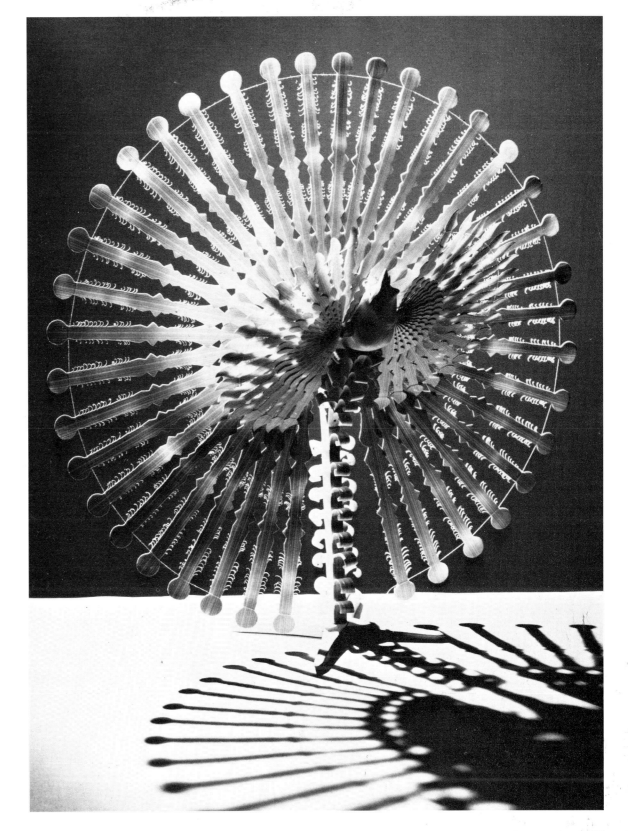

500. Splint bird made by the bird carver Carl Thyrstedt, Sorunda, Södermanland, 1957.

Woodcrafts

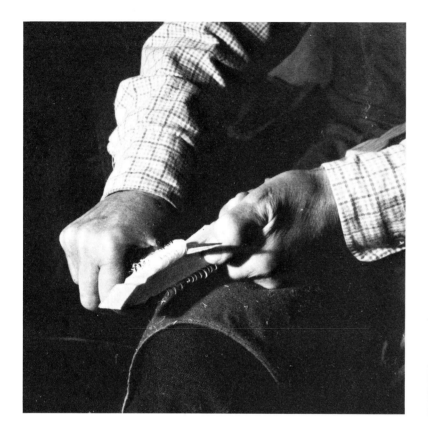

low relief. The boards were no doubt made by professional carvers. Quite naturally, women's tools and implements provided the greatest challenge for the imagination and skill of male wood-carvers, since these articles traditionally were courtship or betrothal gifts. Mangling boards, washing beetles, distaffs, harness pulleys, wooden stretchers or temples, hayrakes, boxes, chests, sewing chests, etc. offer a rich field for studying the decorative treatment and ornamentation of wood. It is a field, however, which so far has remained largely unexplored.

Horses and horse furniture have often inspired a competitive formal display, figuring prominently at holidays, in churchgoing, wedding marches, funeral processions, and trips to town and market (fig. 27). The striving to own the best and fastest horses was reflected in a corresponding striving to outdo one's neigh-

bors in horse harnesses and vehicles. Harness saddles (figs. 506, 507) and other parts of the harness (such as fig. 567) provide one of the richest creative outlets in folk art. Here, animal figures and forms appear in great and imaginative variety: horses' heads, dragons' heads, snakes, lions, and sea horses are the central motifs, often in combination with other flanking motifs. There is a marked difference between the locally developed types in Götaland, northern Sweden, eastern Sweden, and western Sweden. The ornamentation has incorporated elements from every major style; Renaissance, baroque, rococo, and Empire have all contributed to the form and color schemes of these harnesses. As in other contexts, the *fäbod* region of northern Sweden as well as the eastern seaboard emerge as distinct production areas. No doubt specialized

501. The bird carver Carl Thyrstedt at work on a splint bird, 1957.

502. Thyrstedt spreads the "quills" in a wing of the bird seen in fig. 500.

503. Mangling boards with carved decoration. The handles on those in the foreground are shaped like horses. Various provinces.

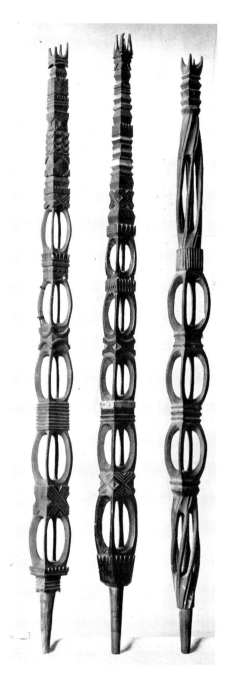

504. Distaffs. Left, with stylized vines in pierced carving; right, with crown, spirals, and scrolls in low relief, pierced work, and engraved linear ornament. Both are painted. Flat distaffs were made in the coastal areas on both sides of the Gulf of Bothnia. Rich variation in their execution is found especially in Roslagen (Uppland seaboard).

505. Distaffs, carved and painted. The pierced, scepter-like distaffs were prevalent in the inland parts of Uppland and northern Sweden.

506. Harness saddle, decorated with lions carved in bold relief and painted. Helgum, Ångermanland.

craftsmen or professionals were responsible for the majority of these items.

Vehicles sported the same near-magical, speed-invoking animals. Upturned runner ends might display stylized horses' heads, while the body of the vehicle would be given animal form with waving mane and open jaws. In his paper "Kyrkåka och kappsläde" ("Church vehicle and racing sleigh"), Gösta Berg maintains that the use of animal figures as the main decorative element on harnesses and vehicles appears to be an ancient custom in Sweden. Prehistoric finds bear this contention out. One of Norway's most impressive archaeological sites, the burial mound at Oseberg, has yielded some sleighs from the ninth century. These ancient sleighs exhibit several formal elements favored by sleigh makers ever since, above all dragons' heads and grotesque masks of trolls and humans.

507. Harness saddle, decorated with contour and low-relief carving and painted. Rödön, Jämtland.

Surface decoration

All woodcrafts share certain characteristic methods of purely decorative surface treatment. The inventory of ornament employed, however, is extremely varied, and has been shaped by continental fashions as well as local traditions. This wide field has not yet been comprehensively treated, as many groups of objects have not been studied either intensively or extensively. The following brief survey is based on the presentation by Sigurd Erixon in his major work *Nordisk kultur: Svensk folkkonst* ("Nordic culture: Swedish folk art") and focuses on the purely formal and technical aspects of wood ornament.

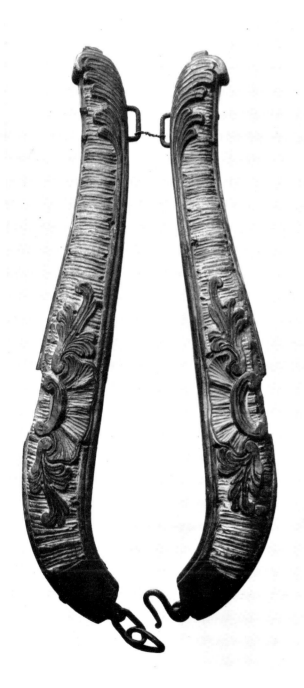

508. Harness hames, decorated with relief carving of rococo type. Ljusdal, Hälsingland.

509. Harness hame, detail, showing one of the animal-head terminals. Stora Kopparberg, Dalarna.

510. Harness hame, detail. One of the animal-head terminals, carved in bold relief and painted. Lister, Blekinge.

511. Drawing of the design on a molded splint *äska,* with a series of cross sections, showing the use of scratch and incised carving. Järeda, Småland. (See also fig. 536.)

Scratch carving and incised carving

Scratch carving is made in one cut with a pointed instrument. Incised carving is made in two cuts with a knife, thereby creating a groove with a V-shaped cross section (figs. 511, 536; color fig. 53). Technically, these two are the simplest methods of decorative treatment of wood surfaces. They are associated with prehistoric and medieval motifs, especially on carved treen and molded wood containers. The ornament takes the form of geometric continuous bands, or overall patterns, zigzag lines, straight or interlaced bands with single or double outlines, diagonally or transversely crosshatched bands, triangles, diamonds, and squares. Scratch carving has also been used to depict figures on boxes, coffers, chests, and on architectural elements, e.g., doors (figs. 512, 513, 535, 537).

Incised carving and scratch carving have been most commonly used in northern Dalarna, Härjedalen, and Uppland. Carved or molded boxes (fig. 512), runic calendar wands, harness saddles (fig. 566), and other parts of the horse harness (figs. 567, 568), handloom pulleys, reeds and temples, distaffs, carved drinking vessels, and serving bowls have been decorated with these techniques. Some of the objects have quite simple decor, others are virtuoso showpieces.

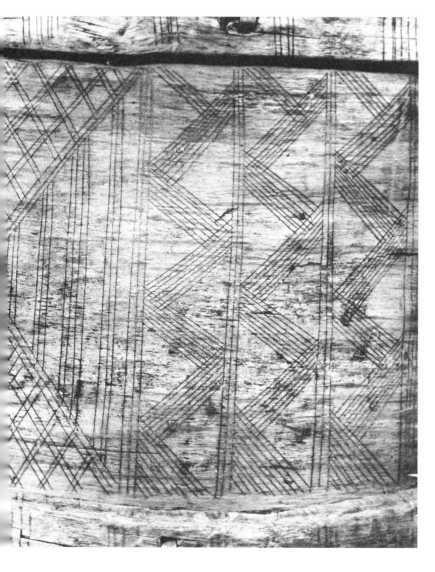

512. Decoration in scratch or line carving on small molded coffer. Delsbo, Hälsingland.

513. Handle in the shape of a horse with single-triangle-cut chip carving on his withers. Älvdalen, Dalarna.

514. Wooden box with chip carving. The lid has a bear claw for a pull and is carved with the date 1574. The inside of the lid is carved with runes and the owner's mark. Värmland. Privately owned.

tical and three oblique cuts. It is a prehistoric technique, which fell into disuse in the romanesque era. In the late Middle Ages, chip carving again became fashionable, and in the seventeenth century it was extremely widespread. In Sweden, it is found mostly in Västergötland, Bohuslän, on the island of Öland, and in Uppland, and, to a limited extent, in Hälsingland and Bergslagen. Chip carving has been used partly as allover repeat patterns, partly in isolated ornament. Allover patterns are found on box lids (fig. 514), mangling boards, cases, bread stamps, and butter molds. Isolated ornaments appear mostly in the form of rosettes or other geometric figures and in plant motifs.

Scratch carving and incised carving
on colored background
Surface decoration achieves a stronger impact by being seen against a colored background. To that end, wood was dyed with alder bark or soot before being carved (fig. 515). This method has been known since prehistoric times in Eastern Europe as far south as the Balkans. In Sweden, it belongs especially in the provinces of Dalarna, Härjedalen, Värmland,

Ornaments of prehistoric and medieval types (color figs. 54, 55) were used as late as the nineteenth century, as is evidenced by an impressive number of dated objects. Late medieval plant ornament with fleur-de-lis and palmetto motifs, romanesque acanthus vines and floral ornament of Renaissance type are often used together on the same object, giving peasant craft its distinct ornamentation.

Scratch carving is often combined with a type of triangular cut in the wood, *uddsnitt* (literally, "point carving"), a single triangle cut in which a wedgelike chip of wood is removed from the surface with two vertical cuts and one oblique cut (fig. 534; color fig. 48), or with a thumbnail-shaped cut, *nagelsnitt* (literal-

ly, "nail carving"), in which a round-bottomed wood chip the shape of a nail is gouged out and removed. Both types have been frequently used throughout Europe since prehistoric times. In Swedish peasant milieu they belong especially in the southern provinces.

Chip carving
In chip carving,[19] a chip the shape of a three-sided pyramid is removed by a double triangle cut, made with a knife or chisel in three ver-

515. The lid of a molded circular box. Engraving and scratch carving create a light pattern on blackened wood. Härjedalen.

and Uppland; also, to a limited extent, in Småland and Halland. A reverse procedure was also followed: instead of the wood, the incised ornamentation was dyed black by being rubbed with soot (fig. 516). Molded wooden vessels of Jämtland and Härjedalen, in particular, are decorated in this fashion.

Wood burning

A similar effect is achieved by burning or branding wood with iron stamps in S-shapes, circles, or dots, combining these elements into geometric patterns (figs. 524, 532). This method has been used in northern Sweden, whereas the burned ornament in Götaland, though employing the same geometric forms as farther north, was made up entirely of dotted lines.

High relief and low relief

Carving in high or low relief emerges with the greatest vitality and frequency in lavish floral ornamentation. In southern and southwestern Sweden, this carving uses baroque forms; in northern Sweden it was inspired by rococo or classicist elements. Painting was used to heighten the plasticity of the relief (figs. 503–10).

Distinct Renaissance ornament in low relief, with some use of the acanthus, was especially prominent in Bergslagen and the Hälsingland-Härjedalen-Jämtland area. It flourished especially on chests, coffers and mangling boards. High relief as well as two-plane low-relief carving are probably associated with a professional production milieu with access to tools and patterns unavailable to home craft production. There have probably existed manufacturing centers, fostering a socially and geographically widespread distribution. A further indication of the professional origin of these objects—mangling boards and chests—is their showpiece nature.

There are a few extant examples of two-plane low relief of prehistoric and early medieval type, e.g., the impressive carving on a chest from Bjuråker in Hälsingland (color fig. 55) and that on a large cylindrical staved vessel with lid from Härjedalen, dating from about

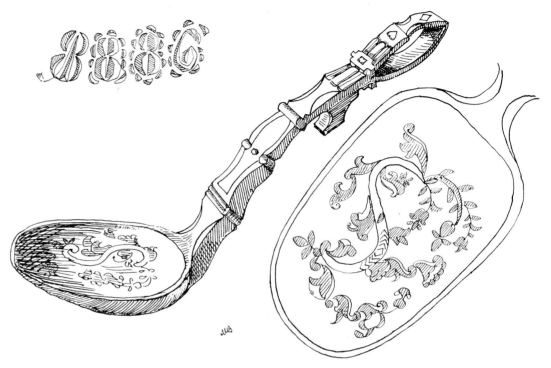

516. Scratch-carved ornament on carved wooden spoon with rubbed-in black dyestuff. Dated 1886, Hede, Härjedalen.

A.D. 1150. Both show purely prehistoric band interlacing and zoomorphic ornamentation in magnificent two-plain low relief. Stylistically, the decoration must be classified as prehistoric, though the carving may be of a much later date. In peasant milieu, especially in northern Sweden, as previously noted, older stylistic elements tend to survive far beyond the point when the style in question has ceased to be fashionable. This phenomenon, style retardation, must be taken into account within all branches of hand and home crafts. Crown rails and carved bowls from Dalarna exhibit the same antiquated decorative scheme of interlaced bands and zoomorphic ornament.

White coopering

In coopering, storage vessels of various kinds are made up of staves, held together by hoops or bands, around one or two solid bases, or

"heads." Hence the term "staved" vessels, deriving from that most important constructive element in coopers' ware, the stave. Though all coopers' ware, from the tiniest saltcellar to barrels and casks, is made with staves, the term "staved" is generally reserved for the products of the so-called white cooper, that is, finely crafted utensils for dairy and household use. Examples are pails, tubs, churns, and piggins. All staves are made by first splitting proportioned wood blocks into rough staves. After shaping with a drawknife and other edged tools in a shaving horse, the staves are planed, beveled, and crozed. In white coopering, the bottom is then fit into the croze—the groove in the staves—whereupon the staves are bound with split withes bent over steam or heat and scarfed together (figs. 519, 520).

A careful choice of materials is fundamental to superior stave work. Preferably, the wood should be free of knots, nonporous, seasoned,

517. Wood carving. Square cheese molds from Uppland and Jämtland; porridge molds and mold for cheese cake of Småland type, all from Småland.

518. Wood carving. Left to right: fulling board with carved date 1623 and the initials H B, Östergötland; felting board for mittens, Värmland; assorted cheese molds of folding type, Bohuslän; butter mold of folding type, Jämtland; and washboard, Värmland.

Woodcrafts

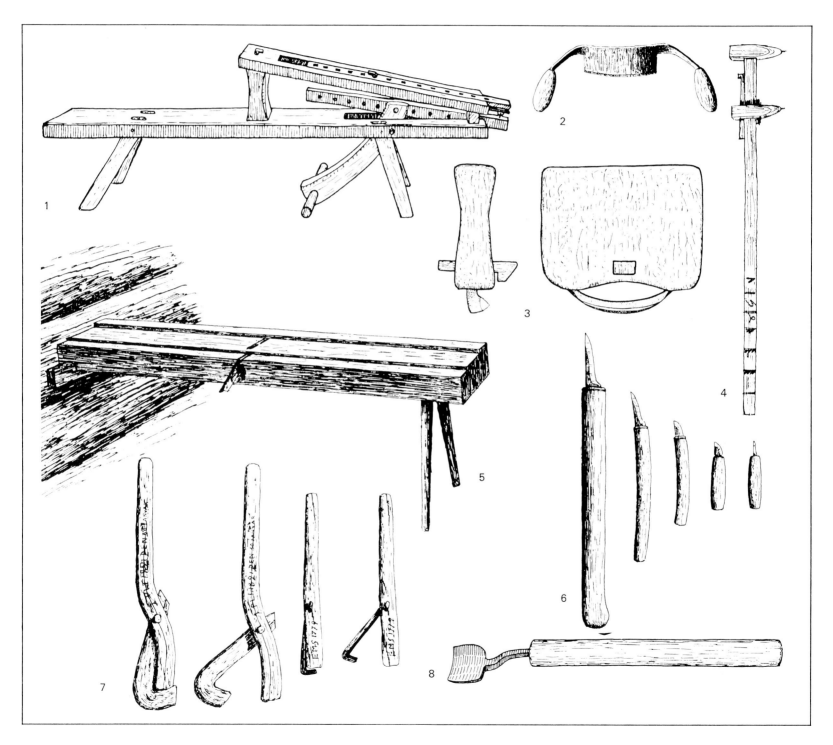

and with a straight grain. In the coniferous forest region, pine and juniper have been generally used, though the more odorless spruce was preferred for milk vessels and butter tubs. In the hardwood region, oak has been considered to yield the best wood for coopering.

The techniques in barrel making or general coopering—so-called wet or dry coopering, depending on the intended contents of the vessel —is largely the same as in white coopering. The difference is that coopering requires more specialized tools and a more systematic organization of the manufacturing process. Certain steps of the process also require different methods, e.g., in barrel making, the staves are preliminarily hooped before the heads are put in. In the Middle Ages, the coopers were already organized as a guild. Tools and techniques spread from the professional milieu to the home craft milieu. There is evidence that coopering techniques existed already in prehistoric times and were known generally throughout Europe.

Home production of coopers' ware has long been intended for sale. For example, as early as 1697 the Peasant Estate required that it be freed from the petty toll levied on its sales of coopers' ware in the towns. This request must no doubt be seen as a confirmation of the important role long played by coopering in the peasant industry. The Coopers' Guild in Kristianstad, Skåne, complained in a petition to the Board of Commerce in the eighteenth cen-

519. Tools for white coopering from Älvdalen and Venjan, Dalarna. (1) Shaving horse for shaping the staves. (2) Hollowing knife or cooper's drawknife. (3) Inside shave for smoothing down concave surfaces. (4) Beam compass for scribing the bottom. (5) Jointer plane for leveling the sides of the staves. (6) Crozing knives for cutting the croze into the staves. (7) Banddogs for prising the hoops or bands into place. (8) Scraper shave for smoothing the inside of the vessel.

520. White coopering. Staved butter tub and dish of variegated wood for decorative effect. Shown at "Slöjd 66" (Handcraft 66), an exhibit at Nordiska Museet in 1966. Privately owned.

521. Pear-shaped staved "canteens" used for milk, beer, and aquavit. Various parts of northern and central Sweden.

522. Butter stand for table use with burned stamped ornament. Three staves extend into carved legs. Västra Vingåker, Södermanland.

tury that the peasants of northern Skåne provided the countryside of the entire province with coopers' ware, thus ruining the market for the professional coopers. In Östergötland the situation was evidently the same. Northern Skåne, southern Småland, and eastern Halland, the forested regions in Östergötland and Västergötland, and the parishes north of Lake Siljan in Dalarna were the leading centers for the production of coopers' ware. Their market areas were the surrounding plains. Products from Dalarna and Västergötland were marketed also in Bergslagen and the provinces around Lake Mälaren.

Usage

White coopering and coopering have been practiced in Sweden as a home craft for home consumption as well as for sale. In these as in other crafts, articles made expressly for sale have generally been characterized by a coarser quality. Most coopered articles made for sale were large vessels, casks, and kegs for beer, milk, and aquavit; also tubs, barrels, and vats. Households always had great need for sturdy vessels for brining meat, for washing, and for laundering. Coopered ware for home consumption was, on the other hand, just as other craft products for home consumption, characterized by more distinctive local types. An example of a locally developed type is the pear-shaped staved "canteen" for milk, beer, or aquavit

(fig. 521). This form was adapted to the mobile life in the *fäbod* region, where provisions and drink regularly had to be carried over long distances.

Many staved vessels are of a formal and ceremonial nature, associated with special holiday customs. Such vessels included staved *kåsor* (large drinking cups with animal-shaped handles) (fig. 498), tankards and stoups for serving ale and aquavit; also butter tubs, variously decorated with carved edge, carved feet, and carved or burnt designs (figs. 521–25). Among the most beautifully decorated and carefully made vessels are the porringers, porridge dishes intended for bringing porridge to women in childbed, to weddings, or to funerals. The porringer is especially ornate in south-

523. Staved tankard with boldly profiled handle, beveled lid, decorative bands, and burned ornament. Östervallskog, Värmland.

524. Staved tankard with lid, decorated with burned ornament. Östervallskog, Värmland.

525. Staved tankard with lid and profiled handle. Rackeby, Västergötland.

western Sweden and in Jämtland and Härjedalen.

Constructional and decorative elements

The constructional elements of staved vessels, the staves and the hoops, also offer unique aesthetic means of expression. The staves have often been used to give a sense of rhythm to the surface, an effect sometimes heightened by the use of alternating woods.

The hooping or banding was also to a high degree executed with expert care and selectivity. This step was one of the most critical in coopering, especially the scarfing of the hoop joints. In some vessel types, such as beakers, a special aesthetic effect was achieved

by completely covering the sides of the vessel with hoops (color fig. 52).

In more carefully made staved vessels, certain functional elements, such as spout (fig. 92), lug or handle (fig. 520), and legs (fig. 522), were actually extended staves. Top and bottom edges were pierced or scalloped. Relief carving, scratch carving, and burned ornament would further heighten the aesthetic impact.

Molded splint containers—svep technique

Molded splint containers are made up of a side of molded splint, or bentwood, a bottom, and, sometimes, a lid. Different woods may be used in the different parts. The molded side, the *svep* (from the Swedish *svepa*, "[to] wrap"),

characteristic of the technique, was made from hardwood in the southern part of Sweden up to the coniferous forest region. In Skåne, Blekinge, and Småland, the preferred woods were oak and beech, combined with each other or with alder and elm. Oak was used especially for large containers. Beech, fairly odorless, was especially suitable for food containers. In northern Sweden birch dominated, combined with pine and spruce for bottom and lid. Various willows were used for small food boxes. In Finland and northernmost Sweden, aspen was the most frequently used wood, in combination with spruce or pine in lids and bottoms. The wood had to be free of knots, straightgrained, and easily split. It was selected with great care and consideration for the particular

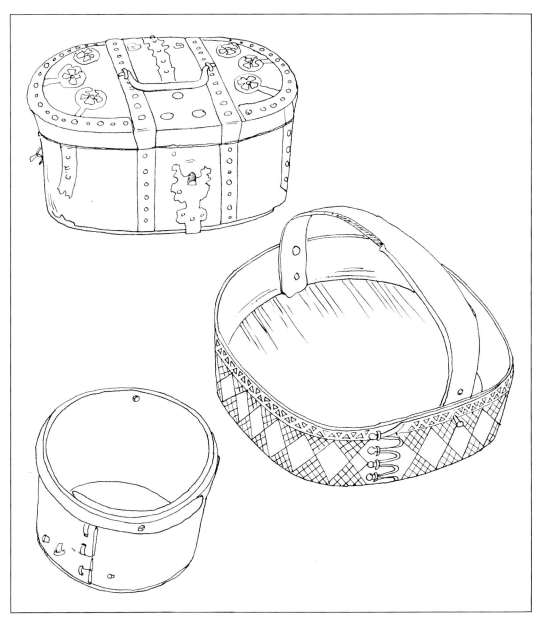

526. Thin wooden splint for a splint box is molded into the desired shape with the aid of two-bar wooden clamps. Valbo, Gästrikland, 1935.

527. The two ends of the molded splint are stitched together. The "thread" of root fibers is inserted into holes made with an awl and pulled through with a pair of tongs. Västerhiske, Västerbotten.

528. Various types of molded containers. Top to bottom: iron-banded molded coffer, molded carrier with curved handle, and measuring cup.

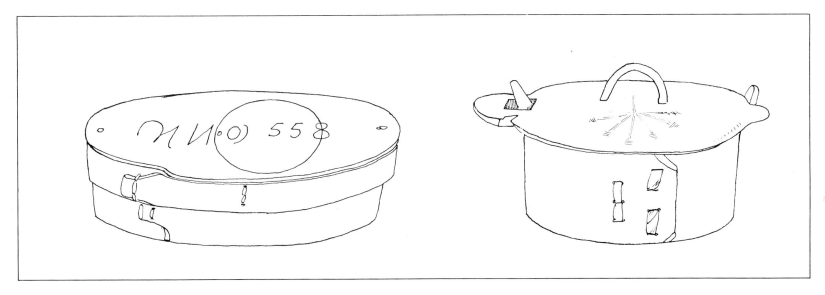

529. Types of molded containers. Left, box with fitted lid; right, *äska* with single-piece lid between two uprights.

intended use of the container. Also, the optimal time of year to fell the trees varied with the particular functional properties desired of the wood.

The splitting of splints, or thin strips, from a larger block of wood required a fairly complicated procedure. The tools used were usually axe, mallet, wedge, whittling knife, and drawknife (figs. 526, 527, 530). An ancient method of removing the splints along the curve of the tree's annual rings has survived to modern times in the region north of Jämtland and Ångermanland and in Finland and the Baltic states. The rest of the country has generally preferred the continental splitting method of more recent origin, which is charac-

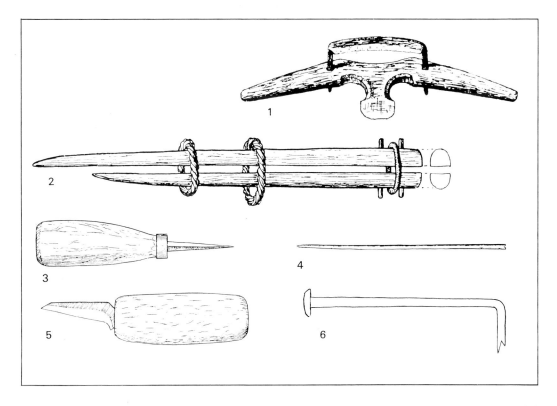

530. Tools for making molded wood containers. (1) Spokeshave for planing the rough splints. (2) Two-bar wooden clamp or vise, for clamping together the two lapped ends. (3) Awl for piercing the lapped ends. (4) Metal scribe for marking the bottom. (5) Knife for rabbeting or shouldering the bottom edge. (6) Jumper for fitting the bottom into place.

terized by the use of special splitting tools, shaving horse, and plane.

Various types of molded containers

One way of grouping molded wood containers is by their respective specific construction details. The various types are: the box with molded fitted lid (fig. 529, left); the *äska,* a box with a single-piece cover snapped into place between two uprights (fig. 529, right); the iron-banded molded coffer with hinged lid and lock (fig. 528, top); the molded carrier with curved handle (fig. 528, center); and, finally, the molded measuring cup without lid (fig. 528, bottom).

The *äska* appears in all of Scandinavia, except among Lapps and Finns. The molded coffer has been in general use north of central Västergötland, in Finland, and in northern and eastern Norway. The molded carrier occurs everywhere in Sweden and Norway, except among the Lapps. The molded box is the most widely distributed of all molded vessels and is found in all the Nordic countries as well as on the Continent.[20]

During the early Iron Age, the art of molding wood containers spread from the Continent to Scandinavia. In Scandinavia, a wealth of forms and functions developed, which have had no counterpart in continental manufacture.

As in the case of other woodcrafts, the making of molded splint containers shows a characteristic distribution: older techniques, functions, and decorations are found in central and northern Sweden, while more recent ones are prevalent in Götaland, influenced from the Continent. In southern Sweden, the manufacture for sale was, above all, geared towards mass production of packing boxes (fig. 533).

Constructional and decorative elements

Characteristic of the molded containers of northern Sweden is that the bottom piece is carved with a narrow projecting rim on which the molded side piece is stood (fig. 531). The molded side overlap is secured with wooden nails. In areas of Finnish or Lapp culture, the overlap was secured with stitches made with root fibers, quills, or reindeer sinews.

531. Two molded boxes with sides and bottoms separated. Left, rabbet-jointed molded sides and bottom—note the projecting rim on the bottom—on a butter dish from the Haparanda area, Norrbotten, dated 1787. Right, butt-jointed molded sides and bottom—note the absence of projecting rim—on a butter dish from Urshult, Småland.

532. Two *äskor.* The large *äska* is a "church box" for transporting finer articles of clothing to and from church. The sides are made from two molded strips. The ends are cut into a row of "lappers" or "fingers," each secured with a fiber stitch; in addition, the sides are joined by three seams in chain stitching next to the "lappers." Burned ornament. The small *äska* is two inches high and made of one molded strip, secured with two stitches. Both *äskor* from Duved, Jämtland.

All over northern Scandinavia the molded container has been used as a provisions box, or lunch pail, a characteristic part of the luggage of the peasant traders of Norrland. In Hälsingland, particularly, large oval boxes, so-called church boxes—used to transport church-going finery to the church village—were quite common in the first half of the nineteenth century (fig. 532). Containers from Jämtland are distinguished by their great variety of shapes and decor. The large molded carriers from this province for the serving of *tunnbröd* (unleavened barley bread, *lefse*) are made without handles.

Small coffers and *äskor* made in northern and western Dalarna come in many ancient shapes and with richly carved decoration. These containers were widely distributed through commercial craft production, especially to the entire Mälaren valley, Närke, Gästrikland, and Hälsingland.

In Dalsland, Värmland, and northern Västergötland, molded containers are characterized by burned ornament of early eighteenth-century type. In Uppland, Södermanland, and Östergötland, two influences can be distinguished. On one hand, there is a northern influence seen in technique and function, e.g., in the molded coffer. On the other hand, a southern influence from the large commercial production centers in Götaland can be seen in standardized shapes and sizes and certain more recent technical features. Such a feature is the bottom construction without projecting rim—that is, the entire bottom piece is fitted inside and flush with the molded side (fig. 531). This construction is, as a rule, found only in Götaland and eastern Svealand. (As mentioned above, molded vessels from northern Sweden have a projecting rim on the bottom). The

533. Molded wooden box, used as wrapping. Addressed to "Fru Svea Myhrman, Rämen, Filipstad" and postmarked July 18, 1871.

534. Molded *äska* with forked lap secured with chain stitching. The edge of the lid is decorated with single-triangle-cut chip carving. The bottom is inscribed MSD i Brunne År 1895 (MSD in Brunne, A.D. 1895).

539. A collection of articles made of birch bark. Those made of bark sheets include: baskets with handles, *dop-kass* (christening bag) or baby carrier, hat, jars, cones, boxes, shoes with birch-bark soles, and doll. Also shown is a bundle of sheets held together by a clip. Objects made of bark strips include: knife sheaths, shoes, boxes, scythe sheaths, salt bottles, butter churns, pack basket, and coil of rope. Northern and central Sweden.

56. Handles and finials of bowls and walking stick, shaped like animal or human heads. Boat-shaped drinking vessel with handle terminating in human head, carved dates 1728 and 1799, Lima, Dalarna; milk bowl, carved and dated 1799, Offerdal, Jämtland; "ale goose" painted to look like a bird, Ragunda, Jämtland; food bowl with carved date 1673, Ytterhogdal, Hälsingland; and walking stick, terminating in fantastic animal head, Östergötland.

57. Boxes of birch bark and molded wood, constructional and decorative elements. Top left, *äska* marked I 1793, Hede, Härjedalen; bottom left and top right, birch-bark boxes from Härjedalen and Värmland; and, bottom right, jewelry box marked SKD ANO 17 Hede, Härjedalen.

Bark sheets

Sheets of bark are bent and folded into cones or square shapes with or without lids. They are sewn together or joined by means of stitches of root fibers or wooden pins. The most original form is the cone, rolled from a single bark sheet. It has been variously used as a drinking cup, for berry picking, as a milk funnel, and also for more permanent storage of milk, flour, fish, salt, tobacco, etc. The cones may be tiny, or they may reach a circumference of up to two feet. Root-fiber stitching on birch-bark containers has, in addition to its important constructional function, also a significant decorative function. Especially pack baskets, baby carriers ("christening carriers"), sewing chests, yarn and stocking baskets, spoon cases, and tobacco jars exhibit a highly elaborate decoration consisting of root-fiber stitches in rhythmically recurring groups and of sewn-on profiled bark bands and wadmal strips of several colors (figs. 539, 542–44; color fig. 57). Birch-bark objects of this kind are found in Västmanland and Värmland, though perhaps mostly in Dalarna, Hälsingland, Härjedalen, and Jämtland. In Västerbotten and Lapp-inhabited areas, they occur more seldom. In Finland, this type of bark craft does not exist, with the exception of simple bark cones among Lapps and Siberian tribes. Research on the subject has shown that this technique reached its most developed form on Swedish territory. It is quite distinctly different from the birch craft in Europe's other birch regions, where only bark-strip weaving is found.

History and distribution

Birch bark is a material which man has been able to utilize without sophisticated tools. Birch bark can therefore be said to have already been an important culture element in the forested regions of Europe, Asia, and North

540. Square boxes of birch-bark sheets. Hede, Härjedalen, and Nås, Dalarna.

541. Round boxes of bark sheets from rowan and birch, laced with root fibers. Klövsjö, Jämtland, and Hede, Härjedalen.

542. Basket of birch-bark sheets. Detail of corner and rim. Nås, Dalarna.

543. Basket of birch-bark sheets. Detail of rim, showing initials and date MOD 1781. Nås, Dalarna.

America in the early Stone Age. Before the climate allowed spruce and linden to spread to the Baltic region, birch bark and pine bark were used as foundation for huts in damp settlements. Birch bark was also used for sinkers—the bark being wrapped around a stone or the like—for roofing, as shrouds for the dead, as a kind of tarpaulin over boats, or as a wrapping material. Preserved items of birch bark from the late Stone Age are boxes, knife scabbards and sword sheaths, pouches, cooking-pot cases, scoops, etc.

Until the present day, birch bark has been used as roofing material, as innersoles in shoes, and as insulation to protect lumber against rot.

However, in modern times the use of birch bark for personal items and household utensils has retreated to a geographically limited area. In Sweden, that area roughly coincides with the *fäbod* region, i.e., the country north of a line from Dalsland to Bergslagen to Gävle in Gästrikland. The same uses of birch bark are also found throughout Finland and in parts of Norway.

Technically related to articles made of birch-bark sheets are articles made of rowan or linden bark. In prehistoric times, the latter were in wide use throughout Europe. They are considered to be related in their development to articles of birch-bark sheets as well as to

containers of wrapped and overlapped, or "molded," birch bark.

Wrapped and overlapped containers of birch bark

As mentioned above, there are birch-bark containers consisting of a side of birch bark wrapped around a bottom of wood. They appear in all of Finland and Scandinavia, and also in large parts of Eurasia and North America.

In Scandinavia, the technique has been used mostly for snuff boxes and tobacco jars—items made fashionable with the introduction of

strips have also been twisted together to form lengths of rope used especially in fishing gear (fig. 539).

A variety of articles has been made by weaving birch-bark strips in a tabby weave. This weave may be used diagonally or perpendicularly to the corners of the article. In this fashion, birch-bark shoes and boots, salt bottles (figs. 545, 547), butter churns, baskets, pack baskets, creels, scythe sheaths, and other things have been made. The bark-strip technique dominated completely in Finland. In Sweden, it is found mostly in areas of Finnish settlement.

Basketry

Indigenous materials used for basketry include various willows, juniper, hazel, birch, spruce, pine, and aspen. Both the wood and the roots

544. Basket, box with lid, and round jar. Birch-bark sheets embellished with scalloped strips, stitching, pieces of cloth, and flakes of mica. Överkalix, Norrbotten; Dalby, Värmland; and Lima, Dalarna.

545. Objects made of woven birch-bark strips: salt bottle and round container from Ramsele, Ångermanland, and knife sheath from Lillhärdal, Härjedalen.

tobacco. It has also been used for, among other things, butter dishes, coffee tins, and butter churns. These containers exhibit a characteristic constructional-decorative element in the joining of the overlapping ends by means of interlocking lappers (fig. 546).

Birch-bark strips

Strips of birch bark have, above all, been used to reinforce other objects by winding or taping. The most impressive example of a bark-wound object is the birch-bark *lur,* or straight horn, a primitive musical instrument, the length of which may vary from two to eight feet. Bark

546. Containers of birch-bark sheets with lapped sides and decoratively interlocking lap ends. Östervallskog, Värmland; Lima, Dalarna.

547. Salt bottle of birch-bark strips. Köla, Värmland.

of these trees have been utilized. It is only in the southernmost parts of Sweden, in Skåne and adjoining provinces, that straw has been used in basketmaking.

There are two basic techniques of basketmaking: upright basket weaving and coiled basketwork.[22] Both techniques are ancient, demonstrably of prehistoric origins. The correspondence between basketry techniques and various textile techniques—weaving, needle looping, and plaiting—is obvious. Undoubtedly these parallel techniques can be traced back to a common, undifferentiated stage, when the same materials and techniques were used to make such varied things as house walls—our oldest prehistoric dwelling types have walls of wattle and daub—vessels, fish traps, and articles of clothing, such as foot coverings and head coverings. The tools required were simple: wooden cleaver, knife to remove the bark and to make weft rods, brakes for stripping the bark off the rods, and skein shave or plane for planing off the pith. Naturally, an ax was also required for the shaping of thicker posts of spruce, pine, or aspen in baskets intended for heavy loads.

Basket weaving

Basket weaving includes basketwork techniques best described in terms of plaiting and weaving. Thus, the side of the "woven" basket is so constructed that one may speak of a warp and a weft. The stakes are the heavier, upright rods, the "warp"; and the weavers or ends are the finer, usually split or shaven, rods which form the "weft" (fig. 549).

In one type of basket weaving, several willow rods are treated as one, forming the interlaced ends of a softly looped plait (fig. 551). Willow braiding forms a sturdy border at the top and bottom edges. The bottom, however, may be further reinforced with radial stakes, on which the ends are worked in a circular fashion.

A willow basket is generally made by weaving flexible twigs, cane rods, or root fibers alternately over and under the stakes of the vertical warp, creating a kind of tabby or basket weave. Sometimes the stakes are set in a wooden base to facilitate the weaving (fig. 21). The stakes may also be supple enough to be bent down at the upper edge, thus reinforcing the border. They may also project above the edge and be decoratively carved.

548. Various "weaves" of coiled basketry. (1) Wrapped coils joined by long stitches over two coils. (2) Short and long stitches, i.e., winding of one coil alternating with stitching over two coils (same principle as in fig. 548:1). (3) Lip work. Each stitch is taken through the corresponding stitch in the preceding coil (similar to Havasupai or Open Poma stitch in Indian basketry). (4) Openwork. Wrapped coils joined by split stitching over two coils, the long stitches splitting the fiber of the long stitches in the coil below.

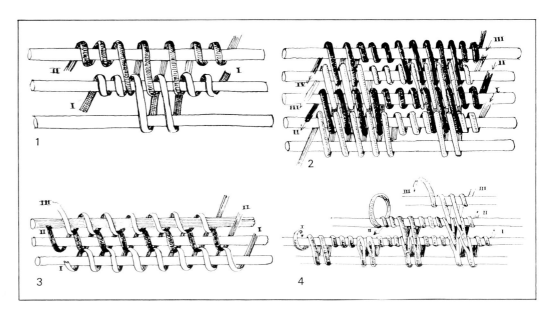

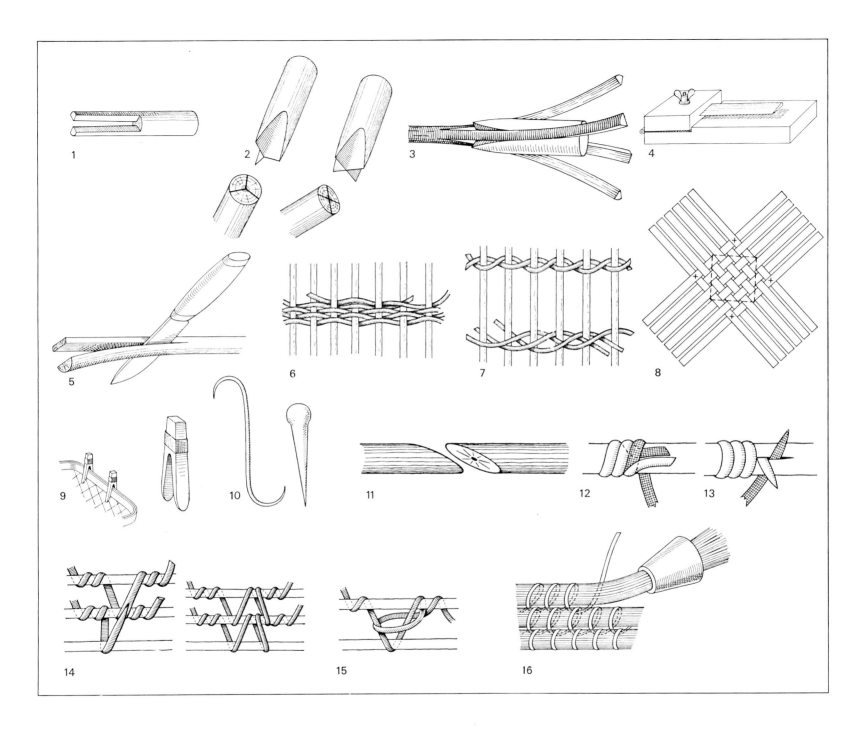

549. Basketwork techniques and tools for preparing basketwork materials. (1) Brakes for stripping willow bark. (2) Weavers, split by cleavers with three or four cutting edges. (3) The cleaver in action. Rod split by cleaver into four skeins. (4) Skein shave for shaving off the inner pith. (5) Splitting the rod with a knife. (6) Piecing of weavers in randing stroke. (7) Strong basket weaves: top, pairing (two-ply twined weave); bottom, upsetting or waling stroke (three-ply twined weave). (8) Sketch of the initial square bottom mat in splint weaving. (9) The rim of the splint basket is clamped over the edge with pincer-like clamps. (10) Left, iron hook for picking up spruce roots; right, awl for threading the wrapping fiber. (11–13) Methods of splicing in spruce-root basketwork. (11) Splicing the coiled rod. (12, 13) Splicing the wrapping fiber. (14) Spruce-root basketwork, pattern created by splitting the long stitches of the wrapping fiber, left, and by "chain stitching," right. (15) Spruce-root basketwork, pattern created by looping the wrapping fiber around itself when making a long stitch over two coils (similar to Mariposa or Knot stitch in Indian basketry). (16) Lip-work technique (cf. fig. 548:3).

550. Skeins are woven into a willow basket with handle. Asby, Östergötland, 1952.

551. Willow baskets in extended weave, with two or more weavers treated as one. Front to back: egg basket, Segerstad, Västergötland; bread basket, Visby, Gotland; and large bread basket, origin unknown.

One type of basket has, in addition to a wooden framework, a skeleton of bent branches or rods outlining the basket. Thus, the basket weaving itself is a minor inset in the basket. The framework is, naturally, especially important in larger pieces such as coach bodies and wicker beds, and in large baskets for heavy loads (fig. 552). Baskets to be carried on the back, pack baskets, frequently have a kind of back-pack frame construction; baskets designed to be carried by two people also required a sturdier frame. Rim, handles, legs, and bottom are important constructional elements reinforcing the woven basket and, at the same time, contributing to its total aesthetic impact.

Woven basket forms
Woven baskets have been made in the shape of round plates or bowls, and round or oval

baskets with a handle. They are widespread throughout Sweden and on the Continent, exhibiting little local variation. These woven baskets were probably the products of a workshop manufacture by indigenous basket makers in cities and towns. They were also imported into the country, above all from Germany. There is clear evidence that basket weaving was practiced also as a home craft. For example, in Augerum parish in Blekinge, where both men and women wove baskets, the production was intended more for household consumption than for the market. The baskets woven there were therefore of local, traditional forms, used as provisions baskets or food hampers. These factors point in the direction of a local manufacturing tradition of some continuity. Moreover, in the same district, the same type of basket weaving is used also for

the edges of fyke nets of spruce root. Two factors argue that basket weaving is of indigenous origin: (1) woven baskets used for food transportation are found throughout the country, and (2) there is evidence that the manufacture of woven baskets dates back to before 1850 (figs. 9, 10).

Splint weaving
In splint weaving, the material used in stakes and weavers is identical: splints split from sapwood of pine or aspen. Technically, the material used in splint-basket weaving requires more specialized tools than other basket weaving. The border or rim, which adds strength and rigidity to the weave, can be formed either by the vertical splints which are folded over and tucked down into the side, or by a bent

withe, or by thicker, though narrower, splints. The sides of the basket can also be made of diagonally woven splints, in which case a distinct border is often missing.

The overwhelming majority of these woven splint baskets has been stout, everyday ware (figs. 552–53, 555). There has been little reason for variation or differentiation, either with regard to function, technique, or decoration. As a result, no local types can be distinguished. Information from various parts of the country indicates that these baskets were standard items, made for sale. There are, however, some splint baskets which clearly were made with greater care in material selection and con-

struction details. These baskets were apparently made in the home for the household's own use (fig. 554).

Splint-basket weaving in Dalarna

In Mora and its neighboring parish Våmhus, splint-basket manufacture occupied a large part of the population. In the wintertime, it was the occupation of practically the entire household. The products of this seasonal craft production were stored to allow the material to dry out in order to better withstand the stress of transportation.

The various types made were large and small

single-handled baskets, egg baskets with lid and two movable handles, and large square baskets with or without lid.

Sales and distribution centers were, as usual, located in the Mälaren valley and adjoining provinces. However, records from Blekinge indicate that Dalarna peasants might sell their wares as far south as southern Småland and northern Blekinge.

As there exists no comprehensive study of basketmaking generally in Sweden, so has there been no systematic investigation either of the use of splints for basket weaving or of the origin and development of this craft. Usually, splint baskets have not belonged among the

555. Man carrying pack basket in splint weave. Brunskog, Värmland, 1940.

household's status-giving furnishings, but have been intended for everyday use. There are therefore few, if any, starting points for an historical overview of the craft. There is some evidence that wall coverings of wood splints were used around the middle of the eighteenth century, in urban milieu as well as in prosperous country homes. These splints were made with the help of a plane and were, in some cases, clearly workshop products. Thus, the home craft cannot be traced very far back. Splints have, however, long been used in combination with the "wrap and overlap," or molded, technique. Functionally and technically, favorable conditions for splint weaving thus existed at an early date. However, the question of the age of splint basketmaking must still be left open.

Splint-basket weaving in southern Sweden

In the forested regions of northern Skåne and adjoining parts of Småland and Blekinge, the manufacture of baskets for sale has at times been quite extensive. This was especially the case with splint-basket weaving in Östra Göinge at the end of the nineteenth century. Apparently, this manufacture is of fairly late date, judging from, among other things, the fact that a plane was used in the making of the splints (fig. 23). The production quickly grew and basket weaving was soon one of the most important industries in Örkened parish.

Basket makers were found on almost every farm, and their products were retailed through a dealer living in the parish. In the years 1875–1900, the manufacture became so extensive that, after the national market had been provided for, there was considerable export to Germany, Denmark, and England. The material was pine and aspen. After the splints had been split from the wood, they were trimmed with a knife. The splints were then woven diagonally (fig. 553). The rim was evened with a knife and fitted with bands of thicker, but narrower, splints. The most common type was a rectangular basket with a transverse handle reaching from one long side to the other. This manufacture seems to have spread to Kyrkhult parish in Blekinge (fig. 9). In Flymen, in east-

ern Blekinge, it appears, on the other hand, to have been introduced by traveling Dalarna craftsmen who went from farm to farm making baskets. In eastern Blekinge this type of basket was thus called *dalkorgar*, "Dalarna baskets." The splint basketmaking in Östra Göinge has, however, probably received an impetus from several directions.

Coiled basketwork

Coiled baskets are built up by one or several spiraling continuous coils of withes, straw bundles, or root fibers (fig. 548). Each coil is attached to the previous one with stitches of a thin fiber or split roots. In southern Sweden, especially in Skåne, another type is found, lip

552. Old woman with large basket for transporting hay. Klövsjö, Jämtland.

553. Splint baskets. Top, rectangular basket without handle, made for household use; left, basket with handle, typical sales item. Dalarna. Right, two school baskets with handle, Småland and Dalarna.

554. Provisions basket, "lunch basket," dated 1857, and knife or spoon basket, both of woven splints with painted decoration. Delsbo, Hälsingland.

556. "Korgmakar-Kalle" ("Basketweaving Charlie") from Adelöv, Skåne.

557. Lip work. Martin Bengtsson of Sandby, Skåne, demonstrates the making of a basket of coiled straw. 1951.

work, in which a roll of straw is used instead of a withe or reed, and the stitching is done by threading linden fiber through the stitch below it on the last made coil, not through the straw itself, which would prove less durable (fig. 557). A third type of coiling consists of winding the covering fiber alternately around one coil—the loose top coil—and two coils—the top coil and the last made coil—thus securing the loose coil to the basket (figs. 548, 549). By combining short and long stitches—over one or two coils—in different ways, various patterns are created.

Coiled baskets occur in all parts of Sweden. To a greater extent than splint baskets they can be traced to certain locales and social milieus because of distinctive features in their function, technique, material, and ornamentation.

Lip work
With regard to the material, the group most easily distinguishable is that of containers made with coiled straw rolls stitched together with thin strips of linden, hazel, or willow—a tech-

nique found only in southern Sweden. The most common household item made in this technique is the beehive, or bee skep, but straw has been used also in chair seats and seedlips, kidney-shaped sowing baskets. Lip work has also been used in more prestigious objects, such as cylindrical food hampers with a lid (color fig. 58), extraordinarily impressive pieces which certainly must have been the pride of maker and owner alike, and magnificent urn-shaped receptacles for grain. Some lip-work receptacles have decorative openwork borders, made by bending the straw coil in zigzag fashion. This type of decoration was apparently borrowed from the coiled reed or withe baskets, an observation supported by the fact that openwork decoration of lip work occurs only in northern Skåne, which is closer to the coiled basketry region.

Coiled baskets of roots and withes

Coiled baskets with long stitches over two coils, creating a solid structure, are more common than coiled baskets with openwork structure (figs. 558–60; color fig. 58). As a rule, the former are not decorated, except among the Lapps who create designs by the use of dyed wrapping fibers, much like what is done in the coiled basketwork of American Indians. Coiled baskets with solid walls have been used as boxes, large containers, food baskets, and cheese forms. Decorative openwork may be made in two ways: knots are made in the wrapping linden fiber, whereby spaces are created between the coils, or a zigzag-bent withe is stitched into the side, between two coils. Knotted decor is limited to Västerbotten and Norrbotten, whereas zigzag decoration is found in coiled basketwork throughout the country, especially on serving plates, serving bowls, and food baskets, which were often made to confer and confirm a certain status. Some local differentiation can be distinguished. Baskets from Skåne have a less lacy openwork than those from other provinces. Baskets from central Sweden are finished with a "picot" edging. In baskets from northern Sweden, the handle is attached on the inside of the basket, with two diagonal stays (color fig. 58). Such is the case also in Uppland and Södermanland, whereas coiled baskets from western Sweden have the handle attached on the outside of the basket and no diagonal stays. Those from Jämtland show more varied openwork, with roundels (fig. 559) which, in turn, may themselves be decorated with openwork in zigzag. There are corresponding forms in Norwegian basketry. Similar but lighter and more supple openwork is achieved by building up the basket entirely with long stitches over two coils. This technique has been used primarily in Härjedalen, Jämtland, Bohuslän, and parts of Väs-

558. Coiled baskets. Left to right: Bread basket of split root fiber, the border and lower zigzag border of dyed root; probably from Hälsingland. Spherical basket with lid, Ådalsliden, Ångermanland; and covered box with pattern created by stitching over two coils, Östergötland.

tergötland, with some occurrence in Hälsingland and Ångermanland. Stitching over two coils offers decorative possibilities even without the use of openwork. By combining long and short stitches in various ways, different patterns are created. Checks, diamonds, triangles, zigzag bands, squares, stars, spirals, and a repeating square pattern covering the entire side of the basket can give an exquisitely decorative effect. These patterns are found above all in the coiled root baskets from northwestern Sweden.

Practical applications

Basketwork has seen a wide range of uses. Baskets have been used for storage and transportation, being especially suited to the latter, as they are among the lightest yet strongest craft products known. Generally, they have been purely utilitarian and therefore less decorated. This is true, for example, of all baskets used for transporting goods, in the home or in the fields: coal baskets, potato baskets, fish traps, creels, food baskets, and baskets for carrying goods to and from market and town.

In the home, they would hold articles of clothing, textile furnishings, yarn balls, and rags In much of the country, cheese forms were made of basketwork. Grain, flour, and bread were also stored in baskets.

Among articles of basketwork may also be counted beds. They are made of woven splints and have six or eight legs. In the forest regions of Östergötland and Södermanland there was an extensive commercial production, aimed at the cities and markets. From the seventeenth century, basket beds are mentioned in inventories from manors and farmsteads in Östergötland, Västmanland, Närke, Uppland, and southern Dalarna, i.e., the particular target areas of marketed craft products.

Low-post beds of this simple type are related technically to the bedsteads found in the Viking ships from Gokstad and Oseberg in Norway. The type is known since the early Middle Ages and is widespread in eastern Europe also. As late as the nineteenth century, these beds were used as simple everyday furnishings in lofts and storehouses.

When baskets were intended for use on a table, as were bread baskets, food baskets, sewing baskets, and spoon cases, more attention was paid to their decorative treatment. This in turn encouraged the development of technical skill and a feeling for design and material which have made basketwork one of the finest Swedish handcrafts.

Basket makers
The majority of those making woodcraft products for sale, whether their products were molded boxes, baskets, or staved vessels, did so because they owned no land or because their land could not support them. They were the unpropertied poor (fig. 556). They might be crippled or handicapped, and unable to work on the farm. In other words, basketmaking was an occupation which did not bestow any measure of social recognition. This was especially so since the work paid very little. In exceptional cases, outstanding skill was able to raise the esteem of a particular craftsman, but hardly that of the profession as a whole. However, it holds true also for basketmaking that

those providing articles for the immediate household's own consumption were far more socially differentiated than those who made baskets for a living.

Sales regions
In the forested regions of Kronoberg county, especially in Blädinge and Söraby parishes, basketmaking for sale was practiced on a large scale as late as the 1860s. The same is true for the districts of Kind, Veden, Bollebygd, Väne, and Kulling, in Västergötland. In the district of Kulling, especially in Hemsjö parish, there was a manufacture of coal baskets, potato baskets, and fish creels of juniper, which were retailed in Sweden as well as in Norway. Around 1900, Hemsjö parish alone delivered around 150,000 coal baskets annually to the railroads. Simple and sturdy basketwork, e.g., pound nets and coal baskets, but also finer work in willow, was made in Örebo county during the nineteenth century. Other forested regions in central Sweden—Östergötland, Nora parish in Västmanland, and Sorunda parish, Södermanland—have had considerable commercial basketmaking. The Jämtland parishes of Sunne, Oviken, and Offerdal were known for their basketry, as were the Lapps for their excellent coiled root basketry.

Horn and bone crafts

Everyday use of horn and bone
Since time immemorial, horn and bone have provided man with versatile materials to be put to any number of uses. Archaeologists have found it justified to speak of one of the prehistoric stages in man's cultural development as the Bone Age. In spite of the fact that man has long since adopted other materials and forms, a great number of words still denoting objects of horn remain in the Swedish, and English, languages, reminding us of the time when animal horn was the natural material for certain objects. As examples may be mentioned inkhorns (ink wells), powder horns, shoehorns, and drinking horns (figs. 562, 564). Generally, the natural form of the bone or the horn defined the material's scope of

559. Coiled baskets of root fiber. Left to right: square basket, stitching over two wooden slats, Järvsö, Hälsingland; circular bread basket used at weddings, Hede, Härjedalen; and cheese basket, Hova, Västergötland.

560. Coiled baskets of root fiber. Left to right: bread basket with four handles, Tännäs, Härjedalen; cheese mold in openwork, Nederkalix, Norrbotten; spherical jar with lid from Tännäs, Härjedalen; and cylindrical jar with lid, Naverstad, Bohuslän.

63. Ironwork from various parts of Sweden. Top to bottom: left, knocker with incised surface decoration, a man's face on the top torus, presumably from a door in Kinnarumma Old Church, Östergötland; door ring from storehouse, Rättvik, Dalarna; door handle, Hede, Härjedalen. Center: chandelier, Älvdalen, Dalarna; escutcheon with knocker in the form of a lion or dog, Högsby, Småland. Right, knocker, similar to the Kinnarumma knocker, but with generally more modeled features, especially the man's face on the torus, Vadstena, Östergötland; gate hinge from Högsby, Småland.

58. Baskets in root fiber and lip work. Left to right, urn-shaped grain receptacle (for grain storage) of coiled straw, Ringamåla, Blekinge; root-fiber baskets with handle, Lillhärdal, Härjedalen, and Rättvik, Dalarna; and circular flat baskets from Hede, Härjedalen, and Glättaryd, Småland.

59. Knife handles of bone with scratch carving, rubbed with black or red dyestuff. Lapp handcraft. Överkalix, Norrbotten; Frostviken, Jämtland; and Jokkmokk, Lappland. Also a needle case from Tännäs, Härjedalen.

60. Spoons of bone with incised decoration. Lapp handcraft, Lappland.

61. Horn spoons from Urshult, Växjö, and Källsjö, Småland.

62. Round canteen for aquavit, wood and bone with incised ornament and the initials PPS MLD. Lapp handcraft, Lappland. Small drinking cups of horn, the smallest with incised carving and the initials AND. Småland.

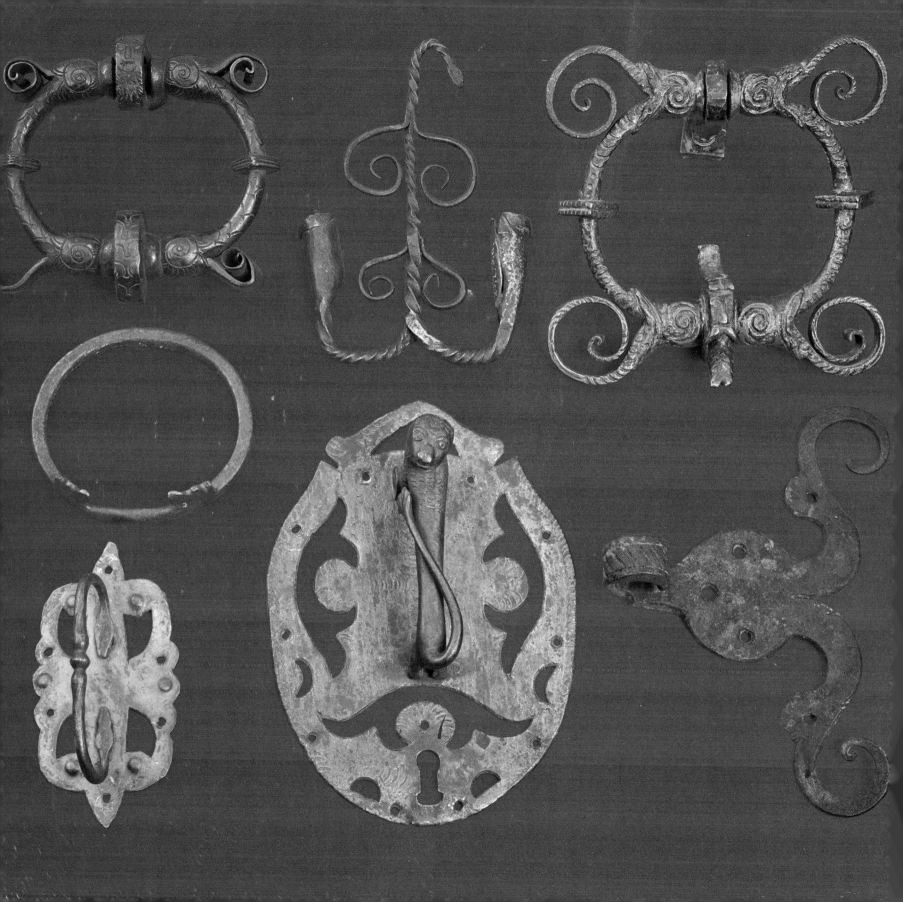

561. Bone craft. Staved canteen with bone trim and bands, blackened ornament; spoons with black or red dye rubbed into the carved ornamentation; dipper of birch with handle and rim of bone; and needle cases. Lapp handcraft, Lappland.

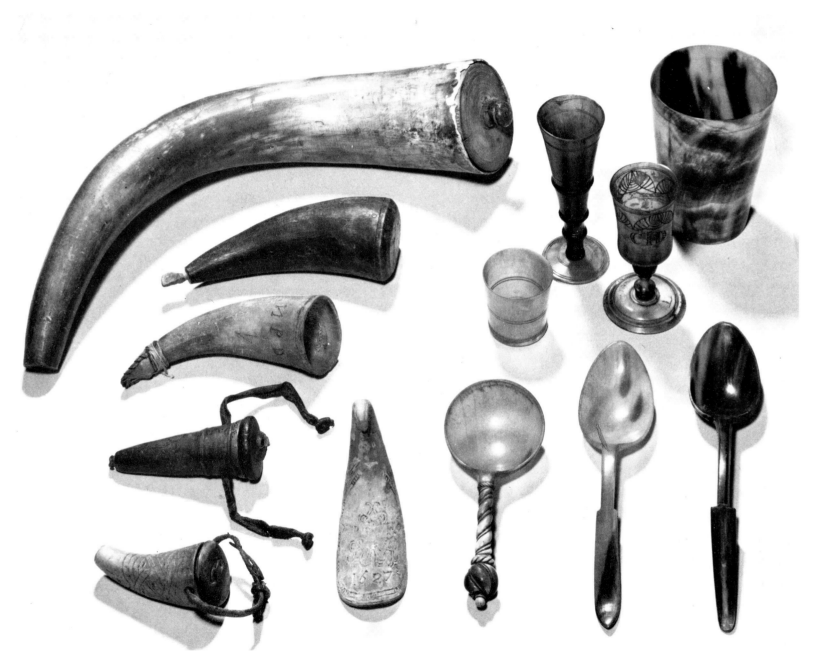

562. Horn craft. Top to bottom: left, powder horns, nursing horn initialed NPD, grease horns, shoehorn dated 1627; right, goblets—one with scratch-carved decor and the initials CID—cups, and spoons. Småland.

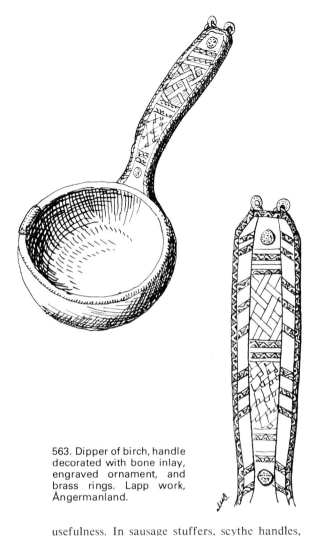

563. Dipper of birch, handle decorated with bone inlay, engraved ornament, and brass rings. Lapp work, Ångermanland.

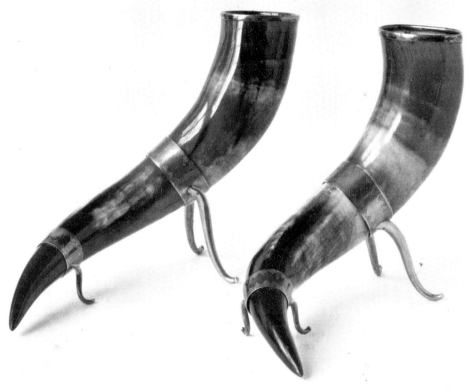

564. Drinking horns of silver-mounted cattle horns, stamped IAO S:t Erik. The Oxehuvud Collection, Nordiska Museet.

565. Lapp shapin knife sheath from reindeer antler. Tärna, Lappland, 1935.

usefulness. In sausage stuffers, scythe handles, nursing horns, drinking horns, and powder horns, the form was perfectly suited to the function. For other purposes, the antlers of deer, elk, or reindeer, or some skeletal bone, were adapted in simple ways to the function at hand.

Distribution

Bone and horn crafts have of course been of greater importance in areas where the raw material was a natural by-product of some regular industry. For example, among the Lapps, reindeer horn was a direct by-product of their main industry, reindeer herding (figs. 561, 563, 565; color figs. 59, 60, 62). In northern Sweden, the predominant cattle-raising industry and a good supply of reindeer and elk horn have stimulated the use of horn and bone

for objects elsewhere made of wood or metal. Thus, there is, in northern Sweden, a varied bone and horn craft, highly adapted to local needs and object types. In southern Sweden, the use of especially cattle horn has given rise to a well-developed craft production for sale. This horn craft was, no doubt, influenced by professional horn work. The former was probably not developed until the 1840s. In southwestern Småland, especially, the population was occupied with making articles of horn. When the manufacture reached its peak, every farmer, cottager, or squatter was involved in one phase or another of production or distribution (fig. 562; color figs. 61, 62).

Forms

The main market area for horn craft was Skåne and Halland, and the preferred product

566. Harness saddle of antler with colored engraved ornament and inscription. Seventeenth century, probably from burgher milieu.

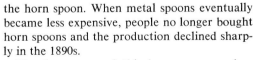

567. Scratch-carved sledge-harness "knees" of bone, inscribed with date and initials ANO 1672 K+I+B+K. Undersåker, Jämtland.

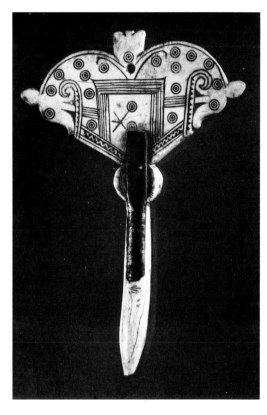

568. Harness pin, used to fasten the traces of the harness to the whiffletree, bone with scratch carving and drilled decor, carved in the outline of horses' heads. Mora, Dalarna.

the horn spoon. When metal spoons eventually became less expensive, people no longer bought horn spoons and the production declined sharply in the 1890s.

The forerunner of this horn-spoon production for sale was no doubt a production for private consumption. Småland farmers, famous for their oxen since the Middle Ages, took naturally to horn craft for household use. In addition to already mentioned articles of horn, there were other household utensils and personal items for which horn was well suited and used: snuff boxes, buttons, horn lanterns, combs, cutlery handles, sheaths, cane handles, sausage stuffers, cookie cutters, tumblers, and bottles.

Decoration

The worker in horn has above all strived to bring out the natural beauty of the material, with its lovely color nuances and the fine sheen of the polished surface. In addition, he has contributed ornamentation in the form of scratch carving, engraving, and the turning of concentric circles and arcs. Drinking horns and powder horns were decorated with carved figures and metal fittings. Scratch-carving ornamentation has been developed to an extraordinary degree in Norrland, above all in Dalarna, Hälsingland, Norrbotten, Västerbotten, Härjedalen, and Jämtland (figs. 567, 568), and especially among the Lapps (figs. 561, 563; color figs. 56, 59, 60, 62). Animal forms, checks, and interlaced bands all link this orna-

mentation to prehistoric and medieval traditions. The more recent acanthus ornament has also found its way into the horn and bone crafter's inventory of design (fig. 566).

Metalwork

Of all metals, iron has been the one most used in handcraft production for home consumption and for sale. It has been used to make tools small and large as well as household utensils. Brass and tin, on the other hand, have been used more sporadically. Like copper, pewter, silver, and gold, they belong mostly in guilded craft production.

There is reason to suppose that the situation

in ironsmithing was similar to that in the textile crafts—i.e., that the large-scale industrial manufacture taking place at the ironworks stimulated the home craft production in the surrounding regions. In the mid-eighteenth century, directors Sven Rinman and Samuel Schröderstierna of the Mining Board sought to improve methods of domestic metalwork in various parts of the country. Among other things, they worked for cooperation between professional smiths and peasant smiths. Thus, not only raw material but also a certain measure of instruction was disseminated from the ironworks.

Consequently, one could expect to find a more developed metalcraft in areas around ironworks. In Småland, the first province in Sweden to extract and export iron, the extraction of iron from lake and bog ore continued to be a peasant industry, from prehistoric times until the end of the nineteenth century. The manufacture of scythes was especially extensive in southern Småland. The market area was primarily Skåne and Öland. In southwestern Småland, alongside agriculture and cattle raising, there was a flourishing production of sundry small metalware, such as sieve mesh, sieves, hairpins, and hooks and eyes, as well as larger farming implements, such as threshers and chaff cutters. Already at an early time, Gnosjö was well known for wire drawing. This important domestic industry received a further boost when water power was introduced around the mid-eighteenth century. In many parts of Småland around 1880, the metalwork of the peasant turned into industrially organized tinsmithing. In Gnosjö, the wire-drawers were similarly industrially organized.

Quite important for neighboring provinces was the export from Småland of unprocessed iron. It is documented that in 1641 Skåne peasants bought iron from Småland, though at that point the export certainly must have been in existence for some time. Certain parishes in northern Skåne frequently bought iron, partly from Småland, partly from ironworks in Skåne, for their production of scythes. Individual smiths would sign their scythes, evidence of a high standard of production reflected in the high esteem in which these smiths were held.

569. Blacksmith at his anvil. Oil painting by Pehr Hilleström, eighteenth century. Privately owned.

A stamp with name, initials, or a trademark—a bear, a heart, sometimes also the date of manufacture—would be put on the heel of the scythe. In the market these scythes were commonly known by their respective trademarks. In this traditional Skåne smithing region, a factory was founded in 1817 for the production of finer ironwork, brass, and cast iron. Workers were called in from ironworks all over Sweden. Production continued until 1839, when the plant was closed down. The craftsmen attached to the factory were then dispersed across parts of northern Skåne, where, as professional or domestic craftsmen, they continued making knives, snuffboxes of brass, curry combs, cow and sheep bells, sadirons, flatirons, mortars, coffee mills, candlesticks, and harness hardware. This handcraft manufacture continued until World War I, after which it gradually died out in competition with intensified industrial production.

Ironsmithing in northern Skåne represents a fairly recent development. About earlier Skåne smithing, on the other hand, very little is known, notwithstanding a wealth of preserved material, primarily in the form of candlesticks (figs. 581–83). In a similar way—using raw material from ironworks close by—a lively craft production for sale sprang up in Halland and Västergötland. It featured scythes, coarse and fine cards, needles, and horseshoes.

In some places the putting-out system gained entry because of the difficulty in securing sufficient capital for raw material. The vital nail manufacture in northern Östergötland (fig. 19) was supplied with raw material by merchant-employers in Askersund in Närke. Due to their need for credit, clock manufacturers in Mora, Dalarna, came under the control of merchant-employers. These, in turn, forced the prices up, whereby the craftsmen in reality became wage earners. This development took place in the first decades of the nineteenth century, at which time mass-production practices and a far-reaching division of labor were established. Clockmaking in Mora does, however, date back to the middle of the preceding century, when Stjärnsund ironworks started turning out their famous clocks based on an invention by the Swedish scientist Christopher Polhem (1661–1751).

Another type of manufacturing organization was exemplified by the tack smithing in Lerbäck, Närke. The farmers would occupy themselves with tack forging in the wintertime only. During that season, some of them even employed extra manpower—farmhands and apprentices—to work in the forge in exchange for food and the use of the smithy one day a week. Shears and scythes were also made here. They were sold all over Sweden, and even exported.

In the nineteenth century, handmade nails were replaced by inexpensive machine-made cut nails, though the former were still turned out on a limited scale as late as 1905.

In Dalarna, as in Småland, iron extraction from bog and lake ore along with iron processing were practiced from prehistoric times. Of great importance, in terms of quantity, was the production of larger and smaller household implements; in terms of quality, building and furniture hardware and household utensils. Iron extraction for household use on any significant scale, the foundation for domestic ironworking, ceased in the eighteenth century. The raw material then had to be supplied from foundries and ironworks. Ironworking was, however, sufficiently extensive as late as 1860 for its products to be listed as prominent trade items north of Lake Siljan (fig. 570). As late as around 1900, several Dalarna parishes were known for their specialized production of such items as horseshoes, cow bells, small rumble bells, sleighs, buttons, and axes.

The following quotation from the Governor's Five-Year Report from Gävleborg county in 1865 offers a description respresentative of the development in Dalarna as well as the Norrland counties.

Concerning the domestic ironmakers' output, especially in the parishes of Ovansjö and Torsåker, it can be said to have noticeably declined, the primary reason being the low price of iron combined with increased daywages. Those ironmakers who own sufficient forest have found it more advantageous to sell their coal to ironworks in the area than to use it themselves. Thus, the domestic ironmaking, since it so little suits current conditions, may with time cease to exist and the peasants in the area entirely devote themselves to the more lucrative agriculture, which heretofore has been neglected on account of mining and metalworking.

In Värmland, the forest won out over the iron. This circumstance initially gave forest-owning peasants great economic advantages, and transformed ironmasters into "lumber-masters." Around the ironworks, however, domestic ironworking had become entrenched. Its most outstanding products, aesthetically speaking, were wrought-iron grave crosses (figs. 572, 573).

In Jämtland, several parishes were known for their metalcraft products for sale. In Västerbotten and Norrbotten, on the other hand, metalworking was carried on stricly as a domestic craft for home consumption.

The Five-Year Reports of the Governors characteristically give quantitative estimates and also account, to some extent, for the types of products turned out. The rural production reportedly consisted overwhelmingly of heavy wrought-iron articles for vehicles, agricultural and other tools, tacks, nails, and horseshoe nails. This output naturally satisfied the big everyday demand. If, however, one looks instead at the types of iron objects still preserved, a partially different picture emerges, dominated by objects made for decorative purposes. The large production of standard wares in regions well supplied with raw materials, i.e., the bog and lake iron districts with domestic ironworking and the districts around the ironworks, provided local smiths with excellent training and much practice. These regions produced smiths of especial talent and skill, who made household utensils and decorative wrought iron with a distinctive local stamp.

Ironwork

On the whole, one may distinguish between two types of ironworking: blacksmithing proper or forged work, and cold metalwork, or bench work. Blacksmithing comprises the making of heavier implements, nails, horseshoes, horseshoe nails, axes, and all kinds of simple hand tools. After heating the iron in the forge, the blacksmith forges it on the anvil, as a rule,

Metalwork

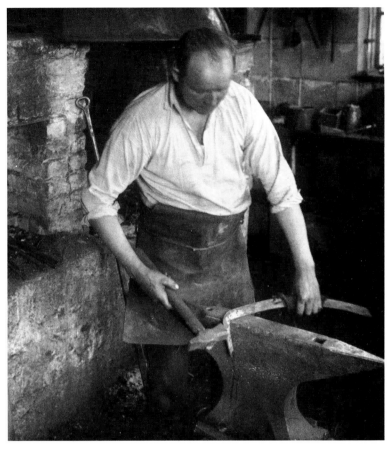

570. Scythe smithing. The part by which the scythe will be attached to the scythe snathe is shaped and hammered over to get a sharp inner corner. Älvdalen, Dalarna, 1927.

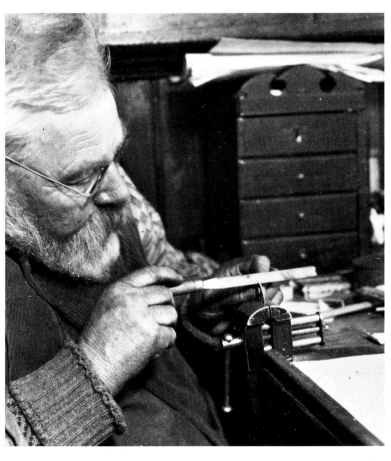

571. Cold metalwork. Clock-maker Myr Anders Andersson filing a gear wheel with a half-round smooth file. Leksand, Dalarna, 1936.

with the aid of hand and sledgehammers (figs. 569, 570). Other principal tools of the blacksmith are an assortment of tongs. With the help of these tools, the smith works the iron by the processes of drawing out or fullering, by upsetting or jumping up, bending, shouldering, brazing, and forge welding. These procedures constitute the actual forging. The finished iron product generally retains the black color thus acquired, hence the term blacksmithing. Cold metalwork (fig. 571) is used primarily in the making of locks, locksmithing, but also for various finer wrought-iron articles, such as keys, mounts, hinges, rifle barrels,

decorative ironwork, etc. The locksmith, as a rule, works the iron cold on a workbench with various tools, the most important of which are file, punch, chisel, hammer, and burin. The treatment with file and polishing steel gives the iron a bright silver-like surface finish. The procedures of cold metalwork belong to a more developed metalcraft, requiring longer training and better workshop equipment, especially various types of files. Cold metalwork was, therefore, usually carried on as a regulated craft or as a small-scale industry. In Sweden, townships and, hence, also craft guilds were slow in coming, whereas on the Continent they

had reached their peak in the Middle Ages. Therefore, Swedish workshop production of any kind, including ironwork, was not influenced by new techniques and styles until well into the sixteenth century. As late as the sixteenth and seventeenth centuries, Swedish ironwork was on the whole still largely influenced by prehistoric and medieval wrought-iron techniques, i.e., blacksmithing. Thus, the iron was worked with tongs, sledgehammer, and hammer. The decorative treatment included splitting and bending the ends of iron bands, twisting of round- or square-section bars, and the use of stout rivet heads. In addition, surface decoration in the form of line-punched flutings (fig. 585) and hammered details helped give Swedish wrought iron its distinctive character.

Thus, it is quite clear that cold metalwork was tied in with vocational training under the aegis of the guilds. On the other hand, Swedish peasant milieu produced, generally and characteristically, only forged work as late as the nineteenth century. Not only heavy agricultural implements, nails, and horseshoe nails were forged, but also ornamental ironwork.

No exhaustive treatment of Swedish ironwork has yet been made. However, some in-depth investigations, above all those by Brynolf Hellner and Sigurd Erixon (see Bibliography), illuminate the subject. They point up what interesting research material is available in Sweden, a country with ironmaking traditions going back more than two millennia. Any presentation of the largely ignored ornamental handcraft ironwork therefore must needs be scanty.

The higher technical standards at the ironworks resulted in a richly ornamental ironwork in the surrounding districts, as evidenced by locally distinctive products. Aesthetically most outstanding are wrought-iron crosses, candlesticks, and locks, all of which have been researched in depth by Hellner and Erixon. Sumptuous and elegant mounts and building hardware, such as weathervanes, gable ornaments, and door mounts for churches and secular buildings, were made in Dalarna, Hälsingland, and Härjedalen. Unfortunately they can only be included in this work in the form of a few illustrations (figs. 584, 585; color fig. 63).

Grave crosses

Wrought-iron grave crosses are found all over Sweden, though they are concentrated in the major ironworking districts of Småland, Bergslagen, Värmland, and Östergötland. Local variations, reflecting different stylistic influences, give this particular group of monuments a prominent place in the history of wrought iron. Since they were made for commemorative purposes, these grave crosses were particularly ornamental in nature.

Grave crosses in central and northern Sweden are of the "ring cross," or Celtic, type, having one or more concentric circles around the intersection of the arms (figs. 573, second from right). In rare cases, a square encloses the intersection. These crosses are made of flat iron bands. They can reach a considerable height, measuring up to thirteen feet, especially in Västmanland, Värmland, and Dalsland. In Jämtland, on the other hand, they are relatively small. Early ring-cross ornaments, similar in design and technique, are found on romanesque church doors. As grave markers, however, ring crosses appear first in the seventeenth century, reach a peak in the eighteenth century, and decline in frequency in the beginning of the nineteenth century. Technically, the decorative form is based on splitting the ends of iron bands and bending these into scrolls or volutes. On the transverse arms and the rings there are short cross bands with similar ornamentation.

In the "triangle cross," the top of the cross and the transverse cross arms are joined by an iron band, giving the cross a triangular outline (fig. 573, left). The type occurs all over Sweden, though concentrated primarily in northeastern Småland. The triangle cross differs from the ring cross technically also, in that the iron bands are not in the plane of the cross but perpendicular to that plane. The decorative curls and scrolls are made by coiling the entire iron band, not by splitting its ends. Triangle crosses date from the end of the eighteenth to the middle of the nineteenth centuries.

The various iron crosses found throughout Sweden are probably but a small part of the original total number of crosses. The cross motif, used as a tomb monument, dates back to stone crosses from the Middle Ages. Wooden crosses have, of course, been far more common, though unable to withstand the ravages

572. Wrought-iron grave cross. The left spire is inscribed LND F. 1735 (LND, born 1735), the one on the right, D. 1807 (died 1807). The central spire carries two inscriptions: top, SIS 1840, and, bottom (incomplete), F 1759 KC—. Nössemark, Dalsland.

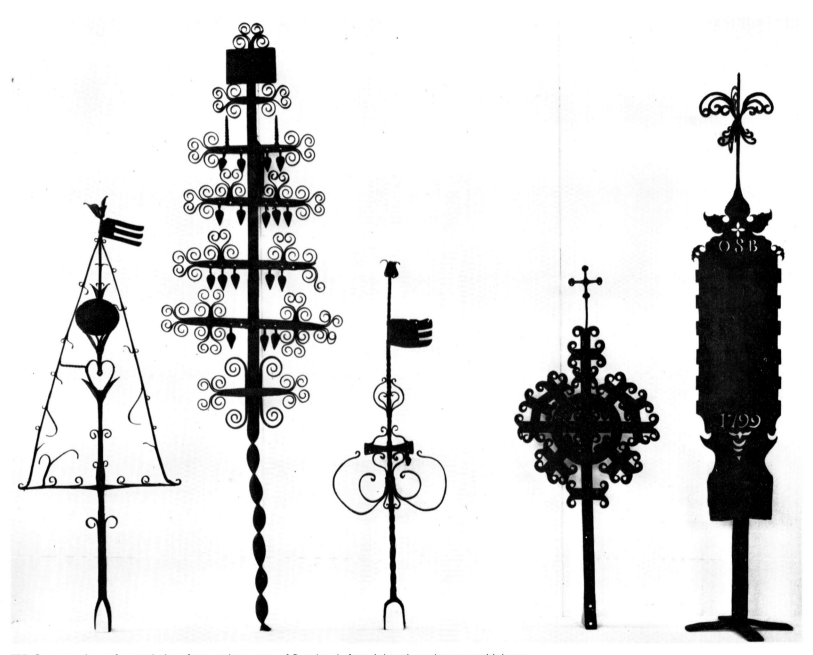

573. Grave markers of wrought iron from various parts of Sweden. Left to right: triangular cross with heart and weathervane, and cross with six transverse arms, leaf pendants, and inscription plaque, both from Ekshärad, Värmland; cross of heart-shaped bent iron topped with weathervane and a flower; cross of Celtic type; and grave marker with inscription plaque, decorative crest with finial, and inscription OSB 1799 in pierced work, all three from Östergötland. The last-mentioned type of grave marker was made by smiths at Boxholm ironworks.

of time. Nameless paupers' graves were always marked with simple wooden crosses. In the latter part of the eighteenth century and all through the nineteenth century, new forms were added. The largest collection of extant wrought-iron grave crosses is found in Ekshärad graveyard (figs. 572, 573), numbering over 200 crosses. Here an interesting local development from 1758 to 1881 can be studied. The first iron cross was wrought only three years after the production had started at the nearby Föskefors ironworks, which gave local smiths easier access to iron.

The crosses in Ekshärad graveyard are made of iron bands. Most of them are many-armed, though a few of them are triangular or of Celtic type with circle or square. The finials vary. They are made up of scrolls and volutes created by the customary splitting of the bar ends. They may also be topped with a flag, a pennant, a plaque with initials in pierced work, a bird, a crown, or some professional attribute, such as a clock on a clockmaker's grave and hammer and tongs on a smith's. The transverse arms are richly decorated with leaf pendants and volutes. On the vertical stem are affixed rectangular plaques with the names of the deceased (fig. 572). When a cross has been used for several generations, several name plaques may be found, one above the other. Some variation from village to village can be discerned. But with one single exception, these crosses have not been identified as the work of a particular master smith. The one signed cross, a ring cross, was "Made by Johan T," in all probability identical with the famous Ekshärad clockmaker Johan Tinglöf (1751–1812). A couple of other peasant smiths are known by name: Erik Jonasson and Erik Nilsson, with the professional nicknames Bössme-Erik ("Riflesmith Erik") and Lellböss ("Li'l Rifle"). Apparently they specialized in making rifles.

The grave crosses were presumably the work of rural smiths. They completely lack hallmarks and manufacturer's stamps, with the exception of a few marked with the Stjärnfors (Värmland) ironworks stamp. These stamped crosses are also distinguished by their professional craftsmanship. They are footed and

have a transverse arm with "draped" decor of Empire type.

Wrought-iron grave markers with vestigial or nonexistent transverse arms are found in northern Småland. They have a heart-shaped outline, leaf-shaped points, and a finial with forked flag (fig. 573, center). At Boxholm ironworks, grave markers were made in the shape of oblong narrow sheets with decoratively outlined pierced crests, topped with flags (fig. 573, far right). They were made at the end of the eighteenth or the beginning of the nineteenth century. Handwrought iron crosses as grave markers are found also in other European countries. The earliest documented examples were made in southern Germany in the sixteenth century. Since that time, this continental production has been primarily located in Germany, Switzerland, northern Italy, and Austria.

Candlesticks and other wrought-iron objects

Ironwork has played a prominent role in the wide range of objects associated with illumination and food preparation, as these require a fire-resistant material. There is an especially great variety of holders for various types of lights. Abundant material is preserved in museums, though it has not yet been systematically inventoried.

The great bulk of holders in everyday use in home and workshop were very simple in design. They were made to hold resinous wood sticks or torches, and rushlights or other lights dipped in resin, pitch, or tallow. They often lack decorative elements, which tends to make them difficult to date (figs. 575–78). Hanging ratchet light holders with the same construction as the notched pot trammel are of prehistoric origin. The same is true for the single or double "crusies," whale-oil lamps, in which the wick floats in the oil. Oil lamps are found especially in southwestern Sweden and on Gotland. Candlesticks for tallow and wax candles received a more decorative treatment, as these candles were luxury items to a high degree associated with the Church, the church service, and holiday celebrations in the home. Thus, it is quite clear that church preferences in the

design and function of lighting devices exerted a strong influence on secular lighting devices. And since the Church long retained antiquated object types, often of medieval origin or associated with medieval traditions, secular ornamental candlesticks were also of medieval character.

Such object types are chandeliers consisting of one or more horizontal rings with candle spikes or sockets. They are decorated with leaf pendants, cut-out crestings in stepped outline, lilies, crosses, and birds. There are also candlesticks with a bird perched on the central stem, diagonally stepped supports which are joined by a double arch and hung with leaf pendants (fig. 576). Formal elements of these medieval types are still present in the peasant ironwork of, especially, Dalarna.

The boat-shaped candelabra from Jämtland are also patterned on medieval models. They have six sockets in a row and a spike in the middle for a bigger candle. The ends are upturned like the prow of a boat and may be topped by a bird or some other decorative feature (fig. 580).

The above-mentioned types are found also in Norway. The Scandinavian types differ from continental types in that they are lavishly trimmed with leaf pendants. In Skåne and adjoining provinces there is a type of tripod candlestick, also in the medieval tradition (figs. 581–83). Candlesticks of this type are preserved in great numbers in Ingelstad district, where, it is supposed, a manufacturing center may have been located. However, no corroborative data about such a center are known. One can merely offer some observations concerning the decorative treatment of these candlesticks, on which the smiths lavished their skill and their artistic aspirations.

These candlesticks usually have a tripod base and are made of band iron. The stem supports two or three arms and terminates in a cross, a star, or some other figure. Arms, feet, as well as the stem may be twisted or embellished with line-punched flutings. The iron bands end in decorative scrolls or spirals. Arms and finials are trimmed with small, predominantly horseshoe-shaped, pendants. Because of the simplicity of their design, the candlesticks are

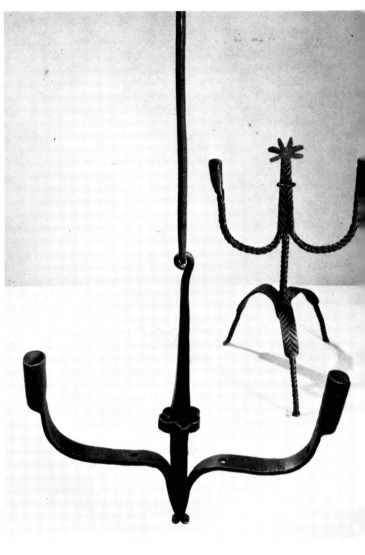

574. Household utensils of wrought iron. Grill from Gärstad, Östergötland; tripod from Möklinta, Västmanland; and three chopping knives, one of them dated 1726, from urban middle-class milieu.

575. Chandelier from Boda, Dalarna, and candlestick from Västmanland, both of wrought iron.

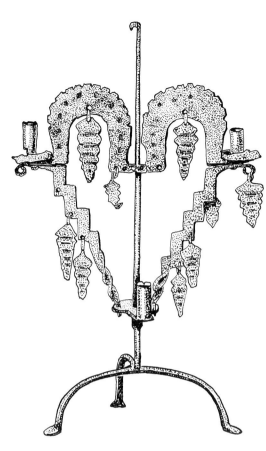

576. Candelabrum of wrought iron, Dalarna.

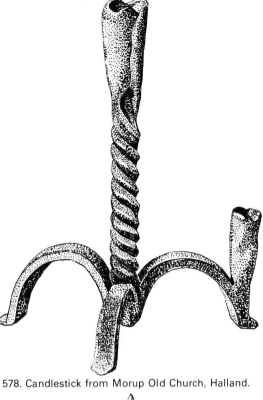

578. Candlestick from Morup Old Church, Halland.

difficult to date. But quite clearly the outstanding ironwork of both Skåne and Dalarna had its origin in the advanced metalcraft of the Middle Ages. We do know that the production in Skåne and Dalarna is of long standing, because a number of these candlesticks in the Nordiska Museet show dates between 1700 and 1800.

The production and usage of the majority of other household iron utensils remain to be investigated. These utensils include roasting spits and skewers, pot hooks, tripods, trammels, hearth cranes, log tongs, pokers, and so forth (fig. 574). Also to be investigated is building hardware in the form of mounts, locks, weathervanes, and gable ornaments, much of which is still in place on secular buildings and churches. These types of hardware offered an opportunity for formal display, which strongly stimulated the smiths' decorative bent. Technically and aesthetically, this type of decoration is of a high standing especially in Dalarna, Hälsingland, Härjedalen, and Jämtland.

In Dalarna some investigations of local metalcraft have been carried out. They point up the importance of a good iron supply combined with a large-scale production of utilitarian ironwork for sale as a growing ground for more aesthetically conscious ironwork. Since prehistoric times Dalarna has been iron country. Bog iron extraction was a true peasant craft and gave the original impetus to peasant ironwork. When this foundation gave way in the middle of the eighteenth century, the iron had to be bought from the ironworks in Bergslagen. Home blacksmithing did continue, but gradually became less profitable and eventually ceased when industrial production forced the prices down, and other, more profitable, sources of income were readily available. The parishes of Älvdalen, Lima, Transtrand, and Hedemora in Dalarna were among the most productive. Around the middle of the eighteenth century, half of the local peasants practiced scythe making as a sideline (fig. 570). A large part of the scythes went to Norway, but most of them were distributed via itinerant peddlers and markets to different parts of Sweden. Other products were nails, cattle bells, dampers, and scissors.

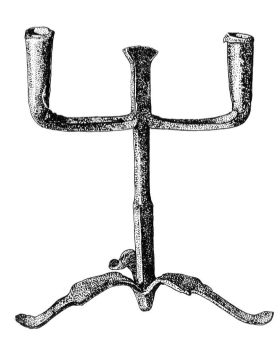

577. Candlestick from Lerdal, Dalsland.

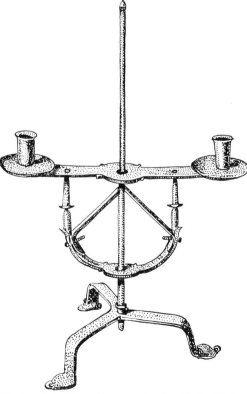

579. Candleholder with central spike. Hede, Härjedalen.

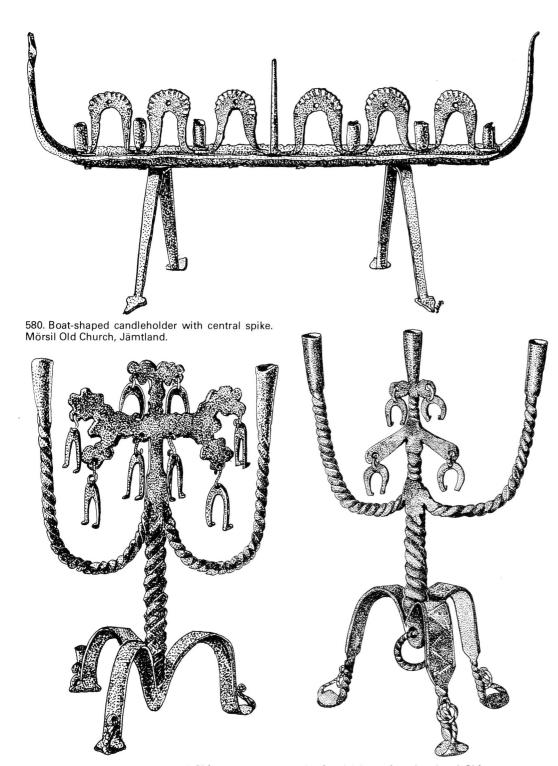

580. Boat-shaped candleholder with central spike.
Mörsil Old Church, Jämtland.

582. Candleholder with central spike. Ingelstad,
Skåne.

581. Candelabrum from Ingelstad, Skåne.

583. Candelabrum from Ingelstad, Skåne.

584. Weathervane of wrought iron, made by Johan Dufva, Forsqvarn. Ösmo, Södermanland, 1803.

585. Door hardware. Straps, strap hinges, and lock of wrought iron. Punched inscription D/1803 (not visible in picture). Dalarna.

Metalwork

In a special investigation "Ett ålderdomligt låssmide i Dalarna och dess härkomst" ("Antiquated Dalarna locksmithing and its origins"), Sigurd Erixon has established that the parish of Lima was the home of many master smiths. The different families developed specialties, passed on from generation to generation. Thus, the making of mounts and locks was localized to Risättra village, where it can be traced from the seventeenth century until the mid-nineteenth century. The products were sold by the peasant craftsmen themselves on sales tours to Västmanland, Dalarna, Härjedalen, Hälsingland, Jämtland, and Ångermanland. No putting-out system ever existed here. Öje village in Malung was especially known for its locks for chests and cupboards. Because ironworking in northern and western Dalarna originated and grew out of prehistoric bog iron processing, the blacksmithing technique in this area retained its ancient character. The distinctive decorative elements were still those of prehistoric and medieval blacksmithing: split bar ends which are bent and scrolled, chased bosses, and decoratively used nails and rivets. Sigurd Erixon writes about the smithing of locks and mounts:

No other ornamental ironwork is as evenly distributed and represents such unbroken traditions through the centuries [as the making of mounts and locks]. This is especially true in Dalarna. Aside from church buildings, nowhere in modern times and original milieus can one hope to find so many at once antiquated and diverse forms, whether of construction or of design.

Appendix   Source of illustrations

Unless otherwise noted, the objects shown in the photographs are all part of the collections of Nordiska Museet. The photographs were taken by the museum's staff photographers, Märta Claréus, Olof Ekberg, Åke Grundström, Lennart af Peterséns, Åke Wintzell and Ulla Wåger. Some of the drawings were made by the museum's draftsmen, M. Berkow, L. Santesson, and J. Cirulis.

In addition, photos showing various milieus and work processes were taken in the field by other museum staff members.

All illustrations are available in the museum's archives.

The photos listed below were taken by other photographers, or are the property of other organizations or private persons. Numbers refer to the figure number in this text.

Märta Brodén, Gävle: 11, 12, 168
Per Flordal, Hälsingmo: 169
Per Jonze: 59
Karl Lärka: 480
Kungl. Myntkabinettet: 166
Malmöhus läns hemslöjdsförening, Malmö: 357, 361, 428
Nationalmuseet, Köpenhamn: 155
Nationalmuseum, Stockholm: 66
Svenska Hemslöjdsföreningarnas Riksförbunds arkiv: 1, 9, 29, 30, 33, 114
Svenska Porträttarkivet: 423

The following sources have graciously permitted the reproduction of the pictures indicated. The number(s) following the source corresponds to the figure number in this text.

Berlingske Haandarbeidsbog, vols. I–II: 396, 397, 398
Cyrus, U. *Handbok i vävning*: 220, 248
Erixon, S. *Svensk byggnadskultur*: 44, 46, 48, 49, 50, 53, 57, 63
Erixon, S. *Atlas över svensk folkkultur* I: 141
Erixon, S. *Svenska kulturgränser och kulturprovinser*: 132, 134, 152
Fataburen 19: 386
Folkliv 1938: 179
Folkliv 1939: 176
Granlund, J. *Träkärl i svepteknik*: 528, 529
Hald, M. *Brikvævning*: 291
Hoffmann, M. *The Warp-weighted Loom*: 174, 175
Ingers, G. *Flamskvävnad*: 220

Johansson, S. *Handledning i knyppling*: 420
Levander, L. *Övre Dalarnas bondekultur: Förvärvsarbete*: 519, 528
Salvén, E. *Bonaden från Skog*: 232
Stora Handarbetsboken: 398, 399, 409
Svenska Turistföreningens årsskrift 1948: 38, 42, 49, 68
Skansens hus och gårdar: 45, 47, 52, 54, 74
Svenskt husmoderslexikon: 549
Tiotusen år i Sverige: 212
Walterstorff, E. v. *Svenska vävnadstekniker och mönstertyper*: 130, 132, 137, 205, 214, 234, 240, 260, 263, 266, 272, 275

Footnotes

Handcraft as a form of production

[1] *Landshövdingarnas femårsberättelser,* the Governors' Five-Year Reports. Every five years since 1755, the governor of each administrative district, *län* (county), has submitted a report on his district, containing, among other things, certain vital statistics about its population.

[2] Names of provinces have not been translated. The reader's attention is called to the map of Sweden which appears on p. 8 and which contains the place names mentioned in the text.

[3] Note the existence in Swedish of two designations for the English "journeyman": *gesäll,* the master's servingman and part of the guild hierarchy, and *gärningsman,* an unguilded craftsman or itinerant artisan. The origin of journeyman and *gärningsman* is the French journée and Swedish [*dags*] *gärning,* respectively, both meaning "a day's work (labor)."

[4] According to Heckscher's *An Economic History of Sweden* (Cambridge, 1963), the Age of Empire extended from 1600 to 1720, the Age of Freedom from 1720 to 1771. The Age of Empire was a period marked by warfare and power politics, the Age of Freedom by peace and growing prosperity.

[5] Gustav Vasa, the founder of the Vasa dynasty, put an end to the Kalmar Union and freed Sweden from Danish rule in 1523. For half a century after the death of Gustav (1560), his three sons, Erik XIV, Johan III, and Karl IX, ruled Sweden successively, followed by Karl's son, Gustav II Adolf, and the latter's daughter, Kristina. Thus the Vasa era can be said to extend from the accession of Gustav in 1523 to the abdication of Kristina in 1654. (See also the list of kings and regents of Sweden in the Appendix.)

[6] Such a market is the Disting Fair in Uppsala, named after the *disablot,* sacrifices at Old Uppsala in pagan times, held every year at the first full moon after Epiphany. Later it was moved to the first week of February and made respectable by being tied in with the Christian holiday of Candlemas. The tradition is perpetuated in an annual fur market at the beginning of the year.

[7] *Härad* (hundred) was the unit in a now obsolete legislative administrative division of the country from Dalarna south, the corresponding unit north of Dalarna being *tingslag.* There were approximately fifty *härad.* Though the *härad* division no longer exists, much of the research material at Nordiska Museet was collected while the *härad* labels were still in use. Perhaps the closest modern equivalent term is "district."

[8] Farms were frequently divided equally among the heirs, resulting in a larger number of smaller farms. Furthermore, the acreage of the farms would be likewise divided, each plot subdivided into smaller plots. As a result, each heir might inherit a large number of small plots in as many different locations.

[9] Heckscher (trans. Göran Ohlin), pp. 189–90.

[10] The "Seven Hundreds" is the collective name for seven districts in Älvsborg county in western Sweden, of especial importance for textile production. (See map of Sweden, p. 8.)

[11] This manual was published in 1828 by J. E. Ekenmark who, with his family, was instrumental in adapting damask patterns for a simpler loom.

Handcraft: Milieu and function

[1] As is pointed out by Nils Keyland and Edward Adams-Ray in *Guide to Skansen* (Stockholm, 1923), the term "fire-house" is in English usage often associated with the central room, the "hall," of the larger dwelling house. The translation of *eldhus* with "fire-house" is nevertheless justifiable, as the two words are analogous (pp. 13–14).

[2] The Swedish word *stuga,* appearing alone or in combinations, is difficult to translate. Originally, it referred to the single-room dwelling house, the fire-house. The terms *parstuga* and *enkelstuga* mean, simply, "a pair of *stugor*" and "single *stuga.*" *Förstuga* is a small room "before" the stuga proper, i.e., a vestibule or entry. However, *stuga* in contemporary usage has become a casual term for either *parstuga* or *enkelstuga,* in other words, synonymous with a fairly small house or cottage, not necessarily limited to one room.

The outstanding characteristic of the Swedish *parstuga* is the joining of two parts with different functions. The type survives in the "parlor" tradition—the seldom-used parlor having developed out of the storage part. The term "two-room house" ("two-room cottage") is not quite adequate in describing the *parstuga,* as it is applicable also to certain American types, e.g. the North Carolina double cabin of the central-passage type with a so-called Dog Run or Possum Trot between the two parts. The latter type features two rooms of equal status and similar function, both equipped with a fireplace on the gable end.

[3] Finns have emigrated to Sweden at various times, settling in so-called *finnmarker* (Finn areas) throughout northern Sweden.

[4] "Tumbler" is here taken in its original sense, i.e., a small cup with rounded bottom which tumbles when it is put down. In this sense, it is a direct equivalent to the Swedish *tumlare.*

[5] The Swedish *öl* denotes various types of malt liquor, the lighter, more bitter beer, as well as the stronger, darker ale. Swedish households would generally drink beer, whereas ale was served only on special occasions, e.g., on holidays.

[6] Though often coinciding or overlapping, names of epochs should not be confused with names of period styles. Thus, Gustavian furniture—so named after the late-eighteenth-century King Gustav III—need not have been made during his reign. In peasant milieu, especially, there has always been considerable selectivity and retardation involved in the acceptance of period styles. A Gustavian chair was manufactured in Dalarna during most of the nineteenth century. This chair type is still made in Sweden.

[7] Rya (rug) is a type of ruglike covering with long pile, although it is today commonly used also to denote the technique associated with rya, i.e., knotted pile weave. The word is throughout this work used in its original sense.

[8] The *lysning* (reading of the banns) takes place on three consecutive Sundays before the wedding. Traditionally, gifts are given at a reception following the *lysning* on one of the three Sundays.

[9] Wooden rails suspended from the rafters. Richly carved, they served symbolic and decorative as well as practical purposes as candle holders or towel bars (see figs. 494 and 495).

[10] *Bonad* was originally a term denoting any textile for interior decoration; nowadays, it is most commonly applied to pictorial representations—painted, woven, or embroidered—intended as decorative wall hangings.

[11] *Dukagång* (swivel weave) a weave brocaded on the counted thread. Provincial variation of discontinuous, or laid-in, brocade, characterized by a pattern striped in the direction of the warp. The brocade filling yarn floats over the ground cloth, the same warp threads tying down all the brocade picks (see further on p. 169).

[12] *Upphämta*—weft-patterned tabby, type "upphämta"; continuous-filling brocade with the pattern weft laid in or shuttled in.

[13] *Rölakan*—a type of laid-in tapestry, with predominantly geometric patterns.

[14] *Krabbasnår*—brocaded tabby, type "krabbasnår"; inlay technique with pattern diagonal in character (see fig. 234).

The products of handcraft

[1] In the Middle Ages, when the production of fine, professionally woven and finished woolen fabrics started, the word cloth—generally denoting "fabric" or "piece of woven or felted stuff"—was also used in a more restricted sense to designate just such fine woolens. Today, this type of fabric is known as broadcloth, an internationally accepted term endorsed by CIETA—the Centre International d'Etudes des Textiles Anciens (Lyons)—though less familiar in the United States than in Canada and Britain. Nevertheless, whenever necessary in this work for the sake of precision, cloth in the sense of fine, finished woolen cloth is referred to as either "fine woolen cloth" or "broadcloth." Wadmal, on the other hand, is the coarser, home-made woolen fabric for everyday use.

There is no corresponding problem of precise terminology in Swedish. The word *kläde*—originally meaning both "fabric" and "professionally finished woolen"—is today used only in the latter, restricted sense, except in a few composite words, e.g. *förkläde* (apron). "Piece of material," on the other hand, is *tygstycke* or *duk*; "fabric" is *tyg.*

[2] The *bussarong* was a bloused shirt with a

round, stand-up collar, somewhat resembling a cossack shirt. It was originally a Navy work blouse, corresponding to the English middy blouse, though without a sailor's collar. Because of its connection with the Navy, it has appeared as a work blouse especially in coastal areas.

[3] *Broderi,* the Swedish word for embroidery, came into the Swedish language from the French in the eighteenth century.

[4] The illustrations will help an English-speaking audience to identify the stitches mentioned in the text. The translator's main references for the English terminology of embroidery stitches are Mary Thomas, *A Dictionary of Embroidery Stitches* (New York, 1935), and Grete Petersen and Elsie Svennås, *Handbook of Stitches* (New York, 1970).

[5] Like Henry VIII of England, his contemporary, Gustav Vasa broke with the Catholic Church and established a Protestant Church. Part of the Swedish Reformation was the dissolution of convents and monasteries.

[6] In Swedish there is a clear distinction between two types of samplers, *märkduk* (monograming cloth) and *mönsterduk* (pattern cloth), the former emphasizing lettering in needlework, the latter various embroidery techniques and pattern motifs. In American usage, no such distinction is generally made. However, whenever a distinction is required in this text, the former will be referred to as a lettering sampler, the latter as a pattern sampler.

[7] The type was popular also in the United States around the same time—found in, for example, splendid bed curtains and canopies—and is today commonly known as crewel work.

[8] Technically, Järvsö work—named after another place in Hälsingland—is identical to Delsbo work. However, Järvsö work has a more characteristic overall pattern, composed of tassel-like shapes.

[9] Most treatments make no distinction between the openwork resulting from the withdrawal of threads in two directions and that based on the cutting away of fabric, both being generally referred to as cut openwork. Here the two techniques are referred to as, respectively, two-directional drawn-thread work and cut openwork. Note also the general inclusion, under the heading "Openwork," of drawn-fabric work, in which no threads are withdrawn from the fabric, but openwork patterns are created by pulling warp and weft threads together in groups with the stitching thread.

[10] While awaiting trial for alleged conspiracy against Erik XIV, five members of the Swedish aristocracy were murdered. They were killed either by the unbalanced King himself, or by his yeomen. Three of the victims were Stures: Svante and his two sons, Nils and Erik.

[11] *Språngsparrlakan,* dialectal, from *laka,* [to] cover, and *sparre,* rafter—". . . so called on account of the use for which they were originally intended, to cover the rafters in the 'sparrastuga' or ceilingless house . . ." (Von Walterstorff, *Swedish Textiles,* p. 76).

[12] I have preferred to use the term *sprang* throughout. The alternative "sprangwork" is probably no more familiar to an American reader, and the term "meshwork," though admirably defined in Verla Birrell, *The Textile Arts* (New York, 1959), has too general and imprecise connotations. Birrell's definition is wide enough to include both meshwork made with bobbins—i.e., a sort of bobbin lace—and that made in a frame, i.e., *sprang.* The precise term would therefore be "meshwork on frame," or "knotless netting on frame," both of which are rather clumsy.

[13] The literal translation of *pinnbandsflätning* is "braiding of bands with shed sticks." The dialectal use of the word *flätning* thus makes no distinction between meshwork and braiding proper. However, *pinnbandsflätning* is meshwork, or *sprang.* Other bands in Swedish folk textile art are true braids, i.e., the "warp" ends pass in a diagonal direction until they reach a border, where they reverse direction.

[14] The Swedish word for tatting, *frivoliteter,* is derived from the French *frivolité.* The origin of the English term is obscure.

[15] Certain British sources use "linen or cloth stitch" and "whole stitch" synonymously—i.e., to designate crossing-twisting-crossing. To avoid any confusion with the double half-stitch, the term "linen stitch" or "cloth stitch" is here reserved for the latter (see fig. 420).

[16] The term *passement* is French. It was used in the Swedish language in the sense of early lace, which further emphasizes the connection between lace and braidwork, from which lace making borrowed techniques, perhaps even patterns.

[17] Funerary cloths are long, sturdy towels, about one foot wide and ten feet long, which were used at funerals to carry the coffin and lower it into the grave.

[18] In English-speaking sources this technique is also given a variety of names, e.g., the generic "knotless netting," "sewing," "circular looping," "coiling," "cycloid coiling," and "interlaced hitch weave." The closest, most specific term in English might be something like "needle-bound coiling," defining tool, process, and the appearance of the product. However, as I do not wish to settle on a fabricated term, I am instead using the more general "needle looping" (Birrell). This has the advantage that it describes the tool, and, to a certain extent, the technique employed. But whereas the Swedish term emphasizes the needle's work of binding together the fabric elements, the English one emphasizes the shape of those elements.

[19] The term "chip carving" generally denotes all carving in which triangular chips of wood are removed, i.e., both the double triangle cut—chip carving proper—and the single triangle cut (*uddsnitt*). To maintain the distinction existing in the Swedish, the two types will be referred to as double-triangle-cut chip carving and single-triangle-cut chip carving, respectively.

[20] This is the type which was brought to America and became one of the most popular and characteristic items of Shaker manufacture in the nineteenth century.

[21] Though obviously related to molded wood containers, these containers of birch bark should, strictly speaking, not be called "molded" as the bark is naturally flexed and need not be forced into the desired curving shape.

[22] Technically, both types may be considered weaves. Thus, for example, the coiled basketry of the Navajo Indians is usually referred to as basket weaving. However, as the upright weaving closely resembles weaving on a loom, the term basket weaving has here been reserved for upright basketwork. Coiled weaves are referred to as coiled basketwork.

Bibliography

What is handcraft?

Forssell, N. *Borås stads historia.* 2 vols. Borås, 1952–53.

Heckscher, E. F. *Sveriges ekonomiska historia från Gustav Vasa.* Stockholm, 1935–49.

Heckscher, E. F. *Svenskt arbete och liv: Från medeltiden till nutiden.* Stockholm, 1941.

Hemslöjdskommitténs betänkande. Delivered 10 December, 1917. Stockholm, 1918.

Ingers, G. *Gästgivaredöttrarna i Everlöv: Slöjd och bohag i en bondesläkt under 200 år.* Kristianstad, 1974.

Nelson, H. *Studier över svenskt näringsliv, säsongarbete och befolkningsrörelser under 1800- och 1900-talen.* Kungliga Humanistiska Vetenskapssamfundets skrifter, no. 63. Lund, 1963.

Nyström, P. *Stadsindustriens arbetare före 1800-talet.* Den svenska arbetarklassens historia. Stockholm, 1955.

Rosander, G. *Herrarbete: Dalfolkets säsongvisa arbetsvandringar i jämförande belysning.* Landsmåls- och folkminnesarkivets i Uppsala skrifter, no. B: 13. Uppsala, 1967.

Sterner, B. "Hemindustribygden i Kinds och Marks härader: Näringsgeografiska studier i en del av Sveriges viktigaste hemindustribygd." *Svensk geografisk årsbok* 1927.

Sterner, M. *Hemslöjd i Sverige. Från Skåne till Norrbotten.* Stockholm, 1933.

Stålberg, H. *Smålands skogs- och träförädlingsindustrier: En näringsgeografisk studie.* Lund, 1947.

Sveriges Hantverk. Edited by Nils Niléhn. Malmö, 1956.

Sveriges officiella statistik (Sweden's official statistics). *Textil- och beklädnadsindustrien: Specialundersökning av Kommerskollegium.* Stockholm, 1914.

Söderberg, T. *Hantverkarna i brytningstid 1820–1870.* Stockholm, 1955.

Söderlund, E. *Stockholms hantverkarklass 1720–1772: Sociala och ekonomiska förhållanden.* Stockholm, 1943.

Söderlund, E. *Hantverkarna.* Vol. 2, *Stormaktstiden, frihetstiden och gustavianska tiden.* Den svenska arbetarklassens historia. Stockholm, 1949.

Troels-Lund, F. *Dagligt liv i Norden.* Copenhagen, 1879 1901.

Utterström, G. *Jordbrukets arbetare: Levnadsvillkor och arbetsliv på landsbygden från frihetstiden till mitten av 1800-talet.* Den svenska arbetarklassens historia. Stockholm, 1957.

Vallin, I. "Västgötaknallar och västgötatyger: Något om innehållet i knallarnas påsar." *Fataburen* 1935.

Settlement and dwelling. Furniture and household articles. Handcraft and cultural milieu

Bengtsson, B. *Skottsbergska gården i Karlshamn: En köpmansgård från 1700-talet.* Nordiska Museets Handlingar, no. 24. Stockholm, 1946.

Berg, G., and Svensson, S. *Svensk bondekultur.* Stockholm, 1934.

Beskow, H. *Bruksherrgårdar i Gästrikland.* Nordiska Museets Handlingar, no. 47. Stockholm, 1954.

Erixon, S. *Atlas över svensk folkkultur.* Vol. 1, *Materiell och social kultur.* Uddevalla, 1957.

Erixon, S. *Folklig möbelkultur i svenska bygder.* Stockholm, 1938.

Erixon, S. *Svensk byggnadskultur.* Stockholm, 1947.

Erixon, S. *Svenskt folkliv.* Stockholm, 1938.

Erixon, S. *Svenska kulturgränser och kulturprovinser.* Stockholm, 1945.

Grenander-Nyberg, G. "Hemtextilier under 1800-talet." *Högsbyboken.* Västervik, 1969.

Hazelius Berg, G. *Gardiner och gardinuppsättningar: En kulturhistorisk studie.* Stockholm, 1962.

Hazelius Berg, G. "Ett Kägleholmsinventarium från 1554." *Från bergslag och bondebygd* 1953.

Hedlund, G. "Sängarnas utstyrsel i Ovansjö under gången tid." *Från Gästrikebygder* 1926.

Hedlund, G. *Dräkt och kvinnlig slöjd i Ovansjö socken 1750–1850.* Storvik, 1951.

Hedlund, M. "Bondehandel i Jämtland under 1800-talet." *Folkliv* 1941.

Hedlund, M. "Jämtlandshandeln och den jämtska folkkulturen." *Folkliv* 1946.

Hofrén, M. *Herrgårdar och boställen.* Nordiska Museets Handlingar, no. 6. Stockholm, 1937.

Hofrén, M. *Pataholm: Kulturhistoriska notiser kring Smålandskustens gamla köpingsväsende.* Nordiska Museets Handlingar, no. 25. Stockholm, 1946.

Kjellberg, S. T. "Bordtäcke." *Kulturen* 1939.

Nylén, A.-M. "Hemslöjd och kulturmiljö." *Annual report for 1959 of Föreningen för Svensk Hemslöjd.* Stockholm, 1960.

Nylén, A.-M. "'Herrgårn' och bygden." *Fataburen* 1954.

Nylén, A.-M. "Textilslöjd." *Rättvik,* vol. 3. Västerås, 1959.

Nylén, A.-M. "Tradition och nutid." *Fataburen* 1961.

Rentzhog, S. *Stad i trä: Panelarkitekturen — ett skede i den svenska småstadens byggnadshistoria.* Nordiska Museets Handlingar, no. 67. Lund, 1967.

Schoultz, G. v. "Till finrummets historia." *Fataburen* 1950.

Skansens hus och gårdar. Stockholm, 1953.

Stavenow, E. *Siden, sammet, läder, lärft: Klädsel på gamla stolar.* Stockholm, 1961.

Strömberg, E. "Historiskt om sänglinnet." *Textilbranschen* 1959.

Walterstorff, E. v. "Bondens bädd." *Svenska kulturbilder,* vol. 5. Stockholm, 1931.

Walterstorff, E. v. "Stugans dragning." *Svenska kulturbilder,* vol. 4. Stockholm, 1931.

The supply of textile raw materials

Bertel, G. "Från djurhud till modern lädervara." *Vår rika värld,* vol. 2. Stockholm, 1949.

Brotherus, H. "Bomull—en världsmakt." *Vår rika värld,* vol. 2. Stockholm, 1949.

Geijer, A. "Textilier och arkeologi." *Svensk naturvetenskap* 1962.

Granlund, J. "Lindbast och träbast: En studie i material och teknik." *Folkliv* 1944.

Hald, M. "The nettle as a culture plant." *Folkliv* 1942.

Hedlund, G. *Dräkt och kvinnlig slöjd i Ovansjö socken 1750–1850.* Storvik, 1951.

Henschen Ingvar, I. "Jämväl i Norden.'" *Fataburen* 1958.

Johansson, S. "Bohuslänsk ullberedning i äldre och nuvarande tid." *Fataburen* 1928.

Keyland, N. "Sentrådsspinning, tenndragning och bältsmyckegjutning hos lapparna i norra Jämtland." *Fataburen* 1920.

Kjellberg, S. T. *Ull och ylle: Bidrag till den svenska yllemanufakturens historia.* Lund, 1943.

Lundmark, E. *En hundraårig bomullsindustri:*

Norrköpings Bomullsväfveri AB och dess anläggningar i Kullen och Gryt 1852–1952. Stockholm, 1952.

Modeer, I. "Öländskt repslageri." *Fataburen* 1928.

Murberg, J. "Anmärkning om kläden och ylletyg, som mäst nyttjades i Sverige i K. Gustaf I:s tid." *Vitterhets-, historie- och antikvitetsakademiens handlingar,* vol. 3. Stockholm, 1793.

Rodenstam, S. "Om lin och nässlor som spånadsämnen." *Jämten* 1917.

Sandklef, S. *Lin och linne.* K. Gustav Adolfs Akademiens Småskrifter, no. 2. Stockholm, 1945.

Sifversson, A.-B. "Om bondkvarter, hälsingegårdar och dalkarlshärbärge på Norrmalm, Stockholm." *Folkliv* 1945.

Sjöberg, N. "Konung Gustaf I:s fatbur på Gripsholms slott." *Fataburen* 1907.

Svensson, S. "Ur beklädnadshandelns historia." *Detaljhandelns bok: Beklädnad.* Stockholm, 1939.

Åström, I. "Några linberedningsredskap." *Folkliv* 1952.

Weaving implements. Fabrics

Axelson, A., and Trotzig, L. *Band.* Västerås, 1958.

Björkman, R. *Stenbergska väfveriet: Ett blad ur Jönköpings historia.* Stockholm, 1908.

Broholm, H. C. *Bronzealderens dragt.* Copenhagen, 1961.

Böttiger, J. *Svenska statens samling af väfda tapeter: Historik och beskrifvande förteckning.* Stockholm, 1895.

Cederblom, G. "Våra äldsta spånadsredskap och deras ättlingar." *Fataburen* 1909.

Cronlund, E. "Upplands ryor." *Rig* 1932.

Danielson, S. "Nordiska vävnader i halvflossa." Mimeographed. Lund: Institutionen för folklivsforskning, University of Lund, 1964.

Engelstad, H. *Norske ryer. Teknikk, form og bruk.* Fortids kunst i norske bygder, no. 2: 1. Oslo, 1942.

Erixon, S. "Redskapsstudier från Gustav Adolfsutställningen." *Fataburen* 1933.

Fischer, E. *Flamskvävnader i Skåne.* Nordiska Museets Handlingar, no. 59. Malmö, 1962.

Fischer, E. *Linvävarämbetet i Malmö och det skånska linneväveriet.* Nordiska Museets Handlingar, no. 52. Malmö, 1959.

Fischer, E., and Ingers, G. *Flamskvävnad.* Malmö, 1961.

Friberg, H. "Småländska prästgårdsvävnader." *Fataburen* 1931.

Geijer, A. "En medeltida altarduk i dukagångsvävnad." *Kulturen* 1943.

Geijer, A. "Mönster och metervara." *Textil,* vol. 2. Hantverkets bok. Stockholm, 1940.

Geijer, A. "Det textila arbetet i Norden under forntid och medeltid." *Nordisk kultur,* vol. 15 A. Copenhagen, 1953.

Geijer, A. "Textila tekniker och termer." *Svenska museer* 1936, no. 1.

Geijer, A. *Ur textilkonstens historia.* Lund, 1972.

Grenander-Nyberg, G. *Hushållningssällskapet och den textila slöjden i Kalmar län för hundra år sedan.* Kalmar läns fornminnesförenings meddelanden: Årsbok för kulturhistoria och hembygdsvård, no. 51. Kalmar, 1963.

Grenander-Nyberg, G. *Lanthemmens vävstolar: Studier av äldre redskap för husbehovsvävning.* Nordiska Museets Handlingar, no. 84. Stockholm, 1974.

Hald, M. *Skrydstrupfundet: En sønderjydsk Kvindegrav fra ældre Bronzealder.* Nordiske Fortidsminder, vol. 3, part 2. Copenhagen, 1939.

Hald, M. "Olddanske Tekstiler: Fund fra Aarene 1947–1955." *Aarbøger for nordisk Oldkyndighed og Historie* 1955.

Hald, M. *Olddanske Tekstiler: Komparative tekstil- og dragthistoriske Studier paa Grundlag af Mosefund og Gravfund fra Jernalderen.* Nordiske Fortidsminder, vol. 5. Copenhagen, 1950.

Henschen Ingvar, I. "Dukagångsdrätten i Skåne." *Kulturen* 1936.

Henschen Ingvar, I. *Svenska vävnader.* Stockholm, 1949.

Henschen Ingvar, I. "Den textila hemslöjden." *En bok om Skåne.* Lund, 1936.

Hoffmann, M. *En gruppe vevstoler på Vestlandet: Noen synspunkter i diskusjonen om billedvev i Norge.* Oslo, 1958.

Hoffmann, M. *The Warp-weighted Loom: Studies in the history and technology of an ancient implement.* Oslo, 1964.

Johansson, S. "Kvinnlig slöjd i Torsby, Lycke och Harestads socknar i Bohuslän." *Fataburen* 1927.

Lithberg, N. *Gotländsk kvinnlig husflit i äldre tider.* Visby, 1924.

Lindblom, A. "Från Bysans lejon till Skånes varulv." *Fataburen* 1932.

Nylén, A.-M. *Folkligt dräktskick i V. Vingåker och Österåker: Material och tillverkning.* Nordiska Museets Handlingar, no. 27. Stockholm, 1947.

Odstedt, E. "Namngivningen och dess principer i dalska textilier." *Rig* 1942.

Odstedt, E. "Vepa, vässel och åkläde, några textiltermer." *Dalarnas hembygdsbok* 1942.

Post, L. v.; Walterstorff, E. v.; and Lindqvist, S. *Bronsåldersmanteln från Gerumsberget i Västergötland.* Stockholm, 1925.

Pylkkänen, R. *The Use and Traditions of Medieval Rugs and Coverlets in Finland.* Helsinki, 1974.

Påhlman, A.-G. "Gammalt—nytt: Vävning med treskaftshästar." *Hemslöjden* 1967.

Rodenstam, S. "Hälsinglands textila hemslöjd." *Svenska Slöjdföreningens tidskrift* 1930.

Salvén, E. *Bonaden från Skog: Undersökning av en nordisk bildvävnad från tidig medeltid.* Stockholm, 1923.

Sirelius, U. T. *Finlands ryor: Textilhistorisk undersökning.* Helsinki, 1934.

Strömberg, E. "Folkliga textilier i Norden med förhistoriska eller medeltida traditioner." *Nordisk kultur,* vol. 15 A. Copenhagen, 1953.

Strömberg, E. "Småländska vävnader och textilhantverk." *En bok om Småland.* Stockholm, 1943.

Strömberg, E. *Textil slöjd: Gruddbo på Sollerön.* Nordiska Museets Handlingar, no. 9. Stockholm, 1938.

Strömberg, E. "Textilt hemarbete i Västerbotten." *Västerbotten* 1936.

Strömberg, E.; Geijer, A.; Hald, M.; and Hoffmann, M., eds. *Nordisk textilteknisk terminologi: Förindustriell vävnadsproduktion.* 2d rev. ed. Oslo, 1974.

Sylwan, V. *Dubbelvävnader.* Medeltida vävnader och broderier i Sverige, edited by A. Branting and A. Lindblom, vol. 1. Stockholm, 1928.

Sylwan, V. *Den skånska dukagångsdrätten.* Göteborgs K. Vetenskaps- och Vitterhetssamhälles handlingar, F6: Series A, vol. 4:7. Göteborg, 1954.

Sylwan, V. *Svenska ryor. Västsvenska textilier—vägledning.* Guide to the Jubilee Exhibition in Gothenburg, 1923.

Bibliography

Sylwan, V. *Svenska ryor.* Stockholm, 1934.

Thordeman, B. "Skogstapetens datering." *Fornvännen* 1948.

Thorman, E. *Duktyg från Flors damastmanufaktur för drottning Sofia Magdalena.* Röhsska konstslöjdmuseets årstryck. Göteborg, 1939.

Thorman, E. *Duktyg från Vadstena.* Stockholm, 1939.

Thorman, E. "Mäster Halfvard Gäfverbergs Ylle- och Linne-Fabrique i Gefle åren 1748–1781." *Från Gästrikland* 1934.

Utterström, G. *Jordbrukets arbetare: Levnadsvillkor och arbetsliv på landsbygden från frihetstiden till mitten av 1800-talet.* Den svenska arbetarklassens historia. Stockholm, 1957.

Vallin, I. "Allmogetextilier på Dal." *Hembygden* 1934.

Walterstorff, E. v. "En bänkdyna i röllakan." *Fataburen* 1930.

Walterstorff, E. v. "Kypertnamn." *Rig* 1942.

Walterstorff, E. v. "Röllakan från Jämtland." *Rig* 1937.

Walterstorff, E. v. *Skaraborgs läns folkliga textilkonst.* Stockholm, 1933.

Walterstorff, E. v. *Svenska vävnadstekniker och mönstertyper: Kulturgeografisk undersökning.* Nordiska Museets Handlingar, no. 11. Stockholm, 1940.

Walterstorff, E. v. *Textilt bildverk.* Stockholm, 1925.

Walterstorff, E. v. "En vävstol och en varpa." *Fataburen* 1928.

Zickermann, L. *Rölakan.* Sveriges folkliga textilkonst: Föreningens för Svensk Hemslöjd samlingsverk över svenska allmogetextilier, vol. 1. Stockholm, 1937.

Band weaving

Axelsson, A., and Trotzig, L. *Band.* Västerås, 1958.

Collin, M. "Gammalskånska band." 2 parts. *Fataburen* 1915.

Hald, M. *Brikvævning.* Copenhagen, 1932.

Hald, M. *Baand og snore.* Copenhagen, 1942.

Hoffmann, M., and Trætteberg, R. "Teglefunnet." (Norwegian.) *Stavanger Museum Årbok* 1959.

Laquist, B. "Iakttagelser rörande de svenska lapparnas bandvävning." *Norrbotten* 1946.

Nylén, A.-M. "Bandvävnad och flätning," from "Textilslöjd." *Rättvik,* vol. 3. Västerås, 1959.

Sylwan, V. "Brickbandet som kulturobjekt." *Fornvännen* 1926.

Needlework and embroidery

Blomquist, K. (Landergren-). "Märkdukar." *Kulturen* 1962.

Blomquist, K. (Landergren-). "Märkdukarnas alfabet." *Kulturen* 1962.

Branting, A., and Lindblom, A. *Medeltida vävnader och broderier i Sverige.* Stockholm, 1928–29.

Brodén, M. *Delsbosöm: Långsöm och tofssöm från Delsbo.* Stockholm, 1974.

Collin, M. "Yllebroderier i Skåneslöjden." *Fataburen* 1923.

Dominicus, E. *Gamla Hallandssöms- och korsstygnsmönster.* Halmstad, 1927.

Fischer, E. *Svensk broderikonst: Ankar Broderibok nr 2 med mönsterblad.* Stockholm, 1952.

Franzén, A.-M. "Broderade agedyner." *Kulturen* 1944.

Garde, G. *Danske silkebroderede lærredsduge fra 16. og 17. århundrede. Med særlig henblik paa de grafiske forbilleder.* Copenhagen, 1961–62.

Garde, G. "Om nogle fragmenter af silkebroderede lærredsduge fra 1600-tallet." *Kulturen* 1962.

Geijer, A. *Albertus Pictor, målare och pärlstickare.* Stockholm, 1949.

Geijer, A. "Pällen med Tage Thotts och Else Ulfstands vapen." *Haandarbejdets Fremme* 20 (1954), no. 1.

Hazelius Berg, G. "Beata Jacquette Ribbings mönstersamling." *Fataburen* 1948.

Hazelius Berg, G. "Väggbeklädnad från Tureholm." *Fataburen* 1943.

Hedlund, G. *Gammal korssöm från Gästrikland.* Malmö, 1925.

Henschen Ingvar, I. "En grupp hängkläden från Nättraby." *Blekingeboken* 1937.

Henschen Ingvar, I. "Robert Douglas bordtäcke." *Östergötlands läns fornminnesförenings tidskrift* 1952.

Henschen Ingvar, I. *Svenska broderier.* Stockholm, 1950.

"Knutet och trätt: Knutet och trätt arbete från Gästrikland." *Svensk Slöjdtidning* 1928.

Keyland, N. "Sentrådsspinning, tenndragning och bältsmyckegjutning hos lapparna i norra Jämtland." *Fataburen* 1920.

Nelson, R. "Broderade hängkläden från västra Blekinge." *Blekingeboken* 1938.

Nylén, A.-M. "Om broderade textilier och dräkter under Vasatiden." *Konsthistorisk tidskrift* 1944, no. 3.

Nylén, A.-M. *Broderier från herremans- och borgarhem 1500–1850.* Stockholm, 1950.

Nylén, A.-M. "Ett eldskärmsbroderi från 1700-talets förra del." *Fataburen* 1943.

Nylén, A.-M. "Historiskt om vitbroderi." *Brodera vitt på vitt,* edited by E. Svennås. Uppsala, 1962.

Nylén, A.-M. *Provböcker och mönsterböcker berättar om hemslöjd på herrgårdar och borgarhem.* Annual report for 1950 of Föreningen för Svensk Hemslöjd. Stockholm, 1951.

Nylén, A.-M. "Textila skatter inventerade i rika Delsbo." *Hemslöjden* 1963.

Rodenstam, G. "Augusta Gripenberg och en hälsingsk prydnadssöm." *Hälsingerunor* 1956.

Schuette, M., and Muller-Christensen, S. *Broderikonsten från antiken till Jugend.* Stockholm, 1963.

Stavenow-Hidemark, E. "Korsstygnsförlagor." *Fataburen* 1959.

Strömberg, E. "Broderade hängkläden från Blekinge." *Fataburen* 1950.

Ugglas, C. R. af. "Till dateringen av våra medeltida mosaik- eller applikationsbroderier." *Fornvännen* 1930.

Thorman, E. *Studier i svensk textilkonst.* Stockholm 1950.

Wintzell, I. *Tråd och söm.* Göteborg: Mölnlycke sytråd AB, 1959.

Sprang. Knot work. Crochet. Braiding. Bobbin lace.

Adelborg, O. "De olika spetstyperna i Dalaknyppling." *Dalarnas Hembygdsförbunds årsskrift* 1923.

Boëthius, G. "Blekingespetsar." *Hemslöjden* 1946.

Branting, A. "Knytning, knyppling och språngning." *Fataburen* 1907.

Broholm, H. C., and Hald, M. "To sprangede Tekstilarbeider i danske Oldfund." *Aarbøger for nordisk Oldkyndighed og Historie* 1935.

Collin, M. "Den äldsta kända flätningen." *Fataburen* 1922.

Collin, M. "Skånska nätspetsar." *Fataburen* 1918.

Coyet, H. *Skånsk hembygdsslöjd.* Lund 1922.

Ehrensvärd, A. "Något om Tosterups-spetsar." *Föreningens för fornminnes- och hembygdsvård i Sydöstra Skåne skrifter,* vol. 2 (1921).

Hald, M. *Olddanske Tekstilier: Komparative tekstil- og dragthistoriske Studier paa Grundlag af Mosefund og Gravfund fra Jernalderen.* Nordiske Fortidsminder, vol. 5. Copenhagen, 1950.

Hedlund, G. *Mönster till knutna och trädda spetsar: Gamla "pinnspetsar" från Gästrikland.* Malmö, 1926.

Henschen Ingvar, I. "Den textila hemslöjden." *En bok om Skåne.* Lund, 1936.

Henschen Ingvar, I. *Svenska broderier.* Stockholm, 1950.

Hörlén, A. "Knyppelskrin och knyppelpinnar i syd-östra Skåne." *Rig* 1969.

Hörlén, A. *Knyppling och knypplerskor i södra delen av Ingelstads härad.* Skrifter från Folklivsarkivet, Lund, no. 5. Lund, 1962.

Ingers, G. *Skånsk knyppling.* Kristianstad, 1966.

Johansson, S. *Knyppling.* Borås, 1964.

Johansson, S. *Traditional Lacemaking.* New York, 1974.

Linnove, A. *Suomalaisen pitsinnypläyksen kehitysvaheita 1500-luvulta—1850-luvulle.* [The stages of development in Finnish lace-making from the 16th century to 1850.] Helsinki, 1947.

Meyerson, Å. "Arkivaliska bidrag om spetstillverkningen i Vadstena." *Rig* 1935.

Nylén, A.-M. "Hilda Lilienbergs spetssamling." *Fataburen* 1942.

Rodhe, G. "Knyppling utan fast mönster." *Rig* 1958.

Thorman, E. *Svenska spetsar.* Stockholm, 1940.

Thorman, E. *Textilkonst i Sverige före år 1930.* Stockholm, 1944.

Trotzig, L. *Knypplade spetsar från Dalarna.* Västerås, 1957.

Needle looping. Knitting

Arbman, H., and Strömberg, E. "Äslevanten." *Fataburen* 1934.

Campbell, Å. "Om ben- och fotbeklädnaden hos allmogen i Norrland." *Rig* 1942.

Collin, M. "Sydda vantar." *Fataburen* 1917.

Hald, M. "Lundavanten." *Kulturen* 1945.

Hansen, H. P. *Spind og Bind: Bindehosens, Bindestuens og Hosekræmmerens saga.* Copenhagen, 1947.

Kaukonen, T.-I. "Valkning av stickade plagg." *Finskt museum* 57. Helsinki, 1960.

Wintzell, I. "Hallandsstickning." *Fataburen* 1957.

Wintzell, I. "Odd Nordland: *Primitive Scandinavian textiles in knotless netting.*" Book review. *Rig* 1963.

Wintzell, I. *Mönster med tradition: Stickat—med tradition.* Stockholm, 1963.

Woodcrafts

Andrén, E. *Möbelstilarna.* Stockholm, 1948.

Berg, G. "Kyrkåka och kappsläde." *Svenska kulturbilder,* vol. 1. Stockholm, 1929.

Berg, G. "Spåntapeter." *Folkliv* 1943–44.

Bergström-Andelius, E. *Om lapska rotkorgar.* Stockholm, 1932.

Biörnstad, A. "Historik: Svarvkonsten—en 1500-årig slöjd." *Svarva i trä,* edited by R. Gustavsson and O. Olsson. Motala, 1959.

Björkquist, L. "En jämtsk selkroksgrupp." *Folkliv* 1943–44.

Bringéus, N.-A., ed. *Arbete och redskap.* Lund, 1973.

Bäckström, S. *Korgtillverkning i Örkened.* Kristianstad, 1953.

Cronlund, E. "Skånsk korgslöjd." *Skånes Hembygdsförbunds årsbok* 1936.

Dryckeskärlen. Catalog from the exhibit "Brygd" (Brew) at Nordiska Museet. Stockholm, 1935.

Erixon, S. "Bolle och kåsa." *Svenska kulturbilder,* vol. 3. Stockholm, 1932.

Erixon, S. *Folkkonsten i Sverige.* Nordisk kultur, no. 27. Copenhagen, 1931.

Eskeröd, A. "Fågelmakaren och hans fåglar." *Fataburen* 1960.

Granlund, J. *Träkärl i svepteknik.* Nordiska Museets Handlingar, no. 12. Stockholm, 1940.

Gårdlund, T. "Om den tidiga svenska träförädlingsindustrien." *Ekonomisk tidskrift* 1941.

Hallerdt, B. "Korgar och korgtillverkning." *Svenskt husmoderslexikon,* vol. 5. Stockholm, 1954.

Hammarstedt, N. E. "Inspirationsfågeln." *Fataburen* 1908.

Hansen, H. P. *Løb og Løbbinding.* Aarhus and Copenhagen, 1927.

Hofrén, M. "Bondesnickaren Zakris Pehrsson." *Fataburen* 1920.

Hofrén, M. "Storsnickare: Ett kapitel ångermanländsk bygdekonst." *Nordsvenska studier och essayer.* Nordiska Museets Handlingar, no. 56. Stockholm, 1962.

Hofrén, M. "Pehr Westman i Utanö och Hemsöskolan." *Nordsvenska studier och essayer.* Nordiska Museets Handlingar, no. 56. Stockholm, 1962.

Kjellberg, S. T. "Svenska selkrokar av trä i Nordiska museet: Försök till gruppering av materialet." *Fataburen* 1926.

Kurvarbeide: Praktisk veiledning. Published by Den norske husflidsforening. Oslo, 1923.

Lagerquist, M. *Pinnstolar: Ett bidrag till Nässjö stolfabriks historia.* Stockholm, 1943.

Lagerquist, M., and Schoultz, G. v. "Stolsnickeriet i Östervåla: En svensk bygdeslöjd." *Folkliv* 1942.

Lekholm, C. G. "Skånska träskor och träskomakare." *Kulturen* 1950.

Levander, L. *Övre Dalarnes bondekultur under 1800-talets förra hälft.* Vol. 2, *Förvärvsarbete.* K. Gustav Adolfsakademiens för folklivsforskning skrifter, no. 11. Stockholm, 1944.

Levander, L. *Övre Dalarnes bondekultur under 1800-talets förra hälft.* Vol. 3, *Hem och hemarbete.* K. Gustav Adolfsakademiens för folklivsforskning skrifter, no. 11. Stockholm, 1947.

Lidström, B. "Träslöjd och korgning i Blekinge." *Blekingeboken* 1939.

Lindström, R., and Olsson, R. "En krönika om sågverksarbetaren." *Svenska sågverksindustriarbetareförbundets minnesskrift* 1947.

Lithberg, N. "Friareskedar." *Rig* 1919.

Lithberg, N. "Svensk korgslöjd." *Rig* 1921.

Nilsson, H. "Halmbindning i spiralteknik." *Kulturen* 1943.

Nodermann, M. *En jämtländsk kyrkmålarfamilj.* Östersund, 1964.

Nylén, A.-M. "Smörställ." *Folkliv* 1950–51.

Schotte-Frödin, A.-S. "Dalhästen och dess tillverkare." *Dalarnas hembygdsbok* 1939.

Ståhl, S. "Sveriges äldsta stolfabrik." *Träarbetaren* 1939, no. 5.

Stålberg, H. *Smålands skogs- och träförädlingsindustrier: En näringsgeografisk studie.* Lund, 1947.

Bibliography

Svedenfors, F. *Vävskedsmakeri och hornslöjd: Två utdöda hemslöjder. Med särskild hänsyn till Sunnerbo härad i Småland.* Svenskt liv och arbete, no. 16. Stockholm, 1952.

Svensson, S. "Friaregåvor och trolovningsskänker." *Svenska kulturbilder,* vol. 5. Stockholm, 1931.

Svensson, S., ed. *Nordisk folkkonst.* Lund, 1973.

Trotzig, D. *Laggningen på Sollerön: Gruddbo på Sollerön.* Nordiska Museets Handlingar, no. 9. Stockholm, 1938.

Valonen, N. "Om näverarbeten i Fenno-Skandinien." *Nordisk kultur,* vol. 14. Copenhagen, 1953.

Wieslander, G. "Skogsbristen i Sverige under 1600- och 1700-talen." *Svenska Skogsvårdsföreningens tidskrift* 34. Stockholm, 1936.

Horn and bone crafts

Fjellström, P. "Lapsk benornamentik." *Norrbotten* 1952.

Huldt, H. H-son. *Mönsterbok för lapsk hornslöjd i Västerbottens län.* Stockholm, 1920.

Manker, E. *De svenska fjällapparna.* Svenska Turistföreningens handböcker om det svenska fjället. Stockholm, 1947.

Svedenfors, F. *Vävskedsmakeri och hornslöjd: Två utdöda hemslöjder. Med särskild hänsyn till Sunnerbo härad i Småland.* Svenskt liv och arbete, no. 16. Stockholm, 1952.

Metalwork

Biörnstad, A. "Mässing i Loshult." *Fataburen* 1955.

Bäckström, S. "Gammalt smideshantverk inom Osby och Loshults socknar." *Skånes Hembygdsförbunds årsbok* 1951.

Erixon, S. "Ett ålderdomligt låssmide i Dalarna och dess härkomst." *Folkliv* 1942.

Erixon, S. *Gammal mässing.* Västerås, 1964.

Hellner, B. *Järnsmidet i vasatidens dekorativa konst.* Nordiska Museets Handlingar, no. 30. Stockholm, 1948.

Hellner, B., and Rooth, S. *Konstsmide: Historia och teknik.* Stockholm, 1960.

Homman, O. "Låssmeder i Lima på 16–1700-talen." *Folkliv* 1942.

Jonsson, O., and Hellner, B. *Smidda järnkors på Ekshärads kyrkogård.* Stockholm, 1932.

Nihlén, J. *Studier rörande äldre svensk järntillverkning med särskild hänsyn till Småland.* Stockholm, 1932.

Nyman, A. "Allmogesmidet." *Skyllberg 1346—1646—1946: Minnesskrift.* Edited by B. Waldén. Stockholm, 1947.

Oldeberg, A. *Metallteknik under vikingatid och medeltid.* Stockholm, 1966.

Sahlin, C. *Allmogesmide i Dalarne. 1764 års undersökning.* Jernkontorets bergshistoriska skriftserie, no. 5. Stockholm, 1936.

Solders, S. *Älvdalens sockens historia.* Vol. 3, *Myrjärn—Hemsmide—Liebruk.* Dalarnas Fornminnes- och Hembygdsförbunds skrifter, no. 9. Stockholm, 1946.

Trotzig, D. "Urmakeriet i Mora." *Dalarnas Hembygdsförbunds årsbok* 1939.

Index

Boldface page numbers refer to illustrations; numbers followed by "F" to color illustrations on the facing page.